England's Landscape

The North West

NORTH
WEST

NORTH EAST

WEST
MIDLANDS

EAST MIDLANDS

EAST
ANGLIA

WEST

SOUTH EAST

SOUTH
WEST

Collins

England's Landscape
The North West

EDITED BY ANGUS J L WINCHESTER

ANGUS J L WINCHESTER
ALAN G CROSBY

SERIES EDITOR NEIL COSSONS

ENGLISH HERITAGE

First published in 2006 by Collins, an imprint of
HarperCollins*Publishers*
77–85 Fulham Palace Road, London W6 8JB

www.collins.co.uk

10 9 8 7 6 5 4 3 2
10 09 08 07

ISBN 10 – 0 00 715577 8
ISBN 13 – 9 78 0 00 715577 4

British Library Cataloguing in Publication Data
A CIP catalogue record for this book is available from the
British Library.

Map on previous page:
The regions: the red lines bound the general areas covered by
each volume.

ACKNOWLEDGEMENTS

SERIES EDITOR
Sir Neil Cossons OBE
Chairman, English Heritage
President, Royal Geographical Society
The series editor would like to acknowledge the contribution of
the following people:

EDITORIAL BOARD:
Professor David Cannadine
Queen Elizabeth the Queen Mother Professor of British History,
University of London

Professor Barry Cunliffe
Professor of European Archaeology, University of Oxford

Professor Richard Lawton
Professor Emeritus, Department of Geography, University of
Liverpool

Professor Brian K Roberts
Professor Emeritus, Department of Geography, University of Durham

ENGLISH HERITAGE EXECUTIVE EDITORS:
Dr Paul Barnwell, *Head of Medieval and Later Rural Research*
Dr Martin Cherry, *Former Chief Buildings Historian*
Humphrey Welfare, *Northern Territory Director*
Graham Fairclough, *Head of Characterisation*

ENGLISH HERITAGE PROJECT MANAGERS:
Val Horsler, *former Head of Publishing*
Adele Campbell, *Commercial Publishing Manager*

All new ground and air photography was taken specifically for
this series. Thanks to: Damian Grady, Senior Investigator of
English Heritage Aerial Survey and Investigation Team, and to
the photographic and dark-room teams in Swindon; Steve Cole,
Head of Photography, and the staff of the English Heritage
Photography team. Archive material from the National
Monuments Record was researched by the Enquiry and
Research Services teams led by Alyson Rogers (Buildings) and
Lindsay Jones (Archaeology/Air Photos). Graphics lists were
managed by John Vallender and Bernard Thomason. Graphics
were produced under the management of Rob Read of 3's
Company (Consultancy) Ltd, by Drew Smith. All other images
were researched by Jo Walton and Julia Harris-Voss.

Publisher & Commissioning Editor Myles Archibald
Production Director Graham Cook
Edited by Catherine Bradley
Designed by D & N Publishing, Hungerford, Berkshire
Indexed by Sheila Seacroft

Printed in Italy by LEGO SpA, Vicenza

Contents

PART IV: LANDSCAPE AND MIND

VOLUME EDITOR'S ACKNOWLEDGEMENTS

The preparation of this book was completed during a period of study leave in 2003–4 granted by Lancaster University. I should like to thank the university and my colleagues in the Department of History for allowing me the luxury of being able to devote myself to this project for six months. Preparing a book with subject matter as wide-ranging as that discussed in this volume could not have been achieved without the help and advice of specialists in an unusually wide range of disciplines. As well as acknowledging the unstinting help of archivists and librarians across the North West, I should like to record my thanks to colleagues and research students at Lancaster University, particularly Michael Winstanley, Ian Whyte, Chris Brader, Lisa Blenkinsop, Gordon Roberts and Bill Shannon. It is also a pleasure to be able to acknowledge helpful discussions with Sharman Kadish of the University of Manchester and Tom Lord of Settle. Writing this volume has been a stimulating and particularly enjoyable exercise, thanks largely to lively interchanges with my co-author, Alan Crosby, and our consultant editor at English Heritage, Paul Barnwell. I have greatly valued their support, encouragement and sense of humour.

Angus Winchester
March 2004

ABBREVIATIONS

CNWRS	Centre for North West Regional Studies, Lancaster University
CRO	Cumbria Record Offices, Cumbria Archives Service
CW	*Transactions of the Cumberland and Westmorland Antiquarian and Archaeological Society*; *CW1*: old series (1866–1900); *CW2*: new series (1901–2000); *CW3*: third series (2001–)
CWAAS	Cumberland and Westmorland Antiquarian and Archaeological Society
LRO	Lancashire Record Office, Preston
PRO	The National Archives: Public Record Office, Kew
RCHME	Royal Commission on Historic Monuments (England)
THSLC	*Transactions of the Historic Society of Lancashire and Cheshire*

Foreword

The landscape of England evokes intense passion and profound emotion. This most loved of places, the inspiration for generations of writers, poets and artists, it is at once both the source of the nation's infatuation and the setting for grievous misunderstanding. For people who visit, the view of England offers some of their most lasting images. For exiles abroad the memory of the English landscape sustains their beliefs and desire for a homecoming.

But for those who live in England the obsession is double edged. On the one hand we cherish the unchanging atmosphere of a familiar place, and on the other make impossible demands of it, believing that it will always accommodate, always forgive. Only in the last half century or so have we started to recognise the extreme fragility of all that we value in the English landscape, to appreciate not only that it is the metaphor for who we are as a people, but that it represents one of our most vivid contributions to a wider culture. At last we are beginning to realise that a deeper understanding of its subtle appeal and elusive character is the key to a thoughtful approach to its future.

The unique character of England's landscape derives from many things. But nowhere is the impact of human intervention absent. If geology and topography set the scene, it is the implacable persistence of generations who since the end of the Ice Age have sought to live in and off this place that has created the singular qualities of the landscape we have today. Not, of course, that the landscape before people was in any sense a static thing; on the contrary, the environment untouched by mankind was and is a dynamic and constantly changing synthesis. Every layer of that complex progression can still be found somewhere, making its own peculiar contribution to the distinctiveness of today's England. It is a compelling narrative. Through this series of regional studies our distinguished contributors – as authors and editors – have distilled something of what has created today's England, in order to decode that narrative.

Unique is an overused term. But it has a special resonance for the landscape of England, both urban and rural. What we hope readers of this series will begin to feel is the nature of the qualities that define the English landscape. Much of that landscape has of course been inherited from cultures overseas, as conquest and migration brought here peoples who have progressively occupied and settled Britain. They created what might be called our shared landscapes, defined as much by what links them to the wider world as through any intrinsically native characteristics. The peoples whose common bonds stretched along the Atlantic seaboard have left a legacy in Cornwall more akin to parts of north-west France or Spain than to anywhere else in England. There are Roman roads and cities and medieval field systems that have their closest parallels in the European plains from whence they derived. Great abbeys and monasteries reflected in their art and architecture, their commerce and industry, a culture whose momentum lay outside these islands. And when disaster came it was a pan-European epidemic, the Black Death, that took away between a third and a half of the people. England's are not the only deserted medieval villages.

And yet, paradoxically, much of what today we would recognise as the quintessential England is only some two or three centuries old. Parliamentary enclosure, especially of the English lowlands, was itself a reaction to an even greater economic force – industrialisation, and the urbanisation that went with it. It has given us a rural landscape that epitomizes the essence of Englishness in the minds of many. The fields and hedgerows surrounding the nucleated villages of the pre-existing medieval landscape are of course quite new when set against the timescale of human occupation. Indeed, when the first railways came through there remained, here and there, open fields where the rows of new hawthorn hedges were still feeble whips scribing lines across a thousand years of feudal landscape.

As Britain emerged to become the world's first industrial nation, its astonishing transformation was at its most visible in the landscape, something new, indigenous and without precedent. It fuelled the debate on the picturesque and the sublime and was a source of wonder to those who visited from overseas. But in its urban and industrial excesses it soon came to be detested by aesthetes, social commentators and a burgeoning class opposed to the horrors of industrial capitalism. What was perhaps the most decisive contribution of Britain to the human race provoked a powerful counteraction reflected in the writings of Ruskin, Morris, Octavia Hill and the Webbs. It was this anguish that a century ago energised the spirit of conservation in a growing band of people determined to capture what was left of the pre-industrial rural scene.

Today the landscape of England is, as ever, undergoing immense change. But, unlike the centuries just past, that change once again draws its energy and inspiration from forces overseas. A new form of global economy, North American in flavour, concept and style carries all before it. The implications for the long-term future of the landscape and the people who live in it are difficult to predict. The out-of-town shopping malls, the great encampments of distribution warehouses crouching like so many armadillos across the rural shires, the growth of exurbia – that mixed-use land between city and country that owes nothing to either – are all manifestations of these new economic forces. Like the changes that have gone before, they have become the subject of intense debate and the source of worrying uncertainty. But what is clear is that a deeper understanding of the landscape, in all its manifestations, offers a means of managing change in a conscious and thoughtful manner.

This was the inspiration that led to this new regional landscape series. To understand the language of landscape, to be able to interpret the way in which people make places, offers insights and enjoyment beyond the ordinary. It enables us to experience that most neglected of human emotions, a sense of place. These books set out to reveal the values that underwrite our sense of place, by offering an insight into how the landscape of England came to be the way it is. If understanding is the key to valuing and valuing is the key to caring, then these books may help to ensure that we can understand and enjoy the best of what we have, and that when we make our own contribution to change it will not only reinforce that essential distinctiveness but will also improve the quality of life of those who live there.

Neil Cossons

1

The Personality of the North West

Generations have trod, have trod, have trod;
And all is seared with trade; bleared, smeared with toil;
And wears man's smudge and shares man's smell ...

Gerard Manley Hopkins[1]

Landscape is about experience of place. Sights, sounds and smells combine to create a 'sense of place', that elusive quality which tells us that one locality is different from another. This book tries to capture something of these intangibles and to give them a clearer definition and context. To do so, we need to explore the history of human activity in creating the landscapes that we experience today.

For many, the dominant impression of the North West is the one captured by Gerard Manley Hopkins' image of an environment worn and exhausted by human industry. Yet the North West also contains wide farming landscapes under clean, rain-washed skies, as well as the wild and windswept majesty of the fell tops and the moors, where the hand of man seems much less in evidence than in other parts of England. In reality, 'the North West' does not possess a single landscape, but a huge diversity within a comparatively small compass. In the two hours it takes to traverse the region on the West Coast main-line railway, the traveller passes through smoke-blackened industrial towns, landscapes scarred by mining and quarrying, grass-rich meadows and pastures, rich red arable lands, coastal salt marsh and bleak, high moorland. In broad terms, the North West embraces two very different areas: those which saw a concentration of settlement and industry from the 18th century (largely but not only towards the south of the region) and those areas from which population drained (largely but not only in the upland and northern parts). Perhaps the first question that needs to be asked is whether anything binds these contrasting landscapes together, distinguishing the region from other parts of England and producing a distinctive north-western sense of place.

For the purposes of this volume, the North West is defined as the region to the west of the main Pennine watershed, stretching from the River Mersey in the south to the Scottish border in the north. In local government terms it consists of the historic counties of Cumberland, Westmorland and Lancashire, and the western fringes of the West Riding of Yorkshire (*see* map p. 2). It forms a long, thin territory, almost 200km (125 miles) from north to south but rarely more than 70km (40 miles) wide, and deeply indented by fingers of sea. If we attempt to distil the key themes which give the landscape of the North West its distinctiveness, the region's physical geography must come first. The lowlands in which human settlement has been concentrated across the millennia form an attenuated strip, hemmed in by the sea to the west and the fells and moors to the east. In places the lowland becomes very narrow, as around Lancaster, where it is little more than 10km (6 miles) wide between the salt marshes of the Lune estuary and the brown moorland of the Bowland fells. In south-west Cumbria, the lowland belt is even more restricted, being

Fig. 1.1 Whitbeck, near Millom, in south-west Cumbria, where the coastal lowland is reduced to no more than a narrow strip hemmed in between the fells and the sea.

reduced to little more than 1km (0.6 mile) where Black Combe presses against the Irish Sea at Whitbeck (Fig. 1.1). Even where the lowlands broaden out into wider plains, in northern Cumbria and in the Fylde and southern Lancashire, the landscape is fragmented by tidal estuaries and peat mosses. Only in the Eden and Lune valleys, Ribblesdale and the Manchester embayment do lowlands extend far inland. The result is that 'core areas', the focus for settlement and political, social and economic institutions across the centuries, are separated from each other by peripheral areas of upland or wetland. These physical barriers gave rise to cultural fragmentation, as different parts of the region looked different ways.

Physical geography also gave the region a diverse and rich resource base, the exploitation of which has contributed to the individual character of the region's landscapes. A variety of mineral resources have been mined and quarried: coal, iron ore, lead and copper, roofing slate, building stone, limestone, clay. The upland environment of the fells and moors has produced magnificent scenery, which has been discovered, sought after and marketed. A long and indented seaboard, opening on to an inland sea, encouraged the development of ports for seaborne trade.

A second characteristic common to the mosaic of landscapes in the North West may be summed up by the term 'marginality'. This refers not just to the physical marginality of a region where environmental constraints limit the scope for agriculture and restrict the possibilities for settlement, though this is one aspect. The upland periphery, frequently a sudden edge, is never far away, marking the boundary between lowlands where arable farming was possible and hill country where cultivation was marginal at best. The limits of human settlement are

reached in the uplands, beyond which empty moorland or mountainside stretches away to the horizon (Fig. 1.2). A comparable margin is found in the lowlands, where peat moss and marsh formed a watery barrier to settlement before the wetlands were drained.

To this physical marginality must be added political remoteness. From the Roman period to the Industrial Revolution, the North West lay distant from seats of power and could be thought of as a frontier zone. Hadrian's Wall marked the limits of Roman power; the region was peripheral to all the centres of power across the early medieval centuries (separated from the heartland of Northumbria by the Pennines; a contested ground between Scottish, Anglo-Saxon and Viking power; on and beyond the fringes of the kingdom of England conquered by William I in 1066). Across the later medieval centuries the Anglo-Scottish border was an active and troubled frontier, dominating life in the northern parts of the region. Only with the growth of Manchester and Liverpool as twin pillars of economic power during the Industrial Revolution did the North West enter the

Fig. 1.2 Needle House, on the headwaters of the River Rawthey, near Sedbergh, the limit of settlement in the uplands deep in the Pennines.

heart of the nation's life. Even then, the northern reaches of the region could still feel almost as remote from those cities as they did from London.

A third aspect of the region's marginality was cultural. The North West exhibits a cultural 'otherness', looking away from rest of England and out to the Irish Sea and beyond. During the early medieval period, it was part of the Celtic-Norse world of the Irish Sea province, with much closer ethnic and cultural ties to the Isle of Man, Ireland and south-west Scotland than to 'mainland' Anglo-Saxon England. Trading links across the northern Irish Sea strengthened in the 17th and 18th centuries, binding together the merchants of Liverpool, Whitehaven and Dublin. Burgeoning North Atlantic and African trade extended horizons further, so that the coast of north-west England became the point of entry to a much wider world (Fig. 1.3). The sea also brought settlers, not only the Scandinavian colonists of the 10th century and the

Fig. 1.3 Sunderland Point, where the River Lune enters the Irish Sea. The port established here in the early 18th century was Lancaster's predecessor, linking north Lancashire with the plantations of America.

Irish immigrants of the 19th, but also smaller numbers of Chinese and Africans, who formed early ethnic minority communities, particularly in Liverpool. An 'otherness' engendered by cultural and ethnic influences coming into the region from the opposite direction to the rest of England was reinforced by the survival of older cultural residues, which had been swept away elsewhere. Most prominent, perhaps, was the survival of Roman Catholicism in lowland Lancashire – arguably the only part of England to remain largely untouched by the Reformation. From the perspective of the southern English social and political elite, the Industrial Revolution reinforced the 'otherness' of the North West. It became synonymous with industrial working-class society, epitomised by a hard, uncouth way of life. As the traditional industries declined, the rapid growth of Asian communities in the Lancashire textile towns in the late 20th century has added another dimension to the cultural complexity of the region.

The distinctive cultural mix of the North West served to heighten the view from outside that the area was truly on the margins: a wet, bleak, border region, which looked away from the rest of England. But this sense of otherness also attracted visitors. By the late 18th century, the picturesque beauty of the Lake District and the sublime horror of the limestone caverns of the Pennines and Peak District had been 'discovered' by travellers seeking to experience the excitement of wild landscapes.

The third key theme which distinguished the North West was, as has been noted already, the impact of the Industrial Revolution. Lancashire is synonymous with the 'dark, satanic mills' of the cotton industry, but the landscape of an industrial society based on textiles was only one expression of the industrial transformation of the century between 1780 and 1880. Coal mining in west Cumberland and south-west Lancashire; the chemical and metal trades of southern Lancashire; the iron and steel industries of southern and western Cumbria; and a host of other industrial specialisms (linen, silk, pottery, glass, linoleum) had a major impact on the region's society and landscape (Fig. 1.4). Yet landscapes of manufacturing were only one aspect of the Industrial Revolution. The needs of the mighty industrial conurbations in the southern parts of the region were felt across the North West. A transport revolution spread a lattice of railways, linking town and country and shrinking perceived distances across the region. The sea and the hills became the lungs of the towns, as the leisure needs of a newly industrial workforce saw the rise of seaside resorts, from Hoylake in the south to Silloth in the north, and the growth of tourism in the Lake District. The demand for water, first for power and later to provide drinking water for the towns and conurbations, led to a frenzy of engineering, as reservoirs and aqueducts gathered the excess rainfall from the fells and moors and took it to the thirsty mills and towns. The impact of the Industrial Revolution is rarely far away in the landscapes of the North West.

Fig. 1.4 Burnley: the urban legacy of industrialisation with the Pennine moors behind.

As a result, it often appears that the landscape of the North West has a narrow time-depth. Little is obviously ancient: the legacies of a distant past are rare – few deserted medieval villages surrounded by ridge and furrow; comparatively few medieval parish churches; few townscapes from before the Industrial Revolution. Large areas of the countryside are the result of the drainage of mosses and reclamation of moorland in the 19th century, while mills, factories and industrial terraces of the 19th century and urban sprawl of the 20th dominate much of the region. Yet look more deeply and the North West's landscape bears evidence of human activity stretching back more than six millennia. Relics of a more distant past abound, from Neolithic stone axe factories, Bronze Age field systems and a rich legacy of forts, roads and settlement sites from the Roman period to Viking age crosses, medieval castles, Tudor manor houses and 17th-century farmhouses. The legacy of those 6,000 years of human activity may be dominated by the last 250, but the Industrial Revolution took place in a landscape in which the framework of settlement (towns, villages, routeways) was already ancient. Today's landscape is the cumulative product of centuries of toil, as successive generations have modified their surroundings, adding and removing features according to the dictates of need, fashion and fancy. The familiar metaphor of landscape as palimpsest (a parchment which has been written on several times, where elements of the older writing show through the more recent layers) is as fitting for the North West as for elsewhere in England.

This book explores the richness of diversity in the landscape of the North West, looking 'under the skin' to see how it has developed over the millennia of human occupation. Its focus is on the contemporary landscape, and its central aim to identify the major historical processes that have moulded the region and to explore the legacy of those processes still visible today. Behind the discussion in the following chapters lies the question, 'How do we understand and interpret the landscape?' To answer that question, the book is divided into four sections, each approaching the relationship between human beings and the environment from a different angle and exploring different layers of meaning in the landscape.

The first seven chapters start from the premise that meaning is to be sought in the essentially utilitarian concerns that lie behind so much of mankind's impact on the landscape. The essential needs for food, clothing and shelter lie behind the cultivation of land and the erection of dwellings, while more sophisticated economic stimuli generate mines, factories, harbours and motorways. Part I (Land and People) paints the broad outlines of the relationship between people and landscape at the regional level. It takes what might be termed a 'human ecology' approach, exploring how human beings fit into the environment of the North West. Why are people more numerous in some areas than others? What resources did the region offer? How did past societies appropriate the land to themselves? The section contains three chapters, the first looking at the natural environment of the North West; the second at the peopling of the region; and the third at the routeways humans have created through the landscape, linking places and giving access to resources.

In order to explain the presence of medieval ridge and furrow, a 17th-century yeoman farmer's stone farmhouse or shops on a town high street, the society and economy out of which they sprang must be understood. The four chapters in Part II (Making a Living), the longest in the book, consider landscape as the product of economic imperatives. Two look at the rural landscape, lowland and upland, where farming has been the driving force; a third explores the rich variety of landscapes created by industrial activity across the centuries; the fourth focuses on the towns and townscapes that result from urbanisation.

Part III (Expressions of the Abstract) explores the landscape at another level. It takes as its starting point the recognition that many landscape features can be thought of as concrete expressions of abstract ideas, even when the primary explanation for their presence may be economic. Why, for example, do so many churches (or cotton mills, or Roman forts, or council houses) look so similar? Is it simply that these forms were the most functional, or do they also encapsulate what was considered to be the most appropriate form for a building of its kind at that point in space and time? In the case of churches, for example, differences in the form of buildings express differences in theology and doctrine. The contrast between the plain preaching box of early 19th-century Dissent and the soaring Gothic spire of mid-19th-century Anglicanism is essentially to do with fashion and the expression of ideas. The three chapters in this section explore the manifestations in the landscape of power and authority (from military might to economic and municipal influences); of faith and the creation of sacred spaces; and of the utopian ideals that underlie so much late 19th- and 20th-century urban development.

The final section (Part IV: Landscapes and Mind) looks at meaning in the landscape from a different perspective. Here the relationship between human beings and landscape is inverted: instead of looking at how humans have affected landscape, this section explores how landscape affects humans and how humans invest landscapes with significance. The first of the three chapters traces the responses evoked by upland scenery and the impact that changing perceptions of mountain and moorland have had, in turn, on the use of the uplands. The second explores the ambivalence inherent in responses to landscapes of the industrial past: are mills, terraces and industrial dereliction symbols of the oppression of the working class or relics of a lost industrial 'golden age'? The final chapter returns to the concept of marginality discussed earlier by examining attitudes to the landscape of the North West held by those in authority at a distance.

NOTES

---

1   Gardner 1982, 27

2

A Patchwork of Landscapes

Behind the layers of human activity across the centuries lies the land itself. It is only possible to comprehend the interaction between past societies and the landscape if the environmental mosaic on which the human story has been played out is first understood. Differences in soil fertility, climate, mineral and vegetational resources, and the ease of movement from place to place have all contributed to patterns of human occupation. This chapter seeks to strip off that veneer of human activity to examine the nature of the land below. Attempting a similar task in his *Guide to the Lakes* (1835), William Wordsworth sought to paint a picture of the land as first encountered by humans, a landscape where hitherto the seasons had turned 'with no human eye to notice, or human heart to regret or welcome the change.'[1] Such an aim, we now realise, was built on a false premise – that landscape untouched by human activity was unchanging. In reality it was, and remains, a dynamic complex, constantly evolving as landform, climate, soils, vegetation and fauna change.

THE LIE OF THE LAND

The long, narrow and fragmented region with which this book is concerned embraces a huge diversity of landscape and landform, from mountainous peaks to broad coastal wetland and marsh. The major contrast is between upland and lowland and the boundary between the two is often strikingly abrupt. The asymmetry of the Pennine spine places the central watershed to the western edge of the range. Sharp, faulted scarps separate the Pennines from the Vale of Eden and the coastal lowlands of Lancashire. Similarly the Lake District dome, a fist of ancient rock pushing up through the surrounding lowlands, is marked by a steep, sudden edge on its western, northern and north-eastern sides. The dichotomy between upland and lowland creates marked differences in climate, which in turn affect soils and vegetation. The lowlands, warmed by proximity to the western sea, receive under 1,000 mm (40 inches) of rainfall each year. Rainfall rises quickly with altitude, reaching 1,600 mm (over 60 inches) in the Lakeland and Pennine dales and more than twice that amount in the heart of the Lake District. As height increases, mean annual temperature drops, giving the uplands a much shorter growing season than the coastal lowlands. Within that basic division lies a greater diversity: in the uplands, where rock lies near the surface, solid geology and the impact of glacial erosion determine the character of landform; in the lowlands, where the land surface is plastered with clays, sands, silts and peat, the character of the landscape is determined by the nature of drift deposited during and after the last glaciation which ended *c.* 10,000 years ago.

In an attempt to provide a simplified sketch of the region's landscape, the following discussion is arranged as a traverse from north to south through the four major landscape divisions in the region: the North Cumbrian lowlands; the Lake District fells; the West Pennines and the Bowland fells; and the Morecambe Bay and Lancashire lowlands (Fig. 2.1).[2]

Sedimentary Formations

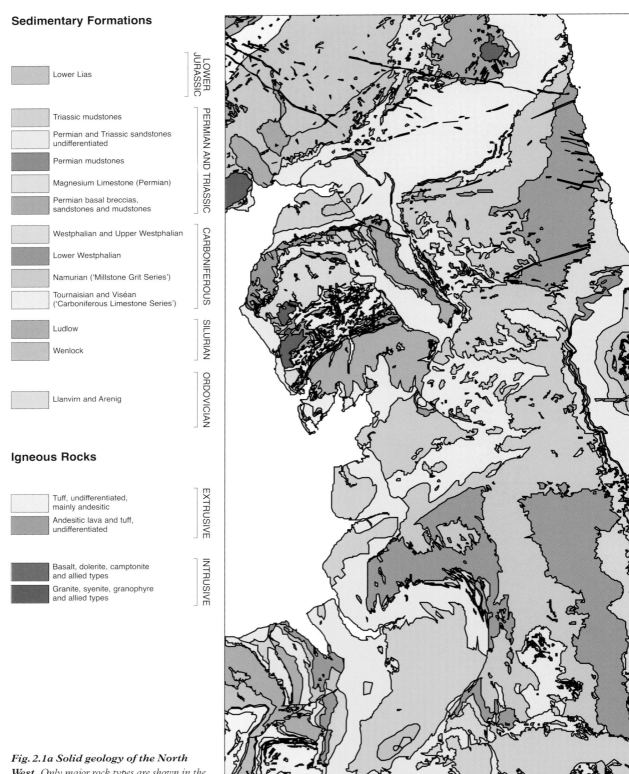

LOWER JURASSIC

Lower Lias

PERMIAN AND TRIASSIC

Triassic mudstones

Permian and Triassic sandstones undifferentiated

Permian mudstones

Magnesium Limestone (Permian)

Permian basal breccias, sandstones and mudstones

CARBONIFEROUS

Westphalian and Upper Westphalian

Lower Westphalian

Namurian ('Millstone Grit Series')

Tournaisian and Viséan ('Carboniferous Limestone Series')

SILURIAN

Ludlow

Wenlock

ORDOVICIAN

Llanvirn and Arenig

Igneous Rocks

EXTRUSIVE

Tuff, undifferentiated, mainly andesitic

Andesitic lava and tuff, undifferentiated

INTRUSIVE

Basalt, dolerite, camptonite and allied types

Granite, syenite, granophyre and allied types

Fig. 2.1a Solid geology of the North West. Only major rock types are shown in the key above (by permission of the British Geological Survey).

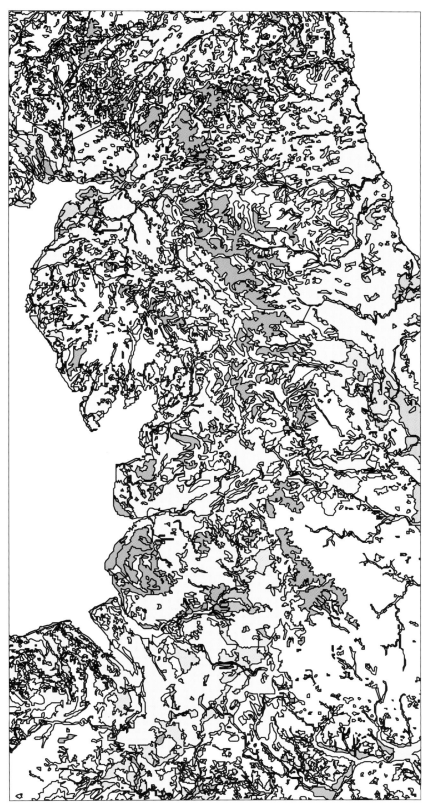

Quaternary Deposits

Landslip

Blown sand

Peat

Lacustrine clays, silts and sands

Alluvium

River terrace deposits
(mainly sand and gravel)

Glacial sand and gravel

Boulder clay and morainic drift

Fig. 2.1b Quaternary deposits of the North West (by permission of the British Geological Survey).

The North Cumbrian lowlands

The swathe of lowland running from the Irish Sea coast in west Cumbria across the Carlisle plain and Solway coast and up the Eden valley is a landscape of glacial and post-glacial deposition containing considerable diversity. The underlying rocks are mostly red sandstone of the Permo-Triassic age, though Carboniferous Coal Measures underlie the West Cumberland plain between Maryport and Whitehaven. For the most part, bedrock is obscured by drift deposits, though an outcrop of the coarse, red Penrith Sandstone forms the ridge of low hills running north from Penrith.

The dominant geomorphological process was deposition of boulder clay by the ice sheets. They flowed out from the Lake District and down the Eden valley, to be diverted west into the Irish Sea basin by ice flowing south from Scotland. This glacial deposition created the classic undulating landscape of drumlins (low, elongated ridges of glacial till), which sweep down the Eden valley and across the Carlisle plain (Fig. 2.2). The drumlins carry fertile clay soils, slowly permeable but wet in winter, land which Thomas Denton, writing of the area between the Caldew and Petteril rivers in 1687, described as 'a very rich & fruitfull clay ground, fitt for corn, hay or pasturage.'[3]

As elsewhere in the lowlands, the character of the landscape owes as much to post-glacial activity as to deposition by the ice sheets themselves. As the ice melted, vast quantities of meltwater spewed under and around static blocks of ice, depositing sands and gravels. In the Cumbrian lowlands these glaciofluvial deposits are particularly significant along the north Pennine edge to the east of the River Eden. Meltwater channels, steep-sided trenches cut through both till and solid rock, survive at the foot of the Pennine scarp, from Croglin to Renwick and between Gamblesby and Kirkland, for example. Meltwater, ponded by ice, created a huge temporary lake ('Lake Eden') in the Brampton area and deposited a belt of sands and gravels around the Pennine edge. The contrast in landscape and soils between this area and the boulder clay plain around Carlisle is striking. Thomas Denton noted how, travelling east from Carlisle, 'the nature of the soyle begins to chainge from a deep, fertill & clayie soyle which lyes all about Carlisle, to a light, hott, sandy earth' in the parishes of Warwick, Wetheral, Hayton and Brampton.[4] The assemblage of deltas, eskers (gravel ridges) and meltwater channels gives these areas a complex, hummocky topography.

A third distinct landscape zone is found along the margins of the Solway Firth, where the very low-lying land was subject to waterlogging and to flooding as a

Fig. 2.2 The Cumbrian lowlands: Newton Reigny, near Penrith. The fields behind the village curve over a typical drumlin ridge.

result of changes in relative sea level. Deep, waterlogged basins between barriers of glacial and glaciofluvial till developed into raised mires containing considerable depths of peat (10m (32 feet) at Glasson Moss), the most extensive of these wetlands being Wedholme Flow, Bowness and Glasson mosses and Solway Moss (Fig. 2.3). The coastal margins, particularly around Silloth and Kirkbride, were subject to fluctuations in sea level, notably a major marine transgression after *c.* 6000 BC, which resulted in the deposition of marine alluvium on which deep, silty soils developed.[5] The resulting landscape is one of islands of drift separated by alluvial flats and peat mosses.

The Lake District massif

The North Cumbrian lowlands are terminated by the Lake District massif. A ring of Carboniferous Limestone laps the margins of the fells, the glacial drift that covers it producing fertile, well drained soils. In the Lake District proper, the character of the landscape is a product of solid geology and glacial erosion. The mountainous dome is composed of three distinct bands of Lower Palaeozoic rocks, each investing the landscape with a different character. The northern fells are composed of rocks of the Ordovician Arenig series (the Skiddaw Slates), which have been eroded into smooth, steep slopes creating great, whale-backed fells such as Skiddaw (931m; 3,053 feet). The centre of the Lake District consists of volcanic lavas and tuffs (the Borrowdale Volcanic series) producing the much more broken and craggy terrain of the high central fells, including Scafell (978m; 3,210 feet) and Helvellyn (950m; 3,118 feet). To the south lies a belt of Silurian Mudstones which have eroded into much gentler, lower lying hills, such as the Furness fells around Hawkshead (rising to 300m; 1,000 feet).

Fig. 2.3 The Solway mosslands, looking from Anthorn to the Solway estuary. Rogersceugh (right centre), a formerly wooded island of drier land in the mosses ('sceugh' is from the Norse word for a wood), stands out as a patch of farmland surrounded by unreclaimed peat moss.

Superimposed on these geological differences are the effects of the last glaciation. During this time, all but the highest fells were blanketed by an ice sheet, which eroded deep into the valleys radiating from the centre of the dome, gouging steep-sided trenches with over-deepened troughs in which lakes have formed (Fig. 2.4). This textbook landscape of glacial erosion includes corries and hanging valleys (often containing tarns such as Angle Tarn, Blea Water and Small Water); side spurs truncated by the power of ice flowing down the central valley; and arêtes (sharp ridges), of which Striding Edge on Helvellyn is the most famous. The fell sides are ice-scoured and almost devoid of drift cover, while the valley floors contain deposits of boulder clay and glaciofluvial sands and gravels. Altitude, high rainfall (up to over 3,000mm (120 inches) per year) and the absence of drift cover on the higher fells have resulted in thin, acidic soils and a craggy, stony environment unsuitable for human settlement. The drift-plastered lower valley

Fig. 2.4 Wasdale Head from Styhead in the heart of the Lake District: a landscape of glacial erosion.

BELOW: *Fig. 2.5 Sadgill, Longsleddale:* a narrow, glaciated trench, with meadows on the valley floor.

sides, by contrast, carry well drained, stony, brown podzols (leached soils), which would have carried mixed oak woodland, while the valley floors are often stony but well drained (Fig. 2.5). The contrast between dale and fells is captured in Thomas Denton's description of the 'narrow but fruitfull dales' north of Kendal surrounded by 'hills mounting up aloft, for the most part covered with wood, or otherwise so rough & rocky that the grass scarce hides the stones.'[6] Leaving the fells and dales, the southern fringe of the Lake District, around Kendal, is an undulating landscape of glacial deposition, from which protrude outcrops of Silurian Mudstones and ridges of Carboniferous Limestone. The soils are fertile and well drained: Celia Fiennes, in her tour of the region in 1698, summed up the landscape of the area as one of 'little round green hills flourishing with corn and grass'.[7]

The West Pennines, Bowland and Rossendale

The uplands rising to the Pennine watershed, which forms the eastern boundary of the region covered by this book, are diverse and attenuated. Separated from the lowlands by a series of steep fault scarps, the dominant geology is Carboniferous, principally Limestone to the north of the Craven Fault and Millstone Grit and Coal Measures to the south. Geology, the different effects of glaciation and the widespread blanket of peat combine to create upland landscapes that differ greatly from those in the Lake District.

The steep fault-scarp of the North Pennines, where a wall of fellside rises to the watershed (reaching 893m (2,930 feet) at Cross Fell), forms a narrow belt of upland beyond the Eden valley. The major areas of limestone upland west of the watershed lie further south, on the plateau around Shap and Orton and in the Yorkshire 'Three Peaks' area between Dentdale and upper Ribblesdale. Both are

Fig. 2.6 The Hodder valley and the Bowland Fells, near Whitewell. Rich *pasture on limestone in the foreground, rising to gritstone moorland beyond.*

characterised by karstic scenery, notably limestone pavements, where ice has scoured clean the surface of resistant strata in the gently tilting beds of limestone. Glacial erosion in these central Pennine areas was not as aggressive as in the Lake District, probably because congested ice flows were unable to move with speed. Some deepened, U-shaped valleys occur (such as the Kingsdale and Chapel-le-Dale valleys near Ingleton), but other areas exhibit few features of erosion by ice. The Howgill fells, for example, a block of older Silurian rocks, contain rounded summits and narrow valleys, with only the poorly developed corrie at Cautley Spout suggesting glacial erosion.

The Craven faults (running roughly parallel to the modern A65 between Kirkby Lonsdale and Settle) separate the limestone uplands to the north from the younger millstone grit moorlands of Bowland and Rossendale to the south. Between the limestone and gritstone hills, however, lies the lowland embayment of Ribblesdale and the lowlands drained by the Greta and the Wenning rivers, eastern tributaries of the Lune. This is another boulder clay landscape of glacial deposition characterised by a swathe of drumlins deposited by ice flowing around and between the surrounding upland blocks.

The Bowland fells are composed of rocks of the Millstone Grit series, their lower slopes plastered with glacial drift and their summits, rising to 560m (1,840 feet), capped with peat (Fig. 2.6). Though not deeply eroded by ice, the three parallel cols along the watershed (at the Trough of Bowland, Salter Fell and Cross of Greet) have been enlarged by meltwater flowing beneath the ice cap. The landscape is one of wet, acidic moorland with waterlogged soils. The rocky western edge of Bowland at Quernmore was described in a survey of 1573 as consisting of 'rockes, skarres, quareis [quarries], mosses, furres [furze] and shake growndes'.[8] Between Bowland and Rossendale lies a landscape of vales and ridges, determined ultimately by fold structures in the Carboniferous rocks, but

Fig 2.7 Lumb in the forest of
Rossendale: *industrial settlements cluster*
along the narrow valley, flanked by a scatter of
moorland farms.

modified by glaciation. The gritstone ridges of Longridge Fell and Pendle Hill
rise above drift-covered limestone vales.

As in Bowland, the Rossendale moors were beneath the ice sheet; boulder clay
plastered the sides of the moors and meltwater deepened the cols (Fig. 2.7).
Glaciofluvial activity also played a significant part in creating the landscape on the
fringes of Rossendale. A complex network of meltwater channels on the slopes of
Knowl Moor behind Rochdale is associated with an extensive outwash of sands
and gravels between Rochdale and Middleton, on which deep, well drained soils
developed. Further deposits of glaciofluvial sands and gravels occur in the
Darwen valley around Blackburn and in patches in the interior valleys (around
Rawtenstall and Bacup, for example) and along the foot of the western scarp
around Wheelton. The interior of Rossendale is dissected by the steeply incised
valleys of the Irwell and its headwaters. Thin acidic soils cover the valley sides and
the moors, rising to 460m (1,500 feet), are capped by peat, which becomes more
extensive on the western edge on Anglezarke Moor and Winter Hill.

The Morecambe Bay and Lancashire lowlands

The swathe of lowland stretching from Morecambe Bay, through the Fylde and south-west Lancashire to the Manchester embayment, is at once both an area dominated by glacial and post-glacial deposition and a landscape of considerable local variety. Apart from the rocky fingers of limestone that protrude into Morecambe Bay (John Leland described the Silverdale area as 'mervelus rokky'), the ridge of Coal Measures rocks, which extends west from the Rossendale fells to Ashurst's Beacon and the Permo-Triassic Sandstone ridge east of Liverpool, the bedrock is largely buried beneath drift deposits, which are up to more than 70m (230 feet) in thickness in places. The character of the landform changes from north to south: in the north, the dominant features are the drumlin swarms around Morecambe Bay, in the Furness peninsula and in the valleys of the Lune and Keer, deposited by ice flowing from the Lakeland massif. The Fylde is characterised by less regular ridges and mounds, separated by flat-floored depressions (Fig. 2.8). In south Lancashire, the spur of higher ground extending from the scarp of the Rossendale fells to Liverpool divides two low lying areas of subdued topography, the south-west Lancashire plain and the Manchester embayment. In both the Fylde and south Lancashire the dominant processes in the creation of the physical landscape were the dumping of drift material as the ice melted, the formation of peat and the effects of sea level changes since the last glaciation. The variety of local landforms is a product of the complexity of these late- and post-glacial processes.

As the last glaciation came to an end around 10,000 years ago, the ice sheet stagnated and melted, dumping material trapped in it and releasing copious quantities of meltwater. The resulting deposits were complex mixtures of clays, sands and gravels, in which blocks of ice were trapped. As these melted, the deposits sagged and slumped and depressions developed where the ice had been. Where drainage was impeded, peat subsequently accumulated in these basins. In the bare, late-glacial landscape the wind whipped up the glaciofluvial sands and redeposited them: over 200km² (77 sq. miles) of south-west Lancashire is blanketed by up to 3m (10 feet) of wind-blown sand, known as the Shirdley Hill sands.

Fig. 2.8 Over Wyre, from Out Rawcliffe towards Pilling. The low, drift-covered ridge in the foreground gives way to rectangular enclosures on reclaimed mossland in the middle distance.

Changes in relative sea level since the last glaciation have had a major impact on the landscape of the coastal lowlands. Comparatively slight fluctuations in sea level could result in significant change along a low lying coast where the tidal range in the estuaries is almost 9m (30 feet) at spring tides and over 6m (20 feet) at mean tides. Between *c*. 7000 and *c*. 4000 BC sea level rose rapidly, covering large areas of south-west Lancashire, the Fylde coast and the fringes of Morecambe Bay.[10] As sea level dropped again and dune belts developed along the modern coastline, impeding drainage from low lying land behind, extensive peat mosses developed between the Alt and Douglas rivers in south-west Lancashire (Fig. 2.9) and at Lytham, Pilling and Out Rawcliffe mosses in the Fylde. These contained stretches of open water, of which the largest was Martin Mere, behind Southport, which covered an area 6.4km (4 miles) long by up to 3.2km (2 miles) wide before it was drained.

These coastal landscapes of mossland and meres restricted and fragmented the drier land suitable for settlement; they also presented hazards. The dune belt fringing the southern Fylde and south-west Lancashire was shifting and unstable, with blown sand destroying land and settlements. Inundations by the sea itself, such as the major flood which washed away over 150 houses and inundated many thousands of acres along the Lancashire coast in December 1720, could cause widespread destruction of life and property.[11] Travel could be dangerous. Martin Mere, according to an old proverb, 'has parted many a man and his mare'.[12] Treacherous pools of standing water pocked the surfaces of the peat mosses: one near Lytham, known as the Cursed Mere because of the cattle drowned there, was described in 1608 as 'a standinge poole or mear in the mosse beeinge deepe of mosse or slitche and covered over with broade leaves'.[13] Further inland, where streams flowed into the plain from the higher ground to the east, the threat of flooding was endemic, as at St Michael's on Wyre in the Fylde, where the Brock and Wyre rivers converged on flat alluvial land and regular flooding of meadows and destruction of hay is recorded in the 16th century.[14] Less common, but more disastrous, were 'bog bursts' in the wet centuries of the Little Ice Age between 1400 and 1800. In these incidents (which are recorded at Chat Moss in 1526, at White Moss (north-east of Manchester) in 1633 and at Pilling Moss in 1744–5, as well as at Solway Moss in north Cumbria in 1771), increased precipitation caused the structure of the peat moss to collapse, causing a flow of liquified peat. Witnesses to the Chat Moss eruption in 1526 'thoght yt had bene domysday' when the flow came tumbling towards them. The liquid peat which flowed into the Mersey 'colowred the water lyck to yncke downe unto Warington'.[15]

These environments, which have been the home of settled human communities for at least 6,000 years, have not been static. The ice left a stark and unstable landscape, subject to slumping and slippage, some of it on a massive scale, in tundra conditions. Huge landslips from this periglacial period are marked by grass-covered

Fig. 2.9 Great Altcar, *strung out along a low ridge surrounded by the reclaimed mosses of south-west Lancashire, with the dune belt at Ainsdale in the distance, fringing the sea.*

lobes on the flanks of the Pennines, in Mallerstang and on the slopes of Whernside and Ingleborough, for example. After *c*. 10000 BC temperatures rose rapidly, reaching values comparable to those of the present day by *c*. 7500 BC and rising above present levels in the Climatic Optimum, which peaked between 7000 and 6000 BC. As the climate warmed up, vegetation spread, and the tundra landscape of the immediate post-glacial period gave way first to open woodland with birch and pine and then to mixed deciduous woodland. By the time humans arrived in significant numbers, during the Mesolithic period, much of the landscape was heavily wooded, except in the highest fells and on the nascent peat mosses. The species composition varied depending on drainage, exposure and the soil parent material: oak predominated on freer draining slopes; ash on limestone; alder on wetter ground in the valleys and on the lowlands. The first major environmental consequence of human activity was woodland clearance, either through deliberate removal or as a result of grazing livestock preventing regeneration. Once woodland had gone, soils were more prone to erosion and to loss of nutrients. On moorland over 400m (1,300 feet), blanket bogs began to develop, where waterlogging allowed peat to accumulate. Some of the Pennine peat bogs appear to have been initiated during a period of wetter climate *c*. 7,000 years ago, perhaps as a result of disturbance to the tree cover by Mesolithic peoples.[16]

A KALEIDOSCOPE OF RESOURCES

The patchwork of landscapes described above offered a wide diversity of resources to sustain life. The soil itself, as the medium nourishing the crops and livestock vital to human survival, may be thought of as the prime resource, but both the native flora and fauna living on the surface of the land and the geological deposits beneath it were also sources of wealth. Until the transport revolutions of the 19th and 20th centuries, communities depended heavily on the resources of their locality and region, so the story of the landscape over most of human history is one of people exploiting their local environment. 'Biological' resources (the native flora and fauna) were particularly significant in the 'pre-industrial' economy, while local geological resources played a major part in the region's transformation during the Industrial Revolution.

The land's renewable riches lay in its biological surface layer. Woodland remained a vital and, as it became scarcer latterly, a jealously guarded resource, yielding not only timber and poles but also bark (oak bark for tanning; willow bark for medicine, for example), twigs and leaves for winter fodder and fuel in the form of charcoal. Other natural vegetation could also be harvested: bracken and heather for thatching; gorse for fuel; rushes for floor covering and to provide wicks for rushlights. The wetland and moorland wastes yielded fuel for the fire in the form of peat. Local ecology led to local specialisms: in the 17th century Borrowdale was renowned for its hazelnuts, and the cliffs at St Bees Head for samphire for use in pickling, for example.[17] The native fauna were also an important food resource: deer in woodland; hares on open ground; wildfowl in the marshes; shellfish (especially shrimps and cockles) in the estuaries. Of particular significance were fish, both from the sea and from fresh water. The migratory patterns of salmon, sea trout and eels made them easy prey in estuaries and inland rivers, while freshwater meres yielded brown trout, perch, pike and char (a rare species found only in the deeper lakes) in the lakes of the Lake District; roach, pike, perch and bream in Martin Mere.[18]

Riches of another kind were to be found in the solid geology, the variety of the region's mineral resources underlying the diversity of its industrial landscapes. The exploitation of a scarce geological resource of high value could transform a locality, adding another layer to the complex landscape mosaic. Outcrops of solid rock are rarely far away (except in coastal lowlands around Carlisle, the

Fylde and parts of west Lancashire) and most of the major rock formations have been quarried for building stone, most notably the 'freestones', both of the Millstone Grit series and the Permo-Triassic Sandstones, which could be cut to shape readily. Where a rock outcrop was found to split into thin slabs, it could be exploited for slates or flagstones for roofing. Limestone could be quarried and burnt, both to sweeten the land and to make mortar for building; boulder clay could be dug for brick-making. The scale of quarrying for building ranges from the small excavations for local use to the vast, cavernous workings which yielded sandstone, lime and slate to create the towns and cities of the Industrial Revolution.

The rocks of the Carboniferous Coal Measures underlying south Lancashire and West Cumberland contained rich seams of coal, the exploitation of which transformed the landscapes of those areas and acted as a magnet for coal-using industries. Metal ores were equally significant. Mineralisation had occurred in both the Carboniferous rocks of the Pennines and the older rocks of the Lake District, producing veins of lead, copper and other ores. Deposits of iron ore were found in association with coal, while haematite, a particularly pure form of the mineral, occurred around Egremont and in the Furness peninsula.

How and why human beings have moulded and modified the landscape can be understood only if the distribution of natural resources is taken into account. Patterns of human activity are determined, at one level, by the location of soils attractive to settlement and of those to be avoided, of environments supporting particular species of plants, animals, birds and fish, and of the rocks and minerals beneath the surface. But such geographical determinism is only part of the story, a necessary but not sufficient explanation for the patterns of human use of the environment. We cannot explain the legacy of human activity in the landscape without understanding the economic stimuli, technological constraints and legal or institutional frameworks that influenced how past societies appropriated the land and assigned it to individuals and communities. It is the interface between the natural environment and these cultural factors that forms the subject matter of the following chapters.

THE FRAMEWORK OF HUMAN OCCUPATION

As a preface to that discussion, let us consider in broad outline how past societies have appropriated the land to their use. The human ecology of the North West may be considered at both a regional and a local level. At the regional level, the environments of the fells and moors and the lowland mosses were hostile to early settlement, with the result that most human activity was channelled into the fragmented lowland areas between these two extremes. The ebb and flow of settlement between the Mesolithic and the early medieval periods, and the consequent impact of human activity on vegetation, is outlined in Chapter 3. The cumulative impact of those millennia of settlement created the framework within which the historic landscape of the past thousand years has evolved. Large areas of the lowlands had been more or less cleared of trees: pollen evidence suggests that very little woodland remained on the Cumberland lowlands by AD 800, and the name of the Fylde (Old English *feld*, 'open country') implies that it was open land by medieval times.[19] But the early medieval landscape also contained areas in which substantial woodland cover remained. Place-name evidence, while not providing a close chronology, can be used to identify those areas where woodland survived by the end of the Anglo-Saxon period (Figs 2.10 and 2.11). The place-name elements *lēah* (Old English, 'clearing in woodland', as in Cadley and Chorley), *skógr* (Old Norse, 'wood', as in Middlesceugh and Myerscough), *viðr* (another Old Norse term meaning 'wood', as in Blawith and Skirwith) and *wudu* (Old English 'wood', as in

Fulwood and Harwood) record the presence of woodland itself, while names referring to pigs, notably the elements *gríss* and *svín* (Old Norse, 'pig', as in Grisedale and Swinside), also indicate woodland, as pannage (payment for pigs grubbing acorns) was a major source of income from woods.

In Cumbria (Fig. 2.10), the place-name evidence suggests that woods survived mainly along the fringes of the uplands: along the North Pennine edge, east of the Eden valley (recorded in names such as Haresceugh, Swindale and Keisley); and on the fringes of the Lake District (where there are several Grizedales, Swinsides and Swindales). Two larger areas of late-surviving woodland can be identified. The first is Inglewood, the wooded core of the medieval royal forest between Penrith and Carlisle, where a scatter of '–sceugh' (*skógr*) names record woodland in the Scandinavian period. The second is on the southern edge of the Lake District, where Furness fells remained heavily wooded in the 16th century and place-name evidence (the township name Woodland and a concentration of names containing the Scandinavian element –*thwaite*, 'a clearing') suggests that the low fells between the River Crake and Kirkby Pool had contained significant woodland at an earlier period.

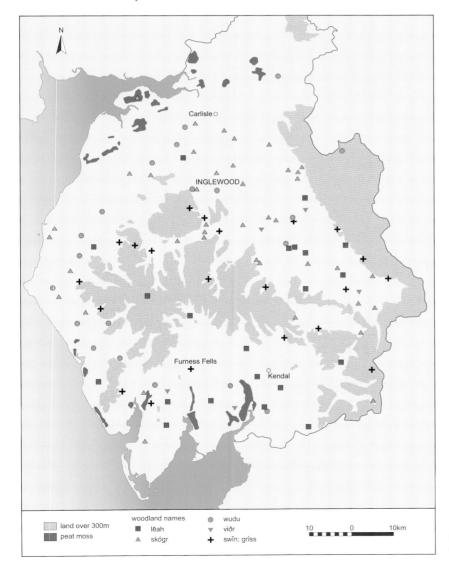

Fig. 2.10 Cumbria: place-names denoting woodland.

Fig. 2.11 Lancashire: place-names denoting woodland.

In parts of Lancashire (Fig. 2.11), the wooded areas may have been more extensive in the early medieval period. The Domesday Book records substantial woodland in the Wigan area, reflected by the numerous woodland place-names in southern Lancashire. Woodland names are also scattered along the foothills of the higher ground. In addition to those plotted on the map are other names recording individual blocks of woodland, such as *shaw* (and its variant *shay*) and *hurst*, which are often found in association with other woodland names, as in the names Stonyhurst, Studlehurst, Crowshaw and Cadshaw, associated with the group of *lēah* names skirting Longridge Fell. The clustering of woodland names suggests the survival of several distinct belts of woodland, as do the names which identify places as being 'in the woods'. The cluster of woodland names around Chorley, for example, is reflected in the names Whittle-le-Woods and Clayton-le-Woods (so-called to distinguish these places from Welch Whittle and Clayton-le-Moors). Similarly, the scatter of woodland names along the western and southern fringes of the Bowland fells is reflected in the name of Woodplumpton, distinguishing it from Fieldplumpton (now Great and Little Plumpton) in the treeless Fylde. When plotted in relation to the inhospitable uplands and the lowland mosses, the distribution of woodland place-names suggests that areas of early settlement were particularly fragmented across southern Lancashire. A swathe of woodland names between Chat Moss and the Rossendale moors separated the Manchester area from the rest of the county, while the woodland around Chorley, wedged between Rossendale and the mosses west of Leyland, divided the lowlands of south-west Lancashire from the Ribble valley.

The combination of physical constraints (in the form of lowland mosses and marsh and upland moorland and fell) and a deep-seated contrast between anciently settled lowland areas and a woodland frontier meant that core areas of human occupation were restricted and fragmented. At a regional level, the contrast between anciently settled lowland cores and the peripheral areas of woodland, wetland and upland is a fundamental feature of the landscape of the pre-industrial North West.

At local level the framework of settlement took account of the character of the soil. Although mineral resources were exploited by 'pre-industrial' peoples from the Neolithic period onwards, past generations in a rural and primarily agrarian society viewed the land from an agricultural perspective. The first requirement to sustain human life was land that was suitable for growing crops. In the environment of the North West, the principal determinants were climate and the natural drainage characteristics of the soil: free- or comparatively free-draining soils were at a premium and determined where settlement took place. In the lowlands, potential arable land was restricted to the islands or ridges of till; in the uplands to free-draining land in the narrow tongues of valley floor. Both in prehistory and in the medieval period settlement was thus constrained by water, avoiding the wetlands and areas of impeded drainage and clinging to the drier islands that had seen settlement by previous generations.

From these arable cores the territory used and appropriated by each community extended out into wetter or steeper land as population pressure increased in medieval times and later drove people to colonise these less-favoured areas. Most communities in the North West also contained within their bounds substantial acreages which remained in a semi-natural state until the 18th or 19th centuries. These 'moors', as they were usually called, were, in Camden's words, 'barren places, which cannot easily by the painfull labour of the husbandman be brought to fruitfulnesse'.[20] In the lowlands, traditional terminology preserved in minor place-names and field-names distinguished between the differing quality of such wastes: *moor* was used of cold, heavy clay land; *carr* described waterlogged land growing a wet woodland of willow and alder; *moss* referred to the peatmoss proper.

The boundaries between communities were drawn to embrace shares in each type of land. This can be seen by examining the boundaries between civil parishes on modern large-scale maps, which are often inherited from those of the medieval townships (the basic units of medieval local administration, consisting of a village and its lands). These administrative boundaries form an invisible web dividing the landscape into blocks of territory, each representing the landed resource belonging to an individual community. Once defined, they tended to form a stable framework of rights in land, parcelling out the patchwork of landforms and soils, and hence influencing patterns of human activity across the centuries.[21]

On the south bank of the Ribble estuary, for example, each of the townships was centred on a village on the clay ridge, but embraced shares of salt marsh by the estuary and of the extensive basin of peatmoss inland (Fig. 2.12). The pattern was repeated elsewhere in the coastal lowlands, creating a framework to the local landscape across the medieval and early modern centuries. Birkdale, near Southport, for example, was described in 1701 as being divided into 'the Heys', that is the enclosed fields on sands and gravels in the centre of the township; 'the Hawes', the sandy wastes between the enclosed land and the sea; and 'the Mosses', the unreclaimed peat moss to the east.[22]

Fig. 2.12 Much Hoole and Little Hoole, Lancashire. *The township boundaries run across the grain of the land, giving each settlement shares of salt marsh and peat moss, as well as farmland on the boulder clay ridge.*

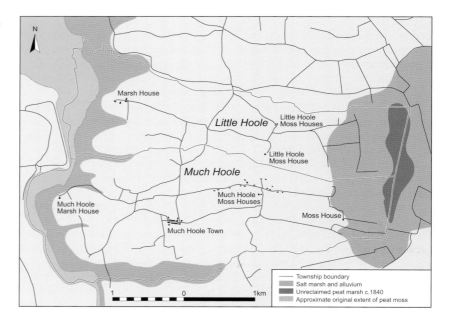

Fig. 2.13 Boredale, near Ullswater: *the limit of enclosed farmland in the uplands, marked by the striking vegetational contrast either side of the 'head-dyke.'*

In the uplands, where altitude, exposure and thinning soils severely limited settlement and cultivation (Fig. 2.13), the boundaries between communities were drawn to give each access to the resources of moorland and fell. These extensive upland wastes formed a vital resource in an environment in which potential crop land was severely limited, since they formed the summer grazing grounds for livestock. In such an environment, the boundaries between communities often followed the watershed along the crest of the fells.

When and how did the boundaries between communities come to be defined? As we shall see in Chapter 3, settled farming communities have lived in the North West for at least 6,000 years, so notions of land ownership and the appropriation of resources stretch back many centuries before the first written record. It is important to remember that the use of land and exploitation of resources are intimately bound up with patterns of land ownership, to the extent that tracing the evolution of boundaries between communities becomes an exercise in charting the process by which ownership rights came to be defined. The communities that grew into the villages and hamlets recorded in medieval sources were not entering on virgin territory: elements of a framework of territorial boundaries were probably inherited from earlier periods, though the extent of such an inheritance is hidden from us. Where land appropriated for agriculture by one community abutted against that cultivated by its neighbours, boundaries will have been set at an early date, often before the earliest written record. It is at the frontiers of medieval colonisation and in the wastes between communities that it is possible to chart the evolution of boundaries in the historic period.

The process was attenuated and accompanied by numerous disputes, particularly over rights in wetland and moorland wastes, where the processes of reclamation and enclosure, discussed in Chapter 6, brought neighbouring communities into conflict. Points of past friction are recorded on the modern map in place-names containing the element *threap* ('a dispute'), such as Threaplands (one of several instances of this name lies close to the boundaries between Newby, Sleagill and Reagill, near Shap, for example), Threap Green (on the boundary between Slaidburn and Bolton-by-Bowland) and Three Post Green (formerly Threapers Green, where the townships of Mawdesley, Heskin and Wrightington met). As population levels rose and the intensity of land use increased, conflicts between communities were resolved by determining clear boundaries defining the territories exclusive to each. Examples abound from the 13th to the 18th centuries, dividing lowland mosses and moors and upland hill grazings: colonisation of moorland at Winscales, near Workington, lay behind the definition of boundaries in the vicinity in 1227 and 1278; disputes over rights to peat prompted the division of the mosses around Downholland in south-west Lancashire in 1532 and 1555. The landscape legacy of this process includes boundary stones and cairns and, on occasion, physical boundaries: in 1277, for example, the fell-top boundary between Rydal and Grasmere was defined and marked by a wall and bank, which can still be traced on Lord Crag.[23] Yet rights over some peripheral wastes remained undefined or disputed until the 19th century, so that the network of territorial boundaries often evolved over many centuries, with some sections being defined only comparatively recently.

Once established, territorial boundaries formed a framework of fundamental importance in the history of the landscape. Not only did they define the agricultural resources available to individual settlements, but, as the boundaries of manorial lordship, they also parcelled out the rights belonging to lords of the manor. These included such lordly prerogatives as fisheries and game, but also (and of particular significance) the mineral rights, the exploitation of which revolutionised large parts of the North West during the Industrial Revolution.

The boundaries between communities transformed a raw, untamed landscape into home, as each community took possession of the resources of a defined tract of territory. The spectrum of local environments within the North West offered a range of potential resources and presented challenges in the form of environmental constraints. As we shall see, human activity accentuated differences in some areas (particularly where the vortex of industrialisation transformed an area offering a particular resource), but levelled them elsewhere (through drainage and reclamation for farming, for example). Yet the resulting mosaic of landscapes moulded by mankind still reflects the diversity of the natural environment.

NOTES

1 de Selincourt 1906, 52
2 The following sections are based on King 1976 and Johnson 1985
3 Denton 2003, 300
4 Ibid, 272–3, 354, 358
5 Hodgkinson *et al.* 2000, 106
6 Denton 2003, 414
7 Morris 1982, 165
8 PRO, DL44/223, m. 2
9 Toulmin Smith 1906–10, IV, 11
10 Tooley in Johnson 1985, 108–9; Cowell & Innes 1994, 76
11 Beck 1953
12 Morris 1982, 161
13 LRO, DDCl/688, evidence of Ric. Rogerley.
14 PRO, DL44/426, m. 2
15 Hodgkinson *et al.* 2000, 121; Hall *et al.*, 1995, 23
16 Moore in Chambers 1993, 217–24
17 Winchester 2000a, 123–38; Denton 2003, 104, 135
18 Winchester 1987, 107–13; Coney 1992, 57–9; Hale and Coney 2005, 105–11
19 Walker 1966
20 Camden 1610, 759
21 For an overview see Winchester 2000c
22 *VCH Lancs*. III, 238n
23 Winchester 1987, 29–30, 163; Winchester 2000a, 29–30; Downholland: LRO, DDM 19/23; PRO, DL5/10, fols 144b–147 (I am grateful to Bill Shannon for the latter references)
24 Morris 1982, 169

THE COLOUR OF THE COUNTRYSIDE

The underlying geology imparts colour to the countryside. Not only do geological parent materials produce soils of varying hues, the character of which affects both natural vegetation and human land use, but locally obtained building materials also impart distinctive colour and character to the built environment. Across the North West the dominant colour changes frequently.

The Carlisle plain and Eden valley are a red country, underlain by rich, pink-brown Permo-Triassic Sandstones. From these derived a reddish glacial drift producing the sticky red ploughsoil of the Carlisle plain and the sandy-coloured glaciofluvial deposits east of Eden (right). The sandstones of the area were easily worked, soft freestones, making excellent building material. The red stone houses of the area struck Celia Fiennes on her journey in 1698: 'The stones and slatt about Peroth [Penrith] look'd so red that at my entrance into the town [I] thought its buildings were all of brick'.[24] Further west, on the Solway lowlands, where rock outcrops are absent, the traditional building material was dull red clay from the glacial drift.

Southern Cumbria, by contrast, is grey and green. Both the Silurian Mudstones and the Carboniferous Limestone weather to hues of grey and, with little land under cultivation, the dominant colours in the landscape are the greens of improved grassland and the browns of bracken and fell grasses (middle right). The 'old, grey town' of Kendal and its surrounding villages are built of limestone (traditionally roughcast in grey, but in the Victorian period sometimes cut and smoothed to ashlar) or of irregular blocks of Silurian rock.

Most of northern and eastern Lancashire and north-west Yorkshire is gritstone country, dominated by shades of brown (below). The sandstones of the Millstone Grit and Coal Measure

series vary in texture, hardness and colour, though they are generally yellower and harder than the Permo-Triassic Sandstones of northern Cumbria. Some are close-grained; others sandier and containing pebbles. The predominant colours are the yellow-browns and grey-browns seen in the 19th-century stone terraces of the textile towns of east Lancashire, but shades of pale grey and pink are also found. In the countryside gritstone farmhouses and dry stone walls are set in a pastoral landscape, where beds of rushes, reflecting the impeded drainage of the boulder clay drift, and brown, bare moorland reinforce the colour of the stone.

In the mosslands of south-west Lancashire, the dominant colours are the blue-black of the drained peat, now rich market garden land, and the blue and white of the overarching sky in this level, windswept landscape (right). The landscape is punctuated by the soft reds and oranges of brick and sandstone buildings.

3

People in the Landscape

It is almost certainly over 10,000 years since human eyes first watched the sun setting over the Irish Sea. Since then countless generations have left their mark on the landscape, temporarily or permanently, intentionally or as an unintended by-product of their activity. Successive migrants have settled the North West – from other regions of England, from Ireland, Scotland and Wales, from mainland Europe, from Africa and from Asia – and have made the region their home, each adding a distinctive flavour to the region's cultural mix. In order to understand the landscape we see today, the outlines of this long history of human settlement need to be grasped. This chapter sketches the peopling of the region from prehistory to the 20th century and identifies the key cultural elements which underlie patterns of human activity.

THE PEOPLING OF A PERIPHERAL AREA

For most of human history, the communities living and working in the region depended directly on the land for their survival. Population levels were low by modern standards (the population of England probably never exceeded 6 million until the 18th century). The transition to an industrial society, particularly the huge social and economic transformations of the Industrial Revolution period (between approximately 1780 and 1880), was accompanied by a demographic sea change: the population of Lancashire increased fivefold between 1801 and 1881.

Land-taking from prehistory to medieval times

The ebb and flow of population levels from prehistory to medieval times can only be seen indirectly (through evidence of woodland clearance and regeneration, or through place-names, for example). In a region containing much agriculturally marginal land, population growth occurred during periods of warmth (in the Bronze Age, during the Roman occupation and in the 'mini Climatic Optimum' of the early medieval centuries), while deteriorating climate was accompanied by population decline, notably in the first millennium BC and in the post-Roman centuries.

The first evidence of a human presence in the North West comes from objects discarded by the hunter-gatherers who roamed the tundra of the late-glacial period. Finds from limestone caves, such as Victoria Cave, near Settle, where stone tools and antler harpoons have been found, and Kirkhead Cave, close to Morecambe Bay near Grange over Sands, suggest that the tundra landscape of the early post-glacial period was traversed by hunters in search of game. Dramatic and very early evidence of such huntsmen comes from the skeleton of an elk, wounded by barbed arrows and other projectiles, which died in a shallow lake near Poulton-le-Fylde c. 10000 BC.[1]

By the time the climate was temperate and the environment heavily wooded, the evidence of human occupation is more extensive. Archaeological evidence from the Mesolithic period (*c.* 8000–4000 BC) comes largely from places on the boundaries between ecosystems, where resources of different environments could be exploited. At Eskmeals, on the Cumbrian coast (Fig. 3.1), where coastal, riverine and woodland environments converged, human groups were gathering by *c.* 5600 BC, and there is evidence of a more settled community, perhaps beginning to domesticate cattle, by 4500–4000 BC. Mesolithic flint tools have also been found inland near fresh water, notably on the limestone plateau surrounding Malham Tarn, around the edges of mosslands in south Lancashire and on the margins of the uplands, such as Anglezarke Moor, on the edge of the Rossendale fells. On the last, a scatter of chert and the possible remains of simple buildings have been interpreted as evidence of seasonal occupation, as bands of people migrated between upland and lowland hunting grounds.[2]

Fig. 3.1 Eskmeals, *in south-west Cumbria, the location of a Mesolithic settlement.*

The scale and nature of human activity in the landscape becomes clearer after settled farming communities were established. Major archaeological remains survive from the Neolithic period (4000–2500 BC), notably the great megalithic monuments such as the Castlerigg stone circle or the henges at Eamont Bridge, near Penrith, while analysis of pollen preserved in peat mosses and lake-bed sediments provides a record of environmental change as a result of human activity. Woodland clearance for Neolithic agriculture is well attested on the west Cumberland lowlands: at Barfield Tarn, near Millom, for example, a drop in tree pollen *c.* 3500 BC coincided with the appearance of weeds, grasses and possibly cereal pollen and with evidence of increased run-off and soil erosion from the margins of the tarn.[3] The Neolithic impact was less pronounced in the uplands, but their presence is attested by the stone axe factories in the heart of the Lake District, manufacturing the tools with which woodland in the lowlands was cleared for farming. The extent of woodland clearance appears to have varied: along the narrow coastal strip of south-west Cumberland it was intense, while elsewhere, around the margins of Morecambe Bay and on Merseyside for example, population levels may have been considerably lower, clearances short-lived and the landscape impact correspondingly less.

Favourable climatic conditions during much of the Bronze Age (2500–700 BC) stimulated a period of intensive settlement, during which much of the landscape may have been occupied and utilised. Population levels were probably significantly higher than in earlier eras. The pollen record shows continuing woodland clearance and a significant change from a predominantly wooded to a largely open environment by c. 1000 BC, recorded from both upland and lowland sites in Cumbria and in the Rossendale moors.[4] The environmental evidence is corroborated by the extensive archaeological remains of Bronze Age activity in the form of cairns and other structures along the margins of the uplands.

Climatic deterioration between c.1000 and c. 500 BC appears to have led to a retreat of settlement and farming activity from the upland margins, and there is some evidence of woodland regeneration. This era of retrenchment was followed during the Iron Age and Romano-British periods by a major phase of settlement expansion and woodland clearance, which is recorded in pollen evidence from across the region. The precise dating of this major clearance phase (sometimes referred to as the Brigantian clearance) continues to be debated, though there is increasing evidence that it began before the Roman occupation. Pollen evidence from sites in Cumbria, the Fylde, Bowland and south-west Lancashire all record widespread woodland clearance in the late Iron Age, continuing into the Romano-British period, implying rising population levels. Deforestation on the unstable slopes of the Howgill fells led to a period of soil erosion and gullying, which has been dated to this period.

Archaeological evidence from the Romano-British period also points to high levels of population. Numerous 'native' farmsteads of the indigenous British population, surviving as earthworks on the fringes of the uplands and as crop-marks in the lowlands, and the extensive *vici* (civilian settlements) attached to the Roman forts suggest that the landscape of the late Iron Age and Romano-British centuries must have been closely settled, with much of the farmland of later centuries already cleared and used.[5] The garrisons of the forts and the communities that grew around them constituted an ethnic mix of people from across the Roman empire (Fig. 3.2).

For the centuries between the end of the Roman occupation c. AD 410 and the Black Death of 1348–9, the evidence of place-names

Fig. 3.2 Roman tombstone from Netherby, north of Carlisle, in memory of Titullinia Pussitta, a 38-year-old woman from Rhaetia (modern Bavaria and north-west Austria), who was probably living in the civilian settlement close to the fort.

and, latterly, of documents can be added to the environmental evidence to reconstruct population trends. This critical period saw the establishment of the rural settlement pattern and the framework of the rural landscape we see today, and the foundation of the region's older towns. Absolute population figures are impossible to calculate, but movements of peoples and the broad trends in population levels can be reconstructed.

It is now generally agreed that the Roman withdrawal did not result in an immediate population collapse. However, there is increasing evidence that some form of demographic catastrophe occurred in Britain during the first half of the 6th century, perhaps associated with climatic deterioration or an environmental crisis in the late 530s. Analysis of pollen from sites in northern Cumbria suggests woodland regeneration during the post-Roman centuries, implying a lowering of population levels in this period.[6] Our knowledge of conditions in the North West between 400 and 650 is extremely hazy, but we can assume the existence of

Fig. 3.3 The Early Medieval North West. *(a) Early Old English place-names; (b) Scandinavian place-names.*

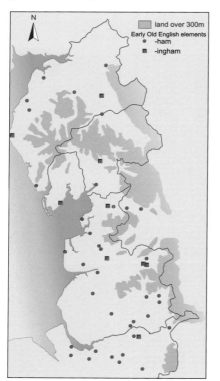

a.

b.

British tribal groups or kingdoms. It is possible (but by no means certain) that parts of the region, perhaps focused on Carlisle, formed the British kingdom of Rheged, which was absorbed into Anglian Northumbria during the 7th century. By the second half of that century, documentary evidence makes it clear that most of the North West fell within the sway of the expanding kingdom of Northumbria.

The extent to which the absorption of the region into Northumbria was accompanied by an influx of Old English-speaking Anglians is debateable. There is a scatter of early (pre-800) Old English names across the lowlands of the North West, such as those containing the elements *ham*, 'a homestead' (Dearham, Heversham, Bispham, Penwortham, Abram, for example), *ingham*, 'homestead of the family of ...' (Hensingham, Aldingham, Padiham, Whittingham) and *ceaster*, 'a Roman fort or town' (Manchester, Ribchester, Lancaster, Muncaster) (Fig. 3.3(a)). But the North West also possesses a particularly strong legacy of names from the Old Welsh language (such as Penruddock, Cark, Charnock, Ince, Penketh), suggesting that the British population retained their identity for some time. It may be that the Northumbrian period involved political suzerainty and the imposition of an Anglian landed class, while the native British population remained on the land. If such an interpretation is correct, the Northumbrian conquest need not have involved large-scale Anglian immigration, nor led to rising population levels.[7]

Northumbrian power had waned by the 9th century and was further weakened by the conquest of southern Northumbria by the Danes in 876. The power vacuum in the North West was exploited by another wave of settlers of Scandinavian descent who entered the region from the Irish Sea. Their activities barely surface in the written record, almost the only direct reference being to the expulsion of a group of Vikings from Dublin *c.* 902 and their subsequent settlement in Wirral. The cluster of Scandinavian names containing the element *–by* ('a settlement or estate') in Wirral and south-west Lancashire probably derives from this event. But Scandinavian place-names are found across the region, particularly in Cumbria (Fig. 3.3(b)). Some names suggest that Danish settlers moved into the Eden valley across Stainmoor from the Danelaw, but the bulk of the settlers appear to have been largely of Norse (rather than Danish) descent. Distinctively Norse words, such as *gill* ('a ravine') and *breck* ('a slope'), abound, and the place-names also show that they had spent time in Gaelic-speaking territory, probably western Scotland, intermarrying with the Gaelic population. 'Inversion compounds' (place-names which use Gaelic word order, such as Aspatria, from *ask*-Patrick, 'Patrick's ash tree'), the presence of Gaelic personal names (Suthan in Greysouthen, Gussan in Goosnargh, for example) and word borrowings, notably the term *erg* ('a summer pasture ground', deriving from the Gaelic *airigh*, incorporated in names such as Sizergh, Grimsargh and Winder), all suggest that the settlers were of mixed Norse and Gaelic blood.[8]

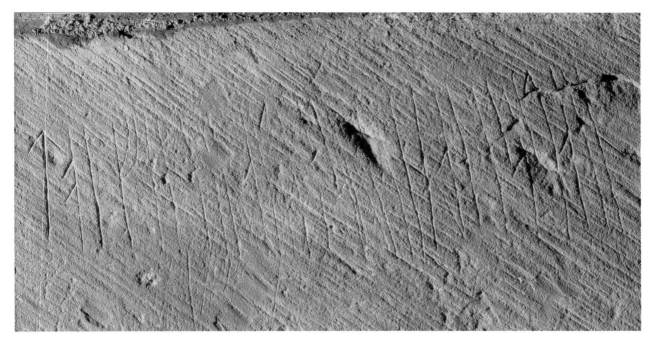

How large was the influx of Scandinavian settlers and what impact did they have on the landscape? These are difficult questions, not only because of the absence of documentary evidence, but also because the Scandinavian influence on language was so strong, particularly in Cumbria, that the presence of Norse elements in place-names does not necessarily demonstrate that these names were coined during the Viking period. The Norse element *thwaite* ('a clearing') continued to be used to create new place-names in the 13th century, for example. Having said that, the 9th and 10th centuries marked the opening of a period of sustained population growth, which continued until the early 14th century. Pollen evidence appears to show a period of woodland clearance approximately coincident with the Viking period in southern Cumbria, which may reflect an intensification of livestock-rearing involving seasonal movement to summer pastures. Such a pattern is suggested by the numerous place-names incorporating the elements *scale* ('a shieling hut'), *seatr* and *erg* (both meaning 'summer pasture').[9]

The communities living in the early medieval North West thus evolved from a diverse ethnic heritage. The legacy of Celtic Britons, Anglian Northumbrians and settlers of mixed Scandinavian/Gaelic blood continued to be seen in personal

Fig. 3.4 Runic graffito, Carlisle Cathedral. Translated, the inscription reads 'Dolfin wrote these runes on this stone'. The carver's Anglo-Scandinavian name and his use of Scandinavian runes reflects the ethnic mix of 12th-century Cumbria.

names in the 12th and 13th centuries (Fig. 3.4). As late as 1270, the inhabitants of the small market town of Cockermouth included two men with the Norse name Lyolf and several more whose fathers had borne Scandinavian names, as well as one with the British name Mungou, the pet name of St Kentigern.[10]

After the Norman Conquest the documentary record becomes much clearer and it is possible to chart the outlines of the major phase of colonisation that accompanied population growth between *c.* 1150 and *c.* 1300. The century of the Conquest itself, the culmination of a period of political turbulence and followed by William's punitive 'Harrying of the North' in 1069–70, appears to have been a period of dislocation: pollen evidence from southern Cumbria hints at a short period of woodland regeneration at this time.[11] But the 12th and 13th centuries saw extensive colonisation across the region. The cultivated area expanded in the lowlands; inroads were made into surviving woodland as new farms and hamlets were established and 'assarting' (clearance for cultivation) took place; on the margins of the uplands shieling grounds were converted into permanent settlements, and in the uplands proper colonisation ran up the dales, so that by 1300 the sites of most post-medieval farmsteads had been occupied. Indeed, there is evidence of pressure on resources and of land hunger by the late 13th century: the impact of assarting on pasture rights led to disputes over rights in land, particularly close to the boundaries between communities, and the presence of numerous landless cottagers is probably another symptom of population pressure.[12]

From Black Death to Industrial Revolution

The 14th century was a demographic watershed in the North West as elsewhere in England. Severe disruption had set in well before the tragedy of the Black Death. Western Europe was swept by famine, resulting from harvest failures in 1315–16, and by cattle plagues in 1319–21. The aftermath of these years is visible in a survey of the barony of Kendal in 1324. Holdings lay untenanted, mills stood idle for much of the year for want of corn, pastures yielded no rent because of a lack of stock: all this suggests economic collapse and a reduction of population.[13] Across the North West, climatic deterioration and widespread sheep disease ('murrain') would have had a heavy impact on a stock-rearing economy in an agriculturally marginal environment.

On top of these longer-term problems came the twin evils of war and pestilence. The Anglo-Scottish border became a hostile frontier when the Scottish raid of 1296 opened three centuries of sporadic warfare. The brunt of the attacks was borne by the far north of Cumbria, but kidnapping, plunder and burning reached deep into the Carlisle plain and Eden valley on several occasions. Less traumatic, but arguably more debilitating, was the requirement to defend the border, which fell more widely on communities across Cumberland, draining men from the land. A few Scottish raids penetrated further south, notably those of 1316 and 1318, when raiding armies swept across the Pennines from Yorkshire into Cumbria and north Lancashire, and the great raid of 1322, when two Scottish armies, converging on Lancaster, surged south as far as Preston.[14]

It was thus a region already weakened and losing population that was devastated by the Black Death in 1349. The scale of the mortality then is open to debate, but there are hints that it may have been as severe as elsewhere, in north Lancashire at least: it was claimed that over 13,000 men and women died between September 1349 and January 1350 in the 10 parishes in Amounderness deanery. Later outbreaks of the plague (notably that in 1361–2, which appears to have been particularly severe in Carlisle diocese) prevented population growth through the late 14th and early 15th centuries.[15] There is scattered evidence of settlement desertion in the late medieval period, such as the deserted village of Stock, near Barnoldswick, or the extensive settlement at Scales on the shore of

Crummock Water, and of settlement shrinkage, such as the empty house platforms at Maulds Meaburn, where one-quarter of the tofts remained 'unbuilt' in 1472.[16]

Recovery, when it came, appears to have been swift. From *c.* 1450 there is evidence of renewed pressure on land and of the growth of the textile industry in Lancashire and southern Cumbria. By 1600 many parts of the region, particularly eastern Lancashire and upland Cumbria, were heavily populated, barely able to support their populations. Holdings of land were often very small; the pastoral bias of the economy meant that communities were dependent on outside supplies of grain, the staple foodstuff; and much of the swelling landless population was dependent on income from spinning and weaving. It was a precarious existence, at the mercy of harvest failures and rocketing grain prices, and local populations were subject to sudden surges in death rates as a consequence. Successive mortality crises, when burials rose to several times the annual average, hit the North West in the century after 1550, related directly or indirectly to the region's susceptibility to harvest failures. The surges in mortality in 1587–8 and 1597 followed successive years of poor harvests and appear to have been famine-related.

The region was hit by another mortality crisis in 1623, when burials ran at up to five times the annual norm in many parishes: significantly, this crisis was not experienced elsewhere in England. There is some explicit evidence for famine, as at Greystoke, near Penrith, where the parish register records the burials of 'a poore hungersterven beger child' and 'a poore man destitute of meanes to live', for example. Grain prices in Lancashire were notably high in 1622 and manor court orders forbidding the poor from congregating at corn mills to seek alms hint at desperation. All these pointers to famine and destitution must be read in the context of a regional economy that had suffered severely from the collapse of the textile trade a few years before. It seems likely that the poor who were dependent on income from textiles suffered extreme dearth and its attendant diseases when the collapse of their income coincided with high grain prices. Fluctuations in grain prices, instability in the textile trades and outbreaks of epidemic disease combined to produce further years of hardship in southern Lancashire, particularly in the later 1640s, in 1654 and 1662. The early 17th century also brought terrifying urban epidemics of plague, hitting Preston in 1630, Manchester in 1645 and Ormskirk in 1648.[17]

The century after 1650 saw much greater demographic stability as the region's economy strengthened and industrialisation began to take hold. Diversification in the textile industries (principally the change from woollens to worsteds and the introduction of cotton, initially woven with wool or linen to produce fustians and cotton-linens) enabled specialisation and intensification of production. Bolton was the focal point of the cotton-using textile trade, from which the development of new mixed cloths spread out to the Blackburn, Oldham and Manchester areas by 1700. These industrialising areas saw a growth and concentration of population, much of it in the countryside where most textile manufacture remained. But industrial towns were also growing substantially by the mid-18th century: Manchester's population stood at over 22,000 by 1773, while other textile towns, such as Bolton, Blackburn and Rochdale, had over 4,000 inhabitants each. The century also saw a population explosion in the ports, as the North Atlantic trade grew: Liverpool, which had under 2,000 people in 1660, had grown to over 34,000 by 1773; Whitehaven, a settlement of perhaps 500 people in the 1660s, had a population of over 9,000 by 1762.[18]

The impact of the three centuries between 1450 and 1750 was to generate increasing divergence between proto-industrial Lancashire and rural Cumbria. As southern Lancashire entered a phase of Industrial Revolution, it became a patchwork of manufacturing specialisations. In contrast (with the exception of woollen textiles in the Kendal area and the collieries and seaborne trade of Whitehaven and its hinterland), Cumbria remained largely rural and agrarian.

The first industrial society

The face of the North West's present-day landscape is, in large part, a product of the major economic and social upheavals of the period referred to in shorthand as the Industrial Revolution. Central to this was the demographic transformation of the century that occurred between 1780 and 1880 (*see* Table 3.1). Not only did the number of people in England and Wales explode (from around 7 million in 1780 to almost 26 million in 1881), but the distribution of population also underwent massive change. In Lancashire and Cheshire, population grew from under half a million in 1751 to over 5 million by 1901, and the counties' share of the national population almost trebled from 5.7 per cent to 14.3 per cent.[19] Industrial towns and cities became magnets for migration, both from neighbouring rural areas and from further afield. While the absolute numbers of people living in the countryside of Cumbria and north Lancashire continued to rise through the initial decades of rising birth rates, most rural communities in these areas had peaked by 1821 or 1831, and declined thereafter. In contrast, the textile towns of central and south-east Lancashire and the areas of heavy industry between Manchester and Liverpool grew rapidly: the populations of Blackburn and Preston grew almost ninefold across the 19th century, while Manchester, Liverpool and Wigan experienced more than fivefold increases.

Table 3.1 Population growth from 1801; census statistics for selected regions.

COUNTY	POPULATION			
	1801	*1851*	*1901*	*1951*
CUMBERLAND	117,230	195,492	266,933	285,338
WESTMORLAND	40,805	58,287	64,409	67,392
LANCASHIRE	673,486	2,031,236	4,406,409	5,117,853

Much of the migration into the growing industrial settlements in Lancashire took place over comparatively short distances, as shown by studies of census returns from individual communities. At Wesham in the Fylde, for example, where two cotton mills were established in the 1850s and a third in 1864, the population of the new mill town was drawn largely from adjacent villages, where there had already been a tradition of handloom weaving. In larger towns longer-distance migration did occur, particularly among the more skilled workforce, who might pursue their specialism across Britain. Manchester and Liverpool drew population from wide hinterlands, attracting incomers from most regions of Britain, while migrants to a smaller town like Lancaster came largely from adjacent counties.[20]

One aspect of migration during the 19th century had a particular impact on the region – the arrival of substantial numbers of immigrants from the Celtic regions of the British Isles. The links between the ports of the North West and Ireland reached back well before the Industrial Revolution, but the hardship of the Irish famine of 1846–7 brought a flood of poor Irish migrants, particularly to Liverpool. The 1851 census recorded that 22 per cent of Liverpool's population had been born in Ireland, and significant proportions of Irish-born were recorded in other towns: 13 per cent in Manchester and Salford; over 10 per cent in Stockport; 8 per cent in Carlisle; 7 per cent in Preston. The bulk of the migrants were manual labourers, and poverty, discrimination and religious separation resulted in a clustering of Irish migrants in particular parts of a town or city. Liverpool's Irish population, for example, consisting largely of labourers and dock workers, was concentrated by 1871 near the docks on the north side of the city. Many Irish also settled in the growing industrial communities of west Cumberland and Furness. In Cleator Moor, the iron-mining capital of west Cumberland, 36 per cent of the population were Irish-born in 1871 (Fig. 3.5). Irish immigration boosted the strength of Roman Catholicism in the industrial towns, but it also imported sectarian rivalries to the areas (such as west Cumbria) where the migrants came largely from Ulster.[21]

Other Celtic territories also contributed to the ethnic mix of the industrial North West. In Cumberland 4.9 per cent of the county's population in 1881 had been born in Scotland. Barrow-in-Furness, one of the boom towns of the 1860s, drew heavily from Scotland, with migrants including engineers and furnacemen from industrial Clydeside and jute workers from Dundee. It also received miners and quarrymen from Wales, Cornwall and the Isle of Man. Liverpool experienced considerable immigration from Scotland and Wales: in 1851 it had 14,000 Scottish-born residents, while in 1871 over 20,000 (more than 4 per cent of the town's population) had been born in Wales. Like the other elements of that cosmopolitan port, the Welsh community was associated with a particular sector of the economy, in this case the building trades. In contrast to the Irish community, the Liverpool Welsh included a significant business elite, who played a leading part in the development of Welsh national consciousness in the late 19th century.[22]

The substantial Irish, Welsh and Scottish elements in the population of the North West by the late 19th century thus added a distinctive Celtic flavour to the region. Migration from further afield contributed smaller, but nonetheless significant, elements to the racial mix. As windows to the wider world, the ports had long been home to ethnic minorities: the slave trade brought a scatter of Africans to the region in the 18th century and Liverpool became increasingly cosmopolitan, with established enclaves of West African seamen (the Kru) and Chinese merchants by the early 20th century. Manchester's Jewish community, which can be traced back to a group established *c.* 1795, was swelled by significant immigration from Russia and Poland in the 1860s. The new Ashkenazi arrivals were concentrated in 1871 in the city's poor Red Bank district, in contrast to the established and wealthy Sephardic community in Cheetham Hill.[23]

By the late 19th century, the region's population was thus weighted heavily to the south. Yet the influence of that industrial heartland was felt across the North West. Ancillary industries, such as bobbin-turning in the woods of southern Cumbria, sprang up in the rural periphery; resort towns grew along the coast, providing lungs for the industrial towns; valleys in the Pennines and Lake District were dammed to provide water for the conurbations. The tentacles of the 'first industrial society' that had grown up in Lancashire spread far, so that few parts of the North West landscape are untouched by the revolutions of the century after 1780.

Fig. 3.5 First World War memorial tablet, St Mary's Roman Catholic church, Cleator. The preponderance of Irish names among the soldiers remembered here reflects the importance of Irish immigration into industrial west Cumberland.

In common with other industrial areas of Britain, the North West suffered in the economic depression of the 1920s and 1930s. Foreign competition and the loss of export markets knocked the Lancashire textile towns from their position of pre-eminence. Exhaustion of coal and iron ore deposits, and the increasing obsolescence of Cumbrian steel-making made west Cumberland the epitome of a 'depressed area' as mines and ironworks closed: the population of Cumberland as a whole dropped by 3.7 per cent between 1921 and 1931. In contrast, the wider industrial base of parts of south Lancashire cushioned towns such as St Helens (dominated by glass manufacture) from the worst.

The transition from an industrial to a post-industrial society was gradual and was accompanied by further movements of population. The textile towns of east Lancashire experienced substantial population loss in the mid-20th century: between 1931 and 1971 Blackburn's population dropped by 17 per cent (from 122,800 to 101,800); Nelson's by 18 per cent (from 38,300 to 31,250). By the 1960s this seepage of people had left an ageing population in the mill towns and a shortage of labour, which led mill owners to recruit young male workers from the Indian subcontinent, bringing a new cultural element to the region's already mixed population. The initial migrants of the early 1960s were young, single men, whose families soon followed them to Britain, creating a youthful and quickly growing population. The Asian community in Blackburn grew from 650 in 1961 to 19,300 by 1990, when it accounted for 15 per cent of the borough's population. By 2001 Lancashire (post-1974 boundaries) contained almost 75,000 people who described themselves as Asian, accounting for 5.3 per cent of the population.[24]

As with previous immigrant communities, the Asians tended to settle in enclaves. The patterns of recruitment meant that many of those who came to a particular town shared a common origin. In Nelson, for example, the immigrants largely came from the Gujurat district of Punjab Province in Pakistan, whereas the majority of Blackburn's Asian population originated in the adjacent Indian state of Gujurat. Many Asian families bought terraced houses in the inner zones of the towns, and religious and ethnic divisions were reflected in the patterns of settlement. In Blackburn, for example, the Sunni Muslim majority was concentrated in the Brookhouse area, while the Hindus and Sikhs settled around Preston New Road. Similarly, the Pakistani community in Oldham favoured Glodwick and Coppice, while Bangladeshis were concentrated in the Westwood and Coldhurst areas. This pattern of settlement by ethnic minorities has resulted in high concentrations of newcomers in the older, inner zones of the textile towns: in 1999 the Asian community accounted for almost half the population of inner Oldham, for example (Fig. 3.6).[25]

THE ROOTS OF LOCAL IDENTITIES

The layers of colonisation and population movements outlined above created a patchwork of local societies, each with its own distinct identity and each set in its own distinctive landscape. Such shorthand descriptions as 'a Lakeland farmer' or 'a Scouser' (a Liverpudlian working man) immediately conjure images of people located in particular places. It is to the roots of such local identities that we now turn.

The creation of the historic counties of Cumberland, Westmorland and Lancashire in the 12th century grouped smaller territories, almost certainly of pre-Conquest origin, into units of county administration. The new counties bore little relation to pre-Norman political and cultural geography, the framework of which is preserved most clearly in the boundaries of the medieval dioceses (Fig. 3.7). Northern Cumbria, south to a line running from the River Derwent through the heart of the Lake District to Stainmoor, formed the diocese of Carlisle, created in 1133 by severing the area from the see of Glasgow, to which it had previously belonged. The new diocese covered 'the land of Carlisle', the territory

OPPOSITE PAGE:

Fig. 3.6 Waterloo Street, Glodwick, Oldham in 1998: immigration from the Indian sub-continent in the later 20th century has contributed new cultural elements to the landscapes of many Lancashire mill towns.

Fig. 3.7 The Medieval North West:
(a) county and diocesan boundaries;
(b) early territories.

OPPOSITE PAGE:
Fig. 3.8 Dunmail Raise, *the large cairn
in the heart of the Lake District, marking
the southern boundary of the pre-Conquest
kingdom of Cumbria.*

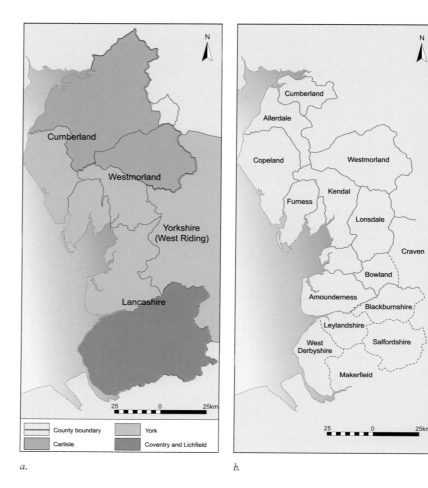

a.

b.

conquered by William II of England in 1092. Glasgow diocese had been the
bishopric of the British kingdom of Strathclyde, and its southern boundary (the
southern boundary of Carlisle diocese from 1133) almost certainly coincided
with the southern limit of Strathclyde power in the 10th and 11th centuries.
Dunmail Raise, the massive cairn on this boundary in the heart of the Lake
District (Fig. 3.8), named after Dunmail or Donald, king of Strathclyde/Cumbria
in the 940s, is thus a boundary marker of great antiquity and significance. To the
north lay territory where British cultural ties remained strong. As well as the
territorial name Cumberland ('the land of the Britons' – originally referring to a
smaller area of the Solway lowlands, south-west of Carlisle), the area contains
both a particularly rich legacy of British place-names, perhaps suggesting that
the British language survived late in enclaves there, and church dedications to
British saints, notably Kentigern, the patron saint of the diocese of Glasgow
(these probably reflecting a sense of Celtic identity in the 10th or 11th century,
rather than dating from the pre-Northumbrian period). Reconstructing pre-
Viking age patterns is fraught with difficulties, but the name Westmorland ('the
land of people dwelling west of the moors') – originally applied to the upper Eden
valley – identifies the territory of an Anglian folk group, as perceived by people in
the Northumbrian heartland to the east of the Pennines.

The Carlisle plain would have formed a natural core area, a tract of lowland,
bounded by the sea and the fells, which probably formed a political, cultural
and economic entity over many centuries. Certainly by the 260s the Roman town
at Carlisle (Luguvalium) appears to have been the focal point of the *civitas*

Carvetiorum, a Romanised tribe called the Carvetii. As we have seen, the town may have formed the core of the shadowy, post-Roman British kingdom of Rheged.

The early political geography of the remainder of the North West is more difficult to reconstruct. The land between the Derwent and the Ribble rivers, consisted of a number of territories forming 'natural' topographical entities, bounded by rivers or watersheds. Their names appear to have been coined in the Anglo-Scandinavian period, since they contain Scandinavian elements: Copeland, between the Derwent and Duddon rivers, is from the Old Norse 'bought land'; Kendal and Lonsdale (the valleys of the Kent and Lune rivers, respectively); Furness ('the headland by the rump-shaped [Peil] island'); Amounderness ('Agmundr's headland'). These territories were a far-flung corner of the medieval diocese of York and were appended to the Yorkshire section of the Domesday Book, suggesting that their links lay towards the Scandinavian kingdom of York in the 10th century. Only the Celtic name Craven (possibly meaning 'scraped land', referring to the exposed limestone scenery) hints at the existence of an earlier, British territorial entity.[26]

To the south of the River Ribble lay territory that fell within the vast Midland diocese of Coventry and Lichfield. Appended to the Domesday survey of the west Midland counties, the 'land between Ribble and Mersey' had been in the hands of the powerful Mercian nobleman Wulfric Spot *c.* AD 1000. Place-names in southern Lancashire also record Mercian influence, the element *bold* (as in Bold and Parbold), for example, being the Mercian equivalent of the Northumbrian *bothl*, meaning 'a high-status dwelling'. Links to Mercia were probably a comparatively recent phenomenon, accompanying the wresting of what later became southern Lancashire from Scandinavian control in the 920s. Until then, the Mersey (Old English for 'boundary river') and its mosslands formed a major political frontier, separating Northumbria from Mercia. The territorial framework of the pre-Conquest landscape between the Ribble and Mersey differed from that further north, consisting of 'shires', large estates focused on a central place, from which they took their name: Blackburnshire, Leylandshire, Salfordshire, for example. The antiquity of these shires is far form clear: hints of an earlier layer of social organisation are provided by the territorial name Makerfield, where a British word meaning 'a wall or ruin' has been combined with the Old English element *feld*, meaning open land.

The political geography of the region on the eve of the Norman Conquest may be compared with deep-seated patterns in the folk culture of pre-industrial society, which can be recaptured by the study of minor place-names and modern dialect. The region is bisected by one of the major divisions in the folk speech of Britain, the boundary between northern and southern dialect forms, which runs roughly from Morecambe Bay to the Humber estuary. To the north, word forms derived from Northumbrian Old English survive: 'stane' and 'hame' instead of 'stone' and 'home'; 'coo' and 'noo' instead of 'cow' and 'now', for example.[27] The fact that the boundary, mapped by the English Dialect Survey carried out in the 1950s, runs through Morecambe Bay, whereas the southern limits of Northumbria originally stretched to the Mersey, reinforces the notion that southern influences have been much greater in Lancashire than in Cumbria and illustrates the cultural contrast between the two areas.

The linguistic pattern is illustrated very clearly by the words for a stream or rivulet (Fig. 3.9). In north-east Cumbria the word is *burn*, the Old English term for a stream favoured in Northumbria (and transported thence into lowland Scotland). Across the rest of Cumbria, the far north of Lancashire and north-west Yorkshire the term used is the Scandinavian *beck*. It is striking that the swathe of land from the Lake District to the Yorkshire Dales is the heartland of the Viking legacy in both place-names and dialect. Scandinavian words, such as *laik* ('to play'), *lea* ('a scythe') and *ket* ('rubbish'), survived almost to the present day in these upland areas.

From Lancaster southwards, the most frequent word for a stream is *brook*, the Old English term common across much of southern and midland England, though Cock Beck near Ormskirk is a reminder of the Scandinavian influence in south-west Lancashire. In general, southern cultural influences were particularly strong south of the Ribble, mirroring the political links discussed above. A striking example of this is the survival in the dialect of southern Lancashire of the Old English form of the pronoun 'she' in the dialect word *hoo*, found in the north-west Midlands and extending into Lancashire. Another is the traditional 'customary acre' used to measure land. In much of the North West the local acre was based on a 21-foot or 7-yard (6.4m) pole or perch, whereas Lancashire south of the Ribble used the larger Cheshire acre based on a 24-foot or 8-yard (7.3m) perch.[28]

There was thus no single folk culture across the whole of the North West. In terms of pre-industrial society, the region may be conceived of as containing three distinct zones: northern Cumbria, where the affinities were more towards Northumbria and Scotland; the upland zone of the Lake District and the Pennine spurs, where a strong Scandinavian legacy survived; and lowland Lancashire, where the links with 'mainland' England were strongest.

Superimposed on that pre-industrial map were the cultural regions that developed as a result of industrialisation. High population densities, the particular patterns of migration found in each industrial heartland and the distinctive lifestyles associated with different industries combined to create strongly individual industrial folk cultures. Underlying them was the bedrock of a powerful and almost monolithic working-class culture, epitomised by life in the mill towns.

The need to forge and reinforce local identities in an age of rapid population growth was expressed in various ways. At regional level, the wave of publication of dialect poetry and prose, which swept across northern England in the second half of the 19th century, proclaimed the personality of Lancashire, which saw more dialect publications than any other English county.[29] At local

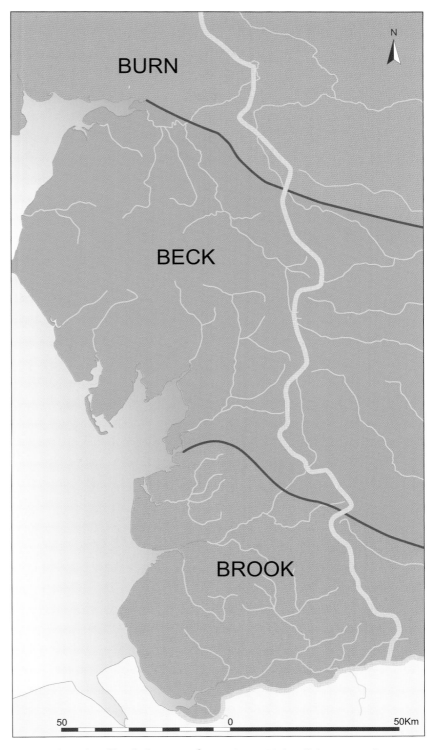

Fig. 3.9 Major dialect zones: the distribution of the three dominant terms for a stream recorded on 19th-century Ordnance Survey maps.

SURNAMES
AND HISTORY

Family names, which had become hereditary in north-west England by the end of the 14th century, moved with their owners. Many surnames were remarkably local in their original distribution, particularly where a surname is a habitation name, often a minor place-name indicating the family's initial place of residence. Such names can provide an

indication of patterns of migration since the later medieval period.

It is also possible to examine more recent immigration by looking at the distribution of names brought into the region from elsewhere (left). The four maps discussed here illustrate both 'native' and immigrant surnames and are based on entries in the 2003 telephone directory.

The indigenous surnames (opposite page top) are both habitation names which originated in particular local areas, though the place-names from which they derived can no longer be identified with certainty. Routledge originated on the Anglo-Scottish border, where it is recorded from the 16th century, especially in the parish of Bewcastle. Even today, almost half of the 219 Routledge households in the North West live in the northern half of Cumbria. The name's Cumbrian origin is also reflected in the concentration of Routledges in Liverpool, which received numerous Cumbrian migrants during the 18th and 19th centuries. However, the surname also spread to Yorkshire, being recorded near Leeds in the 17th century. The minor concentrations of Routledges in Manchester, Bury and Rochdale probably represent movement across the Pennines, rather than direct migration from north Cumbria.

Bamber is a much more numerous surname, represented by over 550 households. Its origins lay in the Fylde, where Bamber, Bamburgh or Bawmber families are recorded in the 16th century in hamlets that were later swallowed up by the growth of Blackpool. By the 17th century there were Bambers across the

Fylde and in villages south of the Ribble, where the family name was transferred to the settlement of Bamber Bridge. The modern distribution remains focused on central Lancashire, with the largest single concentration in Preston and a persistence in rural communities in the Lancashire lowlands. Although the surname has spread across the region, it remains strongest in its heartland: it is striking how quickly the number of Bambers declines as one moves east of Preston, reflecting the separate identity of the east Lancashire towns.

Migration from Ireland in the 19th century is visible in the large numbers of Irish surnames in the North West today. One of these, the comparatively rare surname McCourt (below left), had a fairly restricted distribution in Ireland, being concentrated in the counties of Louth and Armagh. In the North West its distribution reflects migration from Ulster: of the 100 McCourts in the telephone directory, more than one-third are clustered along the Cumbrian coast,

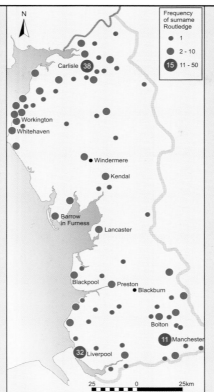

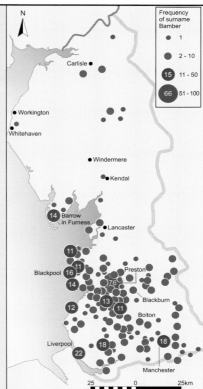

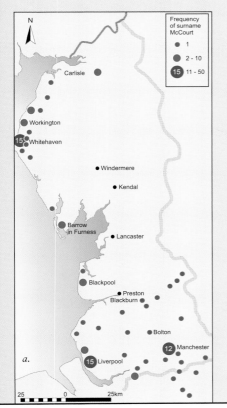

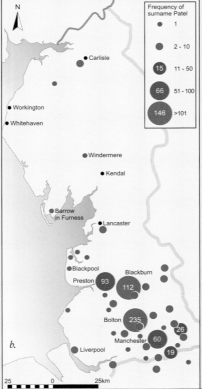

while the only other major concentrations are in Liverpool and Manchester, both of which had substantial Irish communities. It is striking that hardly any of the McCourts are found in rural areas, reflecting the predominantly urban nature of Irish immigration.

The most numerous surname illustrated here is the most recent arrival. Patel (left) originated in Gujurat as an occupational surname, meaning 'village leader', and arrived in the North West as a result of Asian immigration to the Lancashire cotton towns in the 1960s. Over two-thirds of the 631 Patel households in the region live in the three towns of Bolton (226), Blackburn (112) and Preston (93). The name's restricted distribution also reflects its recent arrival: it remains heavily concentrated in industrial south-east Lancashire, with very few Patels living elsewhere in the region.

level, existing folk customs might be re-modelled: the custom of begging food at Easter, for example, developed into an elaborate ritual involving music, dancing and recitation of verses in parts of the region, especially in the Lancashire textile towns. Rushbearing (the ritual summer procession of children bearing flowers and fresh rushes to be strewn on the church floor) was recorded from the 17th century from southern and eastern Cumbria through the western Pennines of Lancashire and the far west of Yorkshire to Cheshire and Derbyshire. By the end of the 18th century the custom had taken a distinctive and more elaborate form in the textile communities of south-east Lancashire and adjacent areas: here the rushes were brought in carts, which came to be spectacularly ornamented. They were communal creations, expressions of fierce local pride and confidence helping to bind together those living in the growing industrial communities.[30]

Urbanisation thus created a patchwork of cultural differentiation across the region. Migrants from the Celtic territories moulded the distinctive 'Scouse' dialect of Merseyside, for example. The west Cumberland coalfield, isolated from the region's other industrial areas, developed a character all of its own. The folk speech of the coalfield bore closer similarities to that of the North East than to other areas: terms such as 'marrow' (pronounced 'marra'), meaning 'companion' or 'workmate', and 'skinch', the truce word used by children in the playground, are unique to west Cumberland and the North East. The cultural and racial mosaic continues to evolve, as witnessed by the developing Asian identity of the former textile towns, reinforcing the contrast between industrial south and east Lancashire and the rest of the region. Landscape is in many ways a product of culture as much as econimics, and reflections of the cultural diversity of the North West across many centuries are to be found in the patchwork of landscapes discussed in this book.

NOTES

1   White 2002, 17; Newman 1996, 19–21; Hallam *et al.* 1973

2   Bonsall *et al.* 1989, 202–3; Newman 1996, 21–30; White 2002, 18–19; Howard-Davis 1996, 153–63

3   Pennington 1970, 67–9

4   Tallis & McGuire 1972

5   Barber *et al.* in Chambers 1993, 225–36; Hodgkinson *et al.* 2000, 323–6; Wells, 2003; Cowell & Innes 1994, 131, 151

6   Barber *et al.* in Chambers 1993, 225–36; Wells 2003, 80

7   Armstrong *et al.* 1950–2; Smith 1967; Mills 1976, 34–43; Phythian-Adams 1996; Kenyon 1991

8   Fellows-Jensen 1985; Edwards 1998

9   Wimble *et al.* 2000, 29; Baldwin & Whyte 1985, 103–17

10 Hall 1977, 78–80

11 Wimble *et al.* 2000, 29

12 Winchester 1987, 42–4, 66–7; Winchester in Crosby 1993, 18–22

13 PRO, C134/81/18, m. 5

14 McNamee 1997, 82–99; Winchester 1987, 45

15 Little 1890; Bouch 1948, 89–91

16 Newman 1996, 118; Winchester 1987, 48–9

17 Appleby 1978, 95–154; Swain 1986, 16–33; Winchester 1986; Walton 1987, 29–30

18 Walton 1987, 61–8; Walton 1989; Collier 1991, 2

19 Lawton & Pooley 1992, 33

20 Ibid, 130–1

21 Ibid, 205–8; Marshall & Walton 1981, 84–6; MacRaild 1998, 38–9

22 Trescatheric 1985, 18; Jones & Rees 1984, 20–43

23 Williams 1976

24 Beattie 1992, 166–78; Hill 1997, 137–41; www.lancashire.gov.uk/environment/lancashireprofile/county

25 Beattie 1992, 177; Law 1999, 345

26 Barrow 1975; Wood 1996

27 Wakelin 1977, 102–3

28 Ibid, 114; Smith 1959

29 Langton & Morris 1986, 204–5

30 Hutton 1997, 200–1, 323–6

4

Moving Through the Landscape

Transport is a crucial theme in understanding the development of the north-western landscape. From the early 18th century, observers were impressed by the increasing scale of the physical monuments of transport, such as bridges and aqueducts, and by man's triumph over the obstacles imposed by nature. But transport also had a wider economic importance; it was an enabling mechanism that stimulated the development of new industries and patterns of activity. Without efficient transport, industrialisation as it emerged in the decades after 1750 would simply not have been possible.

The similes employed in the 18th and 19th centuries to describe transport networks are significant. Terms such as webs, sinews, arteries and veins not only imply the binding together of disparate areas, but also reflect the sense of dynamic power which so impressed contemporaries. North-west England was especially influential in shaping these perceptions because here much pioneering work on turnpike roads, canals and railways was accomplished. Even in the 20th century, however, parts of the North West were not easy ground for new transport routes.

The physical pattern of the region's transport networks was extensively determined by the lie of the land. Geographers often used to write of 'natural routeways', a concept with a certain validity. Any topographical map of the region suggests that some routes would inevitably be favoured, for to stay dryshod and avoid unnecessary climbing were considerations from the earliest period of human occupation into the modern age. Thus in the Pennines the gaps between major upland blocks (for example, the narrow gorge between Littleborough and Todmorden) were obvious through routes. Such 'natural' alignments tend to have a concentration of transport modes from all periods. Preston and Lancaster, for example, grew at the lowest bridging points of the Ribble and Lune rivers, so the transport links take a direct line between them, but their course is shaped by physical factors. Immediately to the east rise the steep Bowland fells, while a couple of miles to the west were great expanses of moss. This route is thus guided by the narrow intervening belt of drier and more manageable land, over which, for much of the 32km (20 miles) between the two towns, the M6 motorway, A6 turnpike (on the alignment of medieval, Roman and prehistoric predecessors), main-line railway and canal run close together (Fig. 4.1).

Fig. 4.1 The M6, turnpike road, railway and canal at Burton in Kendal: the concentration of different transport routes along narrow belts of countryside, guided by topographical constraints, is a distinctive feature of the upland/lowland interface in the region.

From the late 17th century the growth of trade and movement, the expansion of towns and, above all perhaps, the exploitation of mineral resources (almost always found in the very areas of difficult terrain hitherto avoided), meant that transport routes could no longer turn aside at mountain slopes or skirt wetlands. 'Unnatural' routeways were needed, giving rise to the challenges faced by the 18th- and 19th-century engineers – the need to cut through hills, cross rather than follow valleys, traverse wetlands and span estuaries – to secure the goal of rich mineral deposits, accommodate major inter-urban flows of goods and passengers and serve an integrated national economic system.

THE ROAD NETWORK

Roman roads

The basic structure of the network of Roman roads (Fig. 4.2) has long been clear, and for centuries has attracted popular and academic attention. The key routes include impressive examples of engineering, but evidence is now emerging for a considerable further network of minor roads. Many country lanes in, for example, the Lune valley and the lowlands of south-west Lancashire may well have Roman antecedents. The backbone of the regional network was a military route, which ran from Manchester to Ribchester and then crossed the high moorlands of Bowland before descending to the Lune valley at Burrow, negotiating the gorge at Tebay and crossing the Shap fells to the Eden lowlands and Carlisle. This survives over long stretches as earthworks or alignments of hedgerows and modern roads. From Jeffrey Hill above Longridge, its arrow-straight line is aligned precisely on the summit of Pen-y-ghent where it peeps above the distant skyline – a perfect example of the engineer's thinking at work (Fig. 4.3). In contrast, little survives of the main parallel lowland road which extended from Middlewich and Wilderspool, via Wigan and Walton-le-Dale to Lancaster, where it turned inland to Burrow. A series of east–west roads linked north-west England with the north-east and Yorkshire, through the Tyne gap, over Stainmore, between the Ribble and Aire valleys and over the high Pennines east of Manchester. Especially evocative are the roads that spanned the central Lake District, carving a potentially hostile territory into manageable chunks and giving relatively swift access from strategically placed forts around the periphery. The walker who uses the path on the north side of the beck along Wrynose Bottom follows the Roman road that climbed giddily from Hardknott fort, over two passes, into Little Langdale and down to the lakeside fort at Ambleside.[1]

Medieval roads and packhorse routes

In the post-Roman period some of these roads were given names: High Street, the most famous of all, identifies not only a road, but also the high mountain ridge along which it ran, while a reference to the road running from Preston out towards Kirkham as *Wattelingestrete* dates from 1284 and is among the earliest records of that name anywhere in England.[2] The fact that stretches of these roads were given special names several centuries after the end of the Roman period clearly indicates that they remained prominent landscape features and continued in use. Some sections, such as the long, straight alignments of the A6 between Penrith and Carlisle, have thus been main highways for almost 2,000 years. They became integral parts of a sizeable and well-used medieval road network, some of which is shown on the 14th-century 'Gough' map of Britain. Among those shown are major routes extending from the River Mersey at Warrington along the main axis of the region to Carlisle, with branch roads to Manchester, over

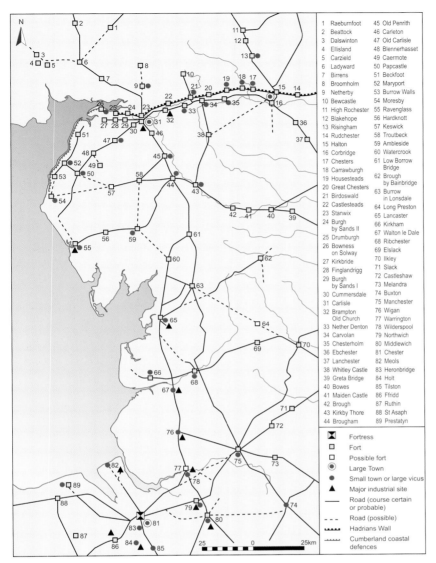

Fig. 4.2 Roman north-west England: *the basic infrastructure of purpose-built roads, military sites and towns is clear; however, substantial sections of road are still uncertain, and in the apparent gaps between were numerous native settlements and 'organic' roads and tracks.*

1	Raeburnfoot	45	Old Penrith
2	Beattock	46	Carleton
3	Dalswinton	47	Old Carlisle
4	Ellisland	48	Blennerhasset
5	Carzield	49	Caermote
6	Ladyward	50	Papcastle
7	Birrens	51	Beckfoot
8	Broomholm	52	Maryport
9	Netherby	53	Burrow Walls
10	Bewcastle	54	Moresby
11	High Rochester	55	Ravenglass
12	Blakehope	56	Hardknott
13	Risingham	57	Keswick
14	Rudchester	58	Troutbeck
15	Halton	59	Ambleside
16	Corbridge	60	Watercrook
17	Chesters	61	Low Borrow Bridge
18	Carrawburgh		
19	Housesteads	62	Brough by Bainbridge
20	Great Chesters		
21	Birdoswald	63	Burrow in Lonsdale
22	Castlesteads		
23	Stanwix	64	Long Preston
24	Burgh by Sands II	65	Lancaster
		66	Kirkham
25	Drumburgh	67	Walton le Dale
26	Bowness on Solway	68	Ribchester
		69	Elslack
27	Kirkbride	70	Ilkley
28	Finglandrigg	71	Slack
29	Burgh by Sands I	72	Castleshaw
		73	Melandra
30	Cummersdale	74	Buxton
31	Carlisle	75	Manchester
32	Brampton Old Church	76	Wigan
		77	Warrington
33	Nether Denton	78	Wilderspool
34	Carvolan	79	Northwich
35	Chesterholm	80	Middlewich
36	Ebchester	81	Chester
37	Lanchester	82	Meols
38	Whitley Castle	83	Heronbridge
39	Greta Bridge	84	Holt
40	Bowes	85	Tilston
41	Maiden Castle	86	Ffridd
42	Brough	87	Ruthin
43	Kirkby Thore	88	St Asaph
44	Brougham	89	Prestatyn

Legend:
- ⬛ Fortress
- ☐ Fort
- □ Possible fort
- ◉ Large Town
- ● Small town or large vicus
- ▲ Major industrial site
- —— Road (course certain or probable)
- - - - Road (possible)
- ▪▪▪▪ Hadrians Wall
- ∿∿∿ Cumberland coastal defences

Fig. 4.3 The high-level Roman road from Manchester to Carlisle, *seen from Jeffrey Hill above Longridge. The road is marked by a striking straight alignment of hedgerows and country lanes, sighted on the summit of Pen-y-ghent, which peeps above the ridge behind Browsholme Hall.*

into Yorkshire and across the ferry at Liverpool to Chester and the Welsh borders.[3] Indeed, most of the region's roads (other than those that were purpose-built in the 19th and 20th centuries) have medieval antecedents but, because so many have been reconstructed repeatedly, it is hard to find examples in something like their original form. Only as unsurfaced green lanes, perhaps where older roads were bypassed by later improvements, do they remain clear. At Hollinshead near Tockholes, for instance, a deeply cut hollow way curving steeply between high banks, its rough surface a watercourse in wet weather, is the medieval road from Bolton to Blackburn. In the early 19th century a new turnpike road was built on a parallel course and the old route fell into disuse except as a bridle path (*see* Fig. 4.8).

Fig. 4.4 **Lancaster Sands** *by David Cox (1783–1859): between 1834 and 1848 Cox painted many watercolour views showing groups of travellers crossing the sands of Morecambe Bay between Hest Bank and Ulverston. His works are perhaps the most evocative reminder of the importance of the route in the period immediately before the opening of the Carnforth–Ulverston railway.*

The majority of the region's medieval bridges have also been rebuilt, either to cater for the heavy traffic of the industrial age or because the original structures were swept away during floods. Almost all the old bridges on the Eden, Lune, Ribble and Wyre rivers were destroyed by flooding at some point over the past four centuries. Some fine examples do survive, such as the Devil's Bridge over the Lune at Kirkby Lonsdale, but no trace now remains of the great medieval bridges across, for example, the Eden at Carlisle and the Mersey at Warrington.

One feature of the medieval road network which continues to fascinate is the sands crossings (Fig. 4.4). Today the routes across Morecambe Bay, from Arnside and Hest Bank to Grange and Kents Bank, remain familiar as a novelty excursion, but in the past they were vital to the communications network. Most of the significant estuaries of the region had long fords and crossings. Those over the Mersey from Hale and Widnes to the Cheshire side were heavily used and, since the deep channel had very strong currents, notably dangerous. Here, as on the shores of Morecambe Bay, local parish registers record a succession of human tragedies, such as that at Runcorn in 1654: 'Richard Jackson and Ellen his daughter were both drowned the 15 day of July ... in going over The Ford at Runcorn to the Colepitt'.[4] In the 17th and 18th centuries there were eight major recognised fords across the Ribble below Penwortham; those from Hesketh Bank to Warton and Freckleton were 2 miles long. After 1603 the crossings of the Solway, from Annan to Bowness and Herdhill, became key sections of cattle-droving routes from Scotland to England. At major crossings expert guides were available, some of them permanently stationed and provided with a 'Guides House', such as that on the north shore of the Ribble at Freckleton Naze. Most sands routes remained in use well into the 19th century, until the developing railway network totally reshaped travel patterns.[5]

As the pace of economic activity quickened in the 16th century, ancient routes were more intensively used and a new emphasis was placed on engineering to overcome physical obstacles. Thus improvements were made on packhorse routes between Lake District valleys. Most passes have evidence of deliberately cut zig-zags, a simple device to ease gradients on these formidable tracks. Examples include Black Sail Pass from Wasdale to Ennerdale and Styhead Pass between Wasdale, Langdale and Borrowdale. Today the passes are used intensively for a quite different purpose, trodden by armies of walkers, but they retained an economic role into the late 19th century because the area was never penetrated by railways.[6] Comparably arduous routes climb the steep, west-facing slopes of the Cross Fell massif into Teesdale. The track from Dufton to Cauldron Snout skirts the cliffs of High Cup Nick, while the one running from Kirkland to Garrigill over the shoulder of Cross Fell reaches over 800m (2,600 feet) above sea level. Use of these high-level routes increased substantially in the 18th century as mining developed on both sides of the watershed.

Packhorse routes were essential to the industrialising economy of south Lancashire (Fig. 4.5). In areas such as Rossendale and the Pennine ranges from Colne to Longdendale they crossed badly drained moorland plateaux, where the tracks were usually paved to give an all-weather surface. The distinctive packhorse bridges, narrow with high arches and very low parapets (so that laden packs would not snag on the stonework), are almost always in a vernacular architectural tradition with little attempt at ornamentation. There are hundreds in the region, from those which are simply slabs of stone to the daringly high Old Lower Hodder Bridge near Slaidburn, with its graceful arch only 2.1m (7 feet) wide, spanning a river notorious for fierce floods (Fig. 4.6). The commodities carried by packhorse included bales of cloth and

Fig. 4.5 The packhorse route climbing Winny Bank towards Fiendsdale Head above Bleasdale (near Chipping): *this carefully-engineered route, which links the lowlands north of Preston with central Bowland and continues into Yorkshire, reaches 445m (1,460 feet) at the top of the slope shown here.*

slippings of yarn, graphite from the plumbago mines in Borrowdale, mineral ores, agricultural produce and even millstones, taken from the quarries at Brindle near Chorley to the Ribble for onward shipment by water.

Packhorses had one great advantage over any other mode of transport. They could cross the wildest passes, wettest moors and loneliest summits, where wheeled vehicles have never been able to go.[7] As a consequence, they remained a familiar sight in more remote areas even after other forms of transport emerged. The poet William Wordsworth casually observed how 'Their panniered train a group of potters goad / Winding from side to side up the steep road'.[8] Not until the entire pattern of economic activity shifted away from the uplands did the need for these routes diminish. It is a reflection of their adaptability and flexibility that packhorses were still at work in the Clitheroe area on the eve of the 20th century, when a local historian, Stephen Clarke, recalled how 'the lime gals which so regularly came into the town from Sabden, Padiham, Burnley and district were a pleasing spectacle as they drowsily bore their dusty burdens along the highways laden with coal, coke, or slates and taking back lime'.[9]

The urbanisation of south Lancashire created other traffic flows. Meat on the hoof came down from Scotland, Cumberland and Northumberland to town markets, or to the Fylde and the Lancashire plain for fattening before sale to the slaughterhouses. Droving was vital to the food supplies of the industrial heartlands for a hundred years, before the railways supplanted the practice in the 1840s. For practical reasons cattle were not driven through villages and settled agricultural land, but instead followed the unenclosed moorlands and dales. A network of drove roads developed across the northern hills, leading down to the Lancashire plain and the head of Airedale (and thence to Leeds and Bradford). These tracks are often still recognisable, despite enclosure of the surrounding moorlands, because of their exceptional width and their alignment, which bypasses settlements. A fine example is the road south from Keasden, near Bentham, which climbs the long slopes of the Bowland fells between walls in places a quarter of a mile apart.

Turnpike roads

As early as the 1630s there were numerous complaints about the damage inflicted on the roads of south Lancashire by large lumbering waggons carrying coal, slate and stone. In 1628, for example, the inhabitants of Chorley claimed that people from other places had 'spoled, decaied, maid fowle and manie of our Cawrseyes broken, by Carrieng and Carteinge of Coales … in unseasonable weather, and at unconveniente tymes'.[10] It is often said that wheeled vehicles were rarely used in the North West before the late 18th century; in fact, they were not only commonplace by 1640, but also central to the developing economy. During the 18th century these acute problems of road maintenance were increasingly tackled by a new administrative device, the turnpike trust, whereby sections of public highway were taken over by private profit-making bodies, under powers granted by parliamentary acts, and upgraded using toll revenues. In north-west England the first trusts were formed in the mid-1720s in south Lancashire, and between then and 1790 most trunk routes and many local roads across the three counties were turnpiked – some 700km (440 miles) in Lancashire alone during this period (Fig. 4.7). Roads were widened, bends were eased, new surfaces laid, and drainage ditches and milestones provided.

After 1790 there was a second wave of turnpike formation in the southern half of the region. It involved a changed emphasis on the construction of entirely new routes in areas such as Rossendale, Blackburn and the Pennines east of Manchester. The rationale for this was that new roads provided easier gradients – heavy industrial traffic was seriously impeded by the steep hills on older roads – and also avoided built-up areas and so accelerated inter-urban movement. The new

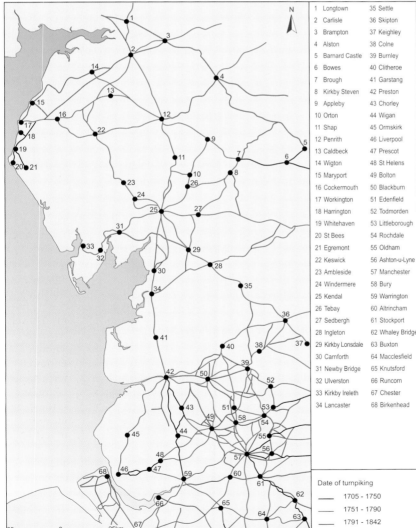

1	Longtown	35	Settle
2	Carlisle	36	Skipton
3	Brampton	37	Keighley
4	Alston	38	Colne
5	Barnard Castle	39	Burnley
6	Bowes	40	Clitheroe
7	Brough	41	Garstang
8	Kirkby Steven	42	Preston
9	Appleby	43	Chorley
10	Orton	44	Wigan
11	Shap	45	Ormskirk
12	Penrith	46	Liverpool
13	Caldbeck	47	Prescot
14	Wigton	48	St Helens
15	Maryport	49	Bolton
16	Cockermouth	50	Blackburn
17	Workington	51	Edenfield
18	Harrington	52	Todmorden
19	Whitehaven	53	Littleborough
20	St Bees	54	Rochdale
21	Egremont	55	Oldham
22	Keswick	56	Ashton-u-Lyne
23	Ambleside	57	Manchester
24	Windermere	58	Bury
25	Kendal	59	Warrington
26	Tebay	60	Altrincham
27	Sedbergh	61	Stockport
28	Ingleton	62	Whaley Bridge
29	Kirkby Lonsdale	63	Buxton
30	Carnforth	64	Macclesfield
31	Newby Bridge	65	Knutsford
32	Ulverston	66	Runcorn
33	Kirkby Ireleth	67	Chester
34	Lancaster	68	Birkenhead

Date of turnpiking

— 1705 - 1750
— 1751 - 1790
— 1791 - 1842

ABOVE: *Fig. 4.6 Old Lower Hodder Bridge*: *the most dramatic and daring of the region's packhorse bridges, this was probably constructed by Sir Richard Shireburn of nearby Stonyhurst in the late 1560s.*

Fig. 4.7 Turnpike roads of north-west England: *the exceptional density of the network in south-east Lancashire contrasts with the comparative lack of roads focusing on Liverpool, while the role of such places as Kendal and Warrington as transport nodes is emphasised.*

roads, the first to be purpose-built since the Roman period, were skilfully engineered, with long straight stretches and sweeping curves which slashed across the grain of the countryside. They exploited the constructional skills that had been developed on the canal network, and even today they impress with their bold alignments and fine engineering. The Preston and Blackburn New Road (1824), passing the half-timbered Samlesbury Hall, almost clips the corner of the building to give maximum directness. Nearby, the Belmont Road (1801) runs between Bolton and Hoghton in a dramatic sequence of straights and curves, swooping up hill and down dale and passing through only two places, Belmont and Abbey Village, both of

Fig. 4.8 The medieval highway from Blackburn to Bolton at Hollinshead near Belmont: in the mid-1820s this narrow lane (in some sections a deeply-entrenched hollow-way) was superseded by a new turnpike road which sliced across the moors and transformed inter-urban access.

which postdate its construction (Fig. 4.8). Between 1790 and 1840 just over 320km (200 miles) of new main road were constructed in the region. In Cumbria the very steep turnpike over Shap was superseded by a completely new alignment extending 13km (8 miles) from Garth Row north of Kendal, while another new turnpike ran from Levens via Newby Bridge to Greenodd, bypassing a very indirect predecessor and beginning the process whereby the Morecambe Bay crossings fell into disuse.[11]

Turnpikes carried heavy inter-urban traffic on trunk routes and allowed major acceleration in coach and stage services for passengers and freight – an essential element in breaking down regional barriers. In 1750 the coach journey from London to Carlisle took about four and a half days, to Manchester three and a half. By 1830 the journeys had shortened to just 32 hours and 18 hours, respectively, almost entirely as a result of turnpike roads.[12] The turnpiking of the rough road from Keswick to Kendal from 1762 opened up the heart of the Lake District to outside visitors. The railway to Windermere carried the process further, but the turnpike first made it possible for visitors to penetrate the heart of England's greatest mountains in comfort, safety and with reasonable speed. It was built for industry and commerce, but the passengers were, in the long run, far more significant.

THE WATERWAYS

The popular perception is that different modes of transport succeeded each other. In the North West, however, they became integrated in a highly complex, multi-layered system, each mode an essential element in servicing the regional economy. The early development of turnpikes coincided with the first phase of waterway improvements. The region's rivers were only navigable for the smallest vessels in the early 17th century, but there were numerous small ports and quays served by coastal shipping (such as Wardleys and Skippool on the Wyre, and Milnthorpe and Haverthwaite on Morecambe Bay). Liverpool and Lancaster served a much wider area and traded with Ireland, Scotland and the Isle of Man. In the late 17th century they began to expand as the Atlantic and American trade grew, while Liverpool also captured much of Chester's coastal and Irish Sea trade and cornered the Cheshire salt business as the Dee estuary silted and the size of trading vessels grew.

Inland trade routes were increasingly reoriented towards these larger ports. The next stage of development was to improve rivers above the tidal limit by building locks and new cuts. Water transport was particularly suitable for low-value bulk commodities such as coal, limestone, salt and grain, and most 18th-century projects were associated with coalfields. They included making the River Douglas navigable from Tarleton to Wigan, and the Mersey and Irwell from Warrington to Manchester. The former allowed coal to be sent downriver for shipment to Liverpool and the small ports of north Lancashire; the latter was vital in furthering Manchester's already rapid growth as a commercial and industrial centre. On both rivers the schemes of the 1720s and later upgradings eliminated long stretches of original channel and reduced others to narrow backwaters. They were completed in 1742, by which time more serious complaints about the inadequacies of transport and the high prices for the carriage of coal were surfacing. More ambitious solutions were needed.

Even as work began on a scheme to make the Sankey Brook, from St Helens to the Mersey, navigable for coal barges, it was decided instead to build a completely new waterway. The Sankey Canal, completed in 1759, was Britain's first true canal of the Industrial Age, though it is overshadowed in the history books by the Duke of Bridgewater's canal (1761), which linked his collieries at Worsley with central Manchester. The success of both, and the engineering prowess of the latter, inspired others. Canals soon threaded their way through the south Lancashire coalfield past Leigh and Hindley, climbed to the summits above Rochdale and Oldham by dozens of locks and tunnelled in Stygian darkness under the Pennine watershed. The Leeds and Liverpool Canal, started in 1766 and completed only in 1816, followed a tortuous route, using the lowest Pennine crossing between Colne and Skipton. It linked a series of booming industrial centres like beads on a necklace, passing from coalfields and cotton towns to the pastoral tranquillity of Craven. Its landscape impact ranged from the straight, mile-long embankment which dominates Burnley town centre to the reservoirs at Foulridge and Colne, built to supply the perpetually water-deficient summit level.

The engineering works on the region's canals are of special note (Fig. 4.9). Standedge tunnel between Marsden and Diggle is the longest in Britain, while a combination of stylish architecture and functional design is demonstrated by the soaring grace of the Peak Forest Canal's Marple aqueduct over the River Goyt. Yet, despite this ability to overcome natural barriers, the waterway network of the North West was geographically restricted and nowhere did it attain the intricacy of the West Midlands canal system. Substantial areas of industrial south

Fig. 4.9 The Lune aqueduct at Lancaster: designed by John Rennie and completed in 1797. One of the architectural triumphs of the canal age, it carries the Lancaster Canal 18m (60 feet) above the tidal river.

Lancashire – notably Rossendale – remained unserved by waterways, which helps to explain the density of the turnpike network in that district; the new roads had no rivals. North of the Ribble only one major scheme came to partial fruition, the Lancaster Canal constructed between Preston and Kendal in 1792–1819. Money ran out before the aqueduct across the Ribble valley at Preston could be built – a pity indeed, since it would have been the most splendid in the country. So while in some parts of the region, such as Leigh, Wigan and Worsley, canals were extremely important in serving existing industries and generating new ones, in others, including most of Cumbria, the Ribble valley and the Fylde, they were largely irrelevant.[13]

As steam power was adopted in the late 18th century, canal bank locations were especially favoured for new industries because of the ease of transporting coal for fuel. Strings of mills lined the canals in places such as Bollington on the Macclesfield Canal and Eanam on the Leeds and Liverpool in Blackburn. Collieries and quarries close to waterways enjoyed a particular advantage – coalpits in the Douglas valley were linked with wharves on the river navigation by early tramroads, while in the Burnley coalfield pits, such as Moorfield at Accrington, immediately adjacent to the canal, had their own wharves. Other coal-using industries followed to canalside locations, such as the numerous coke ovens found along the canal through east Lancashire and the gasworks in many towns. The best local example of urban growth generated by a canal was at the junction of the main line of the Leeds and Liverpool with the Rufford Arm which linked to the Ribble estuary. The development of stables, wharves and workshops prompted the emergence of a small town, Burscough, in what had previously been an entirely agricultural area. The great hump of the canal bridge still dominates its main street, and Top Locks, where the canals meet, retains its late 18th-century architecture, though fortunately not its atmosphere – a main commodity unloaded here was night soil from the privies of Liverpool, brought by barge to be spread on the fields of west Lancashire as a fertiliser (Fig. 4.10).[14]

Fig. 4.10 The Leeds and Liverpool Canal at Burscough Top Locks: the Rufford branch, shown here, opened in 1781 and replaced an earlier river navigation. Burscough, hitherto an insignificant village, grew into a small town after it became a canal port and junction. Note the recessed corner of the cottage (right), designed to reduce the fraying of barge-ropes as horses climbed to the adjacent bridge.

DOCKS AND HARBOURS

The sprawling canal network of south Lancashire, Cheshire and north-west Derbyshire ultimately fed into the port of Liverpool. A minor fishing and trading place in the mid-16th century, Liverpool had become what its mayor proudly called 'the third port of the kingdom' by 1699, and then went on to greater glory as arguably the largest port in the entire world. This was of fundamental importance to the North West as a whole. Without Liverpool, the region's industrialisation could scarcely have happened as it did – and without industrial development the sensational growth of the city would have been impossible. For generations the Liverpool shipping interests were at loggerheads with inland (especially Manchester) merchants, but they depended upon each other in a way that neither liked to acknowledge. The construction of the town's first wet dock, opened at the mouth of 'The Pool' itself in 1721, was the signal for massive expansion in port facilities, a process which encouraged and was stimulated by the simultaneous growth in key industries in the hinterland – coal mining, cotton textiles and salt production. Liverpool experienced a dramatically rapid increase in population, becoming one of the world's largest cities by the middle of the 19th century. The foreshore was reclaimed above and below the old town, and by 1835 there were 15 major docks. On the eve of the First World War the waterfront extended for almost 11km (7 miles), with other docks higher up at Garston and across the river at

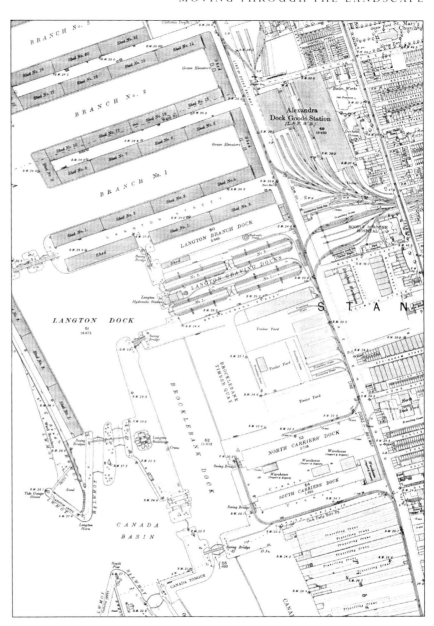

Birkenhead and Seacombe. The dock estate was threaded by miles of railways and sidings, backed by ranks of warehouses and linked by tunnels to the main railway network at Edge Hill and Kirkdale (Fig. 4.11). Even today, photographers' images of the waterfront in the late 19th century, with crowds of dockers and long lines of carts and horses working beneath thick forests of masts and rigging, convey something of the wonder which this man-made landscape inspired.[15]

The smaller ports of the region could not realistically challenge their far larger rival, but schemes were regularly put forward by local interests with ideas well in excess of prudence. The first major new harbour in the region had been at Whitehaven (1634), which after 1666 became the centrepiece of an ambitious plan by the Lowther family to develop their estates with coal mining and a new planned town. It was very successful and was instrumental in stimulating expansion of coal mining in west Cumberland, where inaccessibility and a very small local population

Fig. 4.11 Part of Bootle docks, 1893.
This stretch of docks was developed between 1850 and 1880 along the reclaimed foreshore of the outer Mersey estuary. The facilities are more spacious, and more efficiently laid-out, than those constructed higher up.

Fig. 4.12 Maryport harbour and planned town*, founded at the mouth of the River Ellen in the early-1750s by Humphrey Senhouse of Netherhall (in the woods, centre left); the mid-18th century town is the grid of straight streets between the trees and the harbour, with later development extending inland beyond the railway.*

had hitherto restrained development. Because the collieries were on the clifftops, it was possible to send coal direct to the harbour via a series of short waggonways and inclines, and trade through Whitehaven grew so rapidly that for a period in the mid-18th century it was Britain's sixth port.[16] The opening up of the coalfield generated further port projects between 1730 and 1760, with new harbours at Workington, Harrington and Parton, each with waggonways from local collieries. In the early 1750s Humphrey Senhouse of Netherhall began to develop a harbour and planned town at the mouth of the River Ellen, to serve the northern third of the coalfield. He called the new settlement Maryport, after his wife (Fig. 4.12).

The relationship between transport and industry was intimate. The building of a harbour at Whitehaven had been the key that unlocked industrial expansion, beginning with coal and extending to other heavy industries. This generated substantial inward migration and population growth, transforming the landscape along a 32km (20-mile) stretch of the coast and coalfield, from Maryport to Egremont. Without transport this could not have happened, but, though in the 1860s and 1870s the local railway lines were the most profitable in Britain, the infrastructure depended so heavily on industry that the collapse of coal and iron in the 1920s spelled instant decline and decay. In sickness and in health, they depended on each other.

The same lesson was painfully learned elsewhere. The Walney Channel had been used for shipping iron ore since medieval times, and tonnages grew steadily as the Industrial Revolution gathered pace. In the 1840s massive new haematite reserves were discovered in Furness, and the resulting boom in mining and industry prompted the development of the new town of Barrow. Because it was confidently expected to become a major industrial centre, its transport facilities were lavishly generous (for example, the third largest acreage of docks in the country after London and Liverpool). They were also hugely expensive – and redundant almost from the outset. The iron boom collapsed as the docks were being finished, the industrial empire was largely stillborn, dreams of an international port to rival Liverpool did not come to fruition, and the town and the Furness Railway Company were saddled with facilities that few wanted to use.[17]

At Preston, a major cotton town almost 32km (20 miles) from the open sea, the textile merchants and borough council (almost the same thing) held that Liverpool dock and shipping interests were 'holding the town to ransom'. They resolved to break the alleged stranglehold and a massive dock, said to be the largest in the country, was built between 1885 and 1892. The Ribble was turned into a tidal ship canal by embanking the channel and Preston became a port of some significance, usefully placed for the industrial centres of east Lancashire. However, the 29km (18-mile) channel required continuous dredging and constant repair; as ships grew in size and the costs of upkeep grew even faster, the viability of the port could not be sustained. It closed in 1981.[18]

Elsewhere, railway companies saw docks and shipping as a natural extension of land routes and a way of keeping control of trade. Carlisle, up the sandy estuary of the Eden, was linked to Port Carlisle by a modestly profitably canal from 1823. In the mid-1840s canal traffic disappeared as a result of railway competition, but a new dock at Silloth, linked by rail with the city, was then promoted as a competitor to Maryport, Workington and Whitehaven. It opened in 1859 and for many decades, served by steamer routes to Liverpool, Dublin and Belfast and dealing in cattle, grain, coal and timber, achieved a quiet success. In Lancashire, Fleetwood was the protégé of Sir Peter Fleetwood Hesketh, who in 1836 founded a new town and port among the sand dunes at the mouth of the Wyre. It became the terminus of the Preston and Wyre Railway (1840) and for a few years its docks were the end of the line from Euston (hence the name *North Euston* for the hotel on the front), linked to Ardrossan on the Clyde by a steamer service. The completion of the line from Carlisle to Glasgow in 1848 put paid to this arrangement, but Fleetwood was very successful as a port, developing a network of steamer services in the Irish Sea and also, rather unexpectedly, becoming the premier English west coast fishing port. The port and its railway were jointly operated by the London & North Western and Lancashire & Yorkshire Railways. In 1904 their arch-rival, the Midland, opened its own competing harbour at Heysham.[19]

These schemes were driven not by clear financial logic, but by speculation, pride or jealous rivalry. All these motives lay behind the most ambitious project of all, the Manchester Ship Canal. The pride of Manchester, self-designated as the world's greatest industrial and commercial centre, combined with the ambition of cotton merchants and a deep-seated mistrust of Liverpool to produce a radical answer to an apparent problem. The city of free trade would become a sea-going port in its own right. Large vessels would sail past Liverpool, ignoring railways and metaphorically thumbing their noses at its shipowners and dock officials. The idea had a long history – in 1825 a ship canal from the Dee to Manchester came close to fruition – but this project was in a different league. Opened in 1894, it was Britain's greatest engineering feat of the age and the daring of the plan and the speed of its realisation still inspire awe. Photography provides a vivid record of its devastating impact on the landscape, as massive cuttings, vast lock chambers, river diversions and high-level viaducts and swing bridges were built (Fig. 4.13). The

Fig. 4.13 The Manchester Ship Canal under construction at Latchford near Warrington (1892): the construction of the canal, with its massive engineering works, had a dramatic and permanent impact upon the landscape of the Mersey valley from Salford to the sea.

Ship Canal turned the twin cities of Manchester and Salford, 56km (35 miles) from open water, into Britain's fourth largest seaport, and provided a remarkable boost to their industrial and commercial life. As great sea-going vessels slid quietly through pastoral north Cheshire to the complex of docks at the eastern end, Manchester was filled with civic pride.[20] The choice of a major new waterway as the solution to its perceived difficulties at the end of the 19th century emphasises the way in which different modes of transport co-existed. Each had its vital role to play in keeping the region's economy moving.

RAILWAYS

Local patriots claim that a reference in 1597 to 'rayles' in a mine at Whiston near St Helens is the first record of railed transport anywhere in Britain. Whatever the truth of this, colliery waggonways were certainly operating in the region by the mid-17th century, and a hundred years later they were a standard feature in the Cumberland coalfield and parts of Lancashire – though nowhere in the North West did they assume the remarkable extent and importance they had in the North East and South Wales. Typically, they were no more than a couple of miles long, self-contained rather than in networks, and linked with the nearest canal, harbour or, less commonly, turnpike road. The final stage in the evolution of railways into an essential mode of transport, of global importance, was effected in north-west England by the construction of the Liverpool and Manchester Railway, the first inter-city line in the world and the first to use steam locomotives as the sole motive power for passenger and freight trains. The Liverpool and Manchester was a pioneer in many senses, not least its emphasis on meeting the huge challenges posed by nature. Whereas the unambitious Stockton and Darlington Railway (1825) had few significant engineering works, the Liverpool and Manchester (1830) impressed the public with the feats of laying a trunk line across the quaking bogs of Chat Moss and hacking away the red sandstone to create the deep, vertically sided cuttings between Huyton and Edge Hill.

The line moulded the image of the railway as conqueror of natural obstacles and reactionary values – heroic in its engineering achievements and its empowering impact. Canals prompted poetic musings, and impressed by the prowess of their builders, but they were slow and silent. Railways, on the other hand, were thrilling and sensational in the noise, smell and speed of steam locomotives. It is easy to forget how liberating the railways were, how revolutionary their effects not just upon the economy and industry, but also upon society and landscape. That, as much as their physical attributes, helps to explain the Victorian passion for them, and the enthusiasm which many writers and artists felt for the new method of transport. Nevertheless, it was not a unanimous infatuation, as John Ruskin's bitter opposition to railways and all they stood for reminds us.

The influence of railways was also more pervasive than that of canals or turnpikes. They produced a drastic reorientation of travel, marketing and production patterns, and were geographically penetrating in a way that canals never were and turnpikes only in part. Just before the First World War, when the railways of the North West reached their maximum extent, the network covered almost every part of the region. The only substantial areas more than 8km (5 miles) from a railway were the central and northern Lake District; the Forest of Bowland; the summit and eastern slopes of Cross Fell and the Pen-y-ghent fells; and the Bewcastle district in north Cumberland. Almost everyone in north-west England was within easy reach of a railway, a fact that had profound implications for the social, economic and physical character of the region (Fig. 4.14).

The railway network, as in the rest of England, grew piecemeal, with no planning or rational investment.[21] Truly unbridled competition never existed – it was always tempered by the parliamentary process and by the self-interest of

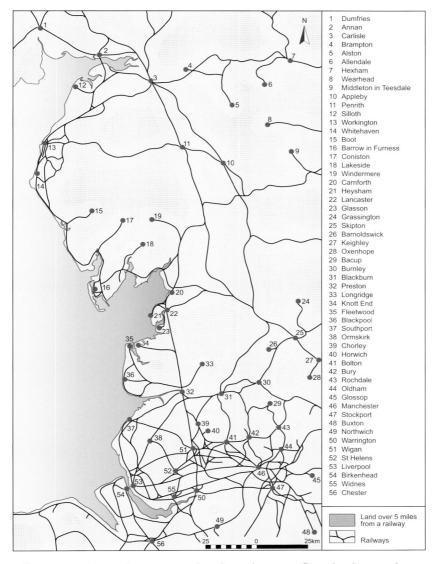

1	Dumfries
2	Annan
3	Carlisle
4	Brampton
5	Alston
6	Allendale
7	Hexham
8	Wearhead
9	Middleton in Teesdale
10	Appleby
11	Penrith
12	Silloth
13	Workington
14	Whitehaven
15	Boot
16	Barrow in Furness
17	Coniston
18	Lakeside
19	Windermere
20	Carnforth
21	Heysham
22	Lancaster
23	Glasson
24	Grassington
25	Skipton
26	Barnoldswick
27	Keighley
28	Oxenhope
29	Bacup
30	Burnley
31	Blackburn
32	Preston
33	Longridge
34	Knott End
35	Fleetwood
36	Blackpool
37	Southport
38	Ormskirk
39	Chorley
40	Horwich
41	Bolton
42	Bury
43	Rochdale
44	Oldham
45	Glossop
46	Manchester
47	Stockport
48	Buxton
49	Northwich
50	Warrington
51	Wigan
52	St Helens
53	Liverpool
54	Birkenhead
55	Widnes
56	Chester

Land over 5 miles from a railway

Railways

Fig. 4.14 The railway network in 1922: *the map emphasises the intricate networks of competing lines woven across south Lancashire and west Cumberland. Elsewhere, only high fells and remote moorlands remained beyond the reach of the railways. The year 1922 was a high-water mark, after which industrial decline and rationalisation rapidly reduced the extent of the system.*

railway companies and promoters – but the region was a fierce battleground between rival undertakings. The massive volume of industrial trade and huge population represented potentially lucrative business: the possibility of capturing some of, say, the coal business of St Helens or the seaside trade of Blackpool was always tempting to newcomers. The result was a tangled confusion of lines in areas such as the south Lancashire coalfield, the industrial zone of west Cumberland and the approaches to Manchester and Liverpool, contrasting with a more comprehensible pattern in, for example, Rossendale and Furness, where the competition was suppressed at an early date and a single company had a monopoly. The prodigious waste of land and capital investment that duplication represented, and the folly of spreading traffic between several rival routes, only became truly apparent when the railways faced the threat of road competition.

The backbone of the network was the main London–Glasgow line, which grew somewhat accidentally from the amalgamation of a series of more local routes. Already by 1840 there was a continuous line of railway from London to Preston and at that stage a critical decision had to be made. Should the line north from Lancaster go up the Lune gorge and over Shap to Penrith; or to Kendal and through the eastern Lake District by long tunnels and dramatic viaducts; or cross Morecambe Bay on a great embankment and follow the coast of Cumberland? Enthusiasts for scenic railway journeys might lament the rejection of the middle option, but the real choice was between Shap or the coast, the latter favoured by the great George Stephenson because it was more or less at sea level throughout, though 48km (30 miles) longer. Exponents of the Shap route argued for its directness, despite the formidable gradients and long climb to the summit. They won the argument, but had the main line crossed the smooth sands of the bay, tunnelled under Furness and snaked up the coast the history of west Cumberland would have been very different: what psychological and commercial barriers would the line have broken down, what economic development might it have sustained? From the 1840s to the 1880s railways threaded deep valleys and lonely shores: the Manchester, Sheffield and Lincolnshire Railway's Woodhead tunnel burrowed for 4km (2½ miles) under the wildest moors on the Yorkshire border; the long line over Stainmore and down Ravenstonedale carried Durham coke to fuel the Furness iron industry, and at Barras spanned the River Belah on England's highest viaduct; the iron-girdered might of the great bridge across the Mersey between Runcorn and Widnes (1864–9) sums up the formidable character of Victorian heavy engineering; and Europe's longest railway bridge was thrown across the Solway from Annan to Bowness (1869) so that Cumberland iron ore could be sent to Lanarkshire. A financial disaster, it survived just 54 years.

In rural areas, after the initial upheavals of construction, railways blended easily into their surroundings. Vegetation clothed embankments and cuttings and the rawness of new structures was soon softened. Even in their early days the great viaducts were widely regarded as embellishments to, rather than blots upon, their surroundings. For the urban industrial heartlands, however, it was a different matter. In mining areas railways came to be a dominating element in the landscape, as skeins of sidings and loops of mineral line wound between houses, across streets and under towering spoil heaps. The amount of land occupied by railway lines could be very substantial – at Hindley, near Wigan, for example, over 10 per cent of the entire area in 1893 – and the effect of these complex networks was to subdivide landscapes and communities, so that large tracts of ground were rendered almost useless, cut off by junctions and loop lines (Fig. 4.15). Railways were greedy for land in towns and cities, where passenger termini, goods yards, carriage sidings and locomotive depots gobbled up the acres. Here railway construction was traumatic, involving wholesale disruption to the urban fabric and massive displacement of population, all of which militated against centrally placed stations. The most extreme example was Manchester, where the building of Victoria and London Road (now Piccadilly) stations in the late 1830s and 1840s resulted in substantial loss of poor quality housing and inferior commercial property, and the construction of the viaducts that linked with these stations cut swathes through the existing built-up area and created major barriers to movement. The process reached a climax with the building of Central station (1876–1880) which, with its attendant viaducts and yards, consumed over 120ha (300 acres) and almost 300 homes. Officially it displaced about 1,300 people – but the true number, in those congested slums, was over 3,000.[22]

Elsewhere, stations were usually situated at the edge of the existing built-up area, because it was easier to route lines through open land skirting the town. At Carlisle, the station was outside the walls at the foot of the rock on which much of the medieval city was built, and at Lancaster it is on the western side of the castle hill, away from the old town. In places such as Oldham, Blackburn, Wigan and Warrington, the stations acted as a new focus for commercial activity, encouraging expansion of the centre in their direction. Stations provided another opportunity for architecture and technology to merge. Many, especially in the industrial areas, were mean and inadequate almost from the start (Preston's was described in 1883 as 'one of the most dismal, dilapidated, disgraceful-looking structures in Christendom'[23]),

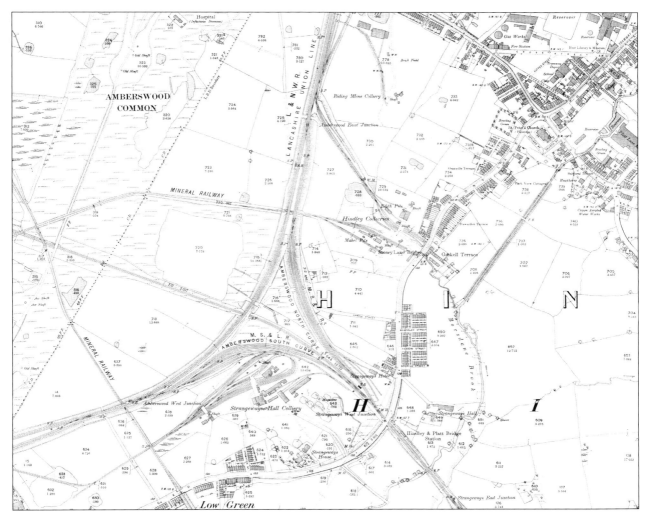

Fig. 4.15 Collieries and mineral railways at Amberswood and Low Green, Hindley, in 1893. The landscape is dissected by railway lines, including those that cross the wetlands and heaths of Amberswood Common. Today all the lines are gone, and there is a large subsidence flash in the centre of the area shown on the extract.

but some companies chose to regard stations as advertisements for their wares and built to high standards. The most noteworthy was the small Furness Railway which, though depending heavily on industrial traffic, built delightful stations of which particularly good examples survive at Ulverston and Grange over Sands.

The real triumphs were the vast stations of the cities. The structural potential of girders and glazing, and the need for all-weather cover and yet airiness to allow clouds of smoke to rise and disperse, gave full scope to engineering achievement. The results could be at once technically brilliant, architecturally splendid, functional and inspirational. As contemporaries noted, these were the cathedrals of the age – temples to a new religion of travel and commerce. The North West has some outstanding examples which, thanks to restoration and cleaning in recent years, are once again places of soaring space and breathtaking spans of glass and girder. Liverpool Lime Street, Manchester Piccadilly and the former Manchester Central (now the G-MEX centre) demonstrate these qualities, but the finest of all – because of its gentle curve and the spaciousness of the platform areas – is Carlisle (Fig. 4.16, *see* p.72).

The railway network acted as a powerful force to shape and mould the region in other ways, some obvious, others more insidious. Agricultural landscapes changed as farming economies were reoriented towards supplying urban markets, using the fast transport that the railways offered. In north Cheshire and

OVERCOMING THE CHALLENGE OF NATURE

The region's railway viaducts, bridges and tunnels were triumphs of construction, but also symbolised the way in which industrial might, harnessed to the driving force of design and innovation, could conquer nature. The landscape, previously an implacable enemy, was tamed and brought to heel. A characteristic of the great age of railway building, from 1830 to 1870, was an outright refusal to opt for the easiest route. When Stephenson drew an almost straight line on a map between Liverpool and Manchester and built a railway which ignored the obstacles in its path he set the tone for later engineers, who disregarded the wise counsels of the cautious. The success of his audacious strategy to cross Chat Moss by floating the line on the unstable peat confounded the sceptics. A contemporary view (right) powerfully conveys the vast emptiness of that quaking land, the railway a single, arrow-straight line drawn across it with a

ruler. For 2,000 years engineers have exploited the Lune gorge (below), a gap in the high fells south of Shap. Through it are channelled not only the main West Coast railway line (joined here by the Ingleton branch line over the curving Lowgill viaduct of 1861), but also a minor road on the east side of the valley (the Roman road from Manchester to Carlisle) and the M6 motorway. The Ulverstone [sic] & Lancaster Railway's viaduct across the Kent estuary (opposite page, top) was built in 1856–7 and, with the longer Leven

viaduct, was instrumental in ending the relative inaccessibility of the Cartmel peninsula and in further boosting the fast-growing Furness iron industry. Above all, there is England's most famous railway, the Settle and Carlisle (opened in 1876). Built because of the fierce rivalry between railway companies rather than for sound financial reasons, it gave the Midland a

separate route to Scotland, not touching the metals of its arch-rival, the London and North Western. The line has the greatest concentration of major engineering works anywhere in Britain, with 16 major viaducts, 10 major tunnels and many miles of cutting and embankment. Perversely, it follows the hardest possible route, along the axis of the Pennines, cutting across the grain of the country and providing the traveller with an unparalleled sense of the physical and human landscape of the backbone of England. The line's outstanding structure, the great Ribblehead viaduct (below) spans the wide moor between high fells, exemplifying the achievement and single-mindedness of the Victorian railway builder.

Fig. 4.16 Carlisle railway station interior: *the airy lightness of glass roofs and strong yet delicate ironwork are complemented by the pale pink of local sandstone in this masterpiece of mid-Victorian railway architecture.*

the Fylde, dairying almost eliminated arable farming. Railways were vital to the continued growth of towns and industry in the 19th century, themes explored further in subsequent chapters. They also contributed to rural depopulation and the decline of minor market centres. People could leave more easily, whether for a day's shopping at a larger market town or permanently as they migrated to the cities. Railways were not responsible for either the initial growth of seaside resorts or the fashion for tourism, but they helped to accelerate these trends with major consequences for the landscape of our region. Blackpool could not have grown as it did without the railway access it enjoyed.

Railways were major agents in another process, the flight to the suburbs and the development of commuting. The growth of places such as Formby and Altrincham was because good rail links encouraged middle-class people to live out of town. While all the modes of transport discussed in this chapter played their part in guiding landscape change, and all had a physical impact upon the region, the scale of change which railways exerted was greater than anything that had gone before.

NOTES

1. For Roman roads, see Shotter 1997, ch. 3 and Edwards in Crosby 1998, 1–28
2. Edwards in Crosby 1998, 28
3. See Higham in Crosby 1998, 29–52
4. Cheshire & Chester Archives & Local Studies, Runcorn parish register transcript
5. Crosby 2000, 28–31; Winterbotham in Crosby 1998, 91–4, 103–5; Hindle 2001, 77–80
6. Hindle 1998
7. Thornber 2002
8. Wordsworth 1904, 4
9. Clarke 1900, 57
10. LRO, QSB 1/42/62
11. For turnpikes see Whiteley in Crosby 1998, Williams 1975, Hindle 2001
12. Pope 1989, figs 5.3 and 5.4
13. For waterways see Hadfield & Biddle 1970, vols 1 and 2
14. Coney 1995, 15–26
15. For Liverpool docks see Ritchie-Noakes 1984, Jarvis 1991
16. Collier 1991, 1–4
17. Marshall 1958, 272–8
18. Hunt 1992, 218–21, 252–5
19. For railway ports see Holt 1986, 212–7, 236–7; Joy 1990, 154–61
20. Kidd 2002, 115–9; Harford 1994
21. For railways, see Holt 1986; Joy 1990
22. Kellett 1979, 150–74, 324–36
23. Hewitson 1883, 205

5

The Farming Landscape

The farming landscape of the north-western lowlands today is largely dominated by rye-grass, forced to luxuriant growth by liberal doses of slurry and cut for silage or hay to provide fodder for the livestock that form the backbone of modern farming in the region. Paradoxically, the most extensive areas of modern cultivation are on the peat lands of western Lancashire, formerly boggy waste land until reclaimed from the moss in the 19th century. Most of the traditional arable lands are now under grass, and this grassland blanket obscures the soil and crop marks that enable us to recapture patterns of pre-medieval farming activity elsewhere in lowland England. However, the landscape we see today preserves many features from the medieval and early-modern periods. As elsewhere, the

Fig. 5.1 Holborn Hill, Great Asby: a 'native' farmstead site of Iron Age or Romano-British date, survives in the centre of the photograph as a fragment of the prehistoric landscape, surrounded by the ploughed, walled fields of the historic landscape.

'Age of Improvement' in the later 18th and 19th centuries resulted in major landscape change, but, in contrast to some other areas, it did not result in a total re-writing of the countryside. Much of the framework of the farming landscapes of Cumbria and Lancashire – villages, farmsteads, lanes and tracks, patterns of field boundaries – is inherited from the medieval and early-modern past.

TIME-DEPTH IN THE COUNTRYSIDE

Behind the historic landscape, however, lies a depth of human occupation stretching back over six millennia. Since settled farming communities first arrived in the Neolithic era, countless generations have been attracted to the same, comparatively scarce, islands of freer-draining soils. The extent to which elements of the landscapes created by prehistoric communities are incorporated into the historic landscape of the North West is far from clear. Some evidence of the pre-medieval landscape does survive, both as isolated earthworks in a sea of later cultivation (Fig. 5.1) and as soil marks in fields that are still under the plough. Relics of the pre-medieval landscape have been identified by aerial photography on drier ridges in south-west Lancashire and in the Solway lowlands, underlying the historic landscape and bearing little relation

Fig. 5.2 'Native' farmstead site at Wiggonby on the Carlisle Plain, showing as a crop mark underlying the modern field pattern. A second crop mark is visible at the top of the picture.

BELOW: **Fig. 5.3 Barnscar,** a settlement site and extensive cairnfield on the western flanks of the Lakeland fells.

to it (Fig. 5.2). Most of this hidden landscape of settlements and associated enclosures in the lowlands is thought to date from the Iron Age or Romano-British period, but excavations have yielded evidence of earlier activity. One such crop-mark site at Plasketlands in Holme St Cuthbert parish has produced radiocarbon dates suggesting Neolithic origins.[1]

In the uplands, tide marks of prehistoric occupation survive from two distinct periods. First are the relict Bronze Age landscapes on the lower fells around the fringes of the Lake District. Extensive cairnfields with associated enclosure walls and huts are found between 200 and 300m (650–1,000 feet) on the fells either side of Eskdale (Fig. 5.3), and on Town Bank, at the head of the Calder valley, for example. The cairns imply field clearance (though some have yielded evidence of burials), the enclosure walls the keeping of livestock. Pollen evidence suggests a pastoral economy and a significant reduction in tree cover. The opening up of the landscape during the Bronze Age, however, sowed the seeds of environmental degradation, from which these areas never recovered and which prevented intensive use by later generations. Deteriorating climate in the period *c.* 1250–800 BC not only led to the abandonment of these upland sites, but also to the leaching of nutrients from the soil, waterlogging and peat formation. The wood-pastures of these hills during the Bronze Age became the ill-drained, acid moorland of later centuries.[2]

Fig. 5.4 Ewe Close, Crosby Ravensworth: one of the best-preserved 'native' farmstead sites. Its name suggests that the tumbled hut circles and paddocks of the Romano-British settlement were later used as sheep pens.

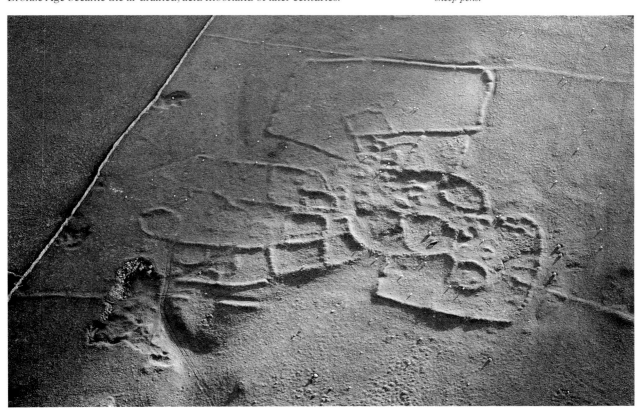

A second tide of occupation occurred during the later Iron Age and Romano-British periods, when pollen evidence suggests widespread woodland clearance, and a ring of settlement sites fringes the uplands and penetrates into the dales. These 'native' earthwork sites tend to survive just beyond the limits of medieval farmland, on the lower slopes of the fells or close to the intake wall along a valley side. They are particularly numerous on the limestone uplands between Shap and Kirkby Stephen; well-known examples include the settlement sites at Ewe Close (Fig. 5.4) and Ewe Locks, near Crosby Ravensworth, on Crosby Garrett

Fell and at Waitby. Sites on the fringes of the Lakeland fells include those on Aughertree Fell near Uldale and on the lower fells in Kentmere; while further settlements lie on the edge of the Pennines between Kirkby Lonsdale and Settle, including the extensive earthworks at Eller Beck and Castle Hill, near Leck.[3] Although some of these 'native' sites (notably those at Crosby Garrett Fell and Eller Beck) are set in contemporary relict field systems, others are not, perhaps suggesting that the fields they used have been incorporated into the field patterns of later occupation.

The apparent unconformity between these relics of prehistoric occupation and the landscape we see today is, of course, found elsewhere in England. The roots of the modern countryside can be traced back to the medieval period, and it is to this historic landscape that we now turn. The key to making sense of the landscape of farms, villages and fields in the North West lies in identifying those areas – around one-quarter of the land surface in the lowlands, but considerably more in the Solway and Lancashire mosses and in the Lakeland and Pennine hills – which survived in a semi-natural state as unenclosed moorland, peat moss or marsh until the 18th or 19th century. This unenclosed common 'waste' was vital to the traditional rural economy, providing summer pasture for livestock and peat for fuel. If we peel off the new landscapes created by wasteland enclosure, mostly after 1750, the way in which the land has been parcelled out between communities, and the relationship of the settlement pattern to the complementary resources of farmland and waste, immediately become apparent (Fig. 5.5). Each township embraces both farmland and moorland. From the villages, funnel-shaped

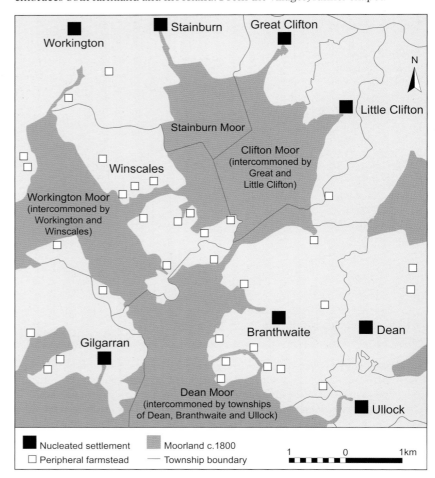

Fig. 5.5 Settlement, fields and moorland before enclosure. By stripping off the fields created by enclosure of moorland in the early 19th century, this maps shows the relationship between farms, fields and open moor in the Cumbrian lowlands inland from Workington.

LEFT: *Fig. 5.6 The 'outgang' leading from Uldale village to Aughertree Fell in the northern Lake District. The margin between the improved grassland of the enclosed fields and the rough grazings contains numerous relics of past human activity: banked enclosures (probably of prehistoric date) and quarrying (probably post-medieval) on the open fell; an earlier head-dyke runs through the farmland at the top of the photograph. The outgang funnel itself is scarred by wheel ruts created by generations of horse-drawn vehicles climbing the steep route up to the fell.*

'outgangs' lead on to the moor (Fig. 5.6); where the township's dwellings are scattered rather than concentrated in a nucleated village, they often lie along the interface between farmland and moorland. Separating the two was that all-important boundary, the head-dyke or ring garth, which kept animals from the growing crops and also marked the division between land appropriated to individual farmers and the unenclosed, common waste. The ring garth boundary reflected the fertility and drainage characteristics of the land, the limit of enclosure representing the point at which altitude, exposure or deteriorating drainage meant that the cost of appropriating land outweighed the benefits of enclosure. Sometimes an island of freer-draining land has been enclosed, with the surrounding cold, wet clays remaining as waste.

Enclosure and reclamation of the wastes has blurred – and often destroyed – the boundary between these two complementary elements: only where upland fellsides remain as open common or in the few surviving

remnants of lowland moor, such as Newby Moor, near Bentham (Fig. 5.7), does the character of the pre-improvement landscape survive. The taming of the fells, moors and mosses since the medieval period is discussed in Chapter 6. A much greater time-depth lies behind the evolution of the core of farmland surrounding villages and farmsteads, and reaching as narrow fingers of enclosure up the dales.

Fig. 5.7 Newby Moor, near Bentham, one of the few surviving examples of an unenclosed lowland moor. The rough grass of the moorland contrasts with the bright green of the enclosed farmland.

VILLAGES, HAMLETS AND FARMSTEADS

The pattern of rural settlement in north-west England includes both areas dominated by nucleated villages and other areas in which villages are few and settlement takes the form of scattered hamlets and dispersed farmsteads. What historical processes lie behind these contrasts? It is striking that nucleated villages and open field farming go hand-in-hand; indeed, the extent of land suitable for ploughing tends to correlate with the size of the units of settlement. Village settlement is generally only found where land suitable for cultivation occurs in large swathes, as on the boulder clay and gravel ridges of the Eden valley or the Craven lowlands. By contrast, dispersed hamlets or individual farmsteads are found in areas of late-surviving woodland, or where potential arable land was fragmented by the presence of mountain, mossland and marsh.

If geographical factors played a part in determining whether farming communities would be clustered into villages or scattered across the countryside, it is clear that other factors must be sought to explain the creation of villages. Nucleated settlements are now seen as to be a product of settlement reorganisation in the later Anglo-Saxon and Norman centuries. The North West contains some striking examples of regular village plans, which must surely indicate deliberate design. The hand of authority is visible in the rectilinear plans of Milburn (Fig. 5.8), Dufton and Temple Sowerby in the Eden valley, or Elswick and Newton in the Fylde, for example. Such villages bear close similarities to the planned villages of Co. Durham and the Vale of York, which have been interpreted as the products of a re-organisation of rural society by manorial lords, perhaps in the aftermath of the Harrying of the North by William the Conqueror in 1069–70.[4] Whether the planned villages of the North West date from re-settlement after the disruption of the 11th century is not known, though Domesday Book's statement that only 16 out 60 vills in the Fylde had any inhabitants is compatible with such a view. Further north, the conquest of 'the land of Carlisle' by William Rufus in 1092 was followed by the planting of southern peasants on the newly conquered lands, a context which might explain the creation of planned villages in the Eden valley and Carlisle plain.

Villages, once established, may have retained their form, but population growth and colonisation in the 12th and 13th centuries added further elements to the settlement pattern as new lands were taken in. The various Newbiggins ('new buildings') in Cumbria and north Lancashire probably date from this period, as do daughter settlements on the periphery of village lands. The hamlet of Mosshouses, on the edge of the mossland north-east of Much Hoole village, had been established by 1296, for example, the hamlets called Moorhouse, on the edge of moorland

Fig. 5.8 Milburn, Cumbria. The closely-packed houses built around the long, rectangular village green form one of the clearest examples of a planned village layout in the North West.

at Burgh by Sands and near Wigton, by the 14th century. This medieval phase of colonisation also created more extensive landscapes of dispersed settlement in areas of woodland and along the margins of moorland and moss.[5]

A second frontier of medieval colonisation lay in the uplands. What distinguished the uplands from other frontiers of colonisation was their status as 'forest' or 'chase' – that is, as hunting grounds belonging to great landholders. The term 'forest' was a legal, rather than an ecological one; they were areas outside (Latin *foris*) the common law, governed by special forest laws, aimed at preserving game. The names of some forests (Skiddaw Forest, Copeland Forest, the Forest of Bowland, for example) survive on the modern map, but forest status extended much more widely during the medieval centuries, covering much of the Lake District and Pennines, the Bowland fells, Pendle and the Rossendale moors.[6]

By the late 13th century, it is striking that, despite being designated as hunting reserves, the upland forests were viewed as pasture grounds, valuable for the income they could yield, whether from direct exploitation as demesne stock farms or from the rents and services of peasant colonists. By 1300 it is possible to think in terms of 'open' forests, which were open to colonisation, and 'closed' forests, exploited directly by the great landowners.

In the 'open' forests the overlords permitted – or perhaps even encouraged – peasant settlement. The process is largely unrecorded (and the chronology far from clear), but it appears that most of the hamlets and farmsteads strung along the Lakeland valleys originated in a phase of colonisation that may have started in the Viking period but certainly continued until *c.* 1300. The final stages of colonisation in remote valleys in the Forest of Derwentfells, between the Keswick and Buttermere valleys, can be glimpsed in the documentary record. Wythop, a small valley tucked away in the fells, remained an uninhabited pasture ground in the mid-13th century, but by 1307 had been 'built on and improved' by its lord, who had had to buy out grazing rights held there by neighbouring landowners. The core of peasant settlement was probably at Old Scales ('the old shielings'), where cultivation terraces provide a reminder of the colonists' attempt to grow

Fig. 5.9 Old Scale, Wythop, a former shieling site, colonised in the late 13th century. The fine flight of lynchets behind the settlement is probably a legacy of medieval cultivation; the narrow ridge and furrow, in contrast, is the result of ploughing in the 19th century.

crops on steep and marginal land (Fig. 5.9). Across the fells to the south, the Newlands valley (the name is significant) was being actively cleared and colonised in the same period. Like Wythop, it had probably been used previously as a summer pasture, as its earlier name (Rogersett, 'Roger's summer pasture') and farm names such as Skellgill and Gutherscale (containing the element *skali*, 'a shieling hut') suggest. The peopling of the forest dales of the Lake District was probably largely a product of the period of rapid population increase in the 12th and 13th centuries, rather than the 'Viking colonisation' that has entered the folklore.[7]

In the 'closed' forests, the roots of the settlement pattern lay in the 'vaccaries' or demesne cattle farms recorded in the 13th and 14th centuries. These were stock farms often running a herd of around 40 cows with a couple of bulls and their young. The Pennines were the heart of vaccary country, in which whole forests appear to have been retained as lordly pastures exploited by demesne stock farms strung out along the dales. Stainmoor Forest, at the head of the Eden valley, contained 12 vaccaries; there were 11 in the wild and narrow valley of Mallerstang chase; 15 in the Forest of Bowland (Fig. 5.10); 20 in Wyresdale; 11 in Pendle Forest; five in the Forest of Trawden; 11 in Rossendale; eight in the Forest of Horwich and several in the Forest of Macclesfield. Even in the more open forests of the Lake District, there were vaccaries in the upper reaches of some valleys, at the head of the Buttermere, at Wasdalehead and in the upper reaches of Ennerdale, Eskdale and Borrowdale.[8]

By the early 14th century, most vaccaries had been leased to tenants, and it was this cessation of direct demesne exploitation that led to a transformation from lordly cattle ranch to hill farming hamlet. In most cases, the former vaccary came to be divided into several smaller holdings, resulting in the creation of hamlets on the site of the former cattle sheds by the 16th century. The four vaccaries at Wasdalehead had become a community of 19 holdings by 1547. In Wyresdale in the Bowland fells each vaccary became a group of farms, either clustered in a hamlet or scattered across the territory, and the boundaries of the vaccary pastures, stretching from the valley floor to the top of the moors, continued to divide the grazing grounds of one hamlet from the next. In the Bowland and Rossendale forests the main phase of subdivision took place in the 16th century. In Bowland 17 tenants held the land of 14 former vaccaries and demesne pastures in 1498; by 1527 the number of tenants had risen to 47 and there is evidence of rapid population growth in both areas later in the century.[9]

If we are right in seeing a re-organisation of settlement in the lowlands soon after the Norman Conquest, and in assigning the roots of settlement in former woodland and upland areas to colonisation in the 12th and 13th centuries, the outlines of the modern rural settlement pattern are approaching 1,000 years old. Hardly anything of the fabric of our villages, hamlets and farmsteads dates from then, of course, but building lines and property boundaries, once established, would have created a stable framework. In many cases, cottages and farmhouses stand within plots laid out many centuries earlier.

The character of the vernacular buildings in the countryside of the North West is determined in part by the nature of local building materials and in part by the ebb and flow of local economies. Though building stone was readily available in much of the region, it was strikingly absent from parts of the drift-covered lowlands. South Lancashire, well-wooded in medieval times, retained a tradition of timber-framed buildings until the 17th century. Relatively few vernacular timber-framed houses survive, however, the majority of timber buildings being gentry manor houses, such as Speke Hall, Rufford Old Hall and Samlesbury Hall. The Fylde and the Solway lowlands possessed neither timber nor stone; here the vernacular tradition was one of low, cruck-framed buildings, covered with thatch and with walls constructed from a variety of materials, including clay (particularly in the Solway lowlands where considerable numbers of 'clay dabbins' survive), cobbles and brick (Fig. 5.11).[10]

ABOVE: *Fig. 5.10 **Harrop Fold**, near Slaidburn, the site of a medieval vaccary on an outlying portion of Bowland Forest.*

*Fig. 5.11 **Baldwinholme, near Carlisle**: an example of the traditional clay-walled, cruck-framed houses of the Carlisle plain, photographed in the late 19th century.*

TOP: **Fig. 5.12 Yew Tree House, Over Kellet**, *a typical example of a farmhouse built (or rebuilt) in the late 17th century and subsequently modified (by having its roof raised). The lintel bears the initials of Richard and Jane Dickinson and the date 1684.*

ABOVE: **Fig. 5.13 Dated lintel, Melling, north Lancashire.** *This unusual and extravagant lintel, inscribed '1684 ROBART', records the construction of a new house, probably as an inn, by Robert Remington (1642–1719).*

The particular mix of ages in the houses and outbuildings of a village or hamlet is essentially a product of capital investment during times of economic prosperity. Across the region there is evidence of a 'great rebuilding' in the 17th and early 18th centuries, notably in the form of solid stone farmhouses; many carry stones that record the date of major building work. The considerable capital investment which these houses represent was made possible by a combination of increasing wealth and security of tenure. Customary tenures, by which most communities in Cumbria, north Lancashire and north-west Yorkshire held their lands, were confirmed and, indeed, strengthened by the mid-17th century, giving tenants security and confidence. At the same time a buoyant livestock trade combined with wealth from trade and industry, particularly textiles, to produce a surplus which could be invested in stone and mortar. The first phase of this 'great rebuilding' was concentrated in the textile districts around Burnley and Colne in east Lancashire, where yeomen-clothiers accumulated considerable wealth from the late 16th century. Further north, fewer farmhouses date from before 1660 and the peak of the rebuilding took place between about 1680 and 1740 (Fig. 5.12). The dynastic pride that lay behind this explosion in building can be seen in the family initials and dates on finely carved door lintels, internal wooden fittings and plaster work (Fig. 5.13).[11]

Few of these sturdy early-modern houses remain unchanged; indeed, date stones, lovingly preserved and re-set, are not infrequently the main surviving evidence. Later phases of prosperity are also visible in the vernacular heritage: farmhouses with symmetrical façades, sash windows and regular quoins in west Cumbria reflect 18th-century wealth; the massive stone barns and shippons (cow houses) of north Lancashire reveal the confidence of farming in the 19th century. Buildings in the countryside also reflect other trends since the 16th century: the winnowing-out of smaller holdings and the concentration of land into fewer, larger farms across the 17th and 18th centuries; a continuing haemorrhaging of population and amalgamation of farms through the 19th and most of the 20th centuries; and a re-population in the late 20th century.

The reduction in the number of landed holdings gathered pace across the 19th and 20th centuries. Unless former farmhouses were in demand for non-farming families (as was the case in some areas during the Industrial Revolution and has been the case again since *c.* 1970), the result was abandoned houses and ruined farmsteads. Even a cursory look around many farmsteads today will yield the tell-tale signs of blocked windows and fireplaces, showing that outbuildings were formerly dwellings. Maps from the 19th century often confirm that what is now a single farmstead was then a small hamlet of two or three houses. Less obvious are the footings of farmsteads deserted in earlier centuries. At the head of the remote and marginal valley of Miterdale, in the western Lake District, are no fewer than four former steadings in various stages of decay (Fig. 5.14). Two, deserted before 1750, survive as little more than footings; the others continued to be inhabited until the 19th century.[12] However, the draw of the countryside in recent decades brought people back to villages and hamlets, and the wealth of retired people, commuters and the internet-dependent has resulted in a new wave of spending on the housing stock and a reversal of almost 200 years of population decline. Desertion has been succeeded by restoration, barn conversion and the subdivision of farmsteads, this time to create private dwellings. The case of one small settlement in the Lake District illustrates these trends. The village of High Lorton consisted of a street of seven farmsteads and five cottages in 1649. By 1840, although six houses had land attached to them, only two were farms of over 20 acres; by 2003 there were no farms in the village and virtually every former outbuilding had been converted into a dwelling.

Fig. 5.14 Miterdale Head, *between Eskdale and Wasdale. The retreat from the upland margins is marked by conversion of farmland to forestry plantation and the desertion of farmsteads.*

FIELDS AND WOODS

The key to understanding the traditional farming landscape lies in appreciating the constraints imposed by water in the soil. Impeded drainage was the greatest block to farming in the lowlands, altitude, slope and poor soils the main constraints in the uplands. Well-drained soils were at a premium to provide the core of arable land on which the staple crops of oats, barley and wheat could be grown. Land for other uses was also needed. Meadows, required to provide the vital crop of hay to keep livestock through the winter, were located on wetter land – too heavy for the plough, but capable of growing a rich crop of grass in the summer. Typically, meadows were located by river sides and on the fringes of arable land, where impeded drainage defeated the plough. Like arable and meadow land, woodland also needed to be protected from grazing livestock if it was to survive, and enclosed woods also fell within the 'anciently enclosed' areas.

Fig. 5.15 Wray, Lancashire: *the field pattern shown on the Ordnance Survey Six-Inch map, surveyed 1844–5.*

Each of these land-use elements exhibited its own history. They can often be identified as distinctive elements in the modern field pattern, as illustrated by the case of Wray in north Lancashire (Fig. 5.15). Here, three distinctive areas can be identified on the large-scale Ordnance Survey map. North of the village are long, thin, strip fields, divided by a network of narrow lanes, stretching across the more level land beside the River Hindburn. These were the arable lands and meadows, and are typical of open field enclosure in the North West. Second, the block of land to the west of the village, containing several areas of woodland, originated as a deer park belonging to the lords of Hornby Castle, as indicated by the curving outer boundary and the names Cold Park Wood and Park Barn. Finally, the rectilinear fields and straight, wide roads running up on to higher ground to the south of the village were the product of the enclosure of moorland by act of Parliament in 1804. The following discussion explores the idea that the history of land use and enclosure since medieval times is reflected in the very fabric of the field boundaries delineating the farming landscape today.

Open-field landscapes

Where farms clustered together into a village or hamlet, there is usually evidence for the existence of an arable open field in which members of the community held shares. Often known in the vernacular as 'townfields' (that is, the fields shared by the members of the township community), the form of these open fields was similar to those elsewhere in lowland Britain: unfenced strips, known as *riggs*, *lands* or (where short and at right angles to the main strips) *butts*, were grouped into furlongs, also called *flatts* or *shoots*, each of which bore a separate name (Fig. 5.16). The strips were ploughed as ridge and furrow, and each

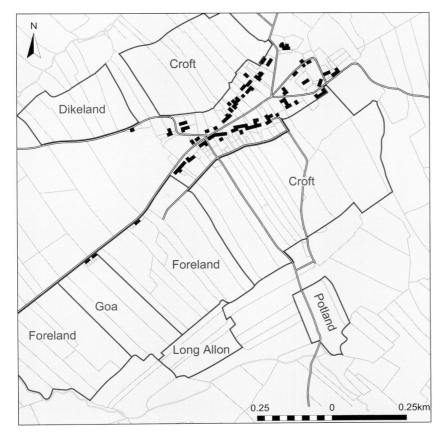

Fig. 5.16 Gilcrux. *The strip fields and the field names given in the Tithe Plan of 1841 preserve the memory of furlongs in the former open fields, enclosed in 1648. The wider, more rectilinear fields to the west of the village (between Dikeland and Foreland furlongs) represent a tongue of moorland converted to outfield cultivation, which was enclosed in 1754.*

farmer's holding would consist of strips scattered through the furlongs in the open field. There were major differences between these open field landscapes and those of the classic Midland type. First, the open fields in the North West generally formed only a core of the community's farmland; second, there is little evidence that systems of crop rotation akin to those found in the classic Midland three-field system were practised.

Most open fields in the North West appear to have been 'infields' – that is, cores of arable land, cultivated intensively. While there is sometimes evidence for more than one open field area attached to a village, there is little indication that the fields were cropped in rotation. Temple Sowerby in the Eden valley had a West Field and a North Field in the mid-16th century, and the neighbouring village of Kirkby Thore had a West Field and a Down Field. Murton, near Appleby, had a Great (or North) Field and two much smaller fields, Little Field and Moor Field in the 18th century; Bowness on Solway an East Field, a West Field and a High Field in 1638; Halton, near Lancaster, an Arra Field, Newfield and Netherfield in 1563.[13] Nowhere is there any suggestion that these were other than topographical names, describing the location of sections of the open fields. Where free-draining land was limited and livestock rearing played a greater part in the rural economy, a smaller core of open field arable could be cropped annually by receiving liberal applications of manure.

The enclosure of these townfields produced one of the most distinctive elements of the north-west English landscape: the narrow, strip-like fields that preserve in their outlines the shapes of the lands and furlongs in the open fields (Fig. 5.17). Enclosure was very protracted, stretching from the 16th century to the 19th, and is only infrequently documented, since it was often a piecemeal process involving exchanges of strips between individuals to consolidate holdings into fewer, wider shares. Obtaining the agreement of all concerned could be fraught with difficulty, as illustrated by a comment on the open fields at Bowness on Solway in 1638:

Fig. 5.17 Blindcrake, flanked by strip fields, preserving the outlines of the village's open fields. The larger, rectangular fields and woodland behind were the demesne lands belonging to the lords of the neighbouring manor of Isel.

There land lyeth very much intermixed & in very small parcells & if it could bee laied togather it would bee much better for the tennantes but I find the freehoulders noe whitt willinge to exc[h]ange & I think it will hardly bee brought to pass.[14]

Occasionally there is evidence of communal action to effect or ease enclosure. In 1567 the manor court jury at Yanwath, near Penrith, ordered the tenants to 'exchaynge theyre landes yn the feldes one withe anotherr so that every tenante may have theyre tenementes yn severall closes', though the fact that the court had to reiterate its decision 10 years later suggests that the process of enclosure was not immediate. A similar order by the manor court at Gilcrux in 1648 probably generated the landscape of strip fields surrounding the village, as the 'Infeild grounds now in Neighbourhood' (that is, held open and subject to common rights after harvest) were 'laid together, every man's by itselfe' (Fig. 5.16). Formal, private enclosure agreements became more common in the 18th century and were responsible for the enclosure of several common arable fields on the Carlisle plain.[15]

More often, however, enclosure is only glimpsed in incidental references. Sir William Norris, who died in 1567, was said to have 'broght the towne feld into closses' at Garston, near Liverpool. At Longton, south of Preston, piecemeal enclosure of the townfields resulted in 1655 in a dispute over a blocked footpath: fields either side of a 'late inclosed Townefeild' had been provided with stiles, but the latest enclosures had none, thus hindering access. Scattered references such as these from both Lancashire and Cumbria suggest that many infields disappeared between the mid-16th century and the end of the 18th. The unplanned and attenuated nature of much of this process meant that small patches of shared land sometimes survived, surrounded by furlongs which had already been enclosed. Over 20 such relics of former townfields survived in the Carlisle plain in 1912.[16]

The strip fields which resulted from the piecemeal enclosure of infields fossilised the structure of the former open fields. The furrow marking the boundary between one owner's lands and those of his neighbour was the property boundary along which the new enclosure fence was built. If strips in the open field possessed the characteristic reversed-S, aratral curve, then the new enclosures would preserve that line (cf. Figs 5.16; 5.17). Sometimes ridge and furrow survives within strip fields to confirm the relationship between pre- and post-enclosure landscapes.

The proportion of a village's farmland held in open fields varied widely. On the Solway lowlands open, shared land was extensive: the three open fields at Bowness on Solway in 1638 covered 115ha (285 acres), and there were other shared fields and meadows around the village. The lands of the nearby hamlet of Cardurnock were almost entirely open, the surveyor noting that 'there is no enclosier to any house in Cardronooke but only small garths'.[17] Elsewhere, a ring of other enclosures lay between the core of the village townfields and the pre-enclosure moorland edge. What was the nature of this land? In lowland Cumbria there is evidence for 'outfields', a category of land intermediate between the intensively cropped infields and the common rough grazings. Outfields were divided into named sections or 'breaks' (there were three in Dean outfield and four at Aspatria and Holm Cultram), which were cultivated in rotation, each being ploughed for, typically, three years and then put down to grass for six years or more. In any one year, then, most of the outfield would be grazed as pasture, but one block would be cultivated in open field strips. Outfield cultivation appears to have survived in Cumberland until the mid-18th century: the outfields at Dean and Gilcrux were enclosed in 1754, those at Aspatria in 1758–9, and that at Seascale in 1764.[18] The resulting enclosures tended to be large and regular (cf. Fig. 5.16).

Although the term 'outfield' is rare in Lancashire, named blocks of land surrounding an infield are found in some villages. A particularly clear example comes from Wharles, near Kirkham (Fig. 5.18). Nothing is known of the medieval field system here (the township was completely enclosed when holdings were first described in detail in 1653), but the field-names recorded then and on the survey of *c.* 1800 show a core of land named Innfield immediately around the hamlet. Except for a strip of wet carr and mossland down the eastern edge of the township, the remainder of the hamlet's territory consisted largely of named blocks (Old Hey; Whinny Hey; Brandhill; Brandearth; Holme), divided into closes held by different members of the community.

Fig. 5.18 Wharles, near Kirkham c. *1800. Field names show a core of infield land, blocks of enclosure of what may have been outfield land and the peat moss and carr on the eastern fringe of the township. (Redrawn from plan in LRO, DDK/Surveys.)*

Early enclosed landscapes

By no means all the farming landscape of the lowlands is the result of enclosure of open fields. Where settlement took the form of dispersed farmsteads, a landscape of enclosed fields had generally evolved before the end of the medieval period. Such landscapes were particularly characteristic of the areas of late-surviving woodland into which the frontier of settlement pushed in the early medieval period, particularly along the fringes of the hills in southern Cumbria, the Ribble valley, the skirts of the Bowland and Rossendale uplands and parts of south-west Lancashire. In these areas blocks of land were granted out across the 12th and 13th centuries, and a landscape of small, irregular fields developed as new enclosures were literally carved out of the woodland. The charters abound with references to 'assarts' (woodland cleared for cultivation), and field-names which continued in use many centuries later preserve the memory of a hard-won landscape, cleared by hand: *thwaite*, the Scandinavian word for a clearing; *ridding* (and the variants *royd* and *rode*), its Middle English equivalent; *stubbing*, a clearing where tree stumps remained. In contrast to the landscapes that resulted from enclosure of open fields, each field bore a different name and many contained the elements *close* or *hey*, indicating an enclosed plot of ground.

An example of such a landscape of woodland clearance is provided by the township of Aighton, Bailey and Chaigley, on the skirts of Longridge Fell. The names of the three hamlets all breathe of woodland: Aighton is 'oak-tree settlement'; Bailey and Chaigley contain the Old English element *leah*, meaning 'woodland' or 'a clearing in woodland'. Early 13th-century charters grant blocks of land explicitly described as 'assarts', their boundaries following cloughs, minor

streams, other assarts and, in some cases, individually identified trees.[19] The post-medieval landscape was a patchwork of irregular closes and scattered farms with patches of woodland, some of the field names (such as Riddings and Stubbings) recording their origins as woodland clearings (Fig. 5.19).

As a result of colonisation, much of the woodland recorded in place-names (cf. Figs 2.10, 2.11) had gone by the end of the medieval centuries, to the extent that the North West became one of the less wooded regions of England. If trees were to survive and regenerate in the face of grazing livestock and the incessant demand for firewood, they had to be protected. Some open wood-pastures remained, particularly in the royal forests of Inglewood and Bowland. In Whinfell Forest, in Westmorland, ancient dying oaks, known as the Three Brothers, survived into the 17th century.[20]

Fig. 5.19 Bailey, on the slopes of Longridge Fell. Woodland names predominate in this landscape of dispersed settlements and small, irregular fields, typical of areas of assarting during the period of medieval colonisation.

By the 14th century, most surviving woodland was enclosed, much of it in seigniorial deer parks. The largest of these were the royal parks, which represented the vestiges of earlier royal hunting grounds (Myerscough, near Garstang, and Croxteth, Toxteth and Simonswood, near Liverpool) and the parks attached to baronial castles (such as those at Cockermouth, Egremont, Kendal and Hornby). Parks offered some protection, but often merely delayed clearance: asset-stripping of timber (as occurred in the parks at Millom Castle and Rose Castle in the 17th century) and the predations of grazing livestock continued to reduce the woodland acreage and many parks (including those at Toxteth, Simonswood, Cockermouth and Kendal) had been disparked and let as farmland by 1700.[21] However, the increasing value of woodland for charcoal production from the 15th and 16th centuries led to strict management of smaller patches of woodland as enclosed coppice woods, particularly in southern Cumbria.

Fields in the dales

Fig. 5.20 The Buttermere valley. In the medieval period the open fields of the village of Buttermere lay between the lakes, with a ring of farmsteads on the lower fell slopes. In the distance, at the head of the lake, was the vaccary of Gatesgarth.

The medieval roots of the upland farming landscape are also still discernible today. Buttermere, in the heart of the Lake District (Fig. 5.20), illustrates the key components of the upland medieval landscape. At the head of the lake, below the steep sweeping slopes of Fleetwith Pike, lay the vaccary of Gatesgarth, represented today by a single large stock farm. The vaccary's meadows lay on the flat valley floor in the bowl of the fells at the head of the lake; to the left of Fleetwith Pike lay

an enclosed park or wood, recorded in the 1260s. The steep and partly wooded fellsides to the right of the lake lay across a manorial boundary in medieval times, but they also contained two large demesne pastures. The dale head was thus a seigniorial preserve, closed to peasant settlement. At the foot of the lake, however, a settled community had grown up by *c.* 1200 and new land continued to be taken in across the 13th century, creating two distinct types of landscape. The clustered village of Buttermere itself was focused on an area of open field arable and meadow on the valley floor between the lakes, represented today by long, narrow fields radiating from the village. On the lower slopes of the fells behind the village lay a ring of farms, set in small irregular enclosures of meadow, pasture and woodland, the product of secondary colonisation in the late 13th and early 14th century.[22]

A similar patchwork of small open fields, irregular fields resulting from colonisation, enclosed woodland and seigniorial enclosures can be found in most Lakeland valleys. Where the valley floor was wide and dry enough, patches of open field arable and common meadows were found, generally associated with a clustered hamlet or village. Open fields on valley gravels, as at Buttermere, are recorded in the 16th century around villages like Braithwaite, Lorton and Wasdale Head. Even Grizedale, a small hamlet deep in the wooded Furness fells, had common fields and meadows on the flat valley floor in the late 17th century.[23] As in the lowlands, these patches of open field deep in the dales disappeared silently through piecemeal enclosure before 1800.

The landscape of hedges, banks and dry stone walls is thus a product of many centuries of piecemeal evolution. As with so much of the English landscape, the position and line of field boundaries are often of much greater antiquity than their fabric. Whether the field pattern is a product of assarting from the waste in the 13th century or of the subdivision and enclosure of formerly shared fields since the 16th, the field boundaries themselves have been repaired and renewed piecemeal by generations of farmers. Much of the look of farmland appears to have been established in the 17th and 18th centuries, as impermanent boundaries (such as 'dry hedges', made of stakes interwoven with brushwood) were replaced by living or 'quick' hedges or by stone walls. In a world of small farms, this process went largely unrecorded, but occasional glimpses are sometimes caught: Isaac Fletcher, a yeoman farmer at Mosser on the north-west fringe of the Lake District, recorded in his diary setting hundreds of thorn bushes between 1759 and 1766 and locating suitable outcrops of stone and employing wallers to construct new walls around some of his higher fields in 1776 and 1777.[24] One distinctive feature of the enclosed landscape of the dales was the management of hedgerow trees to provide additional fodder for livestock in the winter. The pollarded ash trees of the Lake District valleys (Fig. 5.21), spaced out along field boundaries, enabled cattle and sheep to continue to graze at the foot of the tree, while a crop of poles grew from the cut top. They provided nutritious additional fodder in the form of the leaves and bark of the crop of poles, which could then be used around the farm. Holly was even more widespread as a supplementary feed (it is recorded from Bowland and the south and central Pennines, as well as the Lake District) and was often planted close to the farmstead.[25]

Fig. 5.21 Pollarded ash trees,
Newlands. *Pollarding enabled a crop of poles to be grown out of reach of grazing livestock.*

The age of improvement

The Agricultural Revolution of the century after 1760 saw widespread landscape change, much of it the result of enclosure and reclamation of the wastes (*see* Chapter 6). But it also involved a re-writing of the farming landscape, as earlier piecemeal enclosures were swept away and replaced by what were seen as functional landscapes more appropriate to 'scientific farming'. The impact of improving landlords on the landscape of the North West should not be overstated: indeed, the absence of wholesale re-planning of the countryside in the 19th century is one of the characteristic features of much of the region. The key determinant was the nature of the tenure by which tenants held their farms. Where estates were let on short leases, as was common in much of lowland Lancashire, the landlords had the power to take the land in hand and to re-organise it according to the doctrines of 'improvement'. Over most of Cumbria and large parts of north Lancashire and north-west Yorkshire, however, the traditional customary tenures effectively prevented manorial lords from taking control of tenanted land. After the tenants' rights in such customary estates were confirmed by courts of law in the 17th century, customary tenures were tantamount to freeholds, in that tenants could buy, sell and pass such properties on to their heirs without hindrance from their landlords. By the 19th century many customary tenants had been enfranchised, making them freeholders. On such manors power to effect landscape change was vested in these small proprietors: unless a manorial lord bought the freehold from his tenants, he was unable to gain control of the land and to improve his estate.

The impact of landlords during the 'age of improvement' is most clearly visible in the Fylde and on the vast estates of the earls of Derby in south-west Lancashire. The Cliftons of Lytham committed vast sums to re-writing the landscape of their estates. Little Plumpton, for example, was completely transformed in a few years by Thomas Clifton in the 1840s. He more or less demolished the village around 1845, replacing the existing farmsteads with a single large steading, including an impressive range of farm buildings arranged around a courtyard and a series of estate workers' cottages built to the pattern found elsewhere on his estate (Fig. 5.22). The field pattern surrounding the village was rationalised by throwing existing fields together into larger blocks of around 8ha (20 acres), and the focus shifted from arable cultivation to livestock rearing. This physical re-writing went hand-in-hand with social transformation. Five tenants had holdings in Little Plumpton in 1809; after reorganisation the land was thrown into two large holdings of almost 165ha (400 acres) each. The new steading in the village was retained in hand and run by a farm steward, brought down from Scotland, while the remaining 160ha (394 acres) was assigned to a tenant at The Hill, a farm outside the village. The 1851 census records 10 households headed by farm labourers as well as a shepherd, also brought in from Scotland. The era of 'high farming' in the mid-19th century thus produced revolutionary change.[26]

Similarly radical re-writing of the landscape occurred elsewhere. At Great Singleton Thomas Miller, a Preston mill owner, rebuilt farmsteads and labourers' cottages, swept away old lanes and field boundaries, undertook a programme of under-drainage and laid out new fields and plantations. The resulting landscape, laid out on a drawing board, was as rectilinear as the products of Parliamentary enclosure. Although re-modelled landscapes are less extensive further north, islands of improvement occur where a pioneering landlord pursued scientific farming. At the heart of such landscapes there often lay a 'model' farmstead of the type built by Clifton at Little Plumpton and Miller at Avenham Hall, Singleton. Generally arranged around a courtyard, these farmsteads were planned for maximum efficiency, particularly in the housing of stock and crops and the collection of manure. Schoose Farm, at Workington (Fig. 5.23), built by

OPPOSITE PAGE:

TOP: *Fig. 5.22 Estate cottages at Little Plumpton*, built to the standard design used on the Clifton family's estates in the Fylde.

BOTTOM: *Fig. 5.23 Schoose Farm, Workington*, John Christian Curwen's 'model' farmstead, complete with its own windmill tower.

MARL PITS

The landscape of the Lancashire plain is peppered with literally thousands of pits and ponds (right), many of which are legacies of the ancient practice of digging marl as a soil conditioner and fertiliser. Marl was used in the North West to describe calcareous clays in the glacial till, which were used to improve soil texture by adding body, the calcareous content sweetening acid soils. 'Marle is a never-failing friend to most lands in this county,' said a Lancashire farmer in the late 18th century and a tradition of marling can be documented back to the 13th century. A local proverb, 'old' when recorded in the 17th century, said, 'he that marles upon sand intends to bye

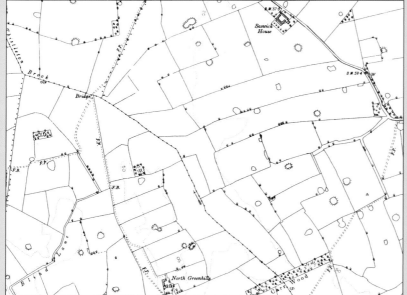

land; But he that marles upon clay throwes all away', suggesting that its principal use was to improve sandy soils. John Holt, in his agricultural survey of Lancashire in 1795, recorded that the general practice in the county was to lay marl on grassland in the summer and to leave it to weather across at least one summer and winter before ploughing it in.[29]

    The pits from which marl was dug destroyed land and frequently flooded: indeed the total acreage of small ponds shown on 19th-century maps across the Fylde and south Lancashire must have been substantial (above). Such slippery-sided, water-filled holes were dangerous, both to man and beast. In 1572 the manor court at Astley, near Wigan, ordered the draining of a marl pit 'wyche is dangerous for menez cattell', and there are numerous records of men being killed in marl pits. Digging

marl was dangerous work to judge by Holt's description of the method of working marl in the 18th century:

> Marle is got by falling it in large clods; this method is expeditious, but requires great caution ... the piece intended to be fallen is undermined, and loosened at each side, by being cut through; long piles are then driven in at the top, and sometimes water is required to insinuate itself into the interstices which the poles have made. The clod falls with such violence as to break the mass into pieces.

By the middle of the 19th century, the availability of other fertilisers, notably imported guano and manure from the conurbations, sounded the death knell for marling. Thinking of the acreages destroyed by flooded marl pits, the agricultural improver, Jonathan Binns, did not regret the demise of 'this expensive and troublesome mode of cultivation'. Since then, many marl pits have been reclaimed, though many still survive (below).[30]

John Christian Curwen *c.* 1800 was at the heart of the 273ha (673-acre) home farm which Curwen saw as a model for agricultural improvement. The annual meetings of the Workington Agricultural Society, founded by Curwen in 1806, included a visit to Schoose, which became 'a mecca for agricultural pioneers from all over the country'. Later in the century Curwen's neighbour, Sir Wilfrid Lawson of Brayton, near Aspatria, re-modelled land at Blennerhasset and created a new model farmstead which he called Mechi Farm, in honour of John J Mechi (1802–80), the agricultural improver and author of *How to Farm Profitably, particularly on stiff, heavy clays* (first published 1857).[27]

Indeed, increasing agricultural productivity on 'stiff, heavy clays' was one of the key challenges facing farmers in the North West during the 19th century and their attempts to overcome it by under-drainage played a major part in creating the rich pastures and silage fields of the modern countryside. Early drains had been constructed of sods, faggots or stone; they had been of limited long-term efficacy and laborious to make. The introduction of clay tiles from the 1820s and, especially, of cylindrical tiles in the 1840s, saw a rapid expansion of under-drainage. Improving landlords built tileries on their estates: by 1851 there were said to be 42 in eastern Cumberland alone. The footings of buildings and boggy patches where clay was dug sometimes mark the sites of the tileries themselves; but the effects of the tiles they produced are far more widespread. Field drains enabled farmers to break out of the straightjacket imposed by the natural drainage characteristics of the soil, and were perhaps the single most important agent in the transition from traditional to modern farming landscapes.[28]

NOTES

1. Cowell & Innes 1994, 131; Higham & Jones 1975; Hodgkinson *et al.* 2000, 110–18, 155–7; Bewley 1992; Bewley 1993
2. Pennington 1970, 72; Wimble *et al.* 2000, 25–6; Leech 1983
3. Higham & Jones 1985, 82–95; Wells 2003, 69–74; Newman 1996, 64–6
4. Roberts 1972; Sheppard 1974
5. Winchester in Crosby 1993, 17; Armstrong *et al.* 1950–2, 128, 334
6. Winchester 2005
7. Winchester 1987, 37–44
8. Winchester 1987, 42–3; Winchester 2000b, 77; Winchester 2003
9. Porter 1975, 45; Tupling 1927, 75–6
10. Watson & McClintock 1979; Jennings 2003
11. Pearson 1985; Machin 1977; Garnett 1988
12. Winchester 1979
13. CRO, WD/Crk/Map II; Tyson 1992; CRO, D/Lons/L5/2/41/53, Whittrigg etc. surveys, fols 52–125; Castle Howard MSS, survey of Halton, 1563
14. CRO, D/Lons L5/2/41/53, Whittrigg etc. surveys, fol. 125v.
15. CRO, WD/Ry, box 42, Yanwath court roll, 9 June 1567, 7 Feb. 1576/7; CRO, D/BD/2/23/1; Elliott 1973, 79
16. LRO, QSP/115/2; Youd 1961, 34–40; Elliott 1973, 76–88; Graham 1913
17. CRO, D/Lons L5/2/41/53, Whittrigg etc. surveys, fols 52–125, 34–44, 47
18. Elliott 1973, 63–7; for Dean, see PRO, C12/1991/4; Gilcrux: CRO, D/Ben; Aspatria: Elliott 1960, 97–108; Seascale: CRO, QRE/1/159
19. Winchester in Crosby 1993, 19–21
20. Denton 2003, 402
21. Ibid, 70, 244; Porter 1975; Cowell & Innes 1994, 134–6; Winchester 2000b, 82–3; Higham 2004, 119–23
22. Winchester 1987, 138–43
23. Winchester 1987, 69; Grizedale: LRO, DDX 398/122
24. Winchester 1994, pp. xx, 315–17, 332
25. Winchester 2000a, 57
26. LRO, DDCl/523; 552; PRO, HO 107/2269
27. *Preston Guardian*, 6 May 1916, p. 6; Hughes 1965, 228
28. Garnett 1849; Davis 2002
29. Holt 1795, 111–17; Lewis 2000, 108, 372. For proverb, see LRO, DDHo/544
30. LRO, DDHm/1, Astley court verdict, 6 Feb. 1572; Holt 1795, 117; Binns 1851, 10

6

Fell, Moorland and Moss

The transformation of the late medieval farming landscape into the patchwork of fields we see today involved not only the enclosure of open fields, described in Chapter 5, but also the appropriation of the wastes. In the North West, fells, moorland, mossland and marsh were brought into individual ownership and, where possible, reclaimed for more intensive agricultural use. This was a process spanning several centuries, involving both piecemeal encroachment and wholesale enclosure. It culminated in a great tide of enclosure and reclamation from the late 18th to the late 19th century – the period of the Agricultural Revolution. As a result, a landscape of fields was created on the many thousands of hectares which had formerly stretched as unenclosed waste between and around the cores of settlement.

LOWLAND MOORS

The wastes most tempting to reclaim were the lowland moors, the common grazings that accounted for one-quarter to one-third of the land surface of many lowland townships. Such moors were generally less well drained than the core of farmland, but they were capable of improvement and were markedly less wet than the mosslands and marshes. Across the North West there is evidence for widespread encroachment on to the lowland wastes in the 16th century, some of it apparently systematic and organised. On the Carlisle plain, the Earl of Northumberland initiated large-scale enclosure at Westward, near Wigton, in 1569, 94 new holdings being created on land which was 'fertill & free from wood', while over 200ha (500 acres) of waste in Inglewood Forest were enclosed in the late 16th century under the encouragement of the chief steward.[1] More widespread were small 'intakes' of moorland: on the Shireburn estates in the Fylde, for example, each of the holdings at Hambleton in 1567 had a few acres of 'new inclosure from Hamleton more and the marshe' totalling almost 55 customary acres (probably *c*. 35ha), and the tenants of Carleton and Norcross had similar, though smaller, intakes from Carleton Moor.[2] There was also wholesale enclosure of moorland, particularly in Lancashire. In the Fylde, for example, the moors at Woodplumpton were enclosed under an agreement of 1573; Whitmoor and Sikefield Moor in Greenhalgh had been enclosed by 1595; and part of Layton Hawes, on the coast near Lytham, had been marked out by sods and assigned for enclosure in 1596.[3] Further east, in the Ribble valley, the enclosure of moorland was proposed in the 17th century: agreement had been reached on the improvement of the common at Alston by *c*. 1630; an unsuccessful attempt was made to embark on enclosing Fulwood Common in 1638, while over 73ha (180 acres) were enclosed from the common at Thornley, near Longridge, in 1681.[4]

The cumulative result of enclosure of moors in lowland Lancashire in the 16th and 17th centuries appears to have been substantial. Whereas most villages in Cumbria and Lancashire north of the River Lune retained unenclosed common moorland until the great wave of Parliamentary enclosure starting in the mid-18th

Fig. 6.1 Croston Finney, a lowland waste described, when it was enclosed in 1725, as being partly overgrown with gorse and furze, and partly mossland. Enclosure created the grid of occupation roads giving access to the newly laid-out fields.

century, little unenclosed waste (other than mossland) survived in lowland Lancashire by 1750. Much of the early-modern enclosure of moors in Lancashire probably took place without formal record, but the legacy of the silent disappearance of the commons remains in field- and minor place-names, notably in the frequent field-name 'Moor Hey' ('enclosure from the moor').

In lowland Cumbria pressure towards enclosure built up across the 18th century, driven partly by the potential for increased profit from reclamation and improvement, partly by the collapse of manorial control of grazing rights on the commons, witnessed in many Cumbrian manors from the 1720s. Early enclosures were by agreement, one of the most extensive being the Low Moor at Hayton, east of Carlisle, containing over 400ha (1,000 acres), enclosed under an agreement of 1704. By the middle of the century the tenants of several Cumbrian manors petitioned their lords for enclosure of their commons, and by the 1760s the first phase of enclosure by private act of Parliament had begun. During the 30 years between 1760 and 1790 over 19,680ha (48,600 acres) of moorland in Cumbria and north Lancashire were enclosed, mainly in four clusters: in west Cumberland; around Carlisle; on the southern fringes of Inglewood Forest; and in the Eden valley (where 10 moors from Culgaith and Stainton in the north to Sandford and Great Ormside in the south were enclosed in the 1770s). Where moorland survived in lowland Lancashire the story was similar: a handful of early enclosures, such as Croston Finney, took place (Fig. 6.1), preceding a spate of enclosure later in the century. The earliest extensive enclosure was at Ellel, near Lancaster, where almost 800ha (2,000 acres) of moorland were divided in 1757.[5]

Much more extensive was the second and greater wave of Parliamentary enclosure across the years of the Napoleonic Wars, when high grain prices encouraged the capital expenditure necessary to convert former moorland to arable. Between 1800 and 1820 over 60,750ha (150,000 acres) of common land were enclosed in Cumbria and north Lancashire, and by 1840 the lowland moors had all but disappeared. The new landscape was created in outline on the enclosure commissioners' drawing boards, and realised by labourers planting hedges and building walls, paring and burning the rough moorland vegetation, spreading lime, ploughing, harrowing and sowing seed. Rectilinear sections of the former common were allotted to individual landowners, resulting in the creation of a landscape of large, straight-edged fields, enclosed by thorn hedges or, where stone was readily available, drystone walls. In many cases the new, rectilinear enclosure landscapes abut unconformably against the less regular features of earlier enclosure. New roads were created, some to define pre-existing routes across the common, others to provide access to the newly allotted fields. Ruler-straight, generous in width and with ample verges, enclosure roads are perhaps the most immediate reminder that one is crossing former moorland. A narrow lane winding out from a village suddenly widens, straightens and runs directly across the former moor until reducing and turning where it enters the next area of pre-enclosure farmland (Fig. 6.2). Though the new fields generally represented additions to existing farms, some new farmsteads were created, their names sometimes recalling the times in which they were built, such as Waterloo

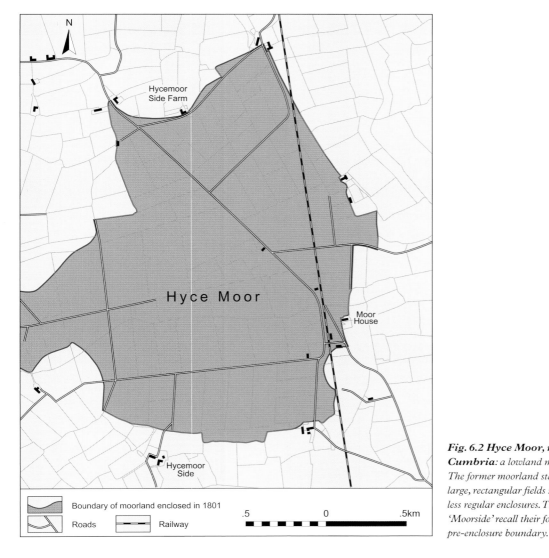

Fig. 6.2 Hyce Moor, near Bootle, Cumbria: a lowland moor enclosed in 1801. The former moorland stands out as a block of large, rectangular fields surrounded by earlier, less regular enclosures. The settlements named 'Moorside' recall their former position on the pre-enclosure boundary.

Farm on Eaglesfield Moor, enclosed in 1815, and the Wellington farms on Brigham Moor, near Cockermouth, and on Brayton Moor near Aspatria, enclosed in 1819 and 1825, respectively.

RECLAMATION OF MOSS AND MARSH

The history of mossland and marshland reclamation also highlights differences in landscape history between Cumbria and Lancashire, epitomised by the contrast between market gardening on the rich black soils of former mosses in south-west Lancashire and commercial peat-cutting on surviving mosses in northern Cumbria. In the former, the market for agricultural produce in the towns of industrial Lancashire (and the availability of night soil from those towns) stimulated a vigorous programme of mossland drainage and reclamation; in northern Cumbria the absence of such stimuli allowed extensive tracts of semi-natural mossland to survive.

The roots of drainage and reclamation of the mosses and carrs (waterlogged scrubland) can be seen in the medieval centuries. As with the lowland moors, considerable hectarages of mossland had been reclaimed before the large-scale drainage schemes of the 19th century. The earliest glimpses of reclamation often come in lawsuit papers, when the enclosure of carr or moss by one landowner infringed the common rights claimed by another. For example, the wet carr land in the depression between the townships of Staining and Weeton-with-Preese, near Blackpool, was the subject of a dispute in 1523, stemming from the digging of a ditch through the carr 12 years previously. John Skillicorn of Preese Hall and his son-in-law, Thomas Singleton of Todderstaffe Hall in Staining (who dug the ditch), appear to have decided to enclose part of the carr between their properties, but their action fell foul of the abbot of Whalley, who, as lord of the manor of Staining, objected to Skillicorn's enclosure. Late 16th-century lawsuit plans provide further glimpses of the process of converting moss into farmland: a plan of Penwortham in 1590 shows land which 'was mosse in awnchient tyme & nowe pasture landes'; one of Greenhalgh in the Fylde in 1595 marks a field of 'arable whitch was mosse' on the edge of Esprick Moss. Such records of piecemeal encroachment on the wetlands probably represent only a fraction of a sustained process whereby new farmland was won by the digging of drainage ditches. The impact of such small-scale extensions of farmland out on to the mosses appears to have been considerable: a total of 525ha (1,300 acres) of mossland was reclaimed in this way on the Molyneux estates in south-west Lancashire in the later 17th century.[6]

The 16th-century examples quoted above are early records of a process that continued until the 19th century. In some townships it resulted in the creation of a landscape of small, irregular fields flanking roughly parallel lanes (sometimes called 'meanygates', i.e. common tracks) reaching out into the moss. Such reclamation by individual farmers contrasts strikingly with the rectilinear and clearly planned landscapes of reclamation in estates dominated by a single landowner. Sometimes the two contrasting landscapes abut each other across an estate boundary, as at the junction between Great Marton Moss and Lytham Moss, near Blackpool, or along the boundary between Catforth and Wharles (Fig. 6.3). Dating these moss lanes and their associated fields is difficult, but some, including Great Marton Moss, appear to have been created in the late 18th or early 19th century. The process was founded on the exercise of turbary (peat-cutting) rights. Each farmer had his own turbary place (known as a 'room', 'dale' or 'dalt'), to which the framework of tracks leading out into the moss gave access. Once peat had been removed, the owner had the right to use the ground below for grazing or cultivation. As each turbary room was worked out, it would be enclosed and reclaimed, while the owner moved on to win his fuel from the next plot of uncut peat, further into the moss.[7]

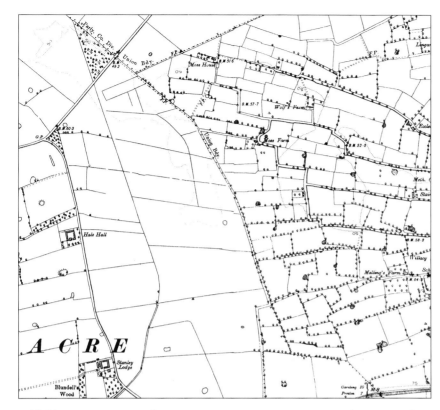

Fig. 6.3 Contrasting patterns of wetland reclamation: *the township boundary between Wharles and Catforth across former mossland in the Fylde in 1844. Wharles (to the left) belonged to the earls of Derby, the pattern of large enclosures reflecting reclamation by a single dominant landowner; the piecemeal enclosure of the mossland across the township boundary reflects the numerous small landowners in Catforth.*

Field patterns on some former mosses suggest a more systematic process of reclamation, even before the era of Parliamentary enclosure. At Hutton and Penwortham, where the mosses appear to have been completely enclosed by the mid-18th century, the blocks of rectangular fields on the former mossland suggest a planned process under the direction of the manorial lords. Lordly direction was certainly central to the reclamation of the wetlands in the Fylde and in south-west Lancashire, and to the drainage of two similarly named lakes, Martin Mere (near Southport) and Marton Mere (near Blackpool). The first major step was when Thomas Fleetwood of Bank Hall obtained an act of Parliament in 1695 to enable him to construct a new cut from Martin Mere to the sea at Crossens, in order to drain the mere. Silting of the floodgates at Crossens prevented the success of this venture and, despite further attempts at drainage after 1778, it was not until the installation of steam pumping in 1850 that the mosslands fringing the mere in Scarisbrick, Burscough, Rufford, Tarleton and Meols could be converted into farmland.[8]

In the Fylde, the transformation of the wetlands behind Blackpool began with the construction of the Main Dyke in 1731, which created a new outflow from Marton Mere to the River Wyre at Skippool. The mere contracted significantly, and most other wetland in the area appears to have been reclaimed by the end of the 18th century. A century after the Main Dyke was built, the Clifton family of Lytham (landlords at the forefront of agricultural improvement) constructed the Main Drain to drain Lytham Moss and adjacent wetlands in 1841. Costing £3,000 and carrying water from 2,400ha (6,000 acres) of land, the Main Drain sought to under-drain both clay and peat soils, consolidating earlier mossland enclosure rather than reclaiming new areas.[9]

The final push in mossland reclamation came with major Parliamentary enclosure in the 19th century. The process is documented in detail for Rawcliffe and Stalmine mosses in Over Wyre, where Wilson Ffrance of Rawcliffe Hall reclaimed 800ha (2,000 acres) under an enclosure award of 1833. Existing drains were deepened; roads were laid out across the moss; new drains were cut at right angles to the roads, dividing the moss into fields of about 1.6ha (4 acres); field drains were laid and lowered at intervals as the moss dried out; finally, the surface of the moss was scarified, ploughed and harrowed and marl was spread on the new fields before cultivation could start (Fig. 6.4). In southern Lancashire, proximity to the conurbations of Manchester and Liverpool encouraged the conversion of mossland to intensive market gardening. Not only did the urban populations offer a market for crops, they and their horses provided a ready supply of manure to fertilise the peat. The reclamation of Chat Moss, which had begun in the 1770s, was boosted by the construction *c.* 1830 of a movable railway to ease the distribution of nightsoil on to the moss. By 1849 about one-third of Chat Moss was under cultivation. The need for a new disposal site for Manchester's nightsoil led to the reclamation of Carrington Moss, where

Fig. 6.4 Out Rawcliffe Moss: *the rectangular fields and straight occupation roads laid out at enclosure in 1833.*

240ha (600 acres) of 'raw bog' survived in 1882; by 1899 the whole of the former moss had been leased to farmers.[10]

Although reclamation for agriculture was the driving force, provision was made for the continuance of traditional turbary rights where peat remained in use as a fuel, as was the case in Cumbria and north Lancashire. In some cases (as in the enclosure of Black Moss, near Egremont, in 1783) long, thin strips of land were allocated as turbary rooms; even where the enclosure award made no explicit allocation, a similar pattern of thin strips assigned for peat-cutting might develop, as around Holm Cultram and on Bolton Fell Moss in northern Cumbria. Furthermore, not all mosslands were reclaimed for agriculture, and where extensive raw peat survived it came to be exploited on an industrial scale as a resource in its own right – as horse litter in the late 19th century and as garden peat in the 20th. Chat Moss and other mosses near Manchester, Winmarleigh and Cockerham mosses in north Lancashire, and Wedholme Flow, Solway Moss and Bolton Fell Moss in north Cumbria were all cut for litter from the 1890s and commercial extraction continues on some of these today.[11]

A second front in wetland reclamation involved the estuarine salt marshes of the region's indented coastline. The wiry salt marsh vegetation, above the normal tidal limit but flooded at spring tides, provided seasonal grazing across the summer months, but the marshes also represented a frontier of potentially cultivable land, if the sea could be kept from them. In 1807 a 5km (3-mile) embankment was built from Cowpren Point to Humphrey Head, enclosing 240ha (600 acres) of salt marsh at the end of the Cartmel peninsula on Morecambe Bay. Two new arable farms, West Plain and East Plain, were established on the reclaimed marsh, though West Plain proved to be short-lived, as the ever-changing course of the River Leven undermined the embankment in 1828, allowing the sea to return.

The most dramatic reclamation took place on the marshes fringing the Ribble estuary, where thousands of hectares of new farmland were created on the south bank between Banks and Hutton. The process began early: at Hutton, for example, fields were being carved out of the marsh in the early 18th century. Alder wood piles were first driven in around the perimeter of the land to be reclaimed to form the core of new embankments. After perhaps a decade free from seasonal inundation, the newly enclosed land could be hedged about, ploughed and reclaimed.

The major phase of reclamation of the Ribble marshes, however, took place in the 19th and 20th centuries. It was intimately linked to the construction of the Ribble Navigation and the development of the port of Preston. By 1850 a dredged channel flanked by embankments had replaced the Ribble's natural course downstream to Freckleton and the confluence with the River Douglas, and the 1880s saw the straightening of the channel and the building of training walls in the lower estuary. The embankment of the upper estuary prevented spring tides from flooding the former marshes; it had the effect of producing dry land out to the centre of the estuary. The newly embanked marsh was vested in the Ribble Navigation Company, but adjacent landowners had the right to purchase it and the result was the creation of many hundreds of hectares of new farmland. The progressive transformation of the estuarine landscape is illustrated dramatically in the township of Hesketh with Becconsall (Fig. 6.5). In the early 19th century, the township's enclosed land was restricted to a narrow ridge, hemmed in

Fig. 6.5 Chronology of marshland reclamation at Hesketh with Becconsall on the Ribble Estuary.

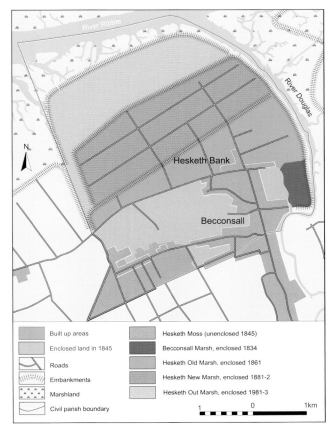

Built up areas		Hesketh Moss (unenclosed 1845)	
Enclosed land in 1845		Becconsall Marsh, enclosed 1834	
Roads		Hesketh Old Marsh, enclosed 1861	
Embankments		Hesketh New Marsh, enclosed 1881-2	
Marshland		Hesketh Out Marsh, enclosed 1981-3	
Civil parish boundary			

between mossland and marsh. Becconsall Marsh, fringing the River Douglas, had already been enclosed in 1834, but much more extensive reclamation took place on Hesketh Marsh as a result of the creation of the Ribble Navigation, where nearly 800ha (2,000 acres) were enclosed in two stages, in 1861 and 1881–2. Hesketh Out Marsh was finally embanked and reclaimed a century later, in 1981–3, extending the enclosed area 3.2km (2 miles) north of the former marshland edge at Hesketh Bank.[12]

THE FELLS AND UPLAND MOORS

The rough pastures of the fells and moors, which form the bulk of the land surface of many upland townships, possess a landscape history all of their own. In an environment largely devoted to grazing on permanent pasture, the time-depth of human occupation is particularly striking, as tangible relics of past human activity litter the hills. Along the boundary between farmland and fell, tide marks of settlement and cultivation reflect the ebb and flow of farming in the marginal upland environment. 'High tides' are represented by the cairnfields of the Bronze Age (Fig. 5.3), the native sites of the Romano-British period (Fig. 5.4), cultivation terraces of the medieval centuries (Fig. 5.9) and 'Napoleonic' ridge and furrow from the early 19th century, when high grain prices pushed cultivation to its limits (Fig. 6.8).

Lying beyond the limit of cultivation, the fells and moors were – and remain – an integral part of the upland farming system. Their primary use as summer grazing for cattle and sheep was the major motive force behind their landscape history, but these marginal areas also provided peat for fuel and a variety of other resources, especially vegetation for use as thatch. Today, the bulk of fell land is in private ownership, much of it the result of Parliamentary enclosure during the 19th century, though significant tracts of common land remain, particularly in Cumbria. In the former counties of Cumberland and Westmorland surviving common waste, most of it on the fells, comprises 11 per cent and almost 26 per cent of the land surface, respectively.

The process of enclosure, dividing the hillsides with a network of drystone walls, stretches back to the seigniorial enclosures of the medieval centuries. Where there had been vaccaries, banks of fellside had often been enclosed to serve as pastures for the vaccary milk herd or other categories of livestock, as in the separate cow, ox, stirk and calf pastures in the forests of Bowland and Trawden, recorded in the early 16th century. Similar fellside enclosures are found at vaccary sites in the Lake District, such as the wall enclosing the corries on the wild northern flanks of Steeple adjacent to Gillerthwaite in Ennerdale and that enclosing the slopes of Robinson, where there was a 'park' or 'wood' attached to the vaccary at Gatesgarth in the 1260s. There were also other seigniorial enclosures such as deer parks, as at the head of the Troutbeck valley, near Windermere, or Musbury Park in the heart of Rossendale Forest.[13]

However, the bulk of the fells and moors were brought into private ownership after 1500. Two distinct phases can be identified: a partial, but nonetheless extensive, enclosure of the lower fellsides during the 16th to 18th centuries; and the wholesale enclosure carried out under acts of Parliament during the 19th century. The key to understanding the enclosure of fell land in the early-modern period lies in the traditional patterns of resource management on the open hills. The fells and moors within the boundaries of most townships were legally 'manorial waste', with the rights in the soil vested in the lord of the manor, while his tenants used the produce of the surface through the exercise of common rights. Tenants had rights of pasture, turbary (the right to cut peat and turf) and estovers (the right to gather woody vegetation and materials such as heather, bracken and rushes). The exercise of these was overseen by the manor court, which made byelaws and other orders controlling and managing their day-to-day use. In practice, local custom, reinforced by the orders of the manor courts, recognised different areas of the waste used for particular purposes. For example, 16th- and 17th-century byelaws from the Lake District manor of Eskdale, Miterdale and Wasdalehead spelt out very clearly how different sections of the vast tract of fell land within the manor were to be used. The lower slopes of the fells, close to the farmsteads, were preserved as cow pastures; the plateau surrounding Burnmoor Tarn, at around 250m (800 feet) above sea level, was assigned to the community's heifers, bullocks and horses; while the high fells, covering the flanks of Scafell and the fells encircling Wasdalehead, were divided into a number of separate grazing grounds (or 'heafs') for sheep. Though there were no physical demarcations in this open, mountainous landscape, it was divided for practical purposes in the minds of the local community.[14]

The result of such management practices in the Lake District was to enable individual farmers to claim exclusive rights on particular sections of the fells, notably the lower fellsides immediately behind their farms, which provided convenient grazing for milking animals. The irregular 'intakes' of rough fell land found on the lower slopes of most Lake District valleys appear to have their origins in such claims: once custom or an order of the manor court established an exclusive right for an individual to use a section of the lower fells as a cow pasture, it was a short step to physical enclosure of that pasture. In Eskdale, most of the cow pastures assigned to individual tenants in 1587 had been enclosed as fellside intakes by 1700.[15]

The process of intaking continued into the 18th century, but could encounter opposition and lead to conflict. The steep fellside behind Boot in Eskdale was the location of a bitter dispute over intaking in the late 18th century. The inhabitants of Boot and a neighbouring farmer, Thomas Tyson of Borrowdale Place, made two large enclosures on Boot Bank in the 1780s, but they were forced to throw these open to the common again as a result of opposition from other farmers. Tyson's enclosure (Fig. 6.6) had blocked the route assigned by the manor court

Fig. 6.6 Boot Bank, Eskdale: the remains of a large fellside intake, deemed illegal and slighted after a lawsuit in 1795.

to a neighbouring farmer to drive his sheep to their heaf. Evidence given by Crispin Pharaoh, the waller who built Tyson's intake, suggests a remarkable degree of informality. Pharaoh started the wall in about 1782 and it took him four years to complete the full 1,100m (1,200 yards). He told the court that 'there was no marks whatever ... to go by for building the fence'; he simply built it 'where it was most convenient to get stone'.[16]

While such piecemeal, opportunistic intaking may characterise many of the Lakeland dales, there is also ample evidence of more systematic enclosure of the lower fells in the 16th and 17th centuries. Communal cow pastures, separated from the common but shared by a group of tenants, are recorded widely from south-eastern Cumbria through upland Lancashire and Yorkshire. Some, as we have seen, appear to be medieval in origin, but the process of enclosure continued in the 16th and 17th centuries: at Mallerstang, for example, a cow pasture near Nateby had been enclosed by 1590, but another at the head of the valley was enclosed in 1694.[17]

The most substantial enclosure of moorland waste in the uplands in the early-modern period took place in the former forests of Bowland and Blackburnshire. Here the impetus behind enclosure was rather different: the tenants saw the potential for agricultural improvement through enclosure of the comparatively gentle moorland, much of it with ready access to lime for improving the quality of the grass. Moreover, their desire to enclose matched the wishes of the Crown, as lord of these former forests, to raise income. In Bowland, nearly 4,000ha (10,000 acres) of moorland were enclosed between the late 1580s and early 1620s. The first phase involved settlements in the Ribble valley, where the southern slopes of the Newton and Easington fells (from Bashall to West Bradford moors) were enclosed by *c.* 1590. Stephen Moor, in Hammerton township east of the River Hodder, was also enclosed at this time. A second and more extensive phase followed the resolution of the copyhold dispute between the Crown and its tenants. It resulted in the enclosure of over 3,000ha (7,400 acres), nearly one-third of which involved the complete enclosure of the Champion, a common rising gently to nearly 300m (1,000 feet) to the east of Slaidburn (Fig. 6.7). The effect of this concerted appropriation of the more fertile, lower fell pastures was to extend the limit of improved land almost to the 300m mark. The new enclosures (which were used as improved grassland rather than for arable cultivation) were regular broad strips, not as rectilinear as the fields created later by Parliamentary enclosure, but recalling their origin in a

Fig. 6.7 Champion, near Slaidburn.
The ladder-like strips of fields date from the enclosure of this common pasture in the early 17th century.

planned process overseen by royal commissioners. In time, new farmsteads were built out on the former commons. Most of the new enclosures covered only the lower slopes of the fells: in the Ribble valley, the upper slopes of the commons belonging to Grindleton, West Bradford, Waddington and Bashall Eaves remained open until 1819.[18]

A similar story of moorland enclosure took place in the Rossendale fells, where the former forests of Blackburnshire were also in Crown hands. After decrees confirming the copyhold tenures of these manors in 1618–19, a series of commissions were established to divide the wastes across the 1620s. From Chatburn, Worston and Pendleton, in the Ribble valley near Clitheroe, through Colne and Burnley to Huncoat, near Accrington, Haslingden and Tottington in the Irwell valley, the moors were divided.[19] This phase of moorland enclosure serves as another reminder of the contrast in landscape history between Lancashire and Cumbria. Whereas extensive tracts of upland common land survived until Parliamentary enclosure in Cumbria, much had already been enclosed in the hills of east Lancashire.

Enclosure of fell and moor by act of Parliament saw the transfer of many thousands of hectares of former common waste into individual ownership. Only sometimes was agricultural improvement the principal aim. The first major phase of Parliamentary enclosure of upland waste was part of the dramatic sweep of enclosure during the Napoleonic Wars, when high grain prices encouraged reclamation. Where they remained open, the lower slopes of the fells offered scope for improvement and cultivation, particularly where the terrain was comparatively gentle. Upland enclosures at this time included fells near Keswick and along the western fringes of the Lake District; the moors on the north side of the Bowland fells; and Longridge Fell. A frenzy of reclamation accompanied many of the enclosures of this period: in 1812 the agricultural pioneer John Christian Curwen, commenting on oats growing on Latrigg, near Keswick, noted 'the disposition to carry the plough much nearer heaven than what was ever dreamed of a few years ago'.[20]

A vivid example of the enclosure and improvement of fell land is provided by the case of Whinfell, on the edge of the Lake District near Cockermouth. The farms at Whinfell were strung out around the skirts of the fell, which rises to 380m (1,248 feet). The 332ha (820 acres) of fell land were enclosed under an award of 1826, following the usual procedures. Occupation roads were laid out, the new allotments were staked out and provision was made for the new owners to enclose their land with either walls or a bank and hedge. To cover the costs of enclosure it had been agreed that the commissioner would allot part of the common for sale. By purchasing some of this land at Hatteringill Head and consolidating his holding by acquiring other allotments from the commoners to whom they had been assigned, John Nicholson, a landowner in a neighbouring township, gained a compact block of 75ha (184 acres) on the fell top. By ploughing, clearing stones and applying liberal quantities of lime, Nicholson converted much of his new holding to arable land and built a new farmstead on it. The memories of a local farmer, William Walker Dixon (1817–1910) of Toddell, give a flavour of the pioneering aspect of Nicholson's attempts to farm the fell. At over 300m above sea level, cultivation was being pushed to the limits. The land was ploughed immediately after enclosure, then heavily limed: 'Many hundreds of cartloads of lime were carted to the fell from Pardshaw Crag'. Dixon recalled helping to house oats from Hatteringill: 'It was very bad weather at the harvest season and, a fine Sunday occurring, the neighbours gathered and assisted John Moffat [Nicholson's tenant] to secure his crop. They put up 14 stacks that day at the entrance to Hatteringill fell, the corn being brought down on sleds.' This activity on the top of Whinfell proved to be short-lived: the 1841 census records John Moffat and his family living at Hatteringill, but by 1851 it was uninhabited and by 1861 had ceased to be recorded as a dwelling. The landscape still bears witness to Nicholson's adventure. The ruins

of the farmhouse are surrounded by land corrugated by the narrow ridge and furrow typical of 19th-century ploughing. Piles of cleared stones are scattered across the fields, and at the entrance to what was Nicholson's property are the circular 'stack bottoms' on which Dixon helped to place the stooks of oats to dry (Fig. 6.8). Crop cultiviation could not be sustained on such marginal land.[21]

The vast majority of upland waste was not capable of improvement for cultivation. Nevertheless, large-scale enclosure of the high fells and bleak moors took place. Much of this occurred during a secondary peak in enclosure awards from the North West, in the middle decades of the 19th century. In Cumbria and Lancashire north of the Lune over 40,000ha (100,000 acres), most of it upland waste, were enclosed between 1840 and 1880 and a trickle of enclosures continued until the end of the century.[22] Enclosure at this period included some of the highest and most remote land in England: the moorlands surrounding Garsdale and Dent (enclosed in 1859); the high fells surrounding Ennerdale (1872); Sadgill Common at the head of Longsleddale (1874), for example. Such enclosures represented a revolution in landholding, without effecting land-use change: the newly walled allotments remained unimproved rough grazing.

The landscape of Parliamentary enclosure in the high fells and moors is typified by large, straight-edged allotments, enclosed by drystone walls running straight up the fellsides (Fig. 6.9). Wide, straight occupation roads gave access to distant allotments and the fellsides are often pocked by small quarries from which the teams of professional wallers obtained their stone. In some of the latest enclosures, wire fences were used in place of walls. On Asby Scar, enclosed in 1874, and along the crest of High Stile and the Haystacks (separating the commons of Ennerdale and Loweswater, enclosed in 1865 and 1872, respectively), for example, the iron straining posts set into stone survive, even where the fencing wire has gone.

Enclosure walls and fences are not the only tangible legacies of the exploitation of mountain and moorland by hill farming communities. The fells are littered with minor features – small buildings, trackways, folds – reflecting centuries of use. Many are the product of the needs of livestock husbandry. The landscape archaeology of sheepfolds has yet to be written, but several distinct types of fold can be identified. First, as in the lowlands, there were the manorial pinfolds, the pounds to which stray livestock were driven by manorial officials. These communal structures varied greatly in size, from the small, stone-walled enclosure by the roadside at the junction between fields and fell at Loweswater to the large, double-celled enclosure known as the Moughton or Mountain Pinfold on the edge of Stockdale Moor to which livestock grazing on the moor across the summer were driven to be sorted each September.[23] Then there were the sheepfolds built for use when gathering individual flocks, usually on a route out on to the common, close to the head-dyke. Some of these were washfolds, built beside a deep pool or 'wash dub' (sometimes created by damming a stream), through which the sheep were forced to swim to clean their fleeces before clipping each summer (Fig. 6.10). A variety of other structures were built to shelter sheep, particularly at lambing time, including small folds

OPPOSITE PAGE:

TOP: *Fig. 6.8 Whinfell, near Cockermouth:* *abandoned cultivation on hill land enclosed in 1826. Narrow 'Napoleonic' ridge and furrow shows the extent of ploughing; the 'stack stands' (see text) are visible in the field beyond the walled access road; the farmstead of Hatteringill, deserted by 1851, lay at the far end of the track.*

BOTTOM: *Fig. 6.9 Enclosure walls on the slopes of Gragareth in Kingsdale, near Ingleton, part of Thornton Fell, enclosed in 1820.*

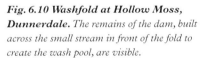

Fig. 6.10 Washfold at Hollow Moss, Dunnerdale. The remains of the dam, built across the small stream in front of the fold to create the wash pool, are visible.

and the short sections of wall, sometimes marked on the Ordnance Survey maps as 'bields'. Some fellside intakes in the Lake District contain hoghouses, small stone sheds built to house young sheep ('hoggs') during their first winter.

Another aspect of the traditional hill-farming economy which has left its mark on the fells was the cutting of peat for domestic fuel. The common right of turbary allowed the community to cut peat for the hearth, and peat was the principal fuel in many upland communities from the later medieval centuries until the transport revolution of the 19th century enabled coal to reach remote valleys. In most manors individual peat 'pots' were assigned to each commoner. The peat diggings themselves are only occasionally obvious (the cut faces now softened and made less visible by the re-growth of vegetation), though removal of peat from enclosed hollows sometimes resulted in flooding, giving rise to the shallow pools on former peat banks on many Lake District fells. Where the peat banks lay on an ill-drained plateau on the fells, as in many Lake District townships, bringing the peat home to the farm involved a difficult journey down a steep and craggy fellside. In many cases, the route to drive livestock from the farm to the fells doubled up as a peat way and was sometimes carefully graded to allow peat (and other produce of the fells, such as bracken) to be brought down by sledge. In some Lake District valleys small, drystone huts, known as 'peat scales', in which cut peats were stored, were built at the top of the fellside, on the edge of the peat-yielding plateau, beside such tracks (Fig. 6.11).[24]

Fig. 6.11 Peat scales, Eskdale. Cut peats were stored in these small dry-stone structures on the fellside, which are found in several Lake District valleys.

Such minor landscape features were all the product of hill farming. Another use of the moors, which has left an extensive legacy in the landscape, grew from the sporting rights retained by the landowning elite. The growing popularity of grouse shooting from the late 18th century resulted in the active management of moorland to create a monoculture of heather, the optimal environment for the red grouse, which lives on young heather shoots. Controlled burning of strips of moorland resulted in the characteristic patchwork of variegated colour and age, typical of the Pennine moors (Fig. 6.12). The distribution of grouse moors in the North West was determined largely by the suitability of the hills for heather growth: vast swathes of the Pennines and the Bowland fells were managed for grouse, whereas only limited patches of the Lake District fells (principally the Skiddaw Slates in the north and the peat moorland around Shap) were so used.

Organised grouse shooting can be traced back to the later 18th century. Shooting parties were a feature of the moors around Ingleborough by the 1790s, and in 1797 the Duke of Devonshire decided to devote several of his moors in the Settle area to grouse shooting. By the middle decades of the 19th century wealthy gentlemen were purchasing upland manors in order to convert them into shooting estates. Bleasdale, for example, on the edge of the Bowland fells, was acquired by William Garnett, the Salford mill owner, who built Bleasdale Tower as a shooting lodge in 1831.[25]

Fig. 6.12 Grouse moor at Bleasdale in the Bowland fells: *the characteristic patchwork created by rotational burning of heather moorland.*

DRYSTONE WALLS

Perhaps the most characteristic features of the upland landscape are the drystone walls, which run up fellsides and across moors, or curve to enclose dale-bottom pastures and meadows. The standard method of construction of drystone walls appears to have been well established by the time of the great surge in wall building during the age of Parliamentary Enclosure. Both older walls built of rounded stones picked from the fields of the valley floor and the enclosure walls on the fells made of angular pieces, freshly quarried, are of essentially the same construction (below left). The wall is double, its two faces locked together by occasional 'through stones' and by a packing of smaller 'pinnel' in the core of the wall. The faces are built with a batter, narrowing towards the top, and the wall is completed by a row of capstones set on edge on the top, sometimes projecting to one side to deter sheep from jumping. This method of construction is found across the uplands of the North West, whatever the parent material: blocks of gritstone, slabs of limestone or irregular lumps of the Borrowdale Volcanic series.

Dating walls presents a formidable challenge, particularly since they are constantly repaired and rebuilt as they collapse. Only rarely do the walls themselves carry dates and these are usually on gateposts, like that in a field beside Ulpha church in the Duddon valley, carrying the date 1766 and the initials 'I G', presumably those of the farmer who built it (above right). The few dated gateposts such as this carry dates in the late 18th or early 19th centuries. Recent work has suggested that older walls, perhaps of medieval origin, may have been wider at the top, their sides more vertical and containing larger stones at higher levels.[26] Closer analysis of surviving walls might yield hints of earlier styles of construction, despite the uniformity of the post-medieval period.

Conventional drystone walls are not the only field boundaries built of stone. In places where large flags could be quarried, walls of vertical stone slabs were constructed. At Wycoller in the former Forest of Trawden, in east Lancashire, slab fences are known as

'vaccary walls' (above), but they are difficult to date and there is no evidence that they were connected with the medieval vaccary there: indeed, an 18th or early 19th-century date has been suggested.[27] Similar stone fences are found in the Lake District, particularly around Hawkshead. They were not as tall as a conventional drystone wall and would certainly not have been sheep-proof. Although any connection with medieval vaccaries is unlikely, such stone fences were probably intended to keep cattle from the growing crops and meadows, rather than to control the movement of sheep.

Some of the earliest dateable walls in the Lake District take another form altogether: a stone facing on the outer side of an earthen bank. Topped with a 'dry' hedge of stakes and brushwood (or a modern wire-netting fence), they were effective barriers to keep livestock out of farmland. Boundaries of this type are found around land known to have been enclosed from the common in the mid-16th century. A moorland intake at Thwaites, near Cold Fell on the western edge of the Lake District, dating from between 1547 and 1578, is enclosed by such a bank. So is Bleak Rigg, a bank of fellside deep in the hills behind Buttermere, which was enclosed c. 1568 (left). In the latter case, the enclosure had decayed and the land reverted to common waste by 1700, so the surviving remains of the stone-breasted bank can be dated more closely than is usually the case.[28]

The heyday of grouse shooting came towards the end of the century, after the revolution in killing power brought by the introduction and refinement of the breech-loading shotgun from the 1870s. As a result of the improvements in weaponry, organised beating, in which grouse were driven towards a line of guns, became the norm, and this generated the most distinctive and numerous structures on the grouse moors, the shooting butts (Fig. 6.13). These small, generally stone-built, C-shaped structures, built in lines across the moors to help conceal the shooters from their prey, survive even where a moor is no longer actively managed for grouse. Other legacies of the sport include lunch huts, built out on the more extensive grouse moors. Where shooting continues, new access roads have been built, running as raw fissures of white across the dark peat and heather, and adding a modern element to the landscape of burning and butts inherited from the 19th century. The fells and moors may appear to be 'natural' landscapes, yet they are as much a product of changing patterns of human use across the centuries as is the farmland of the plains.

Fig. 6.13 A row of grouse butts on moorland at Tatham Fells on the northern edge of Bowland.

NOTES

1 Appleby 1978, 35; Denton 2003, 179, 260
2 LRO, DDSt, rentals & surveys, box 1
3 LRO, DDX/354/23; PRO, MR 430; LRO, DDX 1562 adds.
4 LRO, DDK/1541/1; PRO, DL44/1173 (thanks to Bill Shannon for this reference); LRO, DDK/1532/14
5 Searle 1993, 138, 149; Graham 1907; Dilley 2000; Whyte 2003, 18–26
6 PRO, DL 3/16, fols 61–9; MPC 4; Crosby 1988, 67; PRO, MR 430; Virgoe 2003, 31–2
7 Middleton et al. 1995, 75, 102
8 Crosby 1988, 74–7; Crosby 2000, 84; Virgoe 2003; Hale & Coney 2005, 125–38
9 Middleton et al. 1995, 104
10 Middleton et al. 1995, 76-7; Hall et al. 1995, 24, 73
11 Hall et al. 1995, 24; Middleton et al. 1995, 81; Hodgkinson et al 2000, 81–2, 141–4
12 Rollinson 1963, 137–9; Crosby 2000, 77–9, 105–8; VCH Lancs VI, 111
13 Winchester 2000a, 72; Winchester 2003, 114; Parsons 1993; Tupling 1927, 15–16

14 Winchester 2000a, 110–11
15 CRO, D/Ben/3/761
16 CRO, D/Ben/3/735, 3/756
17 Winchester 2000a, 69
18 Porter 1978
19 Tupling 1927, 155–8, 253–4
20 Curwen 1812, 107
21 CRO, QRE/1/11; reminiscences of W W Dixon, in possession of W D Brooker, Aberdeen; PRO, HO 107/2484; RG9/3936
22 Whyte 2003, 23
23 Loweswater Pinfold at NY 1291 2167; Moughton Pinfold at NY 089 090: Winchester 2000a, 96–7
24 Winchester 1984; Winchester 2000a, 130–1
25 Done & Muir 2001, 198; LRO, DDQ, box 26, 'Bleasdale Tower journal', 1838–54
26 Lord 2004; Lemmey 2003
27 Taylor 1983
28 Winchester 1987, 143, 151; Winchester 2000a, 65

7

Landscapes of Industry

That the most prominent landmark in the ancient city of Carlisle is not the cathedral but the soaring 90m (300 feet) high Dixon's chimney (1836), or that the great cement works at Horrocksford dominates the view north across the Ribble valley from Pendle, is testimony to the omnipresence of industry and its impact upon the region's landscape. However, contrary to the popular view, industry is not a recent phenomenon in the North West. It evolved over many centuries and the Industrial Revolution, far from appearing from nowhere, was in reality an acceleration of long established trends. Many historians identify a phase of 'proto-industrialisation' from the early 16th century, in which domestic and craft trades expanded in many parts of the region.[1]

INDUSTRY BEFORE THE INDUSTRIAL REVOLUTION

The earliest surviving industrial landscapes seem far from the impact of man. At several sites in the central Lake District, Neolithic prospectors identified outcrops of a hard volcanic ash that was ideal for stone axes. The most famous are those at the top of the screes which cascade down the south side of the Langdale Pikes. There, in a breathtaking location below towering crags, the rock was quarried 5,000 years ago (Fig. 7.1). Axes were roughed-out in situ, to be

Fig. 7.1 Langdale prehistoric axe factory: the stone was quarried from outcrops at the base of the crags of Pike o' Stickle, and the tools were shaped on working floors at the top of the long screes that sweep down the very steep slopes of Great Langdale.

finished elsewhere, so that waste material and discarded failures litter the screes, and some of the upper tongues of debris are almost entirely man-made. The stone of the Langdale axes is easily identifiable; numerous examples have been found across northern Britain and as far away as the south coast, demonstrating that long-distance trading routes operated as early as the Neolithic period.[2]

The evidence in the modern landscape for Roman industry is limited. At major sites such as Wilderspool on the Mersey (the largest industrial centre in the Roman north) and Walton-le-Dale, excavation has revealed evidence of a variety of industrial processes, but the intensive nature of later development has effectively obliterated the superficial traces of the Roman period. Wilderspool produced pottery, textiles, ironware and lead items, including the large shallow pans used for evaporating brine at the Cheshire salt springs. The fuel for these industries was coal, which was mined during the Roman period in the neighbourhood of Wigan. Whether the Romans exploited any of the mineral resources of the Lake District is debatable, though lead and silver were certainly worked just beyond the region, in the North Pennines, Wharfedale, Flintshire and the Peak District. Extensive Roman potteries are known from, among other places, Scalesceugh south of Carlisle, Brampton and Quernmore near Lancaster, but here, too, the modern landscape cannot be said to bear any obvious imprint.[3]

Furthermore, none of these places, important though they were in the heyday of Roman control, was occupied after AD 400. The industries vanished completely, and it was seven centuries before their medieval successors emerged anew. Textile production had attained a regional importance by the 13th century, when there are references to fulling mills (where woven cloth was cleaned and finished) in places such as Garstang, Manchester and Rochdale, and in many locations across Cumberland and Westmorland. Though local woollens were comparatively coarse, markets developed beyond the North West, and by 1450 cloth from Kendal and Manchester was being traded as far away as London, Coventry and Southampton. In these towns, and others such as Bolton, Bury, Blackburn and Rochdale, textile production reinforced and augmented the existing role as market centres, contributing to an acceleration in population growth.[4] Flax and hemp were widely grown in the damper lowland areas and used for making linen and canvas. Warrington, Ormskirk, Kirkham and the Wigton area of Cumberland were important local centres for sailcloth, an industry which expanded rapidly after 1660 as the sea-borne mercantile trade of the region grew. In the late 16th century cotton began to appear, first as a minor ingredient of the mixed fibre cloth known as fustian, but assuming an increasingly important role over time. The landscape evidence for these medieval and early modern textile industries is generally limited, though ponds which were used for retting (processing flax and hemp) have been identified in areas such as the Ribble valley and parts of Westmorland.[5]

The medieval iron industry has left a legacy of early industrial sites in Furness and in the western valleys of the Lake District, such as Ennerdale. Heaps of slag mark the sites of charcoal-fired open hearths, known as 'bloomeries', where iron was smelted. For example, there were many such hearths along the western shore of Coniston Water, and they are also known from Lancashire: lumps of slag on the beach at Hackensall, opposite Fleetwood, mark the site of a bloomery operated by Cockersand Abbey in the 15th century. On the coasts of Lancashire and Cumberland the production of salt (by evaporating seawater) is recalled in names such as Saltcotes (Lytham) and Salt Coates (Abbey Town, north Cumberland), which mean 'dwelling of the salters'. Some of these workings date from the late medieval period, but salt pans on the Cumbrian coast and the shores of Morecambe Bay continued in use into the 18th century. At Swarthy Hill, south of Allonby, the remains of saltpans survive as circular embanked enclosures (Fig. 7.2).[6]

During the period of 'proto-industrialisation', landscape change became more pervasive. In south Cumbria, iron-working increased rapidly in scale and complexity during the late 17th and early 18th centuries. New, water-powered forges and primitive blast furnaces, more efficient and productive than bloomeries, opened at, for example, Cunsey Beck, Spark Bridge and Rusland, recalled in names such as Force Forge. The gunpowder industry also emerged as an important element in the economy of the southern Lake District, at places such as Elterwater and Low Wood near Haverthwaite. These industries used enormous quantities of charcoal, and to satisfy the increased demand the existing woodlands along the shores of Windermere, Coniston Water and Esthwaite Water were intensively exploited by coppicing – a method familiar throughout England, but hardly seen on this scale anywhere else. Deep within the modern descendants of these woodlands, often identifiable by the name 'Coppice' or 'Hag', are hundreds of circular platforms with thick layers of burnt material, the 'pitsteads' of the charcoal burners, and the associated kiln sites where potash (used as an alkali in the textile industry) was produced by burning chopped vegetation. The coppice woods were originally protected and managed to serve the needs of industry, but ironically are now perceived and treasured as part of the 'natural' landscape of southern Lakeland (Fig. 7.3). Coniston Water was once a busy industrial waterway, as the ever-observant poet Wiliam Wordsworth noted in 1788: 'along the shady western marge, / Coasts, with industrous oar, the charcoal barge'.[7]

In south Lancashire highly specialised metalworking crafts were well developed by the middle of the 16th century, fuelled by local coal. Wigan grew rapidly with the expansion of the brass and pewter trades, for which it was the most important centre in the north: in the 1660s, with about 4,000 people, it was the third largest town in the region. Here, industry was concentrated in a closely packed quarter of workshops and foundries at Scholes, beside the Douglas east of the town centre. Further south, Prescot was one of England's leading centres for the production of watch parts, such as tiny springs and minute cogs; Chowbent and Atherton specialised in nail-making; while at Leigh and Tyldesley chain links, locks and bolts were made. By 1700 Warrington was the centre for pin making, and in the

Fig. 7.2 Saltpans at Crosscanonby, on the coast between Silloth and Maryport: the circular structures and debris mounds of this medieval and early modern saltworking site lie immediately behind the beach. Across the main road are the partly-excavated remains of one of the Roman fortlets which extended in a chain down the Cumberland coast.

Fig. 7.3 Coppice woodland on the eastern shore of Coniston Water, with the heights of Selside and Bethacarr Moor in the background; these woods were cropped by charcoal-burners until the late 1930s.

mid-19th century it had the world's largest trade in files and other hand tools. In all these places the work was carried on by individual skilled craftsmen, giving rise to a congested urban landscape in which workshops, forges and hearths were crammed into the backyards of cottages and town houses.[8]

Spinning and weaving were ever more important, and in the early 18th century their growth was a key factor in the development of the rural economy. Both were still domestic activities, but the increased demand for yarn and cloth was such that many farming families, who had traditionally spun and woven purely for their own needs, began to produce fabric on a commercial basis. In many households textiles became as important as farming and a dual economy emerged. At Penwortham, across the Ribble from Preston, 32 per cent of men in the 1720s were described as 'weaver', though most also farmed, while in 1831, 53 per cent of all males in Hutton, an entirely rural township immediately to the west, were engaged in 'manufacturing'.[9] The impact on landscape is perhaps not immediately apparent, but it was crucial. A double income meant that farming families could be sustained on relatively limited areas of land, so that the typical landscape of rural Lancashire in the 18th century was one of small farms, with cottages occupied by families who derived most of their income from the domestic textile trades.

Fig. 7.4 Top o' th' Lane, a hamlet of handloom weavers' cottages in the parish of Brindle near Preston: the entirely rural setting of this group of some 20 cottages is characteristic of handloom-weaving in mid- and south-east Lancashire between 1760 and 1840.

In places such as Yate and Pickup Bank near Darwen, and in the Trawden area, mining and quarrying were also available as sources of employment. There, on the moorland fringes, an industrialising economic structure was associated with a fast-changing social framework. Impoverished newcomers and squatters carved out little fields from the waste and built cottages, supporting their households by farming, handloom weaving and other small-scale industrial employment. A pattern of tiny holdings interspersed with patches of moorland and rough grazing emerged – an untidy, semi-industrial landscape whose character is distinctive even today. As the spinning industry was mechanised from the 1760s onwards the demand for yarn grew to unprecedented levels, but weaving was still a domestic trade. For three-quarters of a century, until steam-powered looms became general, handloom weaving enjoyed great prosperity throughout east and mid-Lancashire. Rural populations increased rapidly, sustained by the higher incomes, and many hundreds of cottages were either purpose-built with loomshops in cellars or attics, or were adapted from existing properties by extensions. The handloom weavers' cottages, generally recognisable by extra-large windows and the addition of a third storey or useable basement, are still very numerous in such areas as Tockholes, Mellor, Osbaldeston and other villages around Blackburn. The isolated rows of such cottages found in open countryside in mid-Lancashire are another powerful reminder of the commercial imperative to cash in on the weaving boom (Fig. 7.4).[10]

INDUSTRIAL TRANSFORMATION

The textile industry

The early stages of mechanisation in the textile industries depended on water power, which remained significant into the mid-19th century. The location of cotton and woollen mills in the decades after the 1760s was therefore essentially determined by the existence of reliable, substantial and fast-flowing rivers and streams. Along many rural watercourses chains of textile mills and other industrial concerns developed in the late 18th century, many of them in surprisingly inaccessible locations where the availability of power outweighed the physical disadvantages. Thus, on the Irwell below Radcliffe three paper mills were crammed into deeply incised meanders of the river; there is almost no flat land for building, but the area possesses abundant supplies of water, so essential two centuries ago. The remote valleys of the Cheesden and Norden Brooks, which rise high on the Rossendale moors and flow into the Roch at Heywood, had a series of important early water-powered sites by 1800. In 8km (5 miles) there were four cotton mills, two fulling mills, a dyeworks, a printworks and four industrial weirs, all but one of these sites long since abandoned. Some rivers, such as the Irwell and Darwen, had so much water-dependent industry that at times of low rainfall serious problems arose, and storage reservoirs were built to maintain a regular supply. Regional water management schemes were a favoured solution: thus the 365-million litre (80-million gallon) Holden Wood Reservoir above Helmshore, completed in 1842, was built by a consortium of Irwell valley mill owners in the Bury and Radcliffe area.[11]

The second stage of mechanisation in the textile industry involved a switch from water to steam, and the adoption of mechanical looms for weaving. The latter brought about the gradual elimination of handloom weaving: though its disappearance was neither swift nor uncontested, it had almost gone by the 1880s. Mechanisation changed not only the internal structure of the industry, but also society itself; the large factories that it spawned were instrumental in creating some fundamentals of the modern world – the factory system itself, offices and financial structures, and new employee–employer relationships. It also impacted, to a remarkable degree, upon the region's landscapes. By the 1830s the classic image of the Lancashire mill town was emerging. Mills were immense buildings by any standards – the Old Mill alongside the Rochdale Canal at Ancoats in Manchester (1798–1806) was seven storeys high, 300m (1,000 feet) in length, illuminated brilliantly by gas, with a workforce of 1,300, equivalent to a small town (Fig. 7.5). Such places were comparable in size to the greatest medieval cathedrals. Clusters of mills, grouped along canals or rivers, formed dominant elements in the urban scene, as well as generating new traffic flows and stimulating the hasty construction of cheap and inferior housing. Already in the 1850s the skyline of every mill town was punctuated by forests of chimneys, themselves remarkable and audacious triumphs of architecture and engineering – in 1850 chimneys 75m (250 feet) high were quite common, but 50 years earlier they would have seemed an impossibility.

By the 1850s, too, the architecture of mills had become almost an art form. Early examples were usually in the vernacular tradition, and in areas such as Saddleworth and Rochdale the 18th-century woollen mills, built of roughly dressed stone, were indistinguishable from larger corn mills – indeed, that was what some had formerly been. The first generation of cotton mills also lacked architectural flair. This quickly changed, partly in response to increasing technological and structural requirements such as cast-iron framing, fireproofing, the provision of engine houses, ventilation systems and efficient internal movement, but also as the sophistication and self-confidence of mill owners grew. They began to see their mills as the equivalent of palaces, while

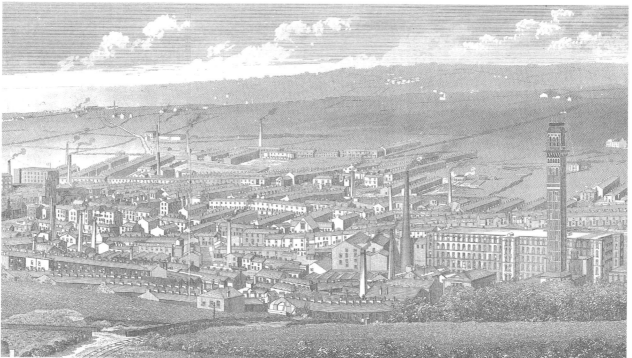

their vast warehouses in centres such as Manchester and Bolton were similarly ambitious in scale and architectural quality. The main source of inspiration was medieval and early Renaissance Italy, consciously or unconsciously drawing upon the example of the city-state – proud, rich, independent and competing with its many rivals. Warehouses for storing cotton and textiles, so utilitarian in function, became Venetian or Florentine *palazzi* in appearance – in Charlotte Street, Manchester, for example, a sequence of commercial warehouses and offices built in 1858–68, or the Watts Warehouse (now Britannia Hotel) in Portland Street, six floors high and modelled loosely on the Fondaco dei Turcho in Venice, but with fantastic detailing which includes Elizabethan English.[12] The Italian theme reached its zenith with the construction, between 1863 and 1870, of the 100m (330 feet) high, massively square, India Mill chimney in Darwen. Designed to replicate the campanile of a *palazzo publico*, it soars high above the rooftops of this otherwise modest mill town, itself a creation of the industrial age (Fig. 7.6).

The third generation of mills were less architecturally flamboyant, but they made up for this with sheer bulk. New technologies of spinning and weaving, developed in the 1880s and 1890s, required a much greater floor space, facilitated by new construction techniques including steel-girder frames. The result was the red brick giants, huge mills particularly associated with Oldham, Bolton and the south-east Lancashire towns. Their uncompromising bulk was offset by symmetry and the grandeur of great chimneys, quirky towers and massive entrance blocks, and they were designed according to modern concepts of efficient layout and planned circulation of goods and people. Examples include the vast Swan Lane mills in Bolton (Fig. 7.7), the largest spinning mills in the world when completed in 1905, and the exceptionally long Nile Mills at Chadderton (1898), which with 22 structural bays of four storeys had so many large windows that it was 'more glass than wall'.[13]

Cotton was king across a swathe of south and east Lancashire, though different towns tended to specialise in certain sections of the industry. In the medium-sized borough of Nelson in 1901, for example, not only was 71 per cent of the entire workforce engaged in cotton, but over 60 per cent were weavers. But while the industry dominated the landscape in places such as Oldham, Blackburn and Burnley, the visual impact of cotton was found in almost every smaller town and many villages. Thus the spread of the rail network, which allowed coal and raw materials to be brought to locations with no 'natural' advantages, led to mills being established at, for instance, Kirkham, Croston and Clitheroe – country market towns which soon acquired 'typical' terraced housing and new working-class quarters. The village of Eccleston near Chorley mushroomed following the opening of a cotton mill in the 1860s. It rapidly became a small town, parts of which resemble chunks of Victorian industrial Lancashire transplanted into the midst of the countryside.

OPPOSITE PAGE:

TOP: ***Fig. 7.5 The great cotton mills beside Rochdale Canal at Ancoats, Manchester (1831)***: *in the centre are A. and G. Murray's Old Mill (1798) and the Decker Mill (1802). This contemporary engraving powerfully conveys not only the impressive scale of the mills themselves, but also their association with the transport infrastructure and urban atmospheric pollution.*

BOTTOM: ***Fig. 7.6 Darwen and the India Mill Chimney (1889)***: *a small mill town in an upland landscape, with terraces of housing creeping up the slopes, a colliery tramroad in the foreground, spiky chimneys, and the great blocks of the mills themselves. To the right is the finest of all monuments to the Lancashire cotton industry, the Italian campanile of the India Mill chimney (built 1867: 100m/ 330 feet high).*

Fig. 7.7 Swan Lane mills, Bolton: *when it was built in 1902–5 the double mill at Swan Lane, south-west of Bolton town centre, was the largest spinning mill in the world, six storeys high and 21 bays long. After a third phase was completed in 1914 it had a total of 330,000 spindles. Red-brick giants such as this characterised the final phase of expansion in the Lancashire cotton industry.*

Other manufacturers

Cotton did not stand alone, for it spawned a multitude of ancillary trades. At the beginning of the 20th century, Platts of Oldham were the world's largest machine manufacturers, specialising in looms and spinning equipment. Bleaching, dyeing and printing were found in many of the valleys between Bolton, Bury and Darwen, where water remained essential for the processing long after it ceased to provide the power. For example, at Belmont, north of Bolton, the bleaching and dyeing works still functions. It is tucked away in a deep cleft south of the village, which itself is a creation of the early 19th century, its rows of model terraced houses built to provide accommodation for employees of the bleachworks.

Other industries serving the cotton trade were more distant. Until the advent of automatic winding of yarn in the late 19th century, wooden bobbins, though prosaic and unremarkable, were essential to the operation of any spinning mill. The making of bobbins, pins, shuttles and other equipment became a staple industry in rural north Lancashire, where small, water-powered bobbin and shuttle mills were found on many streams from the Ribble northwards, in areas such as Knowle Green and Chipping. In the southern Lake District the expansion of this trade came as a godsend, helping to substitute for the dying charcoal burning and iron industries in the early 19th century. The Stott Park Bobbin Mill (Fig. 7.8) at the southern end of Windermere operated until the 1960s: it is now preserved as a working museum, recapturing a humble trade which was once essential to Lancashire's industrial might.[14]

Fig. 7.8 Stott Park Bobbin Mill, Finsthwaite: the last working survivor of the numerous small rural mills which used local coppice wood to produce equipment for the cotton industry. Opened in 1835, and in its heyday producing 250,000 bobbins a week, it is now preserved and managed by English Heritage.

Industrialisation in south Lancashire, away from the main textile areas, gave rise to new landscapes, which were superimposed upon the existing agricultural and small town framework. These transformed riversides and in some places coalesced to produce industrial belts characterised by a multitude of plants and ancillary land uses such as railway sidings and waste tips. This pattern of development was perhaps most striking along the Mersey valley, where the arteries of the river and the associated canals encouraged large-scale industrial development. At Bank Quay and Atherton's Quay in Warrington, for example, a substantial industrial zone was developing by the 1740s, on flat land by the river at the head of navigation for sea-going vessels. With a glassworks, copper-smelter and wireworks, pottery, corn mills, salt refinery and lime kilns, it demonstrated the powerful attraction of accessibility – none of the raw materials for any of these trades was available in the immediate vicinity, and most had to be imported by water. By the late 19th century some of these early ventures had disappeared, but they had been replaced by, among others, the great Crosfield's soap and chemical works (where Persil was invented in 1909) and one of the world's largest ironworks, which produced bedsteads and mattress springs, railway engine wheels and axles, girders, valves and castings.[15]

From the late 18th century the proximity of the Cheshire saltfields and Lancashire coalfield, together with ready access to imported raw materials via Liverpool, encouraged the growth of chemical manufacturing in Widnes, Runcorn and St Helens; candles and soap at Bromborough and later Port Sunlight; and a wide range of processing and refining industries, such as major breweries at Wilderspool and St

Fig. 7.9 The interior of the Ravenhead casting hall, St Helens, *in the late 1790s, showing molten glass being poured onto the casting table. The painting (after Joseph Wright of Derby) captures the atmospheric quality and powerful architecture of the building, the largest industrial structure in late-18th century Britain.*

Helens, tanneries at Arpley and Howley above Warrington and sugar refineries and flour milling in Liverpool. After the opening of the Ship Canal a major new steelworks was built at Irlam (1912), while the first stages of what would become the huge petrochemical industry were emerging at Eastham before the First World War. A nascent glass industry can be identified in south Lancashire in the early modern period, with furnaces recorded between 1580 and 1700 at Haughton Green near Denton, Bank Quay in Warrington, Thatto Heath and Liverpool. After the 1760s the industry increasingly concentrated on St Helens, where the coalfield provided fuel; thick deposits of pure Shirdley Hill sand were nearby at Windle and Rainford; and soda-ash came from the infant chemical industry. At Ravenhead in 1773 the British Plate Glass Company completed what was for some decades the country's largest industrial building (Fig. 7.9), a casting hall 103m (113 yards) long and 46m (50 yards) wide. With its dim recesses of soaring arches and long nave-like hall, the structure bore a remarkable resemblance – to use a familiar analogy – to a medieval cathedral, towering above the nearby cornfields.[16]

Industry became the dominant landscape element along the lower Mersey, as any view of Runcorn and Widnes from the high-level bridge demonstrates today. Between 1847 and 1855 seven large chemical works opened in Widnes and their massive waste tips began to encroach upon adjacent farmland: for every ton of soda produced, 12 tons of waste were dumped in toxic sterile mounds (known locally as 'chemics') on the fringes of the town. In the 1850s legislation required hydrochloric gases – hitherto poured out into the atmosphere to rot the clothes, houses and bodies of the populace – to be condensed into liquid acid. Since this had little commercial value, the manufacturers discarded it: in the 1870s three-quarters of the acid was poured undiluted into local brooks. By the early 20th century the chemical works of Widnes extended along the north shore of the river for over 6km (4 miles) and an observer in 1955 described how 'their glass and chemical works are concentrated on sites of enormous area, littered with chimneys and the surrealistic devices of complicated heavy industries and fantastic mountains of slag on which a few blades of grey grass struggle for life'.[17] This was perhaps the worst legacy of environmental degradation as a result of manufacturing industry anywhere in the region.

Quarrying

The growth of towns and cities generated new demands for stone, brickclay, flagstones and slates, and coal for domestic and industrial fuel. By 1800 the fellsides of the Lake District were being quarried to provide roofing slates for urban south Lancashire, and the coalfields of west Cumberland supplied the hearths of Dublin. Extractive industries had an immediate and traumatic impact upon landscapes and today substantial areas show evidence of past workings.

Although documentary evidence is very scanty, small quarries were already a typical feature of the landscape in all upland areas by the early 17th century, but they only supplied limited local markets. From the 1720s, improvements in transport facilitated long-distance movement of building materials and after 1800, for example, the demand for flagstones for many hundreds of miles of pavement and countless backyards led to the destruction of whole hillsides in Rossendale. The 'Haslingden slates' were ideal for the purpose and small existing quarries at Musbury, Cowpe, Great Hameldon and Edenfield were massively expanded. Around Facit and Whitworth an area of hillside 3km (2 miles) by 1km (half a mile) has been quarried away (Fig. 7.10). From here, two centuries ago, heavily laden stone-wagons trundled down the turnpikes to towns on the plain below. Elsewhere, canals provided the main means of transport – thus the extensive quarries at Parbold Hill, close to the Douglas Navigation (1742) and the Leeds and Liverpool Canal (1774), were linked to wharves by tramroads.

Fig. 7.10 The quarries at Britannia and Facit, north of Rochdale: quarrying was carried on here since the medieval period, but expanded massively in the early 19th century. The partly-vegetated quarries and waste tips along the valley above Cowm Reservoir (left) contrast with sprawling modern workings on Holden Moor. In the foreground is the track of a tramway incline, which took stone down to the Bacup–Rochdale railway line.

Roofing for thousands of new houses stimulated the long-established slate industry in the Lake Counties, so that it became a major influence upon the landscape in areas such as Honister and Coniston. There are extensive surface workings – at Tilberthwaite, for example, vast, vertical-sided holes such as Hodge Close – but also underground excavations, as at Loughrigg. The quarry faces and the associated tips of loose clattering debris, ruined sheds and derelict tramways produce melancholy landscapes with a stark beauty. The largest slate quarries were at Kirkby in Furness, on the east side of the Duddon estuary. Here the workings, owned by the Earl of Burlington, developed very rapidly from the late 18th century and now cover over 500ha (2 sq. miles). They were linked with a quay on the estuary by a tramway incline, so were particularly well placed for the shipment of slate in the pre-railway age – indeed, the Furness Railway (1846) was originally designed to link the quarries with the harbour at Barrow.[18]

The region's varied geological structure yielded many other workable building and construction stones. The Shap quarries, one of the most intrusive and yet dramatic features to be seen from the main West Coast railway line, have been working since the early 19th century, but after 1846 rail access created a national market – parts of the Thames embankment and Southampton docks, for example, are built of Shap granite. Similarly, the extensive quarries which chewed away the western end of Longridge Fell near Preston were connected to the rail network in 1840, and Longridge stone was used to build the Albert Dock in Liverpool. Agricultural improvement stimulated demand for limestone, burned to provide lime for top-dressing, and extensive new quarries opened in areas such as Burton in Kendal and Kellett, Clitheroe and the southern edges of the Yorkshire Dales around Settle. In the 19th century, a relatively narrow seam of limestone east of Burnley and Colne was worked by hushing, whereby dams were built on the hillside and then breached so that the impounded water tore down the slopes, ripping away the overburden to expose the workable rock. Repeated hushing produced massive scarring of the landscape, making an intricate pattern of conical hillocks and deep gullies above Shedden, Hurstwood and Wycoller. These activities in turn gave rise to another distinctive landscape feature, the lime kilns found in large numbers across the region – particularly good ones can be seen around Cow Ark and Whitewell in the Ribble valley, and at Whitbarrow and Levens on the north shore of Morecambe Bay – while the limestone quarries at Horrocksford and Clitheroe were responsible for the development of cement manufacturing, now one of the region's major rural industries. The Castle Cement works at Clitheroe is among the most prominent and controversial industrial sites in the North West, while the impact of continued quarrying here and in places such as Over Kellett and Horton in Ribblesdale excites heated debate because of the conflict between landscape protection and economic advantage.

Mining for ores

Mining for lead and copper in the Lake District, the Cross Fell massif and the western Yorkshire Dales remained on a small scale until the mid-18th century, when industrialisation generated new demands for metals and for ores used in the glass, pottery and chemical industries (Fig. 7.11). For a period of about 150 years, until overseas reserves were opened up, these were major mining areas.

Fig. 7.11 Goldscope mine, Newlands, near Keswick: one of the oldest mines in the Lake District, Goldscope was worked mainly for copper from at least the mid-16th century, initially by the German adventurers and the Mines Royal Company in the latter part of Elizabeth's reign. The spoil heaps visible here are largely a product of 19th-century workings.

Most present-day landscape evidence dates from 1750–1880, although a limited amount of mining survived until the late 20th century. The impact is perhaps most obvious in the Coppermines valley above Coniston, where the mines covered a great spread of steep fellside around the main working area, with its washing and dressing floors, crushers, waste tips and storage yards. On the slopes of Coniston Old Man, Wetherlam and Swirl How old workings are everywhere – long-disused levels, miners' paths down giddy slopes and overgrown dumps of spoil. Water-power was used for processing and for raising ore from the deeper shafts, and by the mid-19th century the supply from the Levers Water Beck was insufficient. A network of leats was constructed, threading the hillsides and redirecting water from numerous gills and becks to feed wheels and washers.[19]

Comparably extensive workings were found at Roughtenghyll and Carrock in the Skiddaw fells, Greenside above Glenridding and in several locations on the western face of the Cross Fell range. Above Knock and Murton, for example, large areas of steep slopes are scored by hushing, which was extremely common in the north Pennines. Some mining sites were in extraordinarily inaccessible places. Thus, the Silverband lead mines, at 700m (2,300 feet), were served by a 5km (3-mile) leat which started at 850m (2,700 feet), just below the summit of Cross Fell itself. To see these haunting remains of past endeavour not only brings home the hardships faced by 18th- and 19th-century miners, but also demonstrates that few parts of the region were without industrial landscapes.[20]

Non-ferrous metal mining, while locally important, did not extend across large tracts of countryside. In contrast, iron mining was a major agent of landscape change in the 18th and 19th centuries. There had been early ironworks around Wigan, where ores were found in association with coal measures, but in the 1830s a combination of more efficient smelting technology and transport improvements, together with rapidly increasing demand, focused attention on the rich haematite deposits in south and west Cumbria. In the 18th century ironworks had already been opened at, for example, Clifton and Seaton in west Cumberland, but exploration revealed vast new reserves of haematite and the resultant mining boom transformed the economy and landscape. In Furness the main early workings were on the limestone ridge at Whittriggs and Lindal behind Dalton, but in the late 1830s new mines opened south of the town and output increased tenfold in a decade, to 300,000 tons in 1851. In that year massive new haematite bodies, the largest then known in the world, were discovered at Park and Roanhead on the east shore of the Duddon, and shortly afterwards their twin was found at Hodbarrow on the other side of the estuary.[21]

The sequel was the opening of iron and steel works and the creation of new communities (Fig. 7.12). Askam grew from 400 people in 1865 to 3,000 in 1873, after the opening of the Park mines and a new ironworks, while Millom, a hamlet of 180 people in 1861, was in 1876 (with 4,000 inhabitants) the largest town in south Cumberland. In west Cumberland the same geological factors created a similar explosion of industry. From 1841 the narrow orefield extending from Egremont to Lamplugh was intensively worked. It had an outstanding advantage, because here coal, haematite and limestone, the three essential ingredients of the iron industry, occurred together. Between 1842 and 1882 nine major ironworks were established in the area between Cleator Moor, Workington and Whitehaven. Mining extended into the Lake District itself: the Knockmurton mines were only 3km (2 miles) from Ennerdale Water and those in Eskdale, briefly important in the 1870s, were within sight of Scafell. In 1882, the peak year, almost 3.25 million tons of ore were raised in west Cumberland and Furness, but then the boom collapsed as the exhaustion of reserves and ferocious competition from cheap imports made mining less economic. The great mines at Park and Roanhead closed in 1918, most of those around Cleator Moor and Egremont by 1925.

The legacies of this mid-Victorian boom were not only Barrow in Furness, 'the English Chicago', and a series of communities along the Duddon and on the bleak

Fig. 7.12 Hindpool ironworks at Barrow in Furness (1878)*: when opened in 1871, this was the largest and most modern ironworks in Europe. It was designed to permit a logical sequence of processing and production stages, with the huge site (1.5km long) integrated by the main line of the Furness Railway and fans of sidings and works tramways.*

plateau behind Whitehaven, left stranded as the tide of industry ebbed, but also a remarkable landscape. Although shaft working was used, opencasting was widespread because the richest ore was found in hugely thick flat 'lenses' of almost pure haematite. The physical impact was thus more extensive, although the purity of the ore bodies meant that the spoil heaps were relatively small. The hills around Dalton and the coastal plain near Askam are pockmarked with pits, their size accentuated by extensive subsidence. In 1893 an area of 320ha (1.25 square miles) north of Dalton had 58 major open pits, the largest 180m (200 yards) across and over 60m (200 feet) deep, together with almost 40 mineshafts, 18 pumping and winding engines and several miles of mineral railways.[22] The existing agricultural landscape was fragmented, with residual patches of fields almost encircled by vast holes. At Hodbarrow the ore body extended beneath the Duddon and in 1905 a curved embankment, 2km (1 mile) in length, was constructed out into the estuary to allow opencasting.

Today many of the pits contain deep pools, and south of Askam the great workings at Park and Roanhead have filled to the brim to form a chain of large lakes (Fig. 7.13). But the most extraordinary legacy is at Hodbarrow where, in the 40 years since mining stopped, the yawning excavation behind the embankment has flooded to create a lake a mile across, now a nature reserve because of its rich bird life. In the ironworking areas of Dalton, Egremont, Cleator and Arlecdon the tracks of long-disused railways wind between pits and spoil heaps amid self-sown woodland, where lumps of purple-grey haematite still lie among the blood-red dust of a vanished industry.

Coal and its impact

The major coalfield in the region extends from Prescot and Whiston through south Lancashire as far as the Pennine foothills around Mossley and Stalybridge, and then northwards through east Lancashire to the edge of the Ribble valley and Pendle. The west Cumberland coalfield was second in importance, and there were smaller outliers in the Lune valley and the area between Ingleton and Bentham; Dent and Garsdale; and the remote area east of Brampton on the Northumberland border. Documentary references to coal mining in areas such as Colne and Rochdale are found from the 13th century onwards, and the industry grew slowly but steadily to achieve an

Fig. 7.13 Flooded ironworkings and spoil heaps at Askam, on the eastern shore of the Duddon estuary: the area shown was part of Pits no. 4 and 5 of the vast Park and Roanhead mining complex, which was developed in the mid-1850s to exploit the richest haematite body then known anywhere in the world.

output in the Lancashire coalfields of about 150,000 tons in 1700. The Cumberland coalfield, with its excellent access to the sea and thus an export trade, achieved its greatest importance in the third quarter of the 18th century, when it produced 7 per cent of the national total and briefly exceeded the absolute and relative position of Lancashire.[23] In south-west Lancashire the opening of canals and turnpikes in the mid-18th century improved accessibility and encouraged expansion of the industry, so that in the county as a whole production grew to some 4 million tons per annum, or 13.2 per cent of the national total, by 1830. Thereafter the region consistently lagged behind, for example, the North East and South Wales. By the end of the 19th century, with the opening up of the rich concealed coalfields of Yorkshire and the East Midlands, its overall position declined though output rose to a peak of almost 27 million tons in 1907.[24]

The earliest areas of significant mining activity were where coal seams were exposed in valley sides, cut through by erosion. Such locations were especially favourable because horizontal adits could be used – these were easier and cheaper to construct than shafts and also drained naturally by gravity. Medieval and 16th-century workings were therefore in places such as Colne, Burnley and Marsden in east Lancashire; Rossendale, with its network of deep valleys; and around Wigan and the Douglas valley. While the physical evidence of early mining has often been obliterated by later workings, there are many places in east Lancashire where hillsides show the typically pitted and disturbed ground of small-scale digging. For example, the prehistoric hillfort of Castercliffe above Nelson is pockmarked with depressions, resembling bellpits, from the early coal industry. In the 17th century more ambitious projects were undertaken, and attention shifted to shaft-working and substantial drainage schemes. Thus in the 1650s Sir Roger Bradshaigh of Haigh Hall built the remarkable Great Sough, a deep-level tunnel, 2km (1 mile) in length, to drain his pits just east of Wigan. In 1716 the region's first steam pumping engine was supplied to a colliery at Whiston near St Helens, and thereafter technological advances encouraged the rapid development of the south-west Lancashire coalfields, helped by fast-rising local demand.[25] By the 1860s some pits in the Leigh and Ince areas were among the deepest in the country.

There was a direct impact on the landscape, with spoilheaps, pithead structures, coalyards and mineral railways, but other effects were more insidious. Subsidence was extensive, gradually producing landscapes of flashes (large, shallow, flooded depressions) in the Leigh, Wigan and Hindley area (Fig. 7.14). Collieries also provided the stimulus to urban growth, and to the creation of pit villages in formerly rural districts. Thus the straggling linear village of Halton Lea Gate near

Fig. 7.14 Scotman's Flash, Wigan:
the largest of the Wigan subsidence lakes, it is almost a kilometre long and is separated from the adjacent Pearson's Flash by the embankment carrying the Leeds & Liverpool Canal, which regularly needs to be raised to prevent collapse as the surrounding ground sinks. The flashes, the consequence of intensive industrial development, are now a nature reserve and major landscape amenity.

Fig. 7.15 Midgeholme and Tindale,
Cumbria: *a fascinating and little-known*
former industrial area between the South Tyne
and Brampton. Numerous small shallow
collieries and quarries dotted the moors, some
linked by tramways with the mineral railway
from Lambley to Brampton. Tracks, former
railways, and small groups of miners' and
quarrymens' cottages are scattered across the
landscape in this view looking west towards
Tindale Tarn.

Brampton (Fig. 7.15) and the appropriately named hamlet of Coal Fell nearby owe their development largely to mining, as do places in west Cumberland such as Moresby Parks and Pica. In Lancashire, Crawford near Rainford is a mining village *par excellence*, entirely a creation of the mid-19th century and named after the owner of its collieries, the Earl of Crawford and Balcarres.

Existing towns and villages, such as Ashton in Makerfield, Westhoughton and Aspatria, grew rapidly once major coal mines were opened in the vicinity. Perhaps the classic case is Skelmersdale, described in perjorative terms in 1907 as 'a particularly bare, unpleasing district, for the most part occupied by collieries, with huge banks of black refuse at intervals amongst treeless fields ... that clay constitutes a large proportion of the sub-soil is evidenced by the large number of brickworks, which do not tend to render the landscape more picturesque'.[26] The population in 1841 was 691, but in the early 1850s large-scale mining began, and by 1891 it was a substantial town with 6,600 people. Here, as in dozens of comparable communities, ill-planned housing and inadequate sanitation inexorably followed industrialisation, and commentators noted how the coal companies that derived such wealth from the mining operations conspicuously failed to put money back into amenities or to contribute to schools and churches. The exploitation of coal was a very mixed blessing for this previously unremarkable community and contributed to its problems in another way – subsidence was endemic, and many buildings in and around the town suffered from structural instability. The terraces amid the fields, the ancient farmsteads cheek by jowl with colliery sidings and spoilheaps, the untidy and haphazard layout of the town centre (the gasworks was next to the town hall) and the way in which mines and railways chopped up the landscape all reflected 50 years of headlong unplanned transformation.

Comparable landscape disruption was found widely across west Cumberland and south Lancashire. In mid-Victorian Oldham there were small coalpits next to the shopping streets and at Burnley the very large Bank Hall Colliery was sunk in 1865 less than half a mile from the medieval parish church. Towering spoilheaps

HARNESSING WATER POWER

Water had been used for industrial purposes for many centuries and, with a dam to impound a pond, almost any stream was potentially a source of power. There was a water-powered corn mill in virtually every community, though many smaller ones closed in the 18th century as a result of increasing competition from commercial millers. Former corn mills were often taken over for other purposes, such as textile production. The time-depth of water power is illustrated by the great millpond at Lostock Hall, between Horwich and Bolton (below), where a water corn mill was in existence as early as 1250.

The principle whereby a waterwheel could drive other mechanisms was applied to a wide variety of industrial processes. At Duddon Forge (bottom) it was exploited to drive bellows, which provided the draught for an early charcoal-fired blast furnace.

The forge, the best preserved 18th-century ironworks in the country (1737), was one of several constructed during a major new phase in the development of the Furness iron industry. In the late 18th century the Chipping Brook, a relatively small stream flowing south from Bowland, was harnessed by a chain of ponds to provide power to a series of industrial sites (opposite page top). In 1893 the highest was the Wolf Spindle and Fly Works, typical of the many rural enterprises that served the Lancashire cotton industry (in 1845 this had been the Wolfenhall corn mill). The lowest of the three sites shown on this extract is still making furniture, as it has been for 150 years, though now it does not use water power. Just beyond the southern edge of the map was a second corn mill, in the centre of Chipping village, so there were four industrial sites on just 1 mile of this little stream.

The final example (above) illustrates how the thirst for water could produce advanced engineering solutions. Dean Mills Reservoir stands dramatically on the edge of the moors above Bolton. It is perched (built out above the level of the adjacent slope, rather than in a valley) and has no feeder stream. Instead a network of 10km (6 miles) of catchment channels drew water from across the slopes of Smithills Moor and Winter Hill. This ambitious project was completed in 1830 to supply the great bleachworks at Halliwell, down in the valley below.

became a feature of the landscape – thus, the 'Three Sisters' dominated the view around the mining village of Bryn near Wigan, while between Hulton and Walkden the huge Cutacre tip, a man-made mountain, swallowed a small valley and buried an intricate medieval landscape of fields, lanes and farms. Opencast mining was important after 1945, though never to the same extent as in Nottinghamshire or Durham. There were substantial opencast workings in the area south of Bolton, around Blackrod, and along the M6 south of Wigan, while in west Cumberland those at Moresby Parks and Weddicar (inland from Whitehaven) have only recently ended; each covered more than 2 square kilometres. Deep mining in the region finished in the early 1990s, with the closure of Parkside Colliery near Wigan, but already the landscape legacy of the industry, stretching back over several centuries, was being systematically obliterated, partly by nature, but mostly by a vigorous programme of 'restoration'.

The major exceptions are where the mines were remote and only of local importance. High on the moors around Darwen and above Rossendale, and on the bleak plateau around Midgeholme east of Brampton, abundant traces survive. For example, at the foot of the television mast high above Horwich, the remains of Holdens and Winter Hill Collieries (consisting of 31 separate shafts and levels in the 1840s) are scattered across the moorland. They were linked by a branching network of access routes, instantly identifiable because their grassed surface contrasts sharply with the surrounding heather and coarse moorland vegetation. Elsewhere it is now almost impossible, except with careful inspection, to identify clear traces of mining in most of the Lancashire and Cumberland coalfields. One could drive from Prescot to Colne and be unaware that the entire route goes through what was once a major mining area. Smooth fields of cindery soil, industrial estates and neat wire fencing now disguise formerly despoiled landscapes. Subsidence hollows have become beautiful reed-fringed lakes, while urban green spaces and newly planted woodland conceal the sites where men, women and children worked and all too frequently died.

NOTES

1   For an overview of geographical patterns of industrial development in the southern half of the region, see Stobart 2004, 32–137

2   Clare in Rollinson 1989, 14–15, gives context

3   Shotter 1997, 40–1, 81–4; Strickland 1995, 28–40

4   Swain 1986, ch.6; Timmins 1998, ch.1; Winchester 1987, 116–19

5   Higham in Roberts 1998; Robinson in Roberts 1998

6   Bowden 2000, 6–11; Taylor 1965; Taylor 1975; Rawlinson-Ford & Fuller-Maitland 1931, 139

7   Bowden 2000, 12–74; Wordsworth 1904, 4

8   Crosby 2002, 79–85

9   Crosby 1988, 86–9; Crosby 2000, 86–93

10 Timmins 1977 and 1993

11 Ashmore 1982; Anon. 1990, 29–33

12 Hartwell 2001, 22–3, 150–1, 191–3

13 For cotton mills see Williams & Farnie, 1992; Calladine & Fricker 1993; Holden, 1998

14 For rural industries see Winstanley 2000; Ashmore 1982; Lowe in Rollinson 1989, 113–21; Marshall 1971, 142–53

15 Crosby 2002, 67–9, 91–7

16 Ashmore 1982; Barker and Harris 1993

17 Millward 1955, 66

18 Virgoe 1994, 90–104; Lowe in Rollinson 1989, 101–8

19 For Coniston copper mining see Holland 1986

20 Adams 1988; Cooper & Stanley 1990, 29–38; Lowe in Rollinson 1989, 109–13

21 Marshall 1958, pts 2, 9 and 10; Bowden 2000, 14–21

22 OS 1:2500 (1893) sheet Lancashire 16/9

23 For the west Cumberland coalfield see Wood 1988

24 Pope 1989, figs 4.1 and 4.3

25 Swain 1986, 163–81

26 VCH Lancs. III, 282

8

Townscapes and Cityscapes

The growth of large urban areas is so closely associated with industry that many people assume that towns barely existed in the North West before the mid-18th century. The reality is different, for most major industrial centres – places such as Bolton, Rochdale and Stockport – were already important 700 years ago. Nevertheless, the region was one of the least urbanised parts of England until the years around 1700; its towns were relatively small and there was no provincial capital equivalent to Bristol or Newcastle. By 1800, however, it was heavily urbanised and in 1901 Lancashire was second only to Middlesex in terms of the percentage of its residents living in urban areas.[1]

PRE-INDUSTRIAL TOWNS

The origin of towns is the subject of continuing historical debate. In the North West, written sources are largely absent until the 12th century, while archaeological work has been patchy. Some towns (notably Carlisle, Manchester and Lancaster) have benefited from excavation of key sites, but many others, such as Preston and Blackburn, have scarcely been touched. It is thus often difficult to pinpoint exactly when a settlement began to acquire urban characteristics, and we are forced to make approximations to a greater extent than is the case in southern England.

Roman towns

There were several Roman towns in the region though only one, Carlisle, was walled. At Wigan and Wilderspool small towns developed in association with major industrial areas, and evidence has accumulated for other civilian settlements (or *vici*) outside the gates of forts. These were sited not only in places where towns reappeared centuries later – as at Kirkham, Manchester and Lancaster – but also in now-rural locations, such as Old Carlisle and Papcastle. It has been suggested that among north-western forts only Hardknott, with its notably inhospitable location, failed to support a civilian settlement. Apart from Carlisle, all these places were essentially unplanned as well as undefended. They grew piecemeal and though some *vici*, such as Ambleside, Manchester and Ribchester, were probably large enough to be considered as towns, they lacked the formal symbols and official identifiers of that status. They did, however, serve as market centres, an essential indicator of urban status in more recent times.

Only rarely did the physical layout of a Roman town determine the form of its medieval successor. At Manchester the Roman settlement and fort were a mile south of the medieval town, but Deansgate, a main element in the later plan, follows the line of the Roman road from Chester to York. Church Street and Market Street in central Lancaster are on the alignments of streets in the Roman settlement, as are Scotch Street and Blackfriars Street in Carlisle.[2] These streets must have remained visible, perhaps even continuing in use, during the post-Roman centuries, becoming urban roads once more as towns grew amid the ruins. However, in contrast to the experience of some places in southern England, there is no incontrovertible evidence of a continuing urban character after the Romans departed.[3]

Medieval towns

Although Carlisle re-emerged as a centre of local importance by the 7th century, when St Cuthbert founded a monastery there, most towns in the region did not appear until around the time of the Norman Conquest (Fig. 8.1). Many grew informally and in an unplanned fashion, evolving from existing rural settlements in the 12th century. Certain attributes help to explain this growth, including the presence of a church or chapel; a meeting place of important routeways; a location on the border of different soils and hence of different agricultural regions; and a position at the head of navigation or a crossing point on a major river. Although none of these was sufficient in itself, a combination of such

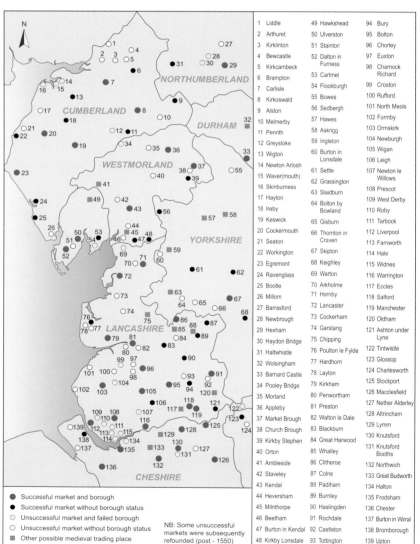

Fig. 8.1 Medieval boroughs and markets: successful markets, with or without borough status, were distributed comparatively evenly (except for the high fells and moorlands of the Lake District, Bowland and the Pennines), but failed ventures were notably concentrated in areas such as south-west Lancashire, the Ribble valley and north Cumberland.

1 Liddle	49 Hawkshead	94 Bury
2 Arthuret	50 Ulverston	95 Bolton
3 Kirklinton	51 Stainton	96 Chorley
4 Bewcastle	52 Dalton in Furness	97 Euxton
5 Kirkcambeck	53 Cartmel	98 Charnock Richard
6 Brampton	54 Flookburgh	99 Croston
7 Carlisle	55 Bowes	100 Rufford
8 Kirkoswald	56 Sedbergh	101 North Meols
9 Alston	57 Hawes	102 Formby
10 Melmerby	58 Askrigg	103 Ormskirk
11 Penrith	59 Ingleton	104 Newburgh
12 Greystoke	60 Burton in Lonsdale	105 Wigan
13 Wigton	61 Settle	106 Leigh
14 Newton Arlosh	62 Grassington	107 Newton le Willows
15 Waver(mouth)	63 Slaidburn	108 Prescot
16 Skinburness	64 Bolton by Bowland	109 West Derby
17 Hayton	65 Gisburn	110 Roby
18 Ireby	66 Thornton in Craven	111 Tarbock
19 Keswick	67 Skipton	112 Liverpool
20 Cockermouth	68 Keighley	113 Farnworth
21 Seaton	69 Warton	114 Hale
22 Workington	70 Arkholme	115 Widnes
23 Egremont	71 Hornby	116 Warrington
24 Ravenglass	72 Lancaster	117 Eccles
25 Bootle	73 Cockerham	118 Salford
26 Millom	74 Garstang	119 Manchester
27 Barrasford	75 Chipping	120 Oldham
28 Newbrough	76 Poulton le Fylde	121 Ashton under Lyne
29 Hexham	77 Hardhorn	122 Tintwistle
30 Haydon Bridge	78 Layton	123 Glossop
31 Haltwhistle	79 Kirkham	124 Charlesworth
32 Wolsingham	80 Penwortham	125 Stockport
33 Barnard Castle	81 Preston	126 Macclesfield
34 Pooley Bridge	82 Walton le Dale	127 Nether Alderley
35 Morland	83 Blackburn	128 Altrincham
36 Appleby	84 Great Harwood	129 Lymm
37 Market Brough	85 Whalley	130 Knutsford
38 Church Brough	86 Clitheroe	131 Knutsford Booths
39 Kirkby Stephen	87 Colne	132 Northwich
40 Orton	88 Padiham	133 Great Budworth
41 Ambleside	89 Burnley	134 Halton
42 Staveley	90 Haslingden	135 Frodsham
43 Kendal	91 Rochdale	136 Chester
44 Heversham	92 Castleton	137 Burton in Wirral
45 Milnthorpe	93 Tottington	138 Bromborough
46 Beetham		139 Upton
47 Burton in Kendal		
48 Kirkby Lonsdale		

● Successful market and borough
● Successful market without borough status
○ Unsuccessful market and failed borough
○ Unsuccessful market without borough status
■ Other possible medieval trading place

NB: Some unsuccessful markets were subsequently refounded (post - 1550)

factors provided the stimulus to urban expansion, while the emergence of a market and a trading role was essential to continued success.

The list of such towns is impressive – from Manchester and Warrington through Preston and Blackburn to Lancaster and Penrith, many leading towns in the region appeared in this way between 1100 and 1250. Market and borough charters, our first written evidence for most, are frequently later than the acquisition of urban characteristics: for example, the first charters for Preston and Lancaster were granted in 1179 and 1193, respectively, but by those dates they were already towns with functioning markets. Characteristic elements can be identified in the plans of these towns. The street pattern was generally irregular – sometimes, as at Penrith and Ulverston, extremely so – but the market place is almost invariably adjacent to the churchyard and situated on a main road to maximise trading potential. A good example is Burnley, which grew within a

Fig. 8.2 Appleby in Westmorland, *untouched by industrial development and little affected by suburban growth, remains a delightful example of a small planned Norman castle borough. The castle is on the high ground in the core of a meander of the Eden, with the broad market street sloping down to the church of St Lawrence close to the bridge.*

curve of the River Brun where it was crossed by the main road towards Yorkshire. The church of St Peter, first recorded in 1122 but founded much earlier, stands beside the bridge, and outside the churchyard gate was the first market place. Typically, it was simply a widening of the road, providing an informal trading space centred on a market cross. At Preston the original market place is still recognisable as a broader stretch of Fishergate, in the centre of the town, next to the parish church founded in the 8th century.[4]

In complete contrast were 'planted' towns, where urban development resulted from a deliberate decision to create a new community, with clearly defined property boundaries, a planned street pattern and a rectangular or square market place. Such planted towns were normally given special privileges as an incentive to settlement and economic development, usually involving the granting of borough status. This introduced the distinctive form of landholding known as 'burgage tenure', based on regularly shaped burgage plots, which were the building blocks of the town. Planned new towns were founded throughout the region and their distinctive layout is often apparent even today, as at Egremont and Flookburgh. Appleby is perhaps the best-preserved example (Fig. 8.2). Boroughgate, the broad main street-cum-market place, slopes down from the castle, edged by burgage plots between which narrow passages lead to a back lane. The old village and church of St Michael were in Bongate ('the street of the bondmen') on the east bank of the River Eden, but the new town lay on the west bank, and the main road was diverted over a bridge and through the market place to maximise passing trade. The new town had its own church, with a characteristically Norman dedication to St Lawrence.

The layout and appearance of Appleby (founded in the early 12th century and chartered in 1179) is preserved because, though the county town of Westmorland, it never became industrialised and remained small. In contrast, the most successful of the hundreds of new towns in medieval England has long been barely recognisable as such, because its astonishing success after 1660 masked its origins very effectively. Liverpool was originally a small fishing community on a low peninsula between the Mersey and 'The Pool', a long-culverted tidal creek curving through what is now the city centre. In 1207 King John granted letters patent creating a royal borough, perhaps intending it as a base for naval campaigns in the Irish Sea. A rudimentary grid pattern of streets was laid out and, though the townscape has experienced overwhelming changes over the ensuing eight centuries, this still forms the framework of the commercial heart of modern Liverpool.[5]

In many existing towns or market villages during the 13th and 14th centuries the built-up area was extended with the same planned character, often contrasting with the informality of the original settlement. In 1310, for example, the abbot of Cockersand was granted a market at Garstang. The market place, a former village green where the road from Over Wyre met the main route from Preston to Lancaster, was edged by an irregular scatter of cottages and crofts, but in the early 14th century a new planned suburb was built northwards along the High Street. The contrast in the two halves of this miniature town is still clear. At Warrington the old market place, beside the ancient church of St Elphin, was superseded in the 13th century by a new planned development at the crossing of two regional highways. A rectangular market place was laid out beside the crossroads, leaving the church and old market place stranded in a backwater half a mile away. In successful towns the volume of trade frequently outgrew the market place and spilled out along adjacent streets, some of which specialised in particular commodities and even derived their names from them (as in Buttermarket and Horsemarket Streets in Warrington).[6] Market places were also reduced in size by the encroachment of buildings, a process which reached its extreme form at Manchester where the medieval market place completely disappeared by 1750.

Not all planted boroughs and chartered markets were successful, for they were speculative ventures and competition from existing places was often very strong, while in more marginal areas the trading potential was always limited.[7] For example, seven medieval markets were chartered in the small district between Chorley and Ormskirk. Those two were very successful, but despite apparently favourable locations on main highways the would-be markets at Charnock Richard, Euxton and Rufford failed to develop. Nor did that at Newburgh, whose name recalls an abortive early 14th-century attempt by the lords of Lathom to found a borough to rival Ormskirk. Strong competition quickly weeded out the weaker contenders, which came too late and much of whose catchment area was thinly populated mossland. In the Eden valley several tiny boroughs died in infancy, victims of comparably harsh commercial realities – Pooley Bridge shows no trace of its erstwhile urban status, Kirkoswald and Greystoke only a hint of it. Thus even the special advantages which borough status gave were no guarantee of success, and many older market towns thrived even without such privileges – examples include Kirkby Stephen, Kirkby Lonsdale and Brampton. In Lancashire, Poulton-le-Fylde has a medieval market place (complete with cross, fishstones, whipping post and stocks) beside a pre-Conquest churchyard. Here the market flourished, though Poulton had neither a borough nor a market charter, and was able to extinguish the competition from two chartered competitors, Hardhorn and Layton (Fig. 8.3).

Fig. 8.3 The market place at Poulton-le-Fylde, photographed in 1990, retains a complete set of early 'street furniture'. At one end stand the stocks, market cross on stepped base, fishstones and whipping post; at the other is the gateway into the raised churchyard of the pre-Conquest parish church of St Chad.

BELOW: *Fig. 8.4 Carlisle in about 1563.* This delicate and skilful scale plan and drawing is the first surviving detailed visual representation of a town in North West England. It was probably drawn as part of a project to restore the city's military defences, at a time of heightened political tension between England and Scotland, but it also includes a great deal of information about the town itself.

Towns in the early-modern period

By 1500 there was a comprehensive network of local market towns, such as Dalton in Furness, Sedbergh and Chorley. Above them stood a range of more substantial sub-regional centres, with increasingly important industrial, administrative and social roles – places such as Preston, Wigan, Kendal and Bolton. At the top of the region's ranking of towns were Manchester and Carlisle (Fig. 8.4), which were becoming significant in national terms. The next 250 years saw the strengthening of this existing pattern and the emergence of new centres drawing their commercial power from the general increase in regional economic activity. Many new market centres were chartered between 1570 and 1720, including Leigh, Haslingden and Padiham in south Lancashire, and Hawkshead, Broughton in Furness, Ambleside and Shap in Cumbria. Although in most cases an informal market probably existed already, the new 'official' status of these places reflects substantial industrial development and population growth in the surrounding rural areas, which augmented their trade and diversified their economic role (Fig. 8.5).

As the towns of the North West grew rapidly during the 17th and 18th centuries, urban living, once the exception, became commonplace. By 1700 these increasingly obvious changes were attracting the interested attention of outsiders, whose contemporary descriptions tell us of the appearance of these towns and the impact they had upon observers. Manchester and Liverpool were now climbing high in the national league

Fig. 8.5 The market green and market hall at Hesket Newmarket, *a small village on the northern edge of the remote Caldbeck Fells. It acquired a market (and the second part of its name) in the early 1750s when, as elsewhere in the region, new commercial activity encouraged market creation, but this did not flourish. Local mining activity failed to generate sufficient economic momentum.*

tables, while places such as Preston, Wigan and Whitehaven were fast moving up the ranks. Statistics derived from the hearth tax returns of the 1660s indicate that Manchester and Salford (with about 2,500 people in the mid-16th century) now had some 6,000 inhabitants, while Wigan, arguably the first major town in England where manufacturing was the dominant sector of the economy, had about 4,000, Preston 3,000 and Liverpool 2,500. By 1730 Manchester with Salford had a population of perhaps 12,000, and in 1760 almost 30,000. In the latter year Carlisle, Warrington and Lancaster each had some 6,000. The unprecedented rate of expansion thus affected towns of widely varied location and character. It was a regional phenomenon of global significance.

Daniel Defoe, writing of Liverpool in the early 1720s, said it was 'one of the wonders of Britain' and commented on how it 'visibly increases both in wealth, people, business and buildings … there is no town in England, London excepted, that can equal Liverpool for the fineness of the streets and beauty of the buildings'. Of Manchester he records that 'the town is extending in a surprising manner; an abundance, not of new houses only, but of new streets of houses, are added, a new church also, and they talk of another, and a fine new square is at this time building. [It is] greater and more populous than many, nay than most cities in England'.[8] Thus a perceptive observer recorded the way in which these towns had appeared sensationally on the national stage, over half a century before the Industrial Revolution. He hints at another aspect of north-western towns. They were becoming notably sophisticated, with elegant architecture and cultural and social amenities befitting their new status. Indeed, north-western towns were in the forefront of the national urban renaissance between 1660 and 1760. Preston was among the first provincial centres where the town council promoted genteel landscaping, laying out gravelled tree-lined walks at Avenham on the edge of the town centre in the 1690s.[9] St Ann's Square in Manchester (1712), to which Defoe alludes, was one of the earliest formal pieces of modern planning in an existing English town. Whitehaven, on the remote coast of west Cumberland, was the first fully planned new town in England since the 14th century (Fig. 8.6).

As towns were extensively rebuilt between 1650 and 1800, brick and stone replaced timber and plaster, slate superseded thatch and medieval irregularity gave way to Georgian grace. In some places this was assisted by acts of God and man. Several, including Lancaster, Warrington and Liverpool, suffered extensive

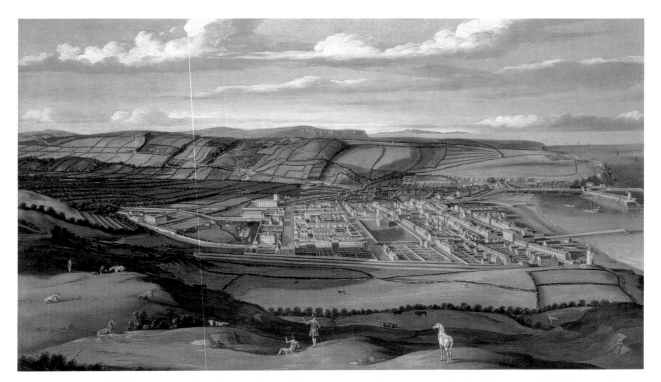

damage during Civil War sieges in the mid-1640s, and Bolton was largely destroyed. Much of central Preston was burned during the street battles which ended the first Jacobite rising in 1715, while Church Street in Lancaster was left in ruins after a great fire in 1698. Little is left in the greater industrial centres to remind us of their physical appearance before the mid-18th century. The few surviving older buildings, notably inns (such as the black-and-white *Barley Mow* at Warrington and *Man and Scythe* in Bolton), can only hint at what is lost, though engravings show that places such as Preston and Wigan had outstanding and impressive half-timbered architecture.

In country towns existing properties were often merely refaced, for only wealthier townsmen had the resources to rebuild completely. A good example is Kendal, where many of the properties facing Stricklandgate and Highgate have 18th- and early 19th-century façades, but earlier fabric to the rear. In towns where commercial life was stagnant only gestures to fashion might be made: much of Garstang High Street comprised single-storey thatched properties as late as the 1840s, while in places such as Kirkham, Brampton and Cartmel the polite architecture of the 18th century was of a homespun variety.

Formal schemes for urban design were of a different order. St Ann's Square in Manchester and Derby Square in Liverpool (1725) were fashionable and exclusive, with modern town houses appealing to the newly moneyed classes. Other places followed suit with squares and terraces. At Lancaster, which in the half century from 1740 enjoyed a period of mercantile good fortune, Dalton Square was laid out in 1783–1820 on the site of the medieval friary, while Preston's Winckley Square was developed from 1799 by and for lawyers and merchants. The epitome of late Georgian developments is in Liverpool, where some of the prodigious wealth and ambition of the powerful America traders was invested in a superior residential quarter on the hilltop above the town. The magnificent terraces and formal layout of the area around Canning Street, Rodney Street and Abercromby Square still form one of England's finest late Georgian townscapes (Fig. 8.7).[10]

Fig. 8.6 **Prospect of Whitehaven from Brackenthwaite,** *by Matthias Read (1736): an exceptionally detailed and informative view of modern England's first planned new town, painted at the stage of its development when the original plan had been implemented but before the major expansion of coal-mining and coal-exporting ravaged the local landscape and environment.*

Fig. 8.7 Rodney Street, Liverpool.
The street was laid out in the mid-1780s and development continued until the 1820s. Here, and in adjacent streets, magnificent rows of terraced houses were built for the elite of the greatest mercantile port in the world, giving them a vantage point high above the town from which to see the long line of docks and the countless masts of the vessels along the shore below.

TOWNS IN THE INDUSTRIAL AGE

As industrial development accelerated, urban growth around existing centres produced startling demographic statistics (Table 8.1; Fig. 8.8). New towns also emerged from nowhere when intensive industrialisation generated population growth in rural areas. Few aspects of the 19th-century landscape history of the region were as dramatic as the creation of, for example, Birkenhead (1901 population 111,000), Barrow in Furness (58,000) or Darwen (38,000), which barely existed in 1801 but were major industrial centres a hundred years later. Numerous smaller places grew from hamlets to become sizeable towns – for example, Carnforth with its railway junction and ironworks, and textile communities such as Shaw, Milnrow, Oswaldtwistle and Brierfield.

With few exceptions, the growth of these places, whether old or new, was unplanned and they developed major problems of poor housing, inadequate sanitation and social deprivation. Yet, alongside the blighted lives of so many of their inhabitants, most also developed a powerful sense of civic pride. They had the resources during their commercial heyday to produce buildings that were among the architectural triumphs of the age. Contemporaries noted the stark contrast between the degradation of slum housing and the splendour of town halls, identifying a gulf between the downtrodden existence of the workforce and the lavish lifestyles of the masters. Such contradictions lie at the heart of the industrial towns of 19th-century north-west England, even if these places were more complex than this might suggest: a host of subtle distinctions of class, occupation, ethnicity and religion distinguished people from their fellow citizens and were mirrored in the townscape.[11]

All over the region, in the fast-growing towns, long years of uncontrolled substandard development were followed by expensive and time-consuming remedial action by new local authorities, paying from the public purse for the manifold faults of private developers and negligent industrialists. St Helens, earliest of the large new towns, was characteristic (Fig. 8.9). It grew from the 1760s, sprawling across the

Table 8.1 *Population growth during the 19th century; census statistics for selected towns.*

POPULATION			
TOWN	*1801*	*1851*	*1901*
LIVERPOOL	84,000	375,000	685,000
MANCHESTER	75,000	320,000	544,000
SALFORD	13,000	85,000	221,000
BOLTON	24,000	61,000	168,000
OLDHAM	21,000	53,000	137,000
PRESTON	12,000	69,000	113,000
CARLISLE	10,000	29,000	49,000

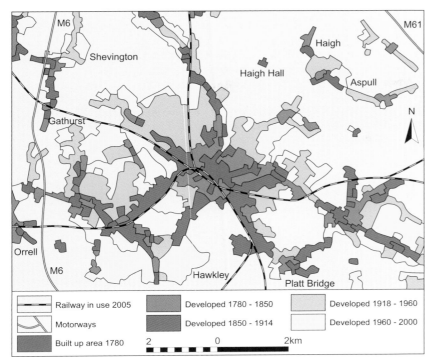

Fig. 8.8 The growth of Wigan 1750–2000: *expansion beyond the medieval core can be traced, with ribbon development in 19th-century industrial areas, the great peripheral council estates of 1918–60, and later municipal projects and private speculative development of the last 40 years. Wigan has coalesced with towns such as Standish and Hindley to produce a conurbation with a quarter of a million people.*

Railway in use 2005	Developed 1780 - 1850
Motorways	Developed 1850 - 1914
Built up area 1780	Developed 1918 - 1960
	Developed 1960 - 2000

2   0   2km

BELOW: **Fig. 8.9 Chimneys and pollution at St Helens (1868):** *an artist's impression of the Pilkington glassworks, collieries and brickworks, a nightmare landscape of chimneys, the cones of glasshouses, belching smoke and visual chaos, summing up the disastrous environmental and social consequences of the unchecked industrial development in many Lancashire towns.*

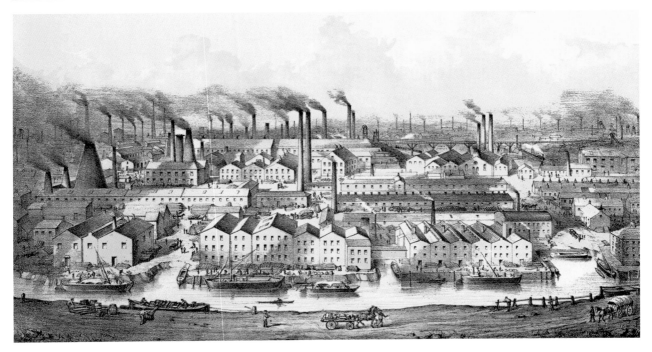

boundaries of four townships so that concerted action, even to plan a coherent street pattern, was impossible. Its delightful name became a byword for squalor. Jerry-built one-up one-down cottages were thrown up on streets of mud and filth, unserved by sewers or piped water and beneath skies darkened with fumes and smoke. Only from 1845, with the establishment of an improvement commission, were serious attempts made to tackle the legacy of problems inherited from the previous 70 years, and not until this child of industry became a borough, in 1868, did the quality of life appreciably improve. Nelson, another new town, grew around a road junction and took its name from the local pub. It was 30 years before the fast-growing cotton town acquired an effective local council, which then struggled to remedy the deficiencies of the immediate past and to foster civic consciousness. The town became a borough in 1890, but it had no heart – no central square or grand town hall – and its focal point was a cluster of eight huge cotton mills. But at least by developing after 1850, Nelson avoided the worst housing problems – of all the Lancashire cotton towns, it had the highest proportion of small, uniform terraced dwellings of 1850–80. In west Cumberland, the most extraordinary growth was at Cleator Moor, where a small village of 760 people in 1840 became a town of almost 11,000 by 1881. It had rudimentary planning – a grid of tiny streets around the central crossroads and market place – but levels of overcrowding in its cottages were high and prosperity was short-lived. By 1891 the population was falling as iron mining declined, and in the 1930s Cleator Moor was among the most depressed communities in Britain.

Housing the industrial workforce

Early population growth in industrialising towns was usually accommodated within the built-up area by developing cramped backlands and burgage plots. Though access was difficult, cottages were built in the severely constricted space, approached by a tunnel entrance or narrow passage from the street. This produced the characteristic 'closed court' layout, especially notorious in Liverpool, but also found in lesser numbers in every industrial centre during the first phase of the Industrial Revolution (Fig. 8.10). Existing buildings might be subdivided, with cellars and attics taken over as living space: Liverpool had a

Fig. 8.10 Court housing on the north side of central Liverpool, 1893.
Between Bond Street and Eldon Street is a sequence of ten-dwelling blind courts of back-to-back houses, each sharing two privies; in Arley Street there are exceptionally small courts of tiny hovels, accessed by a narrow covered passage; and west of Vauxhall Street the rear wall of single-room houses is also the wall of the tannery. This area was perhaps the most overcrowded and insanitary in the entire region.

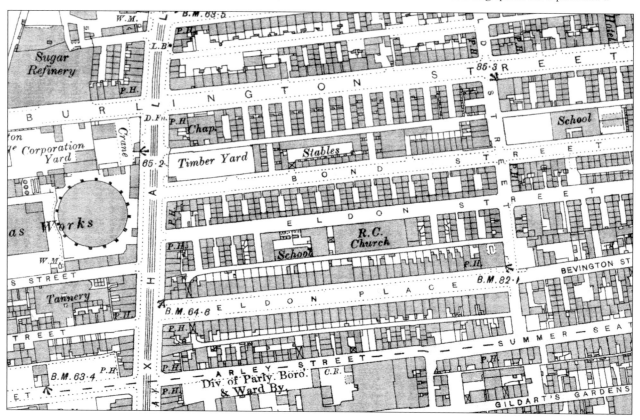

particulary shameful record for cellar-dwellings, with over 27,000 people living in such accommodation in 1848, but all larger towns possessed numerous examples. Levels of overcrowding were fearsome, exacerbated in many places by a massive influx of poverty-stricken Irish in the years after 1846: for example, in Warrington in 1851 one tiny house in a town centre court accommodated 25 people, all but one Irish-born.

In the late 1840s circumstances began to change the way in which towns developed. The direct links between insanitary housing, polluted water and high mortality were recognised by central government, and the first tentative steps taken towards public health provision and housing regulation. By the 1870s local authorities, armed with a range of statutory and voluntary powers, began to enforce building standards and this, together with the campaigning activities of social reformers, produced significant improvements in housing design and quality. Back-to-backs, blind or closed courts and cellar dwellings were slowly eliminated from the 1870s onwards, though the process took over half a century. The result of these improvements was the building of regular terraced (or 'byelaw') housing, now in the popular perception inextricably associated with the Industrial Revolution. Appearances deceive, for most terraced housing was built long afterwards, when towns were already large. It tends to be found in a broken ring around the perimeter of pre-1870 built-up areas and in larger places the main zones of byelaw housing were the formerly separate rural townships beyond the limits of the mid-Victorian town: for example, Openshaw in Manchester, or Kirkdale and Wavertree in Liverpool. The byelaw housing of the 1870s and 1880s represented a tremendous improvement on what had gone before. There were toilets (albeit in the back yard) and piped water, and by the 1880s all new houses had more effective heating, cooking and washing facilities, and most had gas supplies.

Terraced housing was normally designed and erected by jobbing builders – a street here, a terrace there, would be developed as landowners sold off property field by field. The streets and housing were fitted into pre-existing boundaries and the image of serried ranks of identical terraces stretching into the smoky distance was rarely matched by reality. Numerous small distinctions between housing types reflected the idiosyncrasies of builders, and local styles and materials. In south Lancashire red-brick was standard, often with terracotta detailing, but in east Lancashire stone was frequently employed for the whole building, and terraces were often built up steep hillsides with a distinctive continuous roofline parallel with the slope, rather than a stepped profile (Fig. 8.11).

Fig. 8.11 Terraced housing in Ormerod Street, Accrington. *The stone-built terraces of the east Lancashire cotton towns, with their continuous rooflines plunging down steep slopes, are quite different in character and appearance from the conventional image of red-brick post-1870 byelaw housing associated with south Lancashire.*

Fig. 8.12 The Beardwood area, on the hilltop north-west of Blackburn town centre, became a favoured residential district for the town's newly-moneyed merchants and industrialists. The plan (1893) shows some of their large and opulent houses, set within extensive wooded and fashionably designed grounds amid the remnants of an older agricultural landscape.

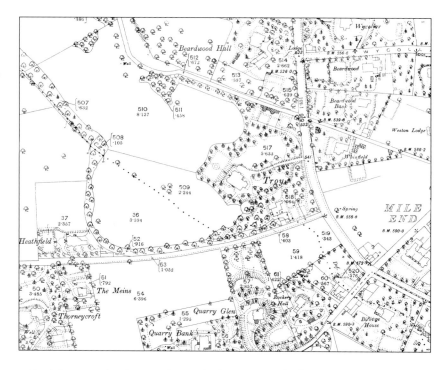

Social segregation became increasingly apparent. Builders and speculators, intent on maximising profit, were careful to choose superior locations (often on hillsides) for better-class housing, while poor housing for the working classes was constructed close to industries and on low lying land. In many towns the more prosperous areas were on the western side, because prevailing winds carried the sooty clouds of industrial and domestic smoke eastwards. The impact of elevation and orientation is sometimes conveyed in textbook fashion. A journey of 2km (1 mile) from the centre of Blackburn, westwards along Preston New Road, runs from the commercial heart of the town through the largely demolished zone of overcrowded working-class housing to tiny semi-detached villas with miniature front gardens. These are followed by larger Victorian semis and finally, on the hill at Billinge, large detached houses in wooded gardens. The largest of these stand away from the busy main road in leafy seclusion (Fig. 8.12). In the contemporary view, houses with little front gardens were associated with white-collar workers such as clerks. They were often on tramway routes, which served the upper working-class and lower middle-class passengers – their inferiors could not afford the fares. The middle classes increasingly chose to separate workplace from home, so their districts were distinguished not only by the better housing, gardens and leafy streets, but also by the absence of industry. The desire for privacy, so powerful in Victorian England as working lives were ever less likely to be spent in isolation, became a vital force in shaping housing areas.

Most industrial towns had at least a small middle-class area, while in the larger towns and cities whole suburbs had that social cachet, 'a nice address'. Areas such as Ashton in Preston and Heaton in Bolton were peopled almost entirely by the middle classes. In some places, restrictive covenants protected the social tone and aesthetic character. Thus, Cressington, Fulwood and Grassington Parks in south Liverpool were shielded from the outside world by gates and walls and managed by mutual trusts.[12] Even Darwen, one of the new mill towns, had its exclusive suburb, though it had relatively few mill-owning families and a below average percentage of professionals such as doctors and lawyers. Whereas at Blackburn the respectable suburbs such as Beardwood were 150–180m

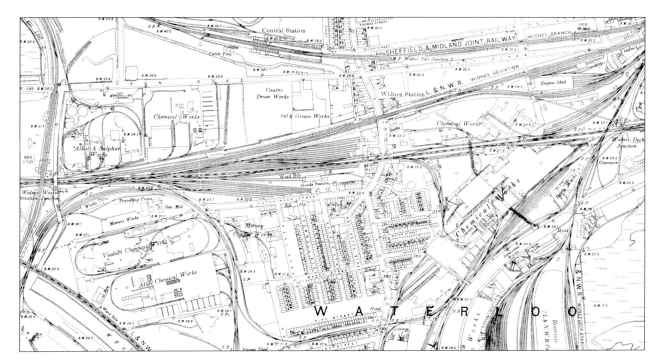

(500–600 feet) above sea level, the south-west end of Darwen, upwind of mills and collieries, was markedly more chilly at 245m (800 feet). Nonetheless, by 1900 in the Bury Fold and Whitehall area there had developed a suburb of splendid stone-built houses, standing in large wooded grounds alongside streams rushing down from the moor. Their names – Spring Bank, Briarwood, Woodlands, Ashdale and Heatherby – are of the type beloved by prosperous late Victorians who had made their way in the world, while the houses reflect the good fortune of at least one sector of society in that golden age of enterprise. Widnes, on the other hand, where small pockets of terraced houses were marooned among ribbons of railway and factories belching acid fumes (Fig. 8.13), was almost alone among the large towns of the region in having no significant middle-class residential area: it was simply too unattractive for those with any social aspirations.

Fig. 8.13 Central Widnes in the mid-1890s was a bewildering tangle of railway lines and huge chemical works, among which the inhabitants of small clusters and pockets of housing somehow managed to live. For many contemporary observers, townscapes such as this exemplified the deplorable and reprehensible downside of the region's industrial progress during the previous hundred years.

Resort towns

North-west England was one of the first areas where seaside resorts developed. The sea might be cold and grey, but this was no deterrent for holidaymakers from mill towns and mining areas. By 1750 several villages were acquiring a reputation for sea-bathing and in the 1790s a string of nascent resorts began to emerge, though some now seem improbable: Widnes and Bootle were both watering places in the mid-18th century, the former noted for the large numbers of ordinary people who came on Whitsunday to swim in the Mersey. Transport improvements assisted the early growth of some towns – Southport was linked by road with the Leeds and Liverpool Canal at Scarisbrick, while Lytham benefited from a private toll road across the marshes from Lea to Freckleton – but the extension of the railway network was the main catalyst for growth. Between 1840 and 1860 railways reached almost every resort between Formby and Silloth, while the expansion of New Brighton was fostered by the ferries which ceaselessly plied across the Mersey from Liverpool.[13]

The townscape of the resorts varied widely, with land ownership patterns being a key determinant. Owners usually set out to encourage a middle-class clientele and

nurture a select character, but success depended on the degree of control they could exert. At Lytham the entire parish was owned by the Clifton family. In the 1830s, after a period of haphazard development, the squire, Thomas Clifton, and his formidable agent, James Fair, asserted control and thereafter leases contained extremely strict clauses dictating the size, materials, character and function of new buildings. Working-class development was strongly discouraged (such as did appear being carefully segregated at the east end, away from the seafront) and the town was provided with amenities such as a market hall, crowned by a graceful clock tower given by Lady Eleanor Cecily Clifton in 1872. During the 1830s and 1840s the dunes behind the shore were levelled to create the smooth sward of The Green (Fig. 8.14). The result was a town which was unusually attractive in appearance, and socially homogeneous and exclusive. When the Cliftons sponsored the development of St Annes in the 1870s they applied these principles from the start. Like other such resorts, Lytham and St Annes became favoured places for retirement and in the 1880s, as rail communication with Manchester and Preston improved, they were increasingly popular as a residential area for wealthy commuters.

In contrast, Blackpool developed in chaotic confusion because it had seven major landowners. No overall plan was ever contemplated, and each landowner built without reference to his neighbours. The street pattern and town centre evolved incoherently, and the architecture was rarely better than mediocre. The town became increasingly 'popular', and from the 1870s attracted workers from the Lancashire textile districts, as well as more distant locations such as Yorkshire and Glasgow. Blackpool was incorporated as a borough in 1876 and the new council single-mindedly promoted holiday interests. It made use of innovations such as electric street-lighting (1879) and the world's first electric tramway (1885), and encouraged a multitude of private ventures including the South Shore entertainments area, the Winter Gardens and, most dramatic of all, the famous Tower (1894). By 1900 Blackpool was dedicated to mass leisure in a way unparalleled anywhere else in the world. The character of the centre and seafront – garish, raucous and inelegant, offset by an occasional splendour such as the Tower – is the unmistakeable consequence of that mid- and late Victorian development (Fig. 8.15).[14]

Some coastal resorts became major towns in their own right: by 1901 Southport and Blackpool, with about 48,000 people each, were larger than Lancaster and not far short of Wigan and Bury. Although local authorities moaned incessantly about the inhibiting effect of railway fares and timetabling, accessibility was a key to this rapid Victorian growth. The size of the resident population meant that the relative dominance of the holiday trade gradually diminished in the half century after 1875. Other resorts, further from conurbations and with no potential for commuter traffic, catered for a local market. Silloth, on the muddy shores of the Solway Firth, was the resort for Carlisle, while Barrovians simply hopped across to Walney Island for their seaside pleasures. Knott End on Sea (the 'sea' being the Wyre estuary) was half-heartedly promoted as a resort, before developing in the 20th century as a retirement and residential area of bungalows and small semis. Seascale in Cumberland was the subject of more ambitious proposals, sponsored by the Furness Railway between 1847 and 1880. These largely failed to materialise (the site was remote and exposed) and a few terraces, boarding houses, a hotel and some villas were all that emerged from a plan for a gracious holiday town. In contrast Grange over Sands, by far the most superior of the resorts, was a great success. Styling itself 'the Torquay of the North', the little town grew after the opening of the railway in 1857 in a casual but unfailingly genteel fashion (Fig. 8.16). Its physical advantages were incomparable. Hampsthwaite Fell, rising behind the town above Morecambe Bay, gave superb views to the fells of Yorkshire and Lancashire; there were delightful country walks from the doorstep; the absence of flat land precluded the development of cheap speculative housing; the railway company landscaped its

TOP: *Fig. 8.14 Lytham Green and windmill: the Green was created after 1835 by levelling a line of sand dunes: the sand was used to raise ground levels on marshes east of the town and make them suitable for building. The windmill, built in 1805, ground corn unloaded from vessels on the beach. It worked until damaged by fire in 1918.*

BOTTOM: *Fig. 8.15 Blackpool from the sea: the Tower (1894) and North Pier (1863) are the most prominent landmarks, with the ill-planned Victorian town centre between the two; beyond are the sprawling 19th century town of terraced housing; the landscaped expanses of Stanley Park, opened in 1926; and the mosslands and low ridges of the Fylde.*

Fig. 8.16 Grange over Sands: when 'The Torquay of the North' emerged as an exclusive resort in the 1860s it had a sandy beach, but because of the shifting topography of Morecambe Bay it is now fronted by extensive saltmarshes. The setting of the town on the wooded slopes of Hampsfell, and its irregular low-density plan, are clear in this view looking north-east from Kents Bank.

shoreside line to provide a pleasant promenade; and the train journey to Preston, Manchester or Bradford was far too long and expensive for any but the wealthiest cotton and woollen merchants, who formed the elite of Grange's population.[15]

The beauties of mountain and lake scenery generated the growth of inland resorts. Foremost among them was Windermere, which developed after the opening of the railway from Kendal in 1846. It had two nuclei, 2km (1 mile) apart: the railway station at the top of the hill and Bowness, with its landing stages on the curving bay at the bottom. Even today that morphology is strikingly clear, with two shopping centres and two sets of visitor attractions separated by a long stretch of residential properties and large gardens. On the slopes, with views across the lake to the wooded hills of High Furness and the arc of mountains beyond, opulent mansions were built in extensive grounds, diversified by natural rocky outcrops and small streams. The largest, designed for Lancashire and Yorkshire industrialists and professional men, are textbook examples of late Victorian and Edwardian 'Arts and Crafts' architecture. Other Lakeland resorts were smaller, their tourist role grafted onto older communities. In 1866 the railway reached Keswick, a long-established market town. Less socially exclusive and more economically diversified than Windermere, it became a significant resort in the late 19th century, even though lakeside landowners would not allow development and to this day the town turns its back on Derwentwater. Remote from conurbations, and a slow 32km (20-mile) railway journey from Penrith, Keswick was less favoured as a high-class residential area, though a sprinkling of expensive houses adorned the lakeside at Portinscale, a mile away on the opposite shore. Ambleside developed even though it had no railway: the dark stone and slate, the vernacular character of its architecture and the narrow central streets all betray its origins as an agricultural village and minor market centre.

Town centres and urban design

In all sizeable towns the 18th and 19th centuries saw major changes in the central area and in many civic pride demanded grand architectural statements (*see* Chapter 9). Commercial zones expanded as rapid population growth increased the volume of retail business, while more general trends, such as the development of the insurance and administrative sectors, meant that office buildings became a major new town-centre land use. Increasing traffic and growing congestion, and the desire to create a more imposing townscape, prompted the widening of streets and the cutting of new ones through the urban fabric. In Manchester, for example, Corporation Street (1848) slashed through a warren of lanes and yards, opening up a large new area for commercial redevelopment. A financial quarter emerged east of the street, dominated by multi-storeyed Victorian and Edwardian office buildings of Portland stone and terracotta, with ostentatious entrances of polished wood and statuary designed to impress with their magnificence (Fig. 8.17).[16]

Fig. 8.17 No.46–48 Brown Street, Manchester: the former Brook's Bank building, designed by George Truefitt in 1868 at the height of Manchester's Victorian prosperity; and (behind) Ship Canal House, built of steel and reinforced concrete, the tallest building in the city when it opened in 1924.

The experience of individual towns varied. During the 19th century Carlisle became a major industrial and transport centre, enhancing its older role as the market town for north Cumberland and east Dumfriesshire. The core of the old city was untouched by blatant change, but development took place to the east and south. New shopping areas emerged adjacent to the railway station, and offices and business premises were built in Lowther Street, a largely new thoroughfare on the line of the demolished walls. In the ancient heart, around the market place, change was insidious, but there was a steady conversion of residential properties to commercial use. In the late 19th century corporate architecture made its presence felt, as banks and other institutions built new premises, architecturally ambitious but alien to the vernacular styles and traditional materials of the region. In Kendal, on the other hand, as in many other less industrialised country towns, change was slower. There was some modest commercial development towards the station, but substantial renewal was conspicuously absent.

With the exception of civic buildings and market halls the renewal and extension of town centres was the product of private initiative. As a consequence, the process was

PUBLIC PARKS

As industrial towns grew, far-sighted individuals and councils regarded public parks as the 'lungs' in which the poorer inhabitants could breathe fresher air. Many urban authorities acquired sites for the purpose, or took advantage of generous gifts of land from philanthropic benefactors. The first public park in Britain was in Birkenhead, laid out from 1843 to designs by Joseph Paxton (right). It was hugely influential, acting as the model and inspiration for urban parks elsewhere in Britain and in North America, and also establishing principles of landscape design which have been employed in countless projects over the ensuing 160 years. It was conceived as one of the two centrepieces of the planned new town of Birkenhead and, after long years of decay and neglect, has recently enjoyed a renaissance.

The half century from 1850 was the heyday of the municipal park. Liverpool's 160ha (400-acre) Sefton Park (1867–72) is the most outstanding in the region. Its superbly landscaped open space serves as a beautiful setting for the expensive villa residences on its perimeter, and it is embellished by the magnificent Palm House (1896), itself a triumph of late Victorian architecture (right), and by splendid ornamental gateways and lodges. When Blackburn received its charter of incorporation as a borough in 1851, the provision of a park was already under discussion. In 1855 the new council began work on a sloping south-facing site of 20ha (50 acres), bought cheaply from the town's leading cotton lord, Joseph Feilden. Corporation Park (opposite page, top) was opened before a crowd of 60,000 in October 1857. It overlooked the town centre and became immensely popular with the working classes, for Sunday afternoon strolls, band concerts and public celebrations. In the mid-1860s it was extended, with landscaped terraces and walks constructed by armies of unemployed mill workers, thrown out of work during the Lancashire Cotton Famine. This, as contemporaries noted, was in every sense a 'people's park'.

During the inter-war years the exodus of the middle classes to the suburbs was matched, in the case of wealthy landowning families, by a flight from the region itself. Industry, smoke pollution, the climate and the encroachment of inferior housing all acted as deterrents to living in Lancashire. Families sold up their estates and moved south to the hunting shires, or north to the Lake District or Scotland. In 1938 the Ainsworth family, owners of the bleachworks at Halliwell, disposed of Smithills Hall at Bolton (opposite page,

bottom), which they had owned since the beginning of the 19th century. Bolton Corporation bought the entire estate and then opened the hall, substantial parts of which date from the 14th century, as a museum. The gardens and grounds became a public park, while most of the estate remained in tenanted agricultural use (though some of the land was used for council housing in the 1960s). Over 60 years later, restored and cherished, Smithills is regarded as 'the jewel in Bolton's crown'.

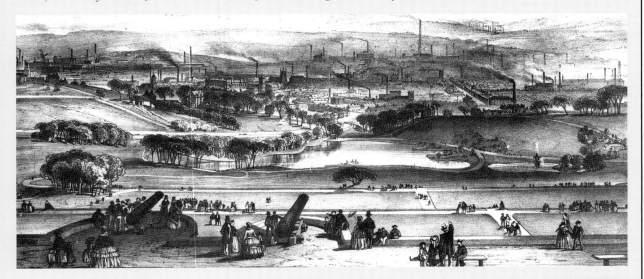

fragmented and rarely produced an overall architectural harmony – though the cumulative effect of imposing buildings could be impressive. A good example in a small borough is provided by Colne where, as the cotton industry flourished, the population doubled to 26,000 between 1891 and 1911, and in 1895 borough status was achieved. The town centre was extensively remodelled to cater for the enlarged population and reflect civic pride. The main road west from the centre was widened and rechristened Albert Road, the council paved the streets with granite setts, and in 1904 an electric tramway was opened. In 1894 a splendid town hall was built at the highest point, dominating the view up Albert Road, and in 1907 the Co-operative Society opened its rival in scale and grandeur, a monumental department store. A private company promoted the cattle market and semi-circular shopping arcade (1905) on backland behind Church Street, at the heart of the medieval town, while the Corporation laid out a new market place to link these retail developments. In the early 20th century a variety of other amenities appeared: a small theatre, a free public library and in 1905, perhaps unexpectedly, England's first purpose-built cinema. Thus by 1913, when it reached the peak of its prosperity and size, Colne had a modern and sophisticated town centre, substantially renewed by a combination of municipal and private action.[17]

Comparable revolutions took place in most other towns. Councils built covered market halls which combined functional efficiency with aesthetic appeal. Those that survive are impressive reminders of municipal patronage of architecture: Preston's slender-columned, open-sided hall (notorious for its icy blasts); the fish market at Warrington, which almost fills the market square; or the chunky sandstone hall at Carlisle. Shopping arcades were a hallmark of Lancashire towns in the second half of the 19th century, their glazed galleries and ornamental entrances adding variety to the urban scene and implying the superior quality of the shops within. Despite urban redevelopment in the 1960s, there are still some excellent examples, such as the exquisite Barton Arcade between St Ann's Square and Deansgate in Manchester, and the Wayfarers' Arcade in Southport.

In 1914 electric trams hummed along streets lined with temples to commerce and retailing. Every building was blackened by the soot of ten thousand chimneys, and every smoking chimney symbolised the industrial might of north-west England. Across large tracts of south and east Lancashire, Low Furness and west Cumberland, urban landscapes predominated, and from adjacent uplands the prevailing impression was of towns, cities and – their inevitable accompaniment – atmospheric pollution. To this day, the smoke-blackened dry stone walls high on south Pennine moorlands reflect the inescapable influence of the town. These urban areas had a host of physical and social problems, and were soon to face huge economic difficulties. The ambitious strategies to remedy them in the 20th century would result in a further transformation of the urban landscape (*see* Chapter 11).

NOTES

1   For overviews of urban landscapes in England, see Waller 2000

2   Shotter 1997, 69–74; Shotter & White 1990, 32–3

3   McCarthy 1993, 14–18, 28–37

4   For medieval towns, see Crosby 1994; Winchester 1987, 121–9

5   Philpott 1989, 35–41

6   Crosby 2002, 16–20

7   For markets, the definitive listing (with sources) is www.history.ac.uk/cmh/gaz

8   Defoe 1971, 541–3, 545

9   Borsay 1989, 162–3 and appendix 6

10   Sharples 2004, 229–50

11   For overview, see Morris in Waller 2000

12   George 2000

13   For resorts, see Walton 1983 and 1992

14   Walton 1998

15   Marshall 1971, 184–95

16   For Manchester see Hartwell 2001; for Liverpool, Hughes 1999, 31–121

17   Crosby 2003

PART III

Expressions of Power

This and the following chapters move to explore a deeper level of meaning in the landscape. So far, we have considered the relationship between society and the environment in functional terms, seeing the landscape as the product of economic imperatives. Yet the landscape abounds with features that cannot be explained simply in functional terms, since they have been constructed to express an abstract idea and to make a public statement. In this chapter the focus is on how features in the landscape may be read as expressions of power and authority.

By definition, those who wield power in human affairs also have the ability to effect landscape change. Expressions of power range from bold statements of military force, such as Roman forts and medieval castles, to the more subtle manifestations of patronage and philanthropy, which produced landscape features perpetuating the memory of the powerful and reflecting glory back on them. The economic power of a great landowner or a 19th-century factory owner; the military might of an Iron Age warlord or a medieval monarch; the powers granted by statute to local authorities in the 19th and 20th centuries – all have left a legacy of major features in the landscape. Many of these are functional structures created on a scale that reflects the resources available to those in power: model farmsteads, cotton mills, motorways, for example. But others reach beyond the utilitarian to celebrate in tangible form the power of those responsible for creating them, and it is these statements of power that form the subject of this chapter.

The aspects of power to be discussed here are threefold: military force; the economic influence of the landed classes and those with wealth from industry; and the civic control of the local governing classes. Other aspects are examined elsewhere in this book, notably religious authority (the subject of Chapter 10) and the intervention of central government (which forms a central theme of Chapter 14). The impact of some aspects of power (that of landowners, for example) can be seen in almost any region, but two forms are particularly distinctive in the landscape of the North West: first, the manifestations of military might associated with the political frontier along the Solway (in both its incarnations, as the limit of the Roman Empire and as the border with medieval Scotland), and second, the wealth and power that came from industry, particularly in the 19th century.

DEFENCE OF A BORDER

Among the earliest manifestations of organised political power in Britain are the military sites of the Iron Age, notably the hillforts which converted prominent summits into defended strongholds. We know little of the political geography of the North West before the Roman period, but the presence of hillforts implies the existence of a structure of tribal power, as their construction presumably required the ability to draw on large resources of labour. Many of the hillforts in the North West are small enclosures, often with only a single defensive ditch, on

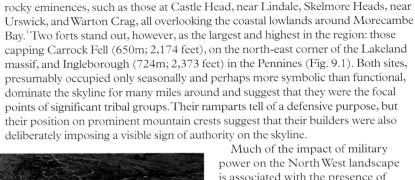

Fig. 9.1 Ingleborough: the ramparts of the Iron Age hillfort and several of the hut circles it encloses are shown up clearly by a light covering of snow

rocky eminences, such as those at Castle Head, near Lindale, Skelmore Heads, near Urswick, and Warton Crag, all overlooking the coastal lowlands around Morecambe Bay.[1] Two forts stand out, however, as the largest and highest in the region: those capping Carrock Fell (650m; 2,174 feet), on the north-east corner of the Lakeland massif, and Ingleborough (724m; 2,373 feet) in the Pennines (Fig. 9.1). Both sites, presumably occupied only seasonally and perhaps more symbolic than functional, dominate the skyline for many miles around and suggest that they were the focal points of significant tribal groups. Their ramparts tell of a defensive purpose, but their position on prominent mountain crests suggest that their builders were also deliberately imposing a visible sign of authority on the skyline.

Much of the impact of military power on the North West landscape is associated with the presence of political frontiers along the Solway Firth in the Roman and medieval periods. By contrast, the political boundaries of the Anglo-Saxon period, running along the Mersey and through the centre of the Lake District, have left few tangible remains. Both the legacy of the Roman military occupation and the medieval castles defending the border with Scotland express the power of a political authority based outside the region and anxious to make its presence known in that critical zone, the outer limit of its authority, where its power was under threat from hostile external forces.

To the Romans, the North West lay on the outer fringes of empire and was threatened by barbarian attack, not only from hostile territory north of the Solway–Tyne frontier, but also along the long, indented coastline of the Irish Sea. The region fell within the 'military zone' of Roman Britain, beyond the villas and towns of the Romanised south. The landscape legacy of the Roman occupation is essentially military: a network of roads linking a series of forts, and the fortified frontier of Hadrian's Wall with coastal defences extending south-west down the Cumbrian coast.

The Roman conquest of the North West took place during the governorships of Quintus Petillius Cerealis (AD 71–4) and Gnaeus Julius Agricola (AD 77–83). Sites which have yielded evidence of this period suggest a movement up the Lancashire lowlands and down the Eden valley to the Carlisle plain: recent dendrochronological evidence shows that the earliest phases of the fort at Carlisle date from AD 72. The late 1st and early 2nd centuries saw consolidation of Roman control, with an extension of the network of forts and roads, including the construction of forts in and on the fringes of the Lake District, suggesting that the Cumbrian massif was brought under Roman control at this time. Evidence from the forts at Papcastle, Caermote and Troutbeck, Ambleside and Hardknott suggests that all were constructed before the reign of Hadrian. The choice of the Solway–Tyne line as a frontier also pre-dated Hadrian. The withdrawal of the army from Scotland c. AD 87 led to the construction of a series of forts (including those at Nether Denton, Brampton and Carlisle) to form a frontier along the Roman road known as the Stanegate. That was replaced in the 120s by the sophisticated frontier complex of Hadrian's Wall, consisting of the wall itself (initially built of turf in the western, Cumbrian section), patrolled from milecastles and turrets and the *vallum*, a wide-

OPPOSITE PAGE:

TOP: *Fig. 9.2 Hadrian's Wall* at Wall Bowers, looking east towards Birdoswald. The modern road follows the line of the wall; only the ditch on its northern side survives. To the right, the line of the *vallum* is clearly visible and the line of the turf wall runs parallel to the *vallum*, diverging from the course of the later, stone wall.

BOTTOM: *Fig. 9.3 Maryport Roman fort*, one of the series of forts defending the Irish Sea coast.

bottomed ditch running roughly parallel to the wall on its southern side (Fig. 9.2). The Stanegate forts were replaced by new forts along the wall itself, such as that at Birdoswald, which supplanted the earlier fort on the other side of the Irthing valley at Nether Denton.[2]

The forts and roads of the imperial power were thus imposed on the region's landscape and must have formed very real symbols of authority to the native British population. For substantial periods during the Roman occupation, particularly in the 3rd century, settled conditions prevailed. Civilian settlements grew up under the walls of the forts, which now housed a policing garrison, rather than a conquering army. Yet the cultural contrast between the forts and the surrounding countryside must have been striking: the great stone buildings constructed of finely hewn masonry, hypocausted bath houses and grand Latin building inscriptions all spoke of foreign power. The buildings, walls and ditches of the 'playing-card' shaped forts and the straight, metalled roads were symbols of imperial authority, built to imported templates and expressing the power of the occupying force (Fig. 9.3). Many centuries after the Roman army left, the legacies of their occupation were among the first relics of the past to fire the imagination of Elizabethan antiquaries, such as William Camden's Cumbrian correspondent, Reginald Bainbrigg, the headmaster of Appleby Grammar School.

As we saw in Chapter 3, the North West as a whole became a peripheral zone in relation to centres of political power for much of the Dark Ages and early medieval period. Its southern boundary, the River Mersey (Old English *maeres ea*, 'boundary river'), probably records in its name its function as the boundary between the Anglo-Saxon kingdoms of Northumbria and Mercia from the 7th century. In the early 10th century, when the kings of the nascent Anglo-Saxon kingdom of England were faced by the threat of incursions by the Scandinavians in the Irish Sea basin,

the Mersey frontier became, briefly, a fortified line of control between English and Scandinavians. A series of forts (*burhs*) was established between 907 and 919 along the Mersey frontier between Chester and Manchester, including those at the strategic crossing points at Runcorn and Thelwall.

Within the region, seats of power in the Dark Ages are difficult to identify. The 5th-century timber hall built within the ramparts of the Roman fort at Birdoswald can be interpreted as the seat of a post-Roman warlord. Shadows of the power of some of the later rulers of pre-Norman Cumbria survive in minor place-names. Dunmail Raise (*see* Fig. 3.8), the huge cairn of stones on the watershed in the heart of the Lake District, takes its name from Dunmail (otherwise Dyfnwal or Donald), king of the Cumbrians in the 940s, and marked, both physically and by name, the southern limit of his power. Castle Hewen, on the edge of Inglewood Forest, may record the name of Owain, the first recorded king of the Cumbrians, while 'Gospatrick's wath', the lost name of a ford near Thursby, probably took its name from the great 11th-century lord of Allerdale, marking as it did the point of entry into Gospatrick's lordship on the main road from Carlisle.[3]

ABOVE: *Fig. 9.4 The motte-and-bailey castle at Burton in Lonsdale*, *centre of the Norman honour of Burton.*

RIGHT: *Fig. 9.5 Mottes, castles and towers in north-west England.*

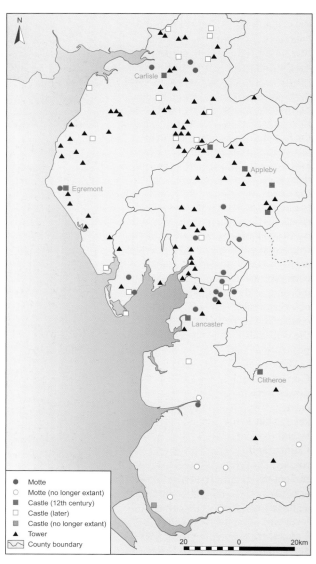

The Norman conquest of the North West was an attenuated process. The area that became Lancashire, together with parts of southern Cumbria, fell within the kingdom William acquired at Hastings; Cumbria north of Dunmail Raise and the Shap fells remained under the suzerainty of the king of Scots until William Rufus conquered 'the land of Carlisle' and expelled its native ruler, Dolfin, in 1092. The most tangible legacies of early Norman power are the motte and bailey castles, earthwork fortifications centred on a raised mound (the 'motte') on which, initially, a wooden tower would be built (Fig. 9.4). The location of motte and bailey castles in the North West is striking (Fig. 9.5). They are concentrated in the utmost fringes of William the Conqueror's kingdom, north of the Ribble and particularly in the Lune valley – the string of seven mottes down the Lune from Tebay to Halton perhaps indicates particular resistance to Norman rule in this frontier region. Further north, mottes are fewer and tend to be associated with the seats of power in the great Cumbrian baronies. Egremont Castle (the motte at the heart of which gives its name to the town, 'the mound by the River *Egre* or Ehen') was the seat of the Norman lords of Copeland barony; tradition states that the motte at Irthington was the original seat of the lords of the barony of Gilsland; Castle Howe, the motte tucked under the hillside at Kendal, appears to have been the precursor of Kendal Castle, the focal point of the barony of Kendal. Similarly, the fine motte and bailey at Burton-in-Lonsdale was the *caput* of the honour of Burton, covering the north-western corner of the West Riding (Fig. 9.4). Others appear to have been more short-lived, legacies of the initial subjugation of the region by the new Norman lords. Many guard river crossings, such as the pairs of mottes at Penwortham and Tulketh, overlooking the head of the Ribble estuary, and at Arkholme and Melling, controlling either end of an ancient crossing of the Lune. These were obvious, visible symbols of authority, controlling movement and imposing the will of the new lords on the local population.[4]

Within little over a century of the Conquest, the key seats of Norman power were marked by sturdy stone castles (Fig. 9.5). Massive square keeps built in the 12th century formed the core of the great royal castles at Carlisle and Lancaster (Fig. 9.6). Less massive, but still imposing keeps were built at the centres of great lay estates at Clitheroe and Appleby. By the early 13th century most of the great lordships of Cumbria and north Lancashire were focused on strong stone castles, such as those at

Fig. 9.6 Lancaster Castle. *The great royal complex at the heart of the city; the Norman keep is now swamped by the congested buildings of HM Prison, of which it forms a part.*

Fig. 9.7 Brougham Castle, the 12th-century keep planted adjacent to the Roman fort.

Fig. 9.8 Yanwath Hall, near Penrith, the late-medieval tower house of the Threlkeld family, probably dating largely from the 15th century.

Cockermouth, Egremont, Appleby, Kendal and Clitheroe, the castles in most cases dominating new boroughs laid out at their feet. A similar relationship between a castle and a new town occurred in the royal borough of Liverpool, where a castle had been built by 1235. These were both strategic fortresses and symbols of authority and control. The barony of Westmorland also contained two further 12th-century keeps, at Brougham (Fig. 9.7) and at Brough-under-Stainmoor, both built on the sites of Roman forts. Along with Appleby they guarded the strategically important trans-Pennine route over Stainmoor.

The outbreak of war between England and Scotland in 1296 ushered in three centuries of sporadic warfare and endemic hostility across the Solway frontier. The far north of Cumbria became a wasted war zone, and periodic Scots raids sweeping across the Carlisle plain and up the Eden valley impoverished those areas as well. Further south the fear of the Scots was more potent than actual attacks, though Bruce's raids down west Cumbria to Furness in 1315 and over Shap to Kendal and Lancaster in 1322 caused devastation, particularly to the towns. The bulk of medieval fortified buildings in the North West date from this period, their distribution (Fig. 9.5) reflecting the level of fear and insecurity, being heavily concentrated in Cumbria and the far north of Lancashire.

Where baronies and other large lordships were not already focused on a castle, new castles were built in the first half of the 14th century: the king granted licences to crenellate (that is, to fortify) to the lords of Gilsland barony and Millom seigniory in 1335 and the lord of Greystoke barony in 1353, which probably give approximate dates for major building work on the castles at Naworth, Millom and Greystoke. Lancashire also saw considerable castle building in the late medieval period, much of it during the 15th century. At Lancaster Castle, the imposing gatehouse was constructed between 1403 and 1413. Lay castles, probably more statements of prestige than vital strongholds, were built at Thurland in the Lune valley (licensed 1402) and Greenhalgh, near Garstang (licensed 1490), while the Stanleys built a massive fortified palace at Lathom between 1459 and 1495, which has not survived.[5]

But the majority of buildings fortified during the 14th and 15th centuries were the halls of lesser manorial lords. These took the form of the characteristic tower houses (or 'pele' towers) (Fig. 9.8), with a stone-vaulted basement and first-floor entrance (tradition stating that, when a Scots raid was imminent, cattle would be secured in the basement while the household retreated to the upper floors from which they could defend themselves and repel the attackers). Most manor houses in northern Cumbria have a late medieval tower at their core, to the extent that Daniel Defoe could describe the journey from Penrith to Carlisle as being 'through a country full of castles, for almost every gentleman's house is a castle'.[6] Tower houses extend south to the margins of Morecambe Bay, suggesting on the face of it that fear of the Scots was prevalent here as well. That may not be the full explanation, however, since towers appear to have become status symbols across the late-medieval centuries. The fabric of some, indeed, suggests that they were built in the late 15th or even 16th centuries, when the threat of major incursions had receded. As substantial stone structures in the countryside, they advertised the presence of a gentry household and may be thought of as symbols of the rising power of the Cumbrian country gentleman (Fig. 9.9). In this respect they mirrored the late medieval moated manorial halls in the less troubled lowlands of south-west Lancashire.[7]

Fig. 9.9 Levens Hall. *The medieval manor house was enlarged substantially in the 1690s, when the formal gardens with their famous topiary were laid out by Guillaume Beaumont for Colonel James Grahme.*

In the far north of Cumbria lawlessness, rather than organised warfare, continued throughout the 16th century. The government's attempts to crush the marauding bands of 'reivers' and to pacify the Borders led to more military building. Thomas Lord Dacre, the warden of the Western Marches, rebuilt and extended Askerton Castle *c.* 1490, and by the later 16th century it had become the residence of the land serjeant of Gilsland, whose role was to command and lead the local inhabitants against Scottish raids. Towers continued to be built in this unsettled area until within a generation of the Union of the crowns in 1603: Brackenhill Tower, in the valley of the Lyne, east of Longtown, is thought to have been built in 1586. The 16th century also saw the final resolution of the dispute over the Debateable Lands, the territory between the Esk and Sark rivers, claimed by both kingdoms. The agreement on a fixed boundary in 1552 was followed by the construction of the Scots Dyke, an earthen bank and ditch over 5km (3 miles) in length, a symbol of the authority of the distant courts of the English and Scottish crowns.[8]

POWER AND PATRONAGE: WEALTH FROM LAND AND INDUSTRY

Tangible expressions of the economic power of the landed classes are widespread in the English countryside. Perhaps the epitome of such manifestations of wealth is the great country houses built between the 16th century and the 19th, set in parkland and dominating the local area – visually, economically and socially. In north-west England the distribution of country houses reflects the contrasting patterns of land tenure within the region. The only significant concentration of the landed estates typical of lowland England was in the south-western parts of

Lancashire. This was a landscape dominated by resident gentry families, where farms were let on leases from the 16th and 17th centuries. The landlord thus retained control over his estate, which enabled him to create the landscape he desired. Such 'closed' villages, dominated by the lord's manor house in its parkland setting, include Rufford, Ince Blundell and Little Crosby.

North of the Ribble, great country houses are few. The owners of the larger feudal estates were generally absentees (like the earls of Northumberland and their successors, who were lords of the extensive estates focused on Cockermouth Castle). At the level of immediate lordship, income from land was limited by the development of customary tenures, which yielded comparatively little income to the lord of the manor, prevented him from taking land into his own hand (except by buying it at market value from his tenants) and gave the tenants a security of tenure akin to that on freehold property. Many of the old gentry families in Cumbria and north Lancashire had modest manor houses, often built around a late medieval tower house, customary tenures denying them the profits from exploiting their estates directly. With a few notable exceptions (such as the impact of the Lowther family at Lowther and the Cavendish family at Holker Hall), the hand of landed power is less visible in the landscape of Cumbria than in other areas of rural England.

Across the North West, landed power overlapped with wealth from industry, as merchants and industrialists acquired land and, with it, the deference due to country gentlemen. This tendency had deep roots. Robert Bindloss, a Kendal clothier, bought half the manor of Borwick, near Carnforth, in 1567 and had acquired the whole manor by 1590, at around which time he extended Borwick Hall, adding an Elizabethan mansion to the existing tower.[9] At a similar date the Brownlows, a family of Bolton clothiers, were extending Hall i' th' Wood, near Bolton. Conspicuous expenditure on grand houses continued through the 18th and 19th centuries. Thomas Patten, a Warrington industrialist, built Bank Hall (now Warrington Town Hall) in 1750. Turton Tower, the Elizabethan manor house near Edgeworth, which had been bought by the Manchester clothier Humphrey Chetham in 1628, was later seen as a suitably manorial home by another industrialist, Joseph Kay, the Preston cotton spinner; he bought it in 1835 and added ornate half-timbering as appropriate to its status and antiquity. Many industrialists' country properties were on a smaller scale, taking the form of villas set in a few hectares of ground. Rural north Lancashire, for example, is peppered with 19th-century Gothic piles, some extending older houses, others built anew. Some were existing medieval towers, swamped by castellated extensions. Thomas Edmundson, a Liverpool merchant, extended Gresgarth Hall, near Caton, c. 1806; the financier Pudsey Dawson gave Hornby Castle its spectacular profile and façade in 1849–52; J P C Starkie, a Lancashire MP, extended Ashton Hall, near Lancaster, in 1856; while Leighton Hall was Gothicised for the Gillow family, Lancaster's renowned cabinet-makers, c. 1810.[10]

Country houses were generally set in a landscape created to reinforce the power and status of their owners. Grounds were landscaped both to heighten the impact of the house and its surroundings from outside and to create prospects and views from the house. In the 17th- and early 18th-centuries, projects to mould the landscape for aesthetic purposes had the effect of drawing the eye towards the manor house, directing attention to the seat of a landed family. An imposing façade and, in particular, the treatment of the principal entrance were critical in dwarfing the visitor and creating a sense of awe at the approach to the physical manifestation of power. Perhaps the most striking example of this in the North West is at Stonyhurst. The core of the house (from 1794 a Catholic seminary and later a public school) is the imposing gatehouse, built by Sir Richard Shireburn in the 1590s, which dominates the west front. A century later Sir Nicholas Shireburn created a landscape to set off his house: between 1696 and 1710 he laid out an entrance drive aligned to the gatehouse, flanked by two long narrow rectangles of

water (known as the 'canals'), and he completed his display of power and opulence in 1712 by heightening the gatehouse with two towering cupolas (Fig. 9.10).[11]

In contrast, the landscaped parks of the 18th and 19th centuries may be thought of as providing a retreat from the world, hiding the house from prying eyes. Such oases of privacy include many of the parks created in the late 18th and 19th centuries, such as those at Scarisbrick and Knowsley. The latter, a medieval deer park, was enlarged in the early 19th century to distance Knowsley Hall further from the world outside. Both Knowsley Hall, the massive Georgian mansion of the earls of Derby, and Scarisbrick Hall, an extravagent Gothic pile designed for the Scarisbrick family by the Pugins, father and son, are big, bold statements of power, but they were intended to be seen by a select few. The sheer scale of Edward Pugin's soaring tower at Scarisbrick, dominating the south-west Lancashire mosslands, was necessary if it was to have an impact from a distance. Hectares of parkland separated the landed elite, giving them a privacy which set them apart and, by distancing them from the world outside, reinforced their authority. The ability to obtain privacy had become, indeed, itself a manifestation of power.[12]

The tension between the desire for separation and the need to project the landed classes' power through physical manifestation in the landscape is illustrated dramatically at Lowther, the seat of the Lowther family, earls of Lonsdale. It is a landscape totally dominated by one family, Cumbria's leading resident landowners since the 17th century. The shell of Lowther Castle, a vast turreted structure built to replace the earlier hall between 1806 and 1814, lies in parkland. The old village of Lowther, which stood around the hall, was removed by Sir John Lowther in the 1680s, rebuilt to the east of the park and renamed Newtown. The church, now isolated in the park, is dominated by Lowther family tombs, and beside the church drive stands a mausoleum which epitomises the self-imposed isolation of the landed elite. Inside it is a life-sized, seated statue of William Lowther, 2nd earl of Lonsdale (d. 1872), 'a picture of loneliness' (as Pevsner put it), dwarfed and imprisoned by the structure that was intended to celebrate his greatness (Fig. 9.11).

The economic power of the landed and industrial elite was also expressed through patronage and benevolence. Endowing almshouses, for example, both alleviated poverty and perpetuated the memory of the founder. The design and layout of the almshouses themselves expressed a number of ideas: accommodation for the residents was generally humble, as befitting the station of the poor; and there were often elements of social control, such as the presence of a warden to oversee the residents and ensure that the rules laid down by the founder were kept, frequently including a requirement to attend the chapel which formed part of the almshouse complex.[13] Over the entrance might be a plaque recording the founder's beneficence, perhaps surmounted by their coat of arms.

Fig. 9.10 Stonyhurst: *the splendour of the great gateway, begun in 1592, topped by Sir Nicholas Shireburn's cupolas of 1712, is accentuated by Sir Nicholas' avenue and canals.*

BELOW: **Fig. 9.11 Lowther Mausoleum, Lowther.** *The statue of the 2nd earl of Lonsdale (d. 1872) in the mausoleum he built in 1857.*

Fig. 9.12 Shireburn almshouses, Hurst Green. *Endowed by Sir Nicholas Shireburn in 1706, and originally built on Longridge Fell, the almshouses were rebuilt (and extended) in their present position in 1946.*

Although most almshouses are restrained buildings, some trumpet the founder's benevolence. Those founded by Sir Nicholas Shireburn of Stonyhurst in 1706 and re-erected at Hurst Green, for example, are approached by a flight of steps, which leads the eye to the central, pedimented bay, topped by urns and carrying the full achievement of the Shireburn arms (Fig. 9.12).

Acts of benevolence have contributed many other features to the landscape. Most are buildings, in both rural and urban settings: endowed schools, libraries, public halls and institutes, for example. Gifts of public parks represented more extensive landscapes of philanthropy. Notable examples from the North West include Lever Park, on the edge of the Rossendale fells at Rivington, created between 1902 and 1911 by Lord Leverhulme for the people of his native town of Bolton, and Williamson Park, in Lancaster, the product of the paternalism of the linoleum manufacturers, James Williamson, father and son. Lancaster's corporation had initiated work to convert the former stone quarries on the moor outside the town into a public park using unemployed labour during the cotton famine of the 1860s. Landscaping was paid for by James Williamson, senior, and the park presented to the town by his son in 1881. James Williamson, junior, financed further improvements (including shelters, a bandstand and a palm house), culminating in the domed Ashton Memorial, opened in 1909, to commemorate his family (Fig. 9.13). The 'grandest monument in England', as Pevsner called it, was only one element of Williamson's largesse to his native town during the Edwardian years: he also donated a new Town Hall (built 1906–9) facing Dalton Square, which he remodelled, erecting on it an imposing statue to Queen Victoria.[14]

CIVIC PRIDE

The activities of the Williamsons in Lancaster illustrate the close connections between industrial wealth and expressions of civic pride. Personal philanthropy contributed significantly to the sense of civic identity and power manifest in the landscapes of Victorian and Edwardian towns. Public buildings continued to be donated by individuals, the corporation then taking over the running costs, as in Lancaster. The imposing Harris Library and Museum, facing Preston's Market Place, is another example of philanthropy being channelled into civic improvement. Built between 1882 and 1893 by the trustees of Edmund Harris, a wealthy solicitor, who had left £300,000 to the town for charitable and cultural purposes, it takes

Fig. 9.13 Ashton Memorial, Williamson's Park, Lancaster. *Lord Ashton's crowning glory to the memory of his family, opened in 1909.*

the form of a Classical temple, dedicated to 'Literature, Arts and Sciences'. To its architect, Alderman James Hibbert, who was chairman of the corporation's free library committee, the ancient Greeks represented the pinnacle of civilisation. His building's Classical architecture not only embodied a rejection of modern artistic fashions, but also made a political statement, a reaction to what he saw as the 'excesses of democracy'.[15]

Most civic buildings were the result of corporate decision-making among the municipal elite. In the textile towns the cotton masters exercised civic power through dominating the membership of municipal corporations, particularly in the middle decades of the 19th century. Eric Hobsbawm has commented on the willingness of 'hard-headed businessmen' to champion and contribute towards the cost of 'those gigantic, awful and very expensive municipal buildings with which northern cities began to demonstrate their superiority over one another after 1848'.[16] Competition between towns – and between political groupings on the councils – fired a blaze of extravagant building, particularly of town halls, of which those in Blackburn (1852–6), Rochdale (1871), Bolton (1873) and Manchester (1877) are the most impressive. Imposing exteriors and lavish interior fittings expressed the power and confidence of the civic leaders and inculcated local pride

MONUMENTS TO POWER

The English landscape is dotted with monuments commemorating the powerful. Vertical structures in prominent positions, reaching skywards, they make a bold statement to future generations, calling them to remember the person they commemorate. They take many forms, from the comparatively simple pillars illustrated here, or the statues gracing town squares, to much grander edifices. Industrial Lancashire sports such substantial monuments as the Peel Tower on Holcombe Hill, near Bury, built by public subscription in 1852 to commemorate Bury's most famous son, Sir Robert Peel, and the ornate clock tower in the town square in Great Harwood, commemorating John Mercer, the self-taught chemist who invented the 'mercerisation' of cotton.

The four Cumbrian pillars illustrated here are less ostentatious. Far from human habitation, on the salt-marsh fringing the Solway at Burgh-by-Sands, stands the monument commemorating the death of Edward I in camp on Burgh Marsh when on his way north to crush Robert the Bruce in 1307 (below left). The square pillar, erected by the lord of Burgh barony, Henry Howard, 6th duke of Norfolk, c. 1685, reflects the growing antiquarian consciousness of the late 17th century. Rebuilt in 1803 by Viscount Lowther, it has kept silent vigil in memory of the power of 'the hammer of the Scots' for over three centuries.

The power of the aristocracy is expressed in perhaps the most remarkable monument illustrated here, the Countess Pillar beside the main road from Carlisle to York (now the A66) at Brougham (below right). This was erected in 1656 by Lady Anne Clifford,

hereditary sheriff and baron of Westmorland, at the point where she parted with her mother, the Countess of Cumberland, for the last time 40 years before. It is thus an intensely personal monument, but one which also makes a very public statement. Lady Anne also left money for an annual dole to be distributed to the poor of Brougham parish on the anniversary of her parting from her mother: the sandstone dole table survives beside the pillar. As well as carrying an inscription and heraldic shields with the arms of Lady Anne's family, the pillar also bears a sundial, a practical aid to travellers along the highway.[19]

A personal statement is also made by the monument to John Wilkinson the ironmaster (d. 1808) at Lindale, near Grange-over-Sands (below). This cast iron obelisk is a symbol of industrial might: Wilkinson designed it himself as his mausoleum and for 20 years it marked his grave in the garden of his villa, nearby at Castlehead. After Castlehead was sold, his body was re-interred in the local churchyard and the obelisk was eventually moved in 1863 to its present site on a hillock overlooking the village. The inscription, drafted in part by Wilkinson himself, commemorates the life of a vigorous industrial pioneer: 'His different works, in various parts of the kingdom, are lasting testimonies of his unceasing labours. His life was spent in action for the benefit of man and, as he presumed humbly to hope, to the glory of God.'[20]

The forward-looking spirit of the Industrial Revolution is also visible in the obelisk on Castle Howe, the Norman motte in Kendal (right). This was erected not to commemorate an individual life, but to celebrate the power of a political idea: freedom. Inscribed 'Sacred to Liberty', it was put up in 1788 to mark the centenary of the Glorious Revolution of 1688. With its wealthy Nonconformist mercantile elite, Kendal was a Whig town; the monument both celebrated Whig ideals and was a bold challenge to the Tory Lowther family's domination of Cumbrian politics.[21]

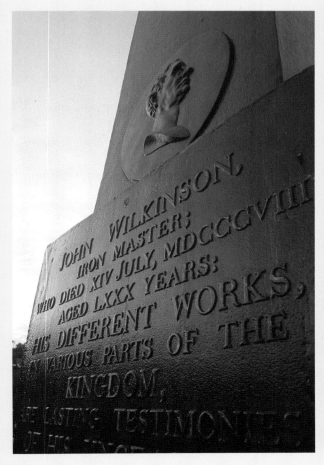

among the townspeople. Rochdale's Town Hall (Fig. 9.14), built 1866–71 at a cost of £155,000, is a secular cathedral in Gothic, dominated by a clock tower, which soared even higher before its upper sections were replaced after a fire in 1883.[17]

The most imposing display of civic power in the North West is the great neo-Grecian assemblage in the heart of Liverpool. St George's Hall, housing a concert hall and two assize courts, completed in 1856, forms the centrepiece, set between a paved plateau and landscaped gardens, in which stand cenotaph, other war memorials, statues and the Tuscan column commemorating the Duke of Wellington. Facing the Hall across William Brown Street is a further group of fine, classical civic buildings: the library and museum (1857–60), Picton Reading Room (1875–9), Walker Art Gallery (1874–7) and Sessions House (1882–4). The civic display was complemented by increasingly confident and imposing commercial buildings. Most iconic is the waterfront skyline on the Pier Head, which greeted passengers arriving by sea. The famous Royal Liver Building

Fig. 9.14 Rochdale Town Hall in 1875: civic Gothic at its most resplendent, completed in 1871 to a design by W H Crossland. The original tower shown here was destroyed by fire in 1883 and replaced by the present, stockier one.

(1908–10), topped by mythical liver birds; the Cunard Building (1913); and the Classical, domed Mersey Docks and Harbour Board offices (1907) form an assemblage recalling the optimism and opulence of Liverpool in its heyday. Both the civic and the commercial express the dignity and majesty of one of the great cities of the British Empire.[18]

Expressions of power in the landscape tend to dwarf the individual human being. Standing beneath the gate of a medieval castle or before the porticoed entrance to a country house or a civic building, the individual cannot fail to be aware of power symbolised in concrete form, whether that power derives from family lineage, military might, industrial wealth or civic authority. A sense of awe is exactly what the builders of these manifestations of secular power intended.

NOTES

1   Newman 1996, 67–8

2   Shotter 1997, 7–50

3   Wilmott 1997, 221–30; Phythian-Adams 1996, 74, 112, 138

4   Higham 1991; Perriam & Robinson 1998, *passim*

5   Newman 1996, 142–3

6   Defoe 1971, 552

7   Perriam & Robinson 1998; Marsh 2000, 266–305; Lewis 2000, esp. pp. 151–4

8   Perriam & Robinson 1998, 130–1, 227, 240

9   VCH Lancs. VIII, 171–4

10 Pevsner 1969b, 50, 92, 147, 267; Champness 1989, 122–4

11 Gerard 1894, 69–72

12 Lewis 2000, 273; Champness 1989, 124–9

13 For almshouse architecture, see Caffrey 2002

14 White 1993, 193; Champness 1989, 144–6

15 Moore 2003; Champness 1989, 137–8

16 Hobsbawm 1969, 112

17 Cunningham 1981, 71–4; Hartwell *et al.* 2004, 594–6

18 Sharples 2004, 49–72

19 Wilson 1997

20 Stockdale 1872, 208–24

21 Kendal Civic Society 1997

10

Places of Prayer

The landscape is full of spaces and buildings dedicated to the spiritual, sacred places set aside for worship. Christian churches and chapels stand in almost every community, often set in 'God's acre', a plot of land put aside to receive the dead and a place where the world of the living encountered that of the spirit. But sacred spaces in the landscape also include both the legacies of pre-Christian religions, windows on to prehistoric religions which are only dimly understood, and the more recent places of worship of other faiths, which are perhaps the most tangible expressions of the cultural diversity of the North West at the beginning of the 21st century. Religious buildings reflect the beliefs of those who built them, so that places set aside for prayer can be read as physical representations of spiritual ideals.

The religious landscape of the North West is distinctive in several respects, the region's physical and cultural marginality forming a thread running through the story. The medieval Christian legacy includes hints of a sub-stratum of Celtic Christianity and a distinctive pattern of large parishes, accentuating the challenge of making religious provision for isolated and scattered rural communities. Since the Reformation, the central theme has been the growth of religious diversity and the importance of religious identity in engendering and sustaining a sense of community. Humble chapels and meeting houses in the countryside; bold and massive Methodist, Congregational and Roman Catholic churches in the industrial towns; and the golden domes of mosques and temples can be seen as successive manifestations of religious consciousness and pride across the centuries. Furthermore, the region's religious diversity had a strong geographical pattern, accentuating contrasts within the regional landscape.

Fig. 10.1 Long Meg and her Daughters, near Little Salkeld, Cumbria. One of the largest stone circles in Britain, this ritual site probably dates from the Neolithic or early Bronze Age.

SHADOWS OF PRE-CHRISTIAN RELIGIONS

Prehistoric ritual sites, such as henges, stone circles and burial cairns, hint at an inner world of ritualised belief in the Neolithic and Bronze Ages that is otherwise lost to us. Clusters of long barrows and stone circles occur in Cumbria, on the coastal strip south of St Bees and in the Eden valley, while Lancashire contains only two known long barrows (both on Anglezarke Moor, near Chorley). The great Cumbrian stone circles of Castlerigg, near Keswick, Swinside, near Millom, and Long Meg and her Daughters, in the Eden valley (Fig. 10.1), probably dating from the 3rd millennium BC, surely mark out spaces which were in some way

Fig. 10.2 Bewcastle: *the church and magnificent Anglo-Saxon cross stand within the ramparts of the Roman fort, which was called* Fanum Cocidii, *(the shrine of Cocidius). At the top of the photograph, also within the fort, are the late-medieval castle and the demesne farmstead.*

special, if not sacred. So must the circular, banked henges known as Mayburgh and King Arthur's Round Table, near Penrith. The likely astronomical alignments of some, at least, of the stone circles, and the fact that sites such as these would have been durable and dramatic features in the prehistoric landscape suggest that these structures delineated important spaces and expressed intangible beliefs.[1]

If our understanding of the sacred places of these prehistoric cultures is tantalisingly elusive, the evidence for the much later pagan religions encountered by the first Christians is equally shadowy. There are hints of nature worship in the place-names Hoff and Hofflunn, near Appleby, and Lund, near Kirkham, which may derive from Scandinavian words referring to sacred places: *hof* meaning a building used for assemblies and ritual feasts; *lundr* meaning 'sacred grove'. Such tentative interpretations hint at a lost landscape of the sacred, partly obliterated by and partly absorbed into Christianity. One of the clearest examples of the re-use of a pagan shrine for Christian worship comes from Bewcastle in the far north of Cumbria (Fig. 10.2). The Roman fort there appears to have been called *Fanum Coccidii*, 'the shrine of Coccidius', a native deity fused into the cult of Mars, and votive plaques to the god have been found on the site. It is possible that the memory of pagan worship lay behind the decision to plant a Christian church within the ramparts of the fort by the 8th century, marked by that masterpiece of Northumbrian sculpture, the Bewcastle cross.

MEDIEVAL PIETY

As in the rest of England, the pattern of places of worship at local level evolved over many centuries. The parochial framework, which carved the countryside into blocks of tithe-paying territory each assigned to a different parish church, was largely in place by 1300 and reflected processes of change from the late Roman period to the 13th century. The location of Christian sites in the Dark Age landscape is suggested by the place-name element *eccles*, derived from the

Celtic ancestor of the modern Welsh *eglwys*, 'a church'. The five *eccles* names in Lancashire, including the Ecclestons near Chorley, near St Helens and in the Fylde, as well as Eccles itself, perhaps imply the survival of an organised pattern of Romano-British churches in these areas, though no tangible remains survive. There are no certain *eccles* names in Cumbria, but there are hints of links with the British church in Galloway in the name of the arguably early religious site at Ninekirk ('Ninian's church'), near Penrith. The scale of the Celtic Christian survival remains an open question: circular churchyards are not necessarily, as is sometimes claimed, synonymous with Celtic sites; many of the dedications to Celtic saints (St Ninian, St Kentigern, St Patrick) may well have been given much later; and excavations on the site perhaps most likely to be a candidate for Celtic survival, St Patrick's Chapel at Heysham, yielded nothing to suggest the presence of a Christian site there before the 8th century.[2]

The first generation of Christian sites in the North West which can be securely identified in the modern landscape are the churches founded during the flowering of Christianity in the kingdom of Northumbria during the 7th to 9th centuries. Identifying such pre-Viking churches is based primarily on the survival of fragments of stone sculpture, but also on the place-name *kirkby* (Scandinavian 'church settlement'), which appears to record places where Scandinavian settlers encountered an existing church. Northumbrian sculpture of this period has been found at 17 churches in Cumbria, including several which were later at the centre of large parishes, such as Brigham and Kendal (formerly Kirkby Kendal), which may be comparable to the Anglo-Saxon minster churches of southern England. Not all pre-Viking sculpture comes from such 'mother church' sites, however: comparatively small parishes, such as Irton in west Cumbria (Fig. 10.3) or Heysham, Halton and Gressingham in north Lancashire also yield such evidence, suggesting an early origin for the parish church sites in those areas. Whether the churches on these sites in the 8th and 9th centuries were serving the pastoral needs of local communities or were small monastic communities remains unclear. Northumbrian monasteries are recorded in documentary sources at Dacre, founded about 727, and at Heversham, from which the community fled in the face of Viking attack in the early 10th century. Pre-Viking stone sculpture survives at both sites.[3]

To judge by the sculptural and place-name evidence, places of Christian worship proliferated during the Viking age, mirroring the great wave of church building by Anglo-Saxon thegns further south. In the North West, almost every medieval parish church site in west Cumbria has evidence of 10th- or 11th-century sculpture, including the masterpieces at Gosforth, which appear to draw on pagan Scandinavian mythology, perhaps in an attempt to draw parallels with themes in the Christian story. Further south, the crosses at Whalley, Bolton and the Manchester area, though less overtly Viking in conception, also date from this period, reinforcing the suggestion that this was a period of church planting. Place-names containing the Scandinavian element *kross* ('a cross'), such as Crosthwaite, Crosby and Croston, suggest the presence of preaching crosses, if not churches, while the name Ormskirk presumably records the Scandinavian name of the founder of one of the major parish churches in south-west Lancashire.

The pattern formed by the parish churches which had emerged by the 13th century, and continued to form the framework of religious provision at local level until the 19th century, was distinctively northern. Whereas in southern England the proliferation of parish churches between *c.* 950 and *c.* 1150 resulted in the provision of a separate parish church and priest for most rural communities, the distribution was much more patchy in the North West. Vast parishes survived, their boundaries sometimes embracing 20 or more separate townships, so that the lattice of parish boundaries was a very open one in most of the region (Fig. 10.4), though single-township parishes did exist, notably in the west Cumbrian coastal strip and in the Eden valley. Some parishes were huge: Whalley parish in east Lancashire

Fig. 10.3 The Irton cross: late Northumbrian sculpture of the early 9th century.

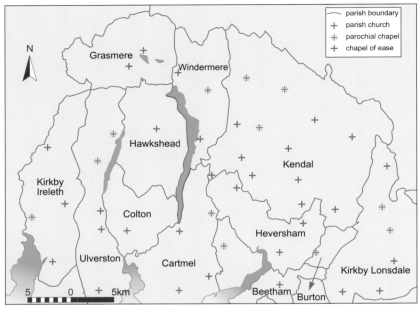

—	parish boundary
+	parish church
⊹	parochial chapel
+	chapel of ease

Fig. 10.4 Parishes in southern Cumbria before the 19th century. *There were even fewer parish churches in this area in the medieval centuries: Grasmere and Windermere separated from Kendal parish in the 14th century; Hawkshead (which, until 1676, included Colton) had been a detached part of Dalton in Furness parish.*

Fig. 10.5 St Michaels on Wyre. *Although a parish church almost certainly stood here in the 11th century (Domesday Book records a vill called 'Michelescherche'), today's church dates mainly from the late Middle Ages. The tower was probably built in the mid-16th century.*

encompassed 43,000ha (over 100,000 acres) and no fewer than 47 separate townships; Kendal parish embraced 25 townships and Kirkham parish 17 townships.

The result, in terms of buildings in the landscape, is that medieval parish churches are comparatively rare in the North West. They tend, moreover, to be sturdy, functional buildings with little of the conspicuous expenditure on chantry chapels, soaring spires and great towers found further south. Although many parish churches preserve evidence for the existence of a stone church from the 12th century, the footprint of the nave and tower dates typically from the 15th or even early 16th century, suggesting a surge of building activity by parish communities in the century before the Reformation. Only in the south of the region did this produce spacious, airy churches typical of the Perpendicular style, notably Sefton church (early 16th century) and the great collegiate church at Manchester (now the cathedral), built across a century from 1420. Further north, the typical parish churches are the long, low, late medieval buildings of the type seen at Bolton-by-Bowland, Churchtown, near Garstang, and Crosthwaite, near Keswick. Many have low, squat towers (Fig. 10.5) or even, particularly in Cumbria, only a humble bell-cote. Writing in 1687, Thomas Denton commented that the 'flatt square steeple' at Skelton, near Penrith, was 'a rare sight in this countrey, except in some few market towns.'[4] Indeed, some church towers in northern Cumbria appear to have had a defensive, rather than a purely religious function, acting as places of refuge in the face of Scottish raids. In 1375 it was reported that the tower of Wigton church had been crenellated without licence. Though it does not survive (Wigton church was rebuilt in 1788), towers without external doorways, with very small windows or with other evidence of defensive purpose, such as internal iron 'yetts', survive at Scaleby close to the border; Burgh-by-Sands and Newton Arlosh on the Carlisle plain; and at Great Salkeld and Ormside in the Eden valley.[5]

Another distinctive aspect of the medieval religious landscape of the North West was a consequence of the pattern of large, multi-township parishes. Distance from the parish church was overcome by building chapels of ease, churches without parochial status in which services were held for outlying communities. Such chapels were founded over many centuries, from the 12th to the 18th, and embraced a huge variety of both institutional arrangements and physical forms. At one end of the spectrum were the tiny, simple chapels in remote dales; at the other churches

which were parochial in all but name. Over time some chapels rose to become fully fledged parishes; others fell into disuse and disappeared.

By the 16th century, the more extensive ancient parishes generally contained one or more 'parochial chapels' – churches which had acquired burial rights and a share, at least, of the tithes from one or more townships within the parish, providing some formal endowment for a clergyman's living. The chapelry of Farnworth in Prescot parish, for example, covered the seven townships in the southern half of the parish. The chapel had been built by *c.* 1200 and operated as a separate parish by 1600, keeping its own registers and being managed by its own chapelwardens. Likewise, the chapel at Lorton (in Brigham parish), recorded from the 12th century, acted in effect as the parish church for five Lakeland townships, two of which (Buttermere and Wythop) possessed subsidiary chapels of ease. The chapel that gave its name to Church, near Accrington, fulfilled a similar function for the southern section of the huge parish of Whalley from the 13th century. Detached portions of vast parishes tended to operate as separate parochial chapelries: Goosnargh and Whittingham townships, detached parts of Kirkham parish, formed the chapelry of Goosnargh; Furness Fells, a detached section of Dalton in Furness parish in the Middle Ages, formed the chapelry of Hawkshead. After the disafforestation of the Pendle and Rossendale forests in 1507, new chapels were built to serve the growing populations of those areas, their comparatively recent origin being recorded in the names of the settlements which grew up around them: Newchurch in Pendle and Newchurch in Rossendale. On the ground, most of these parochial chapels appear similar to ancient parish churches: substantial structures, many of which (Hawkshead, Broughton near Preston, Goosnargh, Great Harwood, for example) display the squat, plain, 16th-century towers typical of northern churches.

At the opposite end of the spectrum are the simple chapels built to serve small, remote, rural communities. These include the typical dales chapels, built 'barn-wise', as bishop William Nicolson put it in the early 18th century – that is, as a simple rectangular structure with no distinction between nave and chancel (Fig. 10.6).[6] Their size reflects the size of the community they were built to serve; some, as at Wasdale Head, Buttermere and Chapel-le-Dale,

Fig. 10.6 Martindale old church: a humble chapel of ease in an upland dale; rebuilt in 1633.

are tiny. Served by readers, often local men with some learning, who supplemented a meagre stipend paid by their neighbours by teaching school in the chapel, such chapels may be thought of as expressions of religious 'self-help'. Some originated in medieval times, but many more are first recorded in the 16th and 17th centuries. They probably reflect a deliberate policy to encourage local communities to build their own chapels: the distance people had to travel to their parish church was cited as one of the problems Chester diocese faced in imposing ecclesiastical discipline in the 1560s.[7]

Parish churches and chapels of ease are not the only legacies of medieval piety in the region's landscape. Monastic houses, which in the North West were generally small and poor, formed islands of prayer, separate from the lives of local communities. Here members of religious orders distanced themselves from the secular world in an attempt to achieve an element of religious purity.

Fig. 10.7 Furness Abbey. The ruins of
this wealthy Cistercian house are the most
extensive in the region.

If hospitals, friaries and collegiate churches
are excluded, the number of houses totalled
12 in Cumbria, nine in Lancashire and one in
Yorkshire (west of the Pennine watershed).
Most orders sought retreat in some form
from ordinary society, but the more rigorous
Cistercians and Premonstratensians, whose
ideal was that monasteries should be built far
from human habitation, were particularly
attracted to the isolation offered by the
physical marginality of the North West. Five
Cistercian houses (Calder, Furness, Holm
Cultram, Sawley and Whalley) and two
Premonstratensian foundations (Cockersand
and Shap) chose deliberately remote
wilderness locations in the region. Furness
(Fig. 10.7), for example, was tucked away in
the 'vale of the deadly nightshade' at the end
of the insular Furness peninsula; Calder
hidden in a steep-sided valley on the edge of
the Lakeland fells; Holm Cultram on an
island of drier ground surrounded by peat
moss and marsh on the Solway plain;
Cockersand, 'standing veri blekely', as Leland
put it, pitting its community against the full
force of the wind from the sea.[8]

Almost all the monastic houses in the region
were founded during the 12th century (the
major exceptions are Whalley, to which a
community founded in Wirral in the 1170s moved in 1283, and Upholland, a
Benedictine priory founded in 1317–18). The poverty of many of the houses was
exacerbated by the troubles of the 14th century, but the surviving remains (and
the evidence for an increase in the numbers of monks at several houses) suggest a
resurgence of vigour in the century before the Dissolution, paralleling the rebuilding
of parish churches at this time. At Whalley the inner gateway and much of the
remains of the conventual buildings date from the late 15th century; at Furness the
east end of the church was rebuilt in the same period, the elaborate, canopied sedilia
expressing opulence and confidence; at Shap, Furness and Upholland great west
towers were built *c.* 1500; Holm Cultram gained its west porch and façade in 1507.[9]

This late flowering of monastic life was, of course, cut short by the Dissolution
in the 1530s. Only the ruins of Furness Abbey vie with the remains of the great
Yorkshire monasteries; in many cases survival of monastic sites has been minimal.
Most poignant, perhaps, are the remains of the Premonstratensian abbey at
Cockersand, on the coast south of Lancaster. Except for a few fragments of wall,
all that survives is the early 13th-century chapter house, perched right on the
edge of the low boulder-clay cliff. Cattle graze on one side, while on the other the
tide ebbs and flows across the sands of the Lune estuary. This incongruous
building is all that survives of a community living on the edge of the world.

One distinctive feature of the legacy of some monastic buildings in the North
West, however, is the retention of part, at least, of the monastic church to serve as
a parish church after the Dissolution. In each case where this occurred in
Cumbria the monks had acquired responsibility to provide pastoral care for the
parish in which their house lay, so that the monastic church or a chapel within it
also served the parish. In the Benedictine houses of Holm Cultram and St Bees
and the Augustinian priory of Lanercost, only the nave ultimately remained in
use, producing strangely truncated churches. Holm Cultram is shorn of its aisles;

at St Bees the chancel survives, but as part of the grammar school, founded in 1583; at Lanercost, choir, crossing and transepts remain as gaunt ruins beyond the altar in front of the blocked crossing arch, though in the 17th and early 18th centuries even the nave was roofless and only the north aisle was kept in repair for services (Fig. 10.8). At Upholland, near Wigan, the chancel of the priory was converted into a parish church. At Cartmel, however, the Augustinian priory church survives intact, partly as a result of continuity in the provision of pastoral care for the parish across the turbulent years of the Dissolution, and partly as a result of restoration by George Preston of Holker Hall in 1618.[10]

Fig. 10.8 Lanercost Priory, near Brampton. The nave of the former monastic church continues in use as a parish church, while the chancel and transepts stand roofless and ruined.

A SPECTRUM OF BELIEF

The majority of places of prayer in the North West date from the centuries since the Reformation and reflect a growing diversity of belief both within and, latterly, beyond the Christian tradition. Much of the post-medieval Anglican landscape of belief in the region was a response to the challenge of achieving religious provision in an environment in which parish churches were few and increasingly failed to reflect the distribution of population. One strategy was to elevate parochial chapels to the status of fully fledged parish churches. Hawkshead, for example, achieved full parochial rights in 1578 and its chapelry of Colton was hived off as a separate parish in 1676. As population grew in the industrialising areas of Lancashire, some of the larger parishes were effectively broken up as chapels gained parochial status. The parish of Croston, which had formerly covered 11 townships, was gradually dismembered, as Hoole became a separate parish in 1642, Chorley and Rufford in 1793 and Hesketh and Tarleton in 1821.[11]

Yet this could not keep pace with population growth and the shifting concentration of people towards the burgeoning industrial regions. Indeed, the rapid growth of Dissenting congregations in the late 18th century highlighted the deficiencies in religious provision by the Church of England. The Church Building Commission, established by act of Parliament in 1818, was granted one million pounds and charged with building 'additional churches in populous parishes'. Its contribution to Lancashire's ecclesiastical landscape was considerable: 19 Commissioners' churches were built in the county before 1830, and a further 62 between then and 1856. They were typically lofty, airy buildings in a generally restrained Gothic style, lit by tall lancet side windows, the interiors fitted with galleries to accommodate a large congregation (Fig. 10.9).[12] The middle decades of the 19th century also saw the rebuilding of many parish churches, including major medieval town churches, such as Preston St John (rebuilt 1853–5) and Bolton St Peter (1867–71). In the countryside, former chapels of ease were elevated to parochial status and replaced by unremarkable Victorian Gothic structures. As a result, many of the region's Anglican churches, both in town and country, are 19th-century buildings, planted in the landscape to reflect contemporary architectural fashions and lacking the regional distinctiveness of earlier churches.

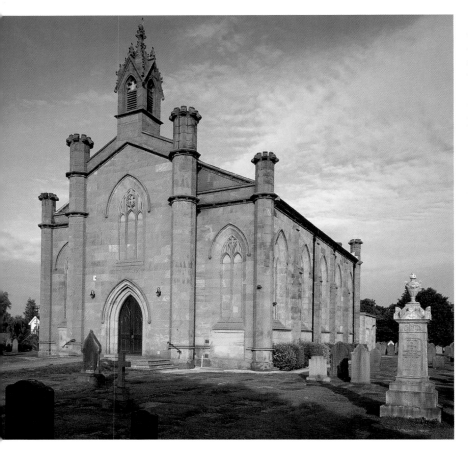

By the 19th century, the Anglican church could claim the allegiance of only a limited proportion of the region's population. A vigorous tradition of refusal to conform to the Church of England from the 16th century, combined with the proliferation of Dissenting congregations during the late 18th and 19th centuries, contributed a richness of religious diversity, which exhibits a striking geographical pattern in the landscape. By 1700 the region was renowned both as the bastion of Roman Catholic survival and as the home of significant concentrations of the Protestant Nonconformist sects which perpetuated the Puritan tradition. The Catholic stronghold was the lowland west of Lancashire, particularly in the Fylde and the south-west of the county, where the old religion was fostered by resident gentry families, religious conservatives, in whose manor houses mass was said and itinerant priests were protected. Roman Catholics were thinner on the ground in Cumbria and in the industrialising parts of south and east Lancashire. These regions, however, contained important pockets of

Fig. 10.9 A Commissioners' church: St John's Church, Burscough, built 1829–31 at a cost of £3,340 to serve the industrial community that had grown up beside the canal at Burscough Bridge.

Protestant Dissent. The textile areas, especially that around Manchester and Bolton, had a long history of Puritan preaching since the late 16th century. When Puritan ministers were ejected from their livings after the Restoration, they often took part of their parish with them, to form the nucleus of a Nonconformist congregation. Further north, in southern Cumbria, northern Lancashire and the far north-west of Yorkshire, a separatist 'Seeker' tradition provided fertile ground for the preaching of George Fox, the founder of Quakerism, in 1652. These areas, together with pockets further north in Cumbria, became an early spawning ground for Quakerism.[13]

The landscape legacy of early Dissent – chapels and meeting houses, some dating from before the Toleration Act of 1689 – reflects that geographical pattern. It also reflects the importance of chapels of ease in the region's religious history. Again and again, these are recorded as the meeting places of Puritan groups. The Westmorland Seekers used the isolated chapels on Firbank Fell and at Preston Patrick for their meetings in the early 1650s, for example. In Lancashire, Nonconformist ministers continued to preach in chapels of ease after being ejected from their livings: James Woods, Puritan minister of Atherton, near Leigh, continued to use the chapel at Chowbent after 1662 and the Dissenting congregation he founded was only dispossessed in 1721. At Elswick in the Fylde, the chapel of ease built *c.*1649 remained in Puritan hands after the Restoration and became the forerunner of the later Independent (now URC) church.[14]

Many of the early Presbyterian, Baptist and Independent chapels were in rural areas, often on the fringes of the parishes from which the Puritan ministers who founded them were ejected. Examples include the Presbyterian church at Penruddock, near Penrith (the present church, dating from *c.* 1789, replaced a chapel built before 1712), which traces its origins to the followers of Richard

Gilpin, the Puritan minister ejected from Greystoke; Tottlebank Baptist church, near Greenodd, an Independent congregation which had followed Gabriel Camelford after he was ejected from the chapel of ease at Staveley in Cartmel; and Rivington Unitarian chapel, built in 1702 for the congregation established by Samuel Newton, ejected from the chapel of ease at Rivington in 1662 (Fig. 10.10).[15]

The meeting houses of the Society of Friends form a distinctive element in the legacy of Dissent in the North West, particularly in the northern parts, where Quaker congregations became established in rural areas in the mid-17th century. They were often in isolated positions, sometimes close to the edge of a parish. A hostile witness, writing about the Cockermouth district in 1687, claimed that Quakerism was a product of distance from the parish church and the controlling hand of the clergy: at Broughton the inhabitants 'dwell so remote from any parish church that most of them, in the late troubles, turn'd Quaker', while at Mosser they were 'allmost all Quakers', being too close to Pardshaw Crag, where Quakers had met in the open air since the 1650s, and 'too far distant from any church.'[16] The resulting rural meeting houses from the late 17th and 18th centuries, such as those at Moorhouse, near Burgh-by-Sands, Pardshaw, near Cockermouth (Fig. 10.11), Mosedale, near Greystoke, Brigflatts, near Sedbergh, and Newton in Bowland, are simple, functional, vernacular buildings, reflecting the distinctive nature of Quaker theology and worship: they were not sacred spaces, but merely structures in which Friends could meet. Most exhibit common and distinctive features, reflecting a uniformity imposed by the sect's strict collective discipline in the 18th and early 19th centuries: windows set high to allow light to flood in but to prevent worshippers being distracted by a view outside; benches of a uniform design; a raised ministers' stand at one end of the room.[17]

The Evangelical Revival, the demographic upheaval of the second half of the 18th century and the gradual relaxation of the restrictions on Roman Catholic worship combined to transform the religious landscape in the century between 1750 and 1850. Many rural Quaker meetings faded away, but there was an explosion of life among other Protestant Dissenters. Meanwhile, the Catholic Relief Act of 1791 allowed Roman Catholics to register places of worship. At first their churches were retiring, unecclesiastical buildings, often in remote locations. With round-arched windows, they

BELOW: *Fig. 10.10 Rivington Unitarian chapel*, *dating from 1703.*

BOTTOM: *Fig. 10.11 Friends Meeting House, Pardshaw Hall*, *near Cockermouth; built 1729.*

resembled Nonconformist preaching boxes rather than sacred spaces in which the mystery of the Eucharist was celebrated. Early examples, tucked away in the countryside, are at Stidd (1789), near Ribchester (Fig. 10.12), Fernyhalgh (1792–4), near Preston, and Dodding Green (1791, replaced by a new church built 1835–7), near Kendal. As late as the 1830s many Roman Catholic churches still eschewed Gothic architecture, but confidence grew after Emancipation in 1829 and, particularly, after the restoration of Catholic dioceses in England in 1850. The ability of the Roman Catholic community to raise its head with pride is epitomised by St Walburge's church, which dominates the Preston skyline. Built between 1850 and 1854, this striking church consists of a vast, hall-like nave and a piercing, slender spire of white stone.[18]

Fig. 10.12 Roman Catholic chapel, Stidd, *near Ribchester, built 1789.*

Fig. 10.13 Penrith Methodist church, *built 1873.*

The century after 1750 also saw an explosion in the number of Protestant Nonconformist chapels, notably in towns and industrial settlements. The evangelical revival spawned a proliferation of sects, separated in many cases by hair-splitting doctrinal differences. The major influence was that of Methodism (which itself fragmented into several, separate 'connexions'), while parts of the North West also proved to be fertile ground for some of the smaller, new, Nonconformist groups. The Inghamites, followers of Wesley's former associate, Benjamin Ingham, gained a following in the Colne area: their chapel at Wheatley Lane, near Barrowford, built between 1747 and 1750, is the earliest in the country. In some of the larger towns almost all of these different denominations were represented by chapels.

Perhaps the main theme in the development of Nonconformist chapels at this time is the growth of confidence and wealth, which is expressed in the buildings themselves in towns large and small. In the Lancashire mill towns the wealth of Nonconformist industrialists contributed to the increasing scale of dissenting churches. Textile masters, bankers and engineers contributed two-thirds of the finance for church-building in Lancashire between 1840 and 1875, though this included contributions to Anglican churches. The Whitehead brothers, mill owners in Rossendale, financed two fine Classical Methodist chapels in Rawtenstall: first the Longholme chapel, built in 1842, and then, after they and others had seceded from the Longholme congregation, the even more solid and sumptuous United Methodist church in Haslingden Road, built 1855–7. Even a small market town such as Penrith can boast ambitious Nonconformist chapels, built in fashionable streets laid out in the mid-19th century on the hillside to the east of the town. The boldest of these, the proud, imposing Wesleyan Methodist church in Italianate style (built 1873) (Fig. 10.13), replaced a humble, late-Georgian preaching box at Sandgate Head, dating from 1815. Though Nonconformist denominations eschewed the Gothic style with its Catholic associations, elements of 'churchiness' had crept in by the late 19th century, especially among the Congregationalists. The former Congregational church at Stonewell, Lancaster (1879–81) and the URC church at Elswick in the Fylde (1873–4), for example, are both Gothic, steepled structures, almost indistinguishable from Anglican parish churches.[19]

Despite the strong ebb tide in religious observance in the increasingly secular society of the 20th century, some of the most eye-catching expressions of faith in the landscape of the North West date from this period. Two great modern cathedrals dominate the Liverpool skyline. The massive and cavernous Anglican cathedral by Sir Giles Gilbert Scott, constructed in sandstone between 1904 and 1978, is often said to be the last great Gothic church in England (Fig. 10.14). It makes a striking contrast to the circular 'wigwam' in concrete and glass of Sir Frederick Gibberd's Roman Catholic cathedral, consecrated in 1967.[20]

But it is the synagogues, mosques and temples of other religious traditions, reflecting the region's increasingly multi-cultural mix, which constitute the most striking recent layer in the religious landscape of the North West. The 19th century saw a proliferation of non-Christian places of worship: Liverpool could boast Jewish synagogues (from 1807), one of the first mosques in the country, the Muslim Institute (founded 1889) and a 'Temple of Humanity' of the atheist Positivists, for example. Particularly significant are the synagogues of Manchester's Jewish community. The most striking surviving Victorian example is the Spanish & Portuguese synagogue in Cheetham, built in 1873–4 (Fig. 10.15). Moorish

Fig. 10.14 Liverpool's Anglican Cathedral *from the air. The last great Gothic building in England towers over the city centre.*

Fig. 10.15 Spanish & Portuguese Synagogue, Manchester, *built in 1874.*

GRAVESTONES

Churchyards and cemeteries are evocative places, where silent tombstones give glimpses of lives long past. Rare before the late 17th century, and only becoming numerous from the decades either side of 1800, grave markers shed light on not only the social and economic history of a locality, but also on changing attitudes to death and commemoration. Gravestones in the North West tend to be plain and unadorned, lacking the rich tradition of symbolism in Scottish graveyards, for example. However, as the four tombstones illustrated here demonstrate, they can be vivid historical records, capturing in stone aspects of the local history of their communities.

Where a parish churchyard contains gravestones from the 17th century, they usually take the form of flat ledgers, carrying an inscription in raised letters. An unusually finely decorated one (its letters incised rather than raised) is that at Colne, marking the grave of the family of Barnard Sutcliffe, a yeoman of Lower Fulshaw, Barrowford (right). The panel is flanked by winged souls ('cherubs') symbolising the flight of the soul into immortal life. As well as recording the burial of Anne, Barnard Sutcliffe's wife, in 1671, and that of Barnard himself three years later, the stone carries at the foot of the main panel the initials of Grace Sutcliffe, his infant daughter who died in September 1673.

The fine slate tombstone to Joseph Dover (d. 1810) at Crosthwaite church (opposite page, top) both exudes confidence in an after-life and makes a statement of social and economic status. The Dover family were members of the local Keswick elite, their wealth deriving from the rural woollen

mills. Daniel Dover commissioned this stone from William Bromley, a member of a Keswick dynasty of stonemasons, whose memorials in the local Skiddaw Slate reached high levels of artistic achievement. The detail of the carving on the Dover memorial is outstanding and is used here to make a statement of faith in immortality: Hope personified (reclining against the anchor which was her symbol) is flanked by the Lamb of God and the dove bearing the olive branch.

The memorial to Tommy Dobson (d. 1910), the huntsman, at St Catherine's church in Eskdale (opposite page, bottom left) stands in marked contrast: the imagery is bold and wholly secular. It is a monument to a local character, put up (in effect) by public subscription ('erected by nearly 300 friends from all parts of the country'). Dobson, a bobbin turner, founded the Eskdale and Ennerdale hunt in 1857 and was master for over half a century. The memorial is a craggy, rough-hewn block of granite, into which has been sculpted a cameo portrait of the huntsman, and from the face of which emerges a scrolled testimonial flanked by the heads of fox and hound and the symbols of the hunt (horn, whip and fox's brush).

Behind the headstone marking the grave of Juliusz F. Mühler (d. 1957) in Lancaster Moor Cemetery (opposite page, bottom right) lies the story of Polish migration to north Lancashire. A close-knit Polish community grew up in Lancaster after the Second World War, some of whom had come to England as part of the army of Polish exiles led by General Wladyslaw Anders. In pride of place, immediately below his name, the stone records that Mühler had been a captain in the Second Corps of that army, which fought alongside the British army in Italy. In a single line, this modern tombstone in a town cemetery provides a reminder that the lives of many new arrivals link the North West to distant places and to the great upheavals of the 20th century.[22]

JOSEPH DOVER Woollen Manufacturer KESWICK, WHO died on the 24ᵗʰ of Sept. 1810 aged 85 years.
Also of E S T H E R his Wife.
who died on the 21ˢᵗ of June 1797 aged 70 years.
Also of Sarah their Daughter who died July the 18ᵗʰ 1768.

Fig. 10.16 Ghosia Jamia Mosque, Nelson: a striking new landmark in the urban landscape, reflecting the growing confidence of the Asian community in east Lancashire.

horseshoe arches and other elements of Islamic-inspired decoration, harking back to the Sephardic Jews' Iberian roots, ensure that it cannot be mistaken for a church. Eastern models inspired other Manchester synagogues, notably the mosque-like South Manchester Synagogue in Fallowfield (built 1912–13), domed and with a minaret-like tower.[21]

The late-20th century saw an increasingly rich array of places of worship in the industrial towns, as ethnic diversity was reflected in a broadening spectrum of faiths. In particular, the growing prosperity and confidence of the Asian community in the textile towns have been expressed in the construction of mosques and Hindu temples. The celebration of eastern faiths increasingly brightens industrial Lancashire with gleaming white minarets and pinnacles and bright colours (Fig. 10.16). In one instance a modern, non-Christian religious community has re-occupied the site of a medieval monastery. The Gothic mansion on the site of Conishead Priory, near Ulverston (a house of Augustinian canons, founded *c.* 1180), became the home of a Tibetan Buddhist community in 1976. In the grounds stands the Kadampa temple, built 1995–7, a light and airy pavilion dedicated to 'the peace and harmony of all living beings'. Like the mosques and Hindu temples of urban Lancashire, this expression of the ideals of an ancient eastern religion is one of the newest manifestations of space dedicated to prayer in the region's landscape.

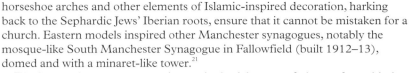

NOTES

1   Higham 1986, 64–74; 107–10

2   Higham 1986, 274–7; Kenyon 1991, 95–7; Potter & Andrews 1994

3   Bailey & Cramp 1988, 2, 10–11

4   Denton 2003, 295

5   Perriam & Robinson 1998, 21, 29, 62–3, 85, 203, 299

6   Ferguson 1877, 109

7   Bouch 1948, 223–4

8   Toulmin Smith 1906–10, IV, 10; Knowles & Hadcock 1971, 117, 119–20, 125, 128, 187, 191; Higham 2004, 203–15

9   Pevsner 1967, 57–8, 287; Harrison *et al.* 1998

10 Summerson & Harrison 2000, 43–59; Pevsner 1967, 57–8, 183; VCH Lancs. VIII, 259, 263

11 *VCH Lancs.* VI, 81; VIII, 374, 386

12 Pevsner 1969a, 29–31; 1969b, 28–9

13 Watts 1978, 509

14 Stell 1994, 72, 75–7, 94

15 Stell 1994, 137–9, 181; Sunderland nd; Colligan 1905

16 Denton 2003, 121, 150.

17 Butler 1999, 888–906

18 Pevsner 1969b, 77, 199–200, 239; Sister Agnes 1949, 56, 65–6

19 Morris 1989, 446; Champness 1989, 122; Pevsner 1967, 174–5; 1969b, 118, 155–6

20 Sharples 2004, 73–90

21 Kadish 2003

22 *The [Morecambe] Visitor*, 15 Oct. 2003, 48

11

The Quest for Utopia

In Chapter 8 we saw how towns and cities of the industrial age were often afflicted by severe social and environmental problems, which developed in the context of unplanned and uncontrolled growth. This 'free for all' was not inevitable, for the principles of good urban design were known and had been tested in practice, but there was no administrative system to accommodate the notion of planning, and no collective will to adopt a principle that so clearly contradicted the prevailing philosophy of *laissez faire* capitalism. Only those individuals or groups with a particular sense of purpose – self-interested or altruistic, sometimes both – sponsored orderly development. For centuries there had been some who, confronted by the disagreeable aspects of the world or the manifest injustices of society, envisaged ideal communities. Now, among social reformers and philosophical dreamers, the increasingly obvious and ubiquitous failings of urban living prompted a new wave of utopianism, where rational design of the landscape was regarded as integral with a carefully structured form for society itself. Others saw more practical reasons for creating planned communities, in which social ambition (while rarely absent) was secondary to more pragmatic motives of economic efficiency or the prosaic provision of simple, decent accommodation.

IDEAL COMMUNITIES

True ideal communities, in which townscape and architecture accorded with coherent social and cultural aims, remained exceptional.[1] Perhaps the finest example in the region is the Moravian settlement at Fairfield, now surrounded by a sprawl of inner suburban housing on the eastern side of Manchester (Fig. 11.1). It was built amid the fields after 1779, the last of seven villages developed by the Church of the

Fig. 11.1 The Square, Fairfield, Manchester: an oasis of tranquillity amid the suburban sprawl of east Manchester, the Moravian settlement retains, to a remarkable degree, an air of solid bourgeois prosperity derived from its central European ancestry.

United Brethren, a Protestant sect which had fled religious persecution in Moravia. The settlement was planned around a gracious central square, with tree-lined streets and solid brick housing which reflects an image of central European bourgeois prosperity: Herrnhut in Germany provided the model. Only church members could live there and the almost timeless tranquillity of the village contrasts sharply with its modern surroundings. It had its own farms, inn, shops, workshops, school and chapel, forming an entirely self-contained, inward-looking community, developed in the context of freedom of worship yet imbued with religious exclusivity.

Other communities originated, like Fairfield, in the specialised aims of particular groups. For instance, the national land societies which flourished in the 1850s sought to influence voting patterns in county constituencies by selling freehold plots (which enfranchised the owners) to would-be Liberal voters. Lancashire has several examples, including Freehold at Chadderton; the Freehold estate in Lancaster; and the Freehold Park estate at Fulwood, in north Preston. At the last, 343 plots were laid out along the gently winding tree-lined Victoria Road, Higher Bank Road and Lower Bank Road – a perfect image of Victorian suburbia, but one which originated in the pragmatic political strategies of the reforming classes of the 1850s.[2] Two generations later, the devastating emotional and physical impact of the First World War produced a fresh wave of optimistic schemes. In 1918, for example, the Lancaster industrialist Herbert Storey gave the house and estate of his late father, Sir Thomas, to develop a village for disabled ex-servicemen and their families. The project, which was to serve both as a commemoration of Sir Thomas and as a memorial to the dead of the Great War, was funded largely from local subscriptions. The Westfield Memorial Village, which opened in 1924, had 35 cottages in an attractively landscaped setting, the work of Thomas Mawson, the Lancaster architect and garden designer.[3]

The massive mental institutions of the 19th century also had utopian origins, in new and idealistic mid-Victorian philosophies of treating mental patients under regimes which were humanitarian, at least in principle, and involved 'useful' work for the able-bodied. Fundamental to these aims was strict segregation from the rest of society. The great public asylums therefore constituted enclosed worlds of their own, planned according to rational design principles, surrounded by woods, a home farm, gardens and recreational areas, and including chapels, graveyards, staff housing and, in many cases, private gasworks and sewage farms. While this might not immediately seem utopian, it was the product of careful and considered thinking by reformers anxious to protect the mentally ill from the jeering public exposure, overt brutality and casual neglect which had so often been their lot.

Classic examples of such developments in the North West included Lancashire's Whittingham Hospital near Longridge (1874), which had its own private railway branch (Fig. 11.2); the huge Prestwich asylum (1851), where in 1900 there were 2,600 resident patients and over 300 staff; and the earliest, Lancaster Moor (opened in 1816), which in the mid-20th century covered 237ha (587 acres), had three farms and accommodated almost 3,000 patients. In the Ribble valley the Lancashire Inebriates Reformatory was opened at Langho in 1904 to accommodate alcoholic women. It became a mental institution in 1920, and in the 1930s was remodelled on the 'working colony' principle, attractively laid out as a village with curving roads and greens on a high spur within a meander of the Ribble. When the philosophy of mental health care changed radically in the late 20th century, the attractive landscaping, seclusion and splendid Victorian architecture of such asylums were enticing to the developers of select private housing schemes.[4]

Benevolent paternalism

In the late 18th century, social idealism was not a hallmark of most landowners and industrialists. Since the outlay on building to high standards and providing amenities for workers could not be directly recouped, expenditure beyond that

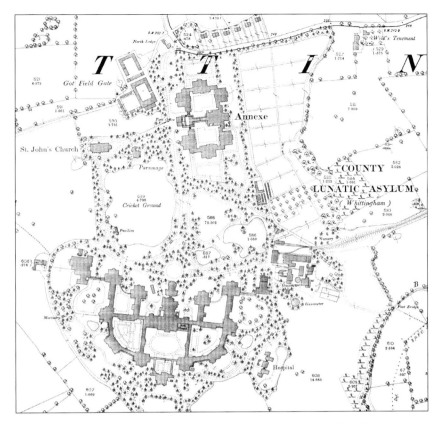

Fig. 11.2 The Lancashire County Lunatic Asylum at Whittingham, between Longridge and Preston, was designed and built in the last quarter of the 19th century as a completely self-contained community. The very generous and imaginative landscaping and monumental buildings are evident from this 1893 plan, which shows the railway station, hospital, gasworks, church and sports facilities.

immediately connected with the business or the estate was usually ruled out. Nevertheless, some made genuine efforts to build decent accommodation for their workers (*see* pp. 194–5), acknowledging that, if nothing else, a healthy and well housed workforce was likely to be more loyal, productive and reliable. Others acted with paternal benevolence, concerned to improve the spiritual and cultural welfare of their employees. Thus, in the Brookhouse area of Blackburn, where a self-contained industrial colony was developed between 1825 and 1845, William Henry Hornby, an immensely wealthy mill owner, paid most of the costs of Brookhouse School (1839, with his crest over the door) for the children of mill workers. He also built Brookhouse Gymnasium, a remarkable though short-lived attempt to provide for workers' recreational and leisure needs. The real problem was that they had no leisure.[5]

In the later 19th century utopian visions, occasionally combined with a vaguely socialist agenda, produced a variety of more coherent principles for urban and community design, as well as a range of practical schemes for their fulfilment. The most famous was Port Sunlight, developed after 1888 by William Hesketh Lever, perhaps the greatest of Victorian industrialists. Using an unpromising area of scrub and marsh near the Mersey shore, he created one of the most enduringly attractive model villages in the world. The community has been described as the product of 'an oppressively paternalistic regime',[6] but its laudable aims included low-cost, high-quality housing for the workers, set in immaculately landscaped surroundings and with a range of social, cultural and community facilities, which even now would be the envy of many a larger town. Much visited by royalty, town planning experts and fellow-industrialists, Port Sunlight made an exceptional contribution not only to images of urban utopia, but also to the philosophy of town planning as it evolved during the late 19th century (Fig. 11.3). It was a formative influence upon the infant Garden City

movement, and thus fed the principles that guided the development of inter-war council estates and post-war new town schemes. Several important early garden city schemes emerged in the region after 1900,[7] among them Vickerstown on Walney Island (Fig. 11.4), built by the Vickers shipbuilding company and including shops, a church, institute, public house and school; Pilkington's Ravenhead Garden Suburb at St Helens (1905), with 500 cottages for workers; and a series of private garden villages in south Lancashire, such as Hollins Green near Warrington (1906–13), Broad Green Garden Suburb

Fig. 11.3 Port Sunlight: the revolutionary nature of this planned ideal community is still impressive, a century and a quarter after it was designed. The lavish amount of open space, meticulously structured layout, and provision of amenities distinguish it from anything that had gone before – and most of what came after. The Lady Lever Art Gallery, cultural heart of the project, is at the centre of this view.

(Liverpool, 1906), Alkrington Garden Village at Middleton; and Burnage Garden Village at Manchester, a 136-house scheme with a recreation area and a community 'pavilion', run by a co-operative partnership. Some schemes involved a similar element of communal management, while others were private speculations as at Chorltonville (Manchester). Here the 15ha (36-acre) garden suburb of winding streets and 'black and white villas' was described as 'an attempt to solve the housing problem of a great city … sunshine and fresh air have been the main considerations in the erection of the houses'.[8]

Exceptionally, some landowners and industrialists had sought to control the development of entire towns. They followed the much earlier example of the Lowthers at Whitehaven, where a meticulously planned new town had been developed between 1660 and 1710, each building being constructed according to strict architectural and social policies drawn up by the estate. The earls of Stamford had ambitious plans for expanding their small market town of Ashton-under-Lyne. Between 1787 and 1803, and again in the 1820s, a geometric pattern of wide

Fig. 11.4 Vickerstown, Walney Island: the company suburb, conceived as a garden city project, is at the western (left) end of the bridge, close to unreclaimed saltmarshes and the remains of the medieval strip fields of Biggar. On the mainland are the planned town of Barrow, with its shipyards and docks, and modern industrial estates (left centre) on the site of the Hindpool ironworks.

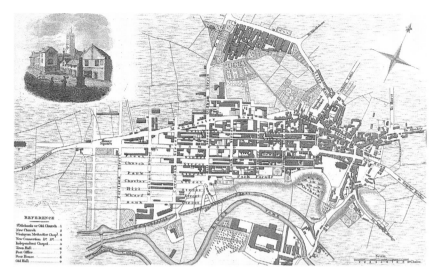

Fig. 11.5 Ashton under Lyne in 1825: the strict geometry of the ambitious planned town of the late 18th century and early 1820s contrasts with the informal and irregular layout of the small medieval market town.

BELOW: *Fig. 11.6 Hamilton Square, Birkenhead (north end of the west side, Mortimer Street corner): following recent restoration after decades of neglect, the impressive architecture and spacious elegance of Hamilton Square are once more apparent. The architect, James Gillespie Graham, had been closely involved with later phases of the Edinburgh New Town and the resemblance between the two projects is clear.*

streets was laid out, linking squares and circuses and with a new church at the western end of the main axis. Building progressed half-heartedly and ultimately the ambition failed because, as Ashton became a major cotton town, the dirty industrial atmosphere did not appeal to those of social standing (Fig. 11.5). A similar fate awaited Birkenhead, where in the late 1830s William Laird, owner of the shipyards that gave it birth, adopted a town plan based on high-class residential areas around Hamilton Square and the outstanding landscape of Birkenhead Park. The vision, which owed much to the New Town of Edinburgh, Laird's birthplace, failed because exceptionally rapid growth outstripped the design, but it was a praiseworthy attempt to build a working town free of contemporary ills (Fig. 11.6).

The vision also faded at Barrow in Furness, created after 1856 under the auspices of the Furness Railway and its megalomaniac general manager, James Ramsden. He envisaged a mighty industrial town and oversaw the building of a planned community with a grid of exceptionally wide streets and with tenement housing on the Scottish model: tall sandstone blocks which added a monumental quality to the growing town. Nevertheless essential amenities were overlooked and the impetus towards careful planning soon waned, because such strategies cost money and were difficult to implement once the initial enthusiasm evaporated. The provision of sewers lagged well behind the construction of housing, and the shopping centre was seriously inadequate. There were no parks, and later dwellings were congested terraced properties without gardens.

OPPOSITE PAGE:

TOP: *Fig. 11.7 Norris Green, Liverpool,* *showing the striking geometric patterns of* *circles and radial roads in the huge municipal* *housing estates, and the broad boulevard routes* *that were designed to incorporate express* *tramways along the central reservation. The* *majority of these estates were developed in the* *interwar period and the early 1950s, though the* *planning concepts predated the First World War.*

BOTTOM: *Fig. 11.8 Land Settlement* *Association smallholding at Dalston,* *near Carlisle. Three estates, at Crofton,* *Broadwath and Dalston, were divided into* *smallholdings in the 1930s, under a* *government-sponsored scheme to provide land* *for the unemployed. The smallholding houses* *with their mansard roofs are a distinctive* *feature of the landscape to the south of Carlisle.*

IMPROVING WORKERS' HOUSING

The story of the collapse of the traditional industries is often told and this is not the place to repeat that sorry tale. Rather, we may consider the physical impact of decline and how attempts to meet the challenge of high unemployment had important consequences for landscape change. None of the old-established industries in the North West escaped. By 1995 coal-mining, with the exception of a few short-term opencasting schemes, had ended; shipbuilding, once central to the economies of Birkenhead and Barrow, was a shrunken remnant; heavy engineering had experienced a succession of major plant closures; the iron and steel industry just held on at Workington but had vanished everywhere else; and the greatest industry, textiles, had dwindled to a shadow. Equally serious, perhaps, was the growing uncertainty over those industries which in the 1940s and 1950s seemed to be the salvation of areas hard-hit by earlier industrial failure – aerospace, vehicle manufacturing and defence were all witnessing plant closures. Long-term promises of stability were no more.

By the beginning of the 20th century, the acute housing problems of the region were at last being tackled. Most local authorities were contemplating direct intervention and some had started modest programmes of slum clearance and new building. Britain's first council houses were built by Liverpool Corporation in 1869 and, for example, Salford Corporation built 701 houses between 1894 and 1914, mostly on cleared sites close to the centre since the borough had little undeveloped land.[9] Some authorities envisaged schemes that went beyond simple 'demolish and rebuild' projects and involved a measure of social policy. Thus, Manchester Corporation's Blackley estate (1902) had high-quality housing, shops and community facilities planned around open spaces, and was a pioneering forerunner of the much larger inter-war schemes.

Since the First World War governments have been major determinants of housing and planning policy. Crucially, between 1918 and the early 1970s, they promoted the housing role of local authorities, a key dimension to the remodelling of urban north-west England. In the optimistic years after 1945 the harsh realities of poor housing, obsolete infrastructure and environmental degradation stimulated policies founded on utopian, and in retrospect often naïve, visions of the future. The apparently irrefutable logic of social and economic theory, founded on the wisdom of experts, would produce infallible solutions. The population would participate willingly, confident that these policies were designed for their benefit by those who knew best. In practice, of course, the benefits often proved elusive and illusory, the solutions generated a new range of problems and the supposed beneficiaries soon demonstrated their antagonism – but there had been a vision. As one early exponent of wholesale urban renewal wrote,

> *Let us hope that [Manchester] will continue her great task of rebuilding the* *city with … energy and vision. Let us hope that we shall have in fifty* *years' time a fine, spacious, and well-planned residential area where the* *slum belt now lies; and that our … satellite garden towns will be models for* *the whole world.*[10]

Characteristically, the projects of the late 1920s and 1930s involved selective clearance of the worst housing, normally dating from before 1870. Replacement housing was built near the edge of the town or, less often, on the site of the cleared dwellings. For example, at Lancaster 10 peripheral estates were built before the Second World War, housing residents displaced by clearance of the picturesque, historic, overcrowded and insanitary courts in the town centre. Preston Corporation constructed 2,847 houses in 1918–39 (twice the number of private houses in the period), most of them semi-detached or in short terraces and mainly in relatively low-density estates, modelled on garden city principles, east and south of the

Victorian town where undeveloped land could be bought at a modest price. Council housing was a key element in reshaping not only Preston's townscape, but also the lives of many of its inhabitants. The most ambitious programmes, not unexpectedly, were those of Manchester and Liverpool. In just 15 years from 1919, Liverpool Corporation built over 22,000 dwellings, of which 96 per cent were in the suburbs. They housed 120,000 people, roughly one-eighth of the city's total population, mostly in low-density estates (such as Norris Green, Clubmoor and Page Moss) which were served by new fast tramway routes along the central reservations of arterial roads (Fig. 11.7). There was, however, a harbinger of the future in the central slum clearance areas where, as redevelopment gathered pace in the later 1930s, five-storey blocks of flats were constructed.[11]

In the countryside, the plight of jobless and emotionally scarred ex-servicemen, and the long-term unemployment of the late 1920s and early 1930s, encouraged 'back to the land' movements. Lancashire County Council was an active supporter of the smallholdings movement before 1914, with 15 schemes accommodating 126 families. After 1918 the programme was extended and a further 121 smallholdings were provided. At Hutton near Preston, for example, 69 holdings were established on 525ha (1,300 acres) of farmland which had been part of the Rawstorne estate, sold and broken up in 1915. The Land Settlement Association (1935), a government-supported national organisation, sponsored three substantial smallholding schemes in Cumberland, at Dalston, Broadwath and Crofton, south of Carlisle (Fig. 11.8). As social and economic experiments these schemes were failures, but their legacy remains today in the distinctive landscape of small bungalows or cottages regularly spaced along country lanes and frequently using then-innovative materials such as ferro-concrete.[12]

In the late 1940s housing policy emerged as a central element in

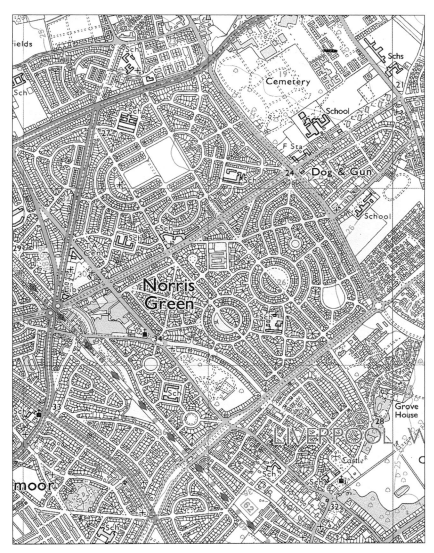

Fig. 11.9 Hulme, Manchester. *This inner city district was razed in 1966–70 and redeveloped with tower blocks and six quarter-mile long crescents of deck-access flats. The scheme was a disaster, socially and architecturally, and in 1991–5 most of it was demolished. This view shows the remaining refurbished tower blocks, with new housing (1997–2005) built around rear parking courts and back gardens. The parkland areas are a legacy of the post-1970 design, but in the new scheme the emphasis is upon private rather than public or communal space.*

regional and local planning strategies. During the 1950s the definition of 'slum' was widened to embrace most Victorian housing in working-class areas, which brought post-1870 byelaw housing within the scope of clearance policies. Since such housing was not in pockets but covered extensive districts around the centre of all larger towns, comprehensive redevelopment, rather than individual clearance schemes, became general. Strategies were devised to cope with the huge displacement of population, as it was rarely possible for more than a minority of residents to stay in the area where they lived. Massive relocation of people was integral to the principle and reality of these policies. The replacement housing could be in peripheral estates; in new and expanded towns elsewhere in the region; or in redevelopment projects built within the cleared areas.

In all these, the utopian vision was paramount. The physical deficiencies of old housing and industrial towns would be swept away; the new housing was to exemplify the best of contemporary architecture and construction methods; and new communities would emerge, which were socially mixed and brimming with opportunity. Central government constantly pressed local authorities to implement such plans, but at the same time imposed its own solutions to the nagging question of expense: industrialised and prefabricated building systems were claimed to be cheaper and more efficient; the construction of tower blocks and multi-decked flats allegedly saved land yet re-created communities 'in the sky'; and compulsory purchase overcame the thorny issue of growing public hostility. It was a truism that the architects, planners and council officers who pushed through these schemes would never contemplate living in such places themselves (Fig. 11.9).

Hardly a town escaped. In places such as Oldham swathes of densely populated and closely built land encircling the central area were flattened, while even larger tracts of farmland on the outskirts disappeared beneath new housing projects. Oldham Council demolished almost 13,600 houses between 1945 and 1974, the peak year being 1968 when 1,200 were cleared. Everywhere, inner city communities of small terraced houses were replaced by concrete flats. At Lark Hill, on the north-east edge of central Blackburn, where the comprehensive redevelopment scheme completed in 1965 centred on three 14-storey tower blocks set in grassed areas, the surviving terraced streets nearby seemed to huddle in their shadow. People were often moved long distances, particularly when local authorities elsewhere in the region signed agreements, under the 'expanded towns' policy, to take 'decanted' population (the impersonality of the term tells its tale) in the hope of reviving their own fortunes. Many residents of Harpurhey and Crumpsall in north Manchester were thus relocated to Darn Hill in the declining borough of Heywood, where 17-storey blocks of flats were built at the edge of town. The new council estates on the fringes frequently involved those experimental and (as it proved) costly construction methods which the government advocated. In 1955 Sholver, 5km

(3 miles) from central Oldham on the Halifax road, was described as 'on the hills above [a] forest of chimney stacks … the plan of the hamlet has probably changed little since the early Middle Ages [and] the cottages and barns are still grouped round a wide central green'.[13] Ten years later, Oldham Corporation began work on a massive new housing scheme there, with 1,780 flats, mostly in concrete blocks on the 'deck' principle. By 1970 the medieval landscape had vanished. Significantly, by 1995 the concrete flats had also vanished, demolished because they were unsafe, deeply unpopular and completely unlettable. Between 1986 and 1999 Oldham alone either pulled down, or gave away to developers for redevelopment, more than 4,000 of its 28,000 council dwellings.[14]

OUT OF TOWN UTOPIAS

The idea of decentralising population to entirely new communities was first put into practical effect by Manchester Corporation. It acknowledged that in order to pursue its slum clearance programme it needed a large number of new council houses, but had almost no undeveloped land within its boundaries. In 1931, therefore, it acquired 3,000 acres of land in north Cheshire and began to build the garden city of Wythenshawe, the most ambitious housing project ever undertaken by a British local authority. It was designed to avoid the problems that were already being identified in peripheral council estates, so shops, schools, a hospital and entertainment facilities were included from the outset, and extensive provision was made for employment in new trading estates. The development was carefully planned with a variety of housing styles and sizes and serious attention to landscaping, and was implemented with astonishing speed. In 1939 the population was already 40,000 and over 8,000 houses had been built. Today this 'city set in a vast woody garden' is home to 150,000 people (Fig. 11.10).[15]

Wythenshawe was the largest of Britain's inter-war garden city schemes, and after 1945 became one of the models on which the new towns strategy was based. The creation of ideal communities, in attractive places, with efficient layouts and good design, was central to government planning policies for 30 years from 1946. The intention was to avoid the glaring mistakes that had recently been made at, for example, Kirkby, where the population grew from 3,000 in 1951 to 52,000 a decade later, as what amounted to a vast council estate, almost entirely occupied by people moved out from Liverpool, was built with minimal facilities and a heavy reliance on tower blocks and walk-up flats. In the North West the first new town was Skelmersdale (1962), intended to revitalise the depressed and environmentally degraded mining area west of Wigan, and to act as a focus for

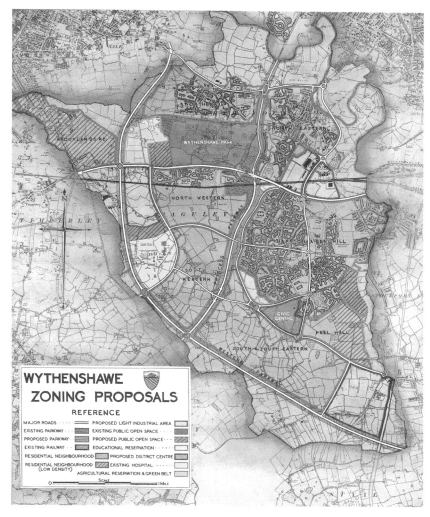

Fig. 11.10 The master plan for Wythenshawe, *from the City of Manchester Plan of 1945 (Nicholas 1945): the plan clearly shows the 10 self-contained neighbourhood units, separated by parkways and expressways and edged with open spaces and green belts, which were fundamental to the design. These planning principles were themselves derived from the Garden City philosophies of the early 20th century.*

Fig. 11.11 Skelmersdale from the slopes of Ashurst Beacon: *the new town was developed on flat ground below the wooded slopes of the Beacon. These are now intensively-used open parkland, still retaining earlier landscape features such as medieval field boundaries.*

overspill population from Merseyside. It was followed by Warrington and Runcorn, which were expansions of existing centres – in the case of Warrington, the economic difficulties and extensive areas of derelict land resulting from the closure of the wartime munitions factories on Risley Moss were the 'negative' reason for the choice of location, and the outstanding potential of a motorway crossroads the positive one. Finally, the Central Lancashire New Town was designated in 1970. It was expected to be the largest in size and population of any British new town, welding three large separate towns – Preston, Leyland and Chorley – into a single city of half a million people.

The varied fate of these towns is illuminating. Skelmersdale never achieved its full promise and acquired an unenviable reputation as one of the least successful new towns. It was designed for the car, with an elaborate road system occupying 12 per cent of the total area, yet had one of the lowest levels of car ownership in Britain, while the industrial areas were slow to grow and factory closures were a recurring problem (Fig. 11.11). In contrast, Warrington, with a strong economic base on which to build, was an outstanding success, growing from 130,000 people in 1971 to almost 200,000 today. Its landscape has been transformed, with extensive new residential areas south of the Mersey and east and west of the old borough. There are numerous peripheral employment centres, with little conventional industry but conspicuously successful office parks, high technology enterprises and large retail parks.[16] The Central Lancashire project was less than half finished when, in the early 1980s, new towns fell out of favour. The masterplan was partly implemented, with new roads constructed around the northern and southern sides of Preston, and with a great deal of new housing there and close to the industrial parks, warehousing and edge-of-town retailing at Fulwood and Bamber Bridge … but the grandiose vision had faded.

These were public utopias, but for many families there was a private heaven on earth for which to aim. Ever since grimy cities began to grow, people, given the opportunity and money, have been striving to escape to cleaner and more attractive places. The suburban development of the 19th century represented an ideal, though the cost of travel to work meant that only the most prosperous could move longer distances. As early as the 1840s wealthy Manchester merchants were relocating to places such as Wilmslow and Alderley Edge, sure in the knowledge that only those of quality could afford the fares to the city. The expansion of places away from the conurbations accelerated between the wars, but after 1955 private motoring gave would-be commuters a much wider choice of towns and villages. The extent of personal mobility which the car permitted has had a profound impact upon the landscape of all rural areas and small towns within driving distance of a major centre.

The smaller Pennine mill towns had seen a long period of growth abruptly terminated with the decline of cotton in the 1920s, and most lost population rapidly from the 1930s onwards. Many country towns also experienced stagnation or even decline in the late 19th and early 20th centuries, as rural depopulation sapped the economic strength of local market centres and older industries waned. Cockermouth typifies their experience. It had 5,775 people in 1851, when its market and administrative functions were reinforced by a substantial woollen industry. By 1911, though, that trade had declined and the town's commercial role stagnated: the population had fallen to 5,203 and not until 1961 did it exceed the 1851 figure. Thereafter commuting and new estate development produced rapid growth: the population grew by 23 per cent between 1961 and 1981, and today exceeds 8,000. Another example is Blackrod, a former mining and industrial town on a hilltop near Bolton, close to the M61 and two stations on the main Preston–Manchester railway. In 1881 its population was 4,234, but by 1961 this had fallen to 3,606. During the next 20 years, however, the town grew by 66 per cent; it now has over 10,000 people, almost entirely as a result of commuter in-migration.

   Such examples could be repeated across the region, as country towns and old industrial centres alike have experienced a sharp reversal of fortunes, with the consequent changes to townscapes. The revitalisation of shopping areas – with designer clothing shops and craft galleries, rather than butchers and bakers (even if candlestick makers are enjoying a new lease of life) – has made a material difference to their character and image. Hitherto unglamorous Ramsbottom, for example, has become a famously fashionable place to live, with restaurants and delicatessens among the cottages which once housed workers in the cotton mills. Every country town is now edged by a brightly coloured fringe of executive housing, trim estates with complex patterns of cul de sacs lined with neo-vernacular architecture, amid the retained hedges and copses, ponds and pathways of an older landscape (Fig. 11.12).

Fig. 11.12 Garstang barely grew beyond its small medieval core (right centre, immediately north of the bridge over the Wyre) until after the Second World War. The very early A6 bypass was opened in 1928. Since the mid-1950s road access has allowed the town to become a popular residential area for Preston and Lancaster commuters, and extensive new housing estates have spread across the adjacent fields.

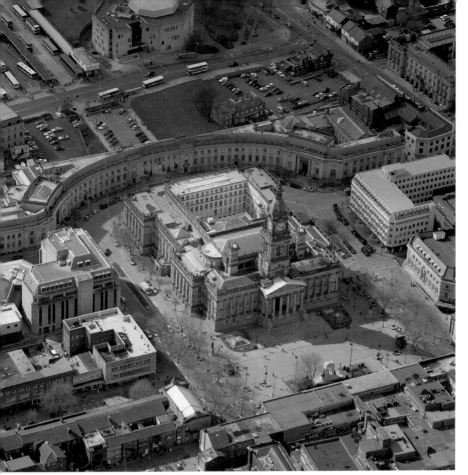

TOWN CENTRE RENAISSANCE

As people voluntarily fled to suburbs and country towns, or were compulsorily shifted to overspill estates, town populations fell sharply. Salford, the most extreme case among the cities, had 234,000 people in 1921: 60 years later it had only 98,000. In many towns central area redevelopment contributed to this trend, because commercial zones were extended at the expense of inner-city residential districts. Some boroughs had started to remodel their centres between the wars: in 1939, for example, Bolton completed its splendid Le Mans Crescent, housing municipal offices, the central library and the museum in a long stylish block that complements the magnificence of the Victorian town hall and is one of England's outstanding examples of inter-war civic architecture (Fig. 11.13). The Second World War reinforced this developing trend: the centres of Manchester, Liverpool, Bootle and Birkenhead were very badly damaged during air raids, and

Fig. 11.13 Le Mans Crescent, Bolton.
This grand classical design, by local architects Bradshaw Gass & Hope, was part of Bolton's late-1930s town centre redevelopment, designed to complement and form a backdrop to the monumentally-splendid Renaissance-inspired town hall of 1866–73. At the same time the town hall was doubled in size, exactly in keeping with the style of the original.

OPPOSITE PAGE:

BOTTOM: ***Fig. 11.15 The market place, Carlisle,*** *exemplifies the sense of repossession of the urban space, which pedestrianisation, and sensitive management of the urban landscape, can bring. With the delightful Old Town Hall of 1669 and 1717 as its focus, the triangular market place is not only physically but also functionally the heart of the city.*

even before the war ended most towns, blitzed or not, were drawing up plans for remodelling in the brave new post-war world.

But whereas before 1939 central area renewal had usually been piecemeal, after 1945 the emphasis switched to comprehensive schemes. Prominent in the thinking of most local authorities was a fervent desire to remove the evidence of the Victorian architectural legacy, now deemed aesthetically (and emotionally) unacceptable. As with the utopian solutions to housing problems, the idealistic late 1950s and 1960s saw almost every significant town indulge in extensive reconstruction. Dual carriageway relief roads took through traffic out of shopping streets, but severed portions of the urban fabric and forced pedestrians underground into subways. Roads came as packages, complete with multi-storey car parks, shopping precincts and office blocks. Some towns adopted redevelopment plans with an almost frightening enthusiasm, as though to conceal a shameful past. At Blackburn the outstanding Victorian market hall and other much-loved town centre buildings were razed and replaced by a shopping centre which soon required extensive rehabilitation and renovation.

Much of the northern part of Manchester's Victorian city centre, badly damaged in wartime air raids, was flattened, and a group of shop and office complexes was built on the site of the medieval market place, crowned by the 'unlovely' Arndale Centre (1972) – instantly dubbed 'the largest public lavatory in Europe' because of its exterior cladding of yellow shiny tiles. It survived the 1996 IRA bomb which put paid to neighbouring shoddy concrete structures.[17] In most larger towns the multi-storey office block became a symbol of the new age, though most were soon regarded with popular dislike: Crystal House (1962), a dull block which dominates Preston's market place, invariably wins local competitions to find the city's most hated building. The failure of the utopian visions of townscape produced in the 1960s and 1970s generated a great deal of general cynicism about planners, architects and their promises.

During the 1980s and 1990s new and very different approaches to urban design and development were increasingly favoured. The erosion of green belts and the inexorable advance of suburbia over farmland on urban fringes; the need to find new uses for derelict or abandoned land within urban areas, as industrial sites and old commercial areas closed or were run down; and the fast-changing nature of the housing market and the social structure of the community (with a rapid rate of household creation) produced in many towns the circumstances for a reappraisal of the role of city centres and urban land. An important catalyst was the success of the Albert Dock project in Liverpool, which had a national impact in fostering the idea of revival by restoration. A reawakened interest in urban living, encouraged by the increasing difficulties in commuting because of road congestion and a public transport system seen as unsatisfactory, popularised the residential conversion of warehouses, mills and churches. Central Manchester, in particular, saw far-reaching changes. Its townscape was extensively altered by an urban renaissance, which saw the emergence of fashionable quarters such as the Canal Street gay village, the expensive apartment zone around Deansgate and the revitalised and enhanced commercial core around St Ann's Square. The 1996 IRA bomb liberated this part of the city from the legacy of the 1960s and unlocked the door to visionary architectural and planning solutions that would otherwise have been elusive (Fig. 11.14), thereby reintegrating the medieval heart of the city with the 18th- and 19th-century shopping areas, allowing new open spaces to be created and introducing eyecatching new buildings. These projects augmented and enhanced a revitalising process already begun by the construction of the Metrolink tram

ABOVE: *Fig. 11.14 New Cathedral Street, Manchester, in 2005.* The reconstruction of the northern city centre after the 1996 IRA bombing involved a praiseworthy, and generally successful, attempt to make the area more attractive and more accessible, both literally and metaphorically. This new shopping street, the main axis of the rebuilding, demonstrates two key themes of the strategy – impressive contemporary architecture and the creation of an extensive traffic-free zone.

PLANNED INDUSTRIAL COMMUNITIES

In rural areas during the late 18th and early 19th centuries water-powered industrial development was often hampered by a lack of labour. One solution was for the proprietors of new industry to provide housing, building what some historians have called 'industrial colonies'. There are many examples of this type of settlement in the region. Characteristically, such places have a planned layout, housing which is better in quality than was usual at the time and a uniformity of design which derives from their 'all in a piece' construction. These villages tend to be closely associated with a single industrial site, very often a textile mill or bleachworks, since mill owners were markedly more philanthropic in this respect than colliery companies or ironfounders.

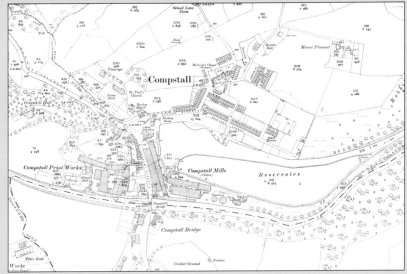

Thus at Calder Vale, north of Preston, a water-powered cotton mill was opened in 1835 by Richard and Jonathan Jackson in a very remote location with no nearby community. Here the owners built a village of four long terraces (above), three on the steep valley sides and one immediately adjacent to the millrace.

The more enlightened employers sought to provide amenities such as schools, institutes, places of worship and greens for drying clothes, as well as gardens, allotments or smallholdings. At Compstall near Romiley (left) the Andrew family developed spinning and weaving mills and a calico printing works in the 1820s. These, too, were water-powered: the very large reservoir and complex of millraces survive almost intact and are now the centrepiece of a country park. The family constructed a model village in the 1820s and 1830s, with a serious and genuine effort to provide for the wider needs of the workforce. Their benevolent paternalism resulted not only in rows of four-roomed cottages, but also a church and Sunday School, and an 'athenaeum' with library and reading room where concerts and improving educational classes were held.[20] Even more ambitious was the village of Bank Top, built by the Ashworths next to their New Eagley Mills (1802) on the northern edge of Bolton (below). Here the village, with rows of cottages, a school, library, newsroom, shops, cricket ground and recreation field, was provided with piped water in 1835 and gas shortly afterwards. It was famed far and wide as an exemplar of employer enlightenment, and visited by many reformers and curious travellers.[21]

Sometimes self-help was mustered, in approved 19th-century fashion, when workers formed co-operative groups or building societies and built small colonies of houses themselves. A good example is the Club Houses at Horwich (right), built in the early 19th century by a terminating building society (one which was wound-up when all its members had been housed). The main employers in the town, the Ridgway family, bleachworks owners, leased out the land.[22] There is evidence that many members of the community – there were about 150 houses in total – were engaged in handloom weaving. Today many industrial colonies are considered to be particularly attractive examples of late 18th- and early 19th-century architecture and planning, and now, as at the time they were built, the contrast with the squalor and overcrowding of the more typical industrial housing is all too apparent.

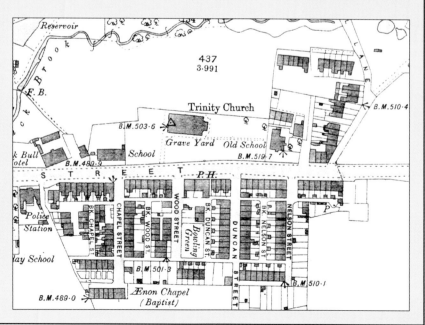

Fig. 11.16 The Trafford Centre: *the fantastic domes and colonnades, and the improbable combination of architectural motifs from every imaginable period and place, give the Trafford Centre an unmistakable character. The seemingly-limitless car parks, link roads and roundabouts create a flat American-style townscape which is greedy of space and visually a desert, in the middle of which the gleaming palace rises as a mirage.*

system and public monuments such as the Bridgewater Hall, the city's new concert venue.[18]

Other towns and cities sought to follow the same principles, though success is closely related to economic drawing power, and in unfashionable or more workaday towns, from Workington to Widnes, the urban renaissance is much less apparent or inevitable. Even so, pedestrianisation of town centre streets everywhere produces a more relaxed environment and helps to counter the attractions of out-of-town shopping centres (Fig. 11.15, *see* p.193). The banal shopping precincts of the years around 1970 were usually remodelled in the 1990s: in Wigan, for example, the 1960s saw extensive redevelopment of the shopping area and the construction of the Wigan Centre, 'the single most inappropriate development the town centre has seen'.[19] In the late 1980s this was itself redeveloped as part of a much larger project, the creation of The Galleries shopping centre, which focuses on the open market place and includes glazed arcades (among them a genuine Edwardian example, Makinson Arcade) and a 'Tudor style' gallery. Such schemes are deemed essential if the commercial vigour of town centres is to be maintained: the Xanadu-like domes and atriums of the Trafford Centre, opened in 1998, not only symbolise late 20th-century car-based shopping patterns, but also represent a powerful threat to retailing businesses in smaller and less thriving towns within a 50km (30-mile) radius (Fig. 11.16). Whether this constitutes utopia is a debatable point, but there can be no doubt that such modern meccas fulfil the aspirations of many people in the region.

NOTES

1   See Darley 1975 for planned and ideal communities and their context
2   Knight & Burscough 1998, 120–34
3   Constantine in White 1993, 203
4   For lunatic asylums see Richardson 2001 and Garside & Jackson, n.d.
5   Crosby in www.cottontown.org
6   Darley 1975, ch.9
7   www.utopia-britannica
8   *Manchester Evening Chronicle*, 7 November 1911
9   Greenall 2000, 254–9
10 Simon & Inman 1935, 165
11 White 2003, 40–4; Hunt 1992, 238–9; Pooley & Irish 1984
12 Crosby 2000, 113–25; www.utopia-britannica
13 Millward 1955, 31
14 Law 1999, 295–310, 340–4
15 Deakin 1989, 137
16 Crosby 2002, 169–82
17 Hartwell 2001
18 Parkinson-Bailey 2000, chs 11–13; Hartwell 2001
19 Hannavy 1990, 165
20 Thelwall 1972; for nearby examples see Calladine & Fricker 1993, 151–9
21 Boyson 1970
22 Timmins 1977, 52–7

The Discovery of the Hills

The simple, whitewashed chapel at Newlands in the heart of the Lake District, set among sycamore trees in a bowl in the mountains, is a place of pilgrimage for many, often reached at the end of a day spent walking in the fells. Tired but elated, walkers come into the church to round off a day of spiritual refreshment. Their one-line records in the visitors' book in the vestry hint at the reverence, a sense of worship even, experienced by so many fell walkers in the mountains. For there is something essentially spiritual about modern reactions to mountain scenery, a personal engagement with the hills, which has its roots in the Romantic movement and the poems of William Wordsworth and others. This chapter traces the responses evoked by the upland landscapes of the North West. Though the Lake District has entered international consciousness as a cultural icon, the call of the Pennine moors and caves should not be forgotten.

THE QUEST FOR MOUNTAIN SCENERY

Before the aesthetic 'discovery' of upland landscapes in the Picturesque movement of the late 18th century, the dominant perception of outsiders to mountain and moorland appears to have been utilitarian. As the uplands were largely unproductive territory, they offered little interest. Daniel Defoe's oft-quoted comment, that the fells possessed 'a kind of unhospitable terror', has been assumed to be typical.[1] However, early perceptions were almost certainly more complex than this. Hills, particularly the most massive, had personalities. William Camden wrote of Skiddaw as though the mountain were a living being, its two heads rising up and 'beholding' Criffel across the Solway. To the anonymous poet praising the Earl of Northumberland's estates in the western Lake District c. 1600, the fells were 'statelie' beings, rearing their 'haughtie heades' to the skies.[2] Affectionate familiarity is suggested by the human names given to some of the more notable eminences, such as Coniston Old Man and Knock Old Man, even if such names developed from the dialect term 'man', meaning a cairn. The brooding presence of the major hills is reflected in local ditties, often recording weather lore. In the late 17th century Carron Crag in Furness Fells was 'an infallible signe of rainy or fair weather', the villagers of Grisedale having a proverb, 'When Mount Charron weares a cap / Graisdale expects a rainey clap / But when its head is low and bair / It betokens weather faire.' Camden recorded a similar local 'prognostication' of a change in the weather according to how 'the misty clouds arise or fall' on Skiddaw and Criffell: 'If Skiddaw hath a cap / Scruffell wots full well of that.' Other couplets reflected local pride in hills which vied to be the highest in the country. From the Pennines came 'Ingleborrow, Pendl and Penigent / Are the highest hills betweene Scotland and Trent'; while Cumbrians claimed (more accurately) that 'Skiddaw, Helvellyn & Casticand / Are the highest hils in all England'.[3] Such folk rhymes confirm that upland scenery evoked a response long before the Picturesque movement. Aesthetic

Fig. 12.1 **Windermere and the Langdale Pikes from Lowood,** *by Julius Caesar Ibbotson (c. 1800–6). The epitome of the Picturesque ideal, contrived by framing the distant fells with the pastoral scene in the foreground, in which cattle chew the cud, maidens relax and a mother and child disembark from a boat. The villa at Brathay, on the opposite shore, was one of the first generation of villas on Windermere, built 1794–6 by George Law, a Jamaica merchant.*

appreciation of the fells themselves is less easy to detect, though the wide 'prospects' over land and sea gained from rising ground in the North West were certainly appreciated in the 17th century.[4]

The roots of the love affair with the mountains of northern England are usually traced to the middle decades of the 18th century. The first explicitly Picturesque description of Lakeland scenery was Dr John Dalton's poem describing the Derwentwater valley, published in 1754. Of the waterfall at Lodore, he wrote, 'Horrors like these at first alarm, / But soon with savage grandeur charm / …I view with wonder and delight / A pleasing, though an awful sight'. Derwentwater and the Keswick valley soon became the epitome of Picturesque charm, the frisson of awe excited by the wild fells and becks juxtaposed with the tamed pastoral landscape of the valley. Dr John Brown's description of Derwentwater, first published in 1766, saw Lakeland scenery in terms of the paintings of the 17th-century French artists Claude Lorraine and Nicolas Poussin: 'delicate sunshine over the cultivated vales' contrasted with 'the horrors of the rugged cliffs, the steeps, the hanging woods and foaming waterfalls' of the fellsides. Picturesque appreciation of upland scenery centred on the dichotomy between the elegance and beauty of lake, woods and fields, and the awe-inspiring 'sublime' quality of the crags and mountains (Fig. 12.1). The Vale of Keswick had both to perfection: 'Beauty lying in the lap of Horror!', as one early visitor put it.[5]

As a result of the effusions of these two clergymen, the Lake District soon became a popular destination for educated tourists in search of scenery. By the end of the 1770s the tour of the Lakes had become popular, its constituent 'stations' formalised by the publication in 1778 of Thomas West's guide to the Lakes.[6] Tourists followed

West's directions to the key viewpoints from which to observe the landscape framed to Picturesque perfection, often mediated through a Claude glass, a tinted mirror in which the view could be composed and admired. Derwentwater and Ullswater resounded to the booms of cannon fired on the lakes so that visitors could marvel at the echoes from the fells; Joseph Pocklington, a Nottinghamshire banker who bought an island and much of the shore of Derwentwater, organised regattas (as well as erecting various extravagant follies on his island). Between 1780 and 1830 large stretches of the shores of Windermere, Derwentwater and Ullswater, the most accessible and celebrated of the lakes, were claimed by villa builders, and even remote Wasdale was not untouched (*see* Fig. 12.3 and pp. 208–9).

The limestone scenery of the Pennines also drew visitors. Caves and chasms had attracted comment since the 17th century, when Charles Cotton and Thomas Hobbes had extolled the wonders of the Peak District. The growing popularity of tours to the Lakes also brought visitors to the karst scenery in Craven. When John Hutton, vicar of Burton-in-Kendal, published his guide to the caves around Ingleborough and Settle in 1781, he explicitly conceived of his work as 'an appendix' to West's *Guide to the Lakes*, aimed at southern visitors, who, he suggested, could visit the caves on their return journey. The caves were curiosities, 'horrid' places to excite pleasurable terror, and were interpreted by reference to the works of Classical writers. Hurtle Pot, a deep dank pothole at Chapel-le-Dale, was the Avernian lake of the Greeks, described in Virgil's *Aeneid*; Gatekirk Cave, a little further up the dale, was the grotto where Diana and her nymphs bathed in Ovid's *Metamorphoses*. Classical literature was their frame of reference, a sounding board to reflect and amplify the resonance of these 'foreign' landscapes on the visitors' educated minds.[7]

Fig.12.2 **Weathercote Cave, near Ingleborough**, *by J M W Turner in 1817–18. The beck cascading into the bowels of the cave evokes the sublime terror with which early visitors invested the limestone country around Ingleton. The Hon. John Byng, visiting in 1792, wrote that 'The cascades of Weathercote fall with a horrid din, filling the mind with a gloom of horror.' (Andrews 1936, 90.)*

Yet the Picturesque, with its allusions to the pastoral world of a Classical golden age, did not fully reflect the disturbing power of these upland landscapes. The Claude glass and the harmonious conceptions of Picturesque beauty were constraints from which those experiencing mountain scenery soon broke free, and by the beginning of the 19th century a full-blooded Romantic love affair with the fells had begun. In both the paintings of J M W Turner (Fig. 12.2) and the poetry of William Wordsworth, the encounter of the human spirit with wild, untamed nature is brought to the fore. To Wordsworth the mountains possessed a teaching and a healing power: the crag above Grasmere, which he and his sister saw high above them during their evening walks, 'often seems to send / Its own deep quiet to restore our hearts.'[8] In 'The Prelude', he described how he had sensed a fellowship with nature since his Lakeland childhood:

> ... In November days,
> When vapours, rolling down the valleys, made
> A lonely scene more lonesome; among woods
> At noon, and 'mid the calm of summer nights,
> When, by the margin of the trembling lake,
> Beneath the gloomy hills I homeward went
> In solitude, such intercourse was mine.[9]

In many ways the nature worship of Wordsworth remains the template for modern perceptions of mountain scenery.

As first the Picturesque and then the Romantic movements awoke a desire to visit areas of mountain scenery, so the 'discovery' of these areas led to their recognition as unique, named landscapes. 'The Lake District' is one such cultural construct, defined conceptually and geographically by ideas of the aesthetic value of landscape. Initially, the 'district of the lakes' was confined to the dales on the central north–south axis through the Lakeland fells: Thomas West's *Guide* of 1778 identified viewing 'stations' on the shores of only four lakes (Derwentwater, Bassenthwaite Lake, Windermere and Coniston Water), and the maps in James Clarke's *Survey of the Lakes* of 1787 only covered Penrith and Ullswater and the central lakes from Bassenthwaite to Windermere (Fig. 12.3). Within a generation, however, the landscape of even the most remote lakes was being painted and described and the whole Lakeland dome was perceived as a distinct, loved landscape. In his guide Wordsworth famously portrayed the unity of the Lake District, its valleys radiating from the central fells 'like spokes from the nave of a wheel.' Although all the valleys soon came to be known, guide books and maps continued to focus on the central lakes. The northern and southern boundaries were generally agreed (Ouse Bridge at the foot of Bassenthwaite Lake and Newby Bridge at the foot of Windermere) but the eastern and, particularly, the western limits were more contentious. Even in the early 20th century, tourist maps frequently omitted parts of the western lakes and valleys (Loweswater, Ennerdale, Eskdale and Dunnerdale), which were the most remote from the main tourist centres and routeways (Fig. 12.4).[10]

The campaign for a National Park focused minds on exactly where the boundary of the Lake District lay. By the 1930s the district was described in terms of a circle centred on High White Stones (now High Raise), on the watershed between Langdale and Borrowdale. H H Symonds reckoned that the 'central Lake District' lay within a 24km (15 mile) radius of that point, while an early attempt to define in detail the boundary of a putative National Park used a 32km (20 mile) radius from High White Stones as an outer limit (Fig. 12.4). As the National Park's long gestation progressed, considerable attention was given to the exact boundary to be designated. Towns and industrial areas were excluded, as was much of the limestone country encircling the Lakeland fells. John Dower, the father of England's National Parks, had a clear idea of what constituted Lake District landscape. Writing in 1942, he excluded the area around St Bees Head on the grounds that it was 'certainly not

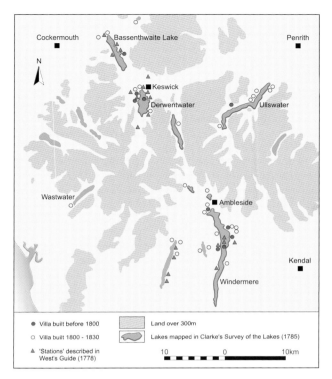

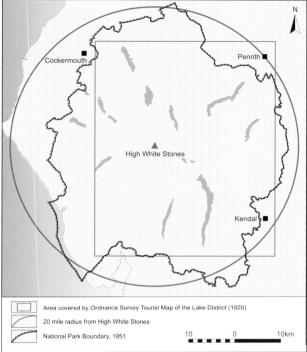

Legend for left map:
- ● Villa built before 1800
- ○ Villa built 1800 - 1830
- ▲ 'Stations' described in West's Guide (1778)
- Land over 300m
- Lakes mapped in Clarke's Survey of the Lakes (1785)

Legend for right map:
- ▢ Area covered by Ordnance Survey Tourist Map of the Lake District (1920)
- 20 mile radius from High White Stones
- National Park Boundary, 1951

ABOVE LEFT: *Fig. 12.3 The Lake District before 1830. The focus on the central lakes (from Bassenthwaite to Windermere) and Ullswater is striking.*

ABOVE: *Fig. 12.4 Defining the Lake District, c. 1920 to 1951. Differing perceptions of what constituted 'the Lake District' lie behind the three boundaries shown here.*

Lake District [being] dullish red-earth country', while the limestone country on the northern fringes of the proposed National Park was also discarded as being 'not real Lake District – its higher ground is bleak limestone pasture, *not* fell-land'. Subjective appreciation of the landscape was paramount: the precise line of the boundary was finally decided by members of the National Parks Commission, staying in the Lake District and touring the periphery by coach.[11]

Since the creation of the National Park in 1951, an official boundary has existed, defining the area subject to the controls of the Lake District National Park Authority, but 'the Lake District' is ultimately a construct of the mind rather than a legal entity. Perceptions of 'the Lake District' retain a certain flexibility to judge by road signs, tourist brochures and estate agents' literature, which often seem to equate Cumbria with the Lake District, even though the National Park embraces less than one-third of the county's area.

IMAGES OF FELL-FARMING COMMUNITIES

The fell country discovered by the outside world from the late 18th century was a peopled landscape, whose inhabitants were an integral part of the visitor's experience of place. Mountain communities have often excited comment, both bad and good. They have been seen variously as backward and uncouth or as morally superior and pure, unsullied by the negative aspects of social change. The 'otherness' of upland communities in Cumbria can be seen in the comments of the Crown surveyors, who reported on the attainted Earl of Northumberland's estates in the western valleys of the Lake District in 1570. The land was 'very populous', they wrote, 'and bredyth tall men and hard of nature … They have but little tillage, by reason whereof they lyve hardly and at ease, which makyth them tall of personage and hable to endure hardnes when necessyte reqyryth'. They were probably thinking of the Cumbrians' fitness for military service on the Border, but a sense of encounter with 'noble savages' is unmistakable.[12]

The discovery of the Lake District in the late 18th century created a myth of 'otherness' that was to endure. Wordsworth's oft-quoted description of society in the upper reaches of the Lake District valleys before the middle decades of the 18th century portrayed society in the dales as an 'almost visionary mountain republic'. 'Towards the head of these Dales,' he wrote, 'was found a perfect Republic of Shepherds and Agriculturalists …'

> *The chapel was the only edifice that presided over these dwellings, the supreme head of this pure Commonwealth; the members of which existed in the midst of a powerful empire like an ideal society or an organised community, whose constitution had been imposed and regulated by the mountains which protected it. Neither high-born nobleman, knight, nor esquire was here; but many of these humble sons of the hills had a consciousness that the land, which they walked over and tilled, had for more than five hundred years been possessed by men of their name and blood.[13]*

Wordsworth was not the first to portray Lakeland society as a precious remnant of a lost rural utopia. To Thomas Gray in 1769 Grasmere was a 'little unsuspected paradise', where 'no gentleman's flaring house' intruded on the 'peace, rusticity and happy poverty' of the scene.[14] John Housman, attempting a thumbnail sketch of his native county in the 1790s, described the inhabitants of the Lake District as

> *the happy people, who inhabit the peaceful dales shut up among the mountains, where labor and health go hand in hand, and luxury and discord have had little opportunity of extending their baneful influence. The behaviour of this class is modest, unaffected and humble … the pure emanation of nature and honesty.[15]*

The key attributes of this idealised mountain society were happy poverty, innocence and independence. It was a society morally superior to that of the mainstream, complementing the mountain scenery in the inspiration it gave to the visitor: 'they have a high character for sincerity and honesty'; 'honesty is the only qualification requisite to entitle its possessor to the best company … so accustomed are they to consider mankind as equal'.[16] Such idealised imagery masked reality, of course, and blurred distinctions which would have marked a much more heterogeneous society than the caricature suggests. Yet as late as 1876, John Ruskin perpetuated the myth. The 'peasantry', which Wordsworth had described 'with absolute fidelity', were, he claimed, 'hitherto a scarcely injured race, whose strength and virtue yet survive to represent the body and soul of England before her days of mechanical decrepitude and commercial dishonour.'[17] The inhabitants of the Lake District were perceived as a precious survival from a lost golden age.

By the late 19th century, that caricature of upland society was being reflected back in vernacular tales and poems by local authors, which were proud and defensive and not averse to taking a swipe at the 'offcomers'. Thomas Farrell (1837–94), the Aspatria schoolmaster who wrote *Betty Wilson's Cummerland Teals*, set his stories in Embleton, on the northern fringe of the Lake District, at some unspecified date in the mid-19th century. The tales are a nostalgic and humorous evocation of rural life before the changes wrought by the railway age, but they also mock visitors. Laughter is provoked at the expense of the botanist (a 'windy-wallet' who 'kent nowt aboot farmin'), whose collected 'spessymens' are accidentally made into a herb pudding; and the gullible London sportsman ('varra polite, [he] ran back an' forret, prancin' like a cat on a het gurdel [hot griddle]'), on whom a local lad played a practical joke, persuading him that crows were pheasants.[18]

An important aspect of the cultivation of a Lakeland identity lay in the identification of Viking roots. The sturdy independence of Lakeland society was seen as a direct legacy of the Scandinavian settlement of Cumbria in the 10th century. The roots of this can be traced back to the Cumbrian churchman and antiquary, William Nicolson (1655–1727), who noted the 'Danish' influence in northern English dialect. The first systematic attempt to argue that the Lakeland dialect preserved the language of the Scandinavian colonists came in 1819–20, when Thomas De Quincey published a series of articles on the 'Danish origin of Lake Country Dialect' in the *Westmorland Gazette*. In 1856 Robert Ferguson's pioneering study attempted to use Lakeland place-names to chart the process of Norse settlement, but it was the work of W G Collingwood (1854–1932), Ruskin's scholarly secretary, which secured Viking roots as a central element in the historical identity of Lake District communities.[19] He saw the dialect of Cumbria, with its rich legacy of Scandinavian words, as the direct descendant of the speech of the Norse colonists a millennium before. As well as a stream of historical work, Collingwood published two works of historical fiction that did much to give prominence to the Viking roots of Lakeland society in the popular imagination: *Thorstein of the Mere: a saga of the Northmen in Lakeland* (1895) and *The Bondwoman* (1896). The theme of *Thorstein* was the persistence of Scandinavian culture and language in the Lake District. It evokes a powerful sense of place by locating an imagined heroic past in a real landscape:

Fig. 12.5 Hawell Monument, Lonscale Fell, near Keswick. Canon H D Rawnsley designed his memorial to two Lakeland shepherds, Joseph and Edward Hawell, deliberately to celebrate the Norse ancestry of fell shepherds. The ring-headed cross copies Viking-age sculpture from west Cumbria, and Rawnsley chose the panel of interlace as a 'symbol of eternity, the endless knot their Norse forefathers used' (Rawnsley 1903, 165). Modern scholarship, however, sees both features as deriving more from the Celtic church than from pure Viking styles.

> *But the Northmen continued in their homes by firth and fell … Even when the Normans had brought all this border country under the feudal yoke, still for many a hundred years the dalesmen used to meet at the Steading-stone by Thirlmere, and kept alive some smouldering memory of their birthright in the country Laws of Wythburn. And everywhere they still had their old manners and their old speech, changing little of either, and that but slowly.*[20]

The legend of the Viking past in Lakeland communities has proved powerful and enduring (Fig. 12.5). It continued to spawn fiction, such as the Lakeland romances of Nicholas Size, whose *The Secret Valley* (1929) was a tale of the resistance to the Norman yoke by fiercely independent Lakelanders, set at Rannerdale, near Buttermere. Collingwood's ideas were also kept alive by William Rollinson (1937–2000), whose lectures and television programmes stressing the cultural ties between Cumbria and Norway captured the popular imagination in the 1980s and 1990s.[21]

Across the 20th century the character with which these myths endowed Lakeland communities became increasingly detached from the reality of life in the uplands. Population drained from most parts of upland Lancashire and Cumbria in the late 19th and early 20th centuries, leaving a legacy of abandoned and decaying farmsteads in windy places. Gaunt and roofless steadings evoked tales of mystery and the supernatural, as well as a nostalgia for an older and purer way of life. The ruined farmstead at Miterdale Head, near Eskdale (Fig. 5.14), became the setting for a ghost story ('the beckside boggle') written by the daughter of an incoming landowning family in the 1880s;[22] while the Saddleworth author Ammon Wrigley (1861–1946) lovingly recreated a picture of life in a now-ruined homestead high on the Lancashire moors, contrasting the hard, healthy life of a handloom-weaving past with the artificiality of modern life:

> *The days are gone, and round us now a world of sham prevails,*
> *The wheel of time keeps rolling on with changes in our dales;*
> *We've homesteads, all veneer and show, with make-believe and pride,*
> *But give to me the simple heart that loves an old fire-side.*[23]

As local farming families were replaced by 'offcomers' – whether commuters, retired people or second-home owners – across the 20th century, attempts were made to grasp the traditional hill farming culture before it slipped away. Wistful evocations of traditional Lakeland life, such as Wren Rumney's story of an archetypical 'dalesman' and Dudley Hoys' portrait of Eskdale, recorded the daily round in loving detail, with a nostalgic pride in being able to share in a vanishing way of life.[24] The 'otherness' of the sheep farmer's life was also portrayed in

Fig. 12.6 **Jarrod and the bastle house** *by Alan Stones (1987). A modern painting, which conveys the perception of hill farming life as masculine and physically taxing: the farmer's strong hands, working with the sheep, seem to grow out of a harsh landscape of bare cobbled yard, gaunt stone bastle house with the North Pennine scarp and Cross Fell behind.*

graphic images. To the romantic category belong the stylised photographs of Lakeland shepherds in the late 19th and 20th centuries, the classic images (such as Joseph Hardman's photograph of Isaac Cookson of Bampton) showing the shepherd alone on the fells, carrying or otherwise tending an individual sheep. Resonances with the Good Shepherd of scripture are intended in the solitary figure braving the elements for the sake of his flock.[25] More recently, a colder realism is portrayed in the admiring celebration of the tough masculine world of the hill farmer in Alan Stones' painting, *Jarrod and the Bastle House* (Fig. 12.6). As the dialect speech and the family ties of the older community have weakened since the 1960s, inhabitants have become separated from landscape. The 'natives' no longer form a major part of the experience of visitors to the Lake District or the Pennines; the focus has shifted to the hills and moors themselves.

THE FREEDOM OF THE HILLS

The 20th century saw the growth of a direct and intimate experience of mountain landscapes, through the development of mountaineering and the outdoor movement. Visitors in the 18th century had climbed the more accessible and prominent fells, such as Skiddaw and Ingleborough, and Coleridge had even written a letter from the top of Scafell in 1799. When Jonathan Otley published the first practical guidebook to the fells in 1823, he included descriptions of most of the major peaks, including Scafell, Gable, Pillar, Helvellyn, Skiddaw and Saddleback, though he noted that neither Saddleback nor Scafell were much visited by strangers at that time.[26]

The challenge of rock climbing in the Lake District fells developed across the 19th century. Its roots can be traced back to the Romantics: Coleridge's descent of Broad Stand on Scafell in 1802 is often cited as the first Lakeland rock climb. Pillar Rock in Ennerdale, conquered by a local shepherd in 1826, became a magnet for early climbers, both locals and visitors, by the 1870s. Wasdale Head, convenient for the highest fells, became the headquarters of the climbing fraternity, the focal point being the small hotel kept by Will Ritson, who cultivated his fame as a character and teller of tall stories. By the 1880s serious exploration of the Lakeland crags had begun, in a partnership between local men, such as the estate agent, John Wilson Robinson (1853–1907) who came from old yeoman stock near Cockermouth, and visitors, who were mostly young, educated town dwellers: professionals, academics and businessmen. The fierce attachment to the highest fells by the well-to-do mountaineering community was reflected in the decision of the Fell and Rock Climbing Club (founded in 1906) to purchase the summit of Great Gable and 1,200ha (3,000 acres) of the surrounding fells and to donate them to the National Trust in 1923 as a memorial to club members who were killed in the First World War.[27]

Underground exploration of the limestone caverns around Ingleborough developed in parallel with the conquest of the crags. Early exploration took place in the middle decades of the 19th century, with local gentlemen like John Birkbeck of Settle and William Metcalfe of Weathercote in Chapel-le-Dale exploring several caves in the 1840s. The age of organised potholing began in the 1890s, key landmarks being the formation of the Yorkshire Ramblers' Club in 1892 and the first complete descent of the most dramatic of the caves, Gaping Gill, near Clapham, in 1895. An increase in the number of potholing clubs from around 1930 led to an explosion in underground exploration, as intrepid explorers crawled and slithered through fissures and subterranean streams to map the complex network of passages and caves deep beneath the hills.[28]

Both rock climbing and speleology were minority pursuits in comparison with the less taxing exploration of upland scenery by ramblers and fell walkers. The industrial communities of the Lancashire textile towns had a long tradition of walking on the moors that rose around them, and books describing 'rambles' into the countryside around industrial Lancashire appeared from the 1840s. The moors gave space and freedom to a people confined to cramped living conditions and toil in the mills. Edwin Waugh (1817–1890), the Lancashire poet of the moorlands, captured the essence of the escape offered by the hills:

> *Away with the pride and the fume of the town,*
> *And give me a lodge in the heatherland brown;*
> *Oh there, to the schemes of the city unknown,*
> *Let me wander with freedom and nature, alone ...*[29]

Yet, for many, rambling was a communal activity. Rambling clubs proliferated in the towns of industrial Lancashire during the 1890s and were characterised by the ethos of working-class improvement current at the time. A convergence of socialist and Christian Nonconformist ideals gave rambling a serious purpose, encouraging a morally and physically healthy use of leisure time, self-discipline and intellectual stimulation. The ramblers of industrial Lancashire engaged in serious discussion during the camaraderie of days spent on the open hills and took an enquiring interest in the environment through which they walked (its botany, folklore and local history, for example).[30]

Rambling took townspeople out into the hills, not only the Pennine moors which formed the backdrop to their daily lives, but also to the Lake District fells and further afield. Its rise brought into focus the potential conflict between landowners' rights and access to the hills. The battle grounds in northern England were largely in the Pennines, where thousands of acres of moorland close to the industrial conurbations were managed for grouse rearing and shooting from the later decades of the 19th century. One of the earliest sustained disputes over access concerned the moors behind Darwen, where an 18-year confrontation was triggered in 1878 by an action for trespass on the grouse moors brought against five men from the town. Open access was eventually achieved in 1896, when the corporation took over the common. More famous was the tension between the owners of grouse moors and walkers in the Peak

Fig. 12.7 Kinder Scout Trespass plaque, Hayfield quarry. *The plaque records the mass trespass on Kinder Scout on Sunday 24 April 1932, when a group dominated by Manchester ramblers confronted gamekeepers on the open moorland.*

District, where huge swathes of the Dark Peak behind Glossop and New Mills were closed to ramblers. The 'veritable fever of rambling' which swept Britain in the 1920s and 1930s generated mounting pressure for access to the Peak moorlands from the Manchester and Sheffield conurbations, culminating in the mass trespass on Kinder Scout in 1932 (Fig. 12.7). The trespass had a strong political aspect (Mancunian ramblers affiliated to the British Workers' Sports Federation sang the Red Flag and the Internationale as they walked) and the scuffles with gamekeepers resulted in charges for illegal assembly and assault.[31]

In the Lake District, by contrast, the survival of unenclosed common wastes and the scarcity of grouse ensured a more relaxed attitude to access by walkers. This was reinforced by an unintended consequence of the 1922 Law of Property Act, which gave the general public a right to take exercise on common land within the bounds of an urban district. As parts of the central fells, including Langdale and Grasmere, lay within the boundary of the Lakes Urban District, access rights on some of the most popular hills were secured. In the burgeoning outdoor movement of the 1920s and 1930s, the fells became a playground, epitomised by Arthur Ransome's popular series of adventure stories set in the Lake District. *Swallows and Amazons*, *Swallowdale*, *Winter Holiday* and *Pigeon Post* capture the excitement of middle-class holidays spent exploring the Lakeland environment and the healthy challenges it presented.

Serious walking in the Lake District was made possible for the ramblers of industrial Lancashire by the provision of organised holidays in simple accommodation. The Co-operative Holidays Association, founded in 1893, for example, offered week-long holidays at its centres in Ambleside and Newlands, near Keswick, which combined long days in the fells with lectures on the area's literary associations, flora and geology. Such hostels were the forerunners of a long tradition of simple living, which included the foundation of the Youth Hostels Association. The YHA grew out of the rambling tradition, having its roots in a special meeting called by the Liverpool and District Ramblers' Federation in December 1929. Its growth was dramatic: by the end of 1931 the YHA had 73 hostels; by 1936 it had 260: the 12 hostels in the Lake District provided nearly 43,000 overnight stays in 1935.[32]

The fashion for outdoor pursuits generated a passionate and intensely personal attachment to the fells: Ewan McColl's song, the 'Manchester Rambler' (written in 1932), declared that 'sooner than part from the mountains, I think I would rather be dead'. Alfred Wainwright (1907–91), brought up in Blackburn, expressed a similar devotion in the first volume of his seven-part walking guide to the Lakeland fells, published in 1955. Fell walking was almost a religious experience: he found 'a spiritual and physical satisfaction in climbing mountains – and a tranquil mind upon reaching their summits, as though I had escaped from the disappointments and unkindnesses of life and emerged above them into a new world, a better world'. His relationship to the fells was personal: 'At the first the hills were moody giants, and I a timid Gulliver, but very gradually … we became acquaintances and much later firm friends'. Like the artist William Heaton Cooper (Fig. 12.8, *see* p.210), he sensed the character of individual fells: Catbells 'has a bold "come-hither" look that compels one's steps'; Hindscarth and Robinson 'turn broad backs to the Buttermere valley and go hand-in-hand together down to Newlands'; Helvellyn is a 'very friendly giant' which inspires affection.

Wainwright's books were his way of expressing his devotion to the fells. The first volume of the series 'was conceived, and is born, after many years of inarticulate worshipping at their shrines. It is, in very truth, a love-letter'.[33] Many of the thousands who walk and climb on the fells and moors of north-west England today would recognise in Wainwright's words something of their own experience of upland landscapes, an encounter between the individual and Nature, first articulated in the North West in the Romanticism of Wordsworth and his contemporaries.

LAKELAND VILLAS

The aesthetic appreciation of the Lakes soon resulted in landscape change, as members of fashionable society sought out choice locations on which to build villas and to create a landscape of perfection. The goal was a lakeside position, set in fields but embowered by woodland, with a view across the lake to the mountains beyond. Even more perfect was an island, where an idealised landscape could be created in an entire and self-contained setting. The first Lakeland villa to be erected in pursuit of the Picturesque

was that on Belle Isle in Windermere (right), built for Thomas English, a London glass founder, in 1774. It was a circular house, a classical, porticoed rotunda set in a formal garden, consciously modelled on a domed temple in one of Claude Lorraine's paintings. In 1781 the island (until then called Long Holme) was bought by the trustees of Isabella Curwen, the heiress of Workington Hall, and renamed in her honour. She removed the formal garden and had the island landscaped by Thomas White in Capability Brown style: a parkland with clumps of trees and a perimeter walk from which to view the fells across the water.[34]

Lyulph's Tower (below), on the northern shore of Ullswater, another of the first generation of Lakeland villas, drew on

medieval rather than classical inspiration. The castellated, Gothic structure was built in 1780 for the Duke of Norfolk as a hunting lodge in Gowbarrow Park. Yet the building was clearly built for the view, its three wings ('three sides of an octagon, like a fire-screen' as Pevsner graphically put it) framing prospects up and down the lake. It was also ostentatiously ornamental, seeking to be a suitably picturesque addition to the lake shore. Its name was a piece of self-conscious historicism, recalling Lyulph, the supposed 1st baron of Greystoke.[35]

A much more self-effacing lakeside retreat was built on the western bank of Derwentwater by Lord William Gordon in the 1780s. Derwent Bay (below) is a retiring villa built by a reclusive aristocrat. Perhaps significantly, Lord William began to enquire about purchasing property on Derwentwater soon after the notorious Gordon Riots of 1780, in which his brother had played a leading part. By 1785, he had bought the whole of the west bank of the lake from Fawe Park to Manesty and by 1790, acting in consort with neighbouring landowners, he had replaced the road linking the farms along the shore with a new road higher up the slopes of Cat Bells. His villa (completed by 1794) consisted of single-storey, pavilion-like rooms with high windows opening on to a tree-framed vista across the lake. He also carried out extensive tree planting, replacing the former patchwork of coppice woods and meadows with a mixed woodland containing 'oak, spruce, silver fir, Weymouth pine, beeches' and other species, traversed by gravelled carriage drives and footpaths.[36]

Of later date and far from the populous Windermere–Derwentwater axis stands the half-timbered villa of Wasdale Hall (right). In 1811 Stansfeld Rawson, a banker from Halifax, purchased five farms at the foot of Wastwater and began a programme of tree planting, which continued until the early 1820s. He surrounded the site he had chosen for his villa with a screen of mixed woodland, the plantations being edged with ornamental trees, such as beech, hornbeam and exotic oaks. In 1829 he built Wasdale Hall on the site of one of the former farmsteads, creating a compact villa in a Tudor style with superb views across the lake to the screes. Like Lord William Gordon, he also diverted the public road, so that it ran behind the house, rather than in front of it.[37]

Fig. 12.8 **Langdale Pikes from Lingmoor,** *by William Heaton Cooper (1938). As a mountaineer and rock climber, Heaton Cooper sought to portray the personality of individual fells. In this painting he saw 'an interesting balance between straight lines and curves, seen as an abstract design yet with the straight lines revealing the "parent" rock, part of the earth's bony structure, and the curves representing the muscles, the debris left behind by glacial action.' (Cooper 1984, 77.)*

NOTES

1   Defoe 1971, 549
2   Camden 1610, 767; Winchester 1987, 116
3   LRO, DDX 398/122; Camden 1610, 749, 767 (which has 'Lauuellin' for Helvellyn)
4   Denton 2003, 100, 113, 148, 338; Anon. 1876, 8
5   Andrews 1989, 180–1; Brown 1767
6   West 1778
7   Hobbes 1678; Cotton 1681; Hutton 1781, pp. [ii], 22–4, 36–7
8   Wordsworth 1904, 148
9   Ibid, 638
10 West 1778; Clarke 1787; de Selincourt 1906, 22; Clark 1994
11 Clark 1994
12 Pollard 1997, 109–13; PRO, E164/37, fol 3 (quoted in Winchester 1987, 1)
13 de Selincourt 1906, 67–8
14 Printed in West 1780, appendix
15 Housman 1800, 67–8
16 Bailey & Culley 1805, 302; Housman 1800, 68
17 Ruskin 1903–12, XXXIV, 141
18 Farrall 1929, 105–11, 5–9
19 James 1956, 77; Roberts 1999; Ferguson 1856; for Collingwood, see Parker 2001; Townend 2000; Wawn 2000, 335–40
20 Collingwood 1895, 297–8
21 E.g. 'A Tale of Two Dales' (Border TV / NRK Norway TV, 1988)
22 Rea, 1886
23 Yates 1923, 325–6
24 Rumney 1911; Hoys 1955
25 Kermode 2003, 12–15
26 Hutton 1781, 29–33; Plumtre 1992, 150; Andrews 1989, 155; Otley 1825
27 Hankinson 1972; 1988
28 Heap 1964; Beck 1984
29 Waugh nd, 175
30 Taylor 1997, 54–90
31 Ibid, 135–8, 229, 258–60
32 O'Neill 2000, 95
33 Wainwright 1955, quotations from introduction; Helvellyn 2; and 'Some personal notes in conclusion'; Wainwright 1964, quotations from Catbells 2, Hindscarth 2
34 Murdoch 1984, 28–9; RCHME 1997, 2–10
35 Pevsner 1967, 160; Murdoch 1984, 38
36 CRO, D/Ben/1/1901–75; Crossthwaite 1881, 41; Murdoch 1984, 36–7
37 Martin 1993, 269–82

13

Industrial Heritage

> *… a tourist in Lancashire has to search for objects of interest, different from those which excited his attention in other lands; he has to contemplate stupendous triumphs of science and art, instead of the wondrous works of nature; he has to deal with the present and the future, scarcely finding time to bestow inquiry or reflection on the past.*[1]

Almost a century after readers of *The Pictorial History of Lancashire* (1843) received that blunt warning, J B Priestley assessed the county's industrial squalor and concluded that it derived from 'More money, more muck; more muck, more money; the only flaw in the system being that the money tended to go in an opposite direction from that of the muck'.[2] In these quotations we see opposite perceptions. To some, especially in the early days, the 'stupendous triumphs' were foremost, but to others, for over a century from the 1840s, the prevalence of muck and absence (for most people) of money represented the besetting failure of the industrial age. Architectural splendours and technological achievement were in sharp contrast to a ravaged environment and ruined society. This chapter looks at the feelings about industry and urbanisation expressed by contemporaries. It then reflects on the heritage industry and our own perceptions of the industrial past, now that the monuments of the Industrial Revolution are regarded as an emotional link with the lives of our forebears.

As a young man William Wordsworth, pioneer of the idea of landscape protection, was not unaware of the fascination of industry. In his earliest major poem, 'An Evening Walk', written in about 1788, he describes slate quarrying in terms which leave no doubt that he recognised, as did many who came after, that however disruptive and destructive of beauty, industry could also be intrinsically compelling. He also identifies the sense that man shrinks to a mere incidental in such landscapes:

> *I love to mark the quarry's moving trains, | Dwarf panniered steeds, and men, and numerous wains: | Now busy all the enormous hive within, | While Echo dallies with the various din! | Some (hear you not their chisels' clinking sound?) | Toil, small as pigmies, in the gulf profound ...*[3]

The dichotomy between the dramatic beauty of industry and its repulsive qualities lies at the heart of Victorian perceptions of industrialisation.[4] Industry also generated moral and social responses which cannot be ignored when contemporary views of landscape are analysed. It could possess *virtue* despite its ugliness, because it represented progress, national glory, scientific achievement and man's victory over nature (Fig. 13.1). For Henry Booth, author of the first description of the Liverpool and Manchester Railway, this conquest was symbolised by the embankment at Roby (unremarkable to 21st-century eyes) which, he wrote

> *strikingly exhibits how much may be accomplished when our efforts are concentrated on one grand object. There is a feeling of satisfaction by no means*

Fig. 13.1 Summit Tunnel on the Manchester and Leeds Railway: *James Tait's 1845 lithograph conveys the sense of rugged drama which contemporaries appreciated in the engineering works of the new railway system, and also emphasises the architectural aspirations of the railway builders.*

common-place, in thus overcoming obstacles and surmounting difficulties, in making the high places low and the rough places plain, and advancing in one straight and direct course to the end in view.[5]

Writing in 1842, at a time of acute depression in the cotton trade, W Cooke Taylor saw smoking chimneys as the mainstay of prosperity for the working population and admitted that he found beauty in the industrialising landscape on the northern edge of Bolton:

The intervening valley is studded with factories and bleach-works. Thank God, smoke is rising from the lofty chimneys of most of them! for I have not travelled thus far without learning … that the absence of smoke from the factory-chimney indicates the quenching of fire on many a domestic hearth, want of employment to many a willing labourer, and want of bread to many an honest family. The smoke creates no nuisance here – the chimneys are too far apart; and it produces variations in the atmosphere and sky which, to me at least, have a pleasing and picturesque effect.[6]

A century later, when cotton was in terminal crisis, Priestley met a Blackburn woman recently returned from exile in the Midlands, who unconsciously made a similar point:

I hardly recognised the place. It's all becoming clean. The smuts are wearing off because so few of the mills are working. The bricks and stone are beginning to show through. I hardly knew the place.[7]

Alternatively, though, industry could be *reprehensible* despite its benefits, because it spawned damaging and destructive elements in society. If progress were to be measured by increased human happiness and well-being, how could industrialisation represent progress?

THE POSITIVE VIEW

Wordsworth again acknowledged the fascination of the new landscapes in a passage from 'The Excursion', published in 1814:

Here a huge town, continuous and compact,
Hiding the face of earth for leagues – and there,
Where not a habitation stood before,
Abodes of men irregularly massed
Like trees in forests – spread through the spacious tracts,

Fig. 13.2 **Manchester from Kersal Moor,** *by James Bourne (1773–1854): this bucolic scene was painted in 1806, when Manchester, although already the possessor of smoking chimneys, could still be viewed as a country town set within the idyllic rural framework of the Irwell valley.*

Fig. 13.3 **View of Manchester from Kersal Moor,** *by William Wyld (1806–89): a version of a view commissioned by Queen Victoria, this painting reveals the potential grandeur of the industrial scene, while keeping a safe distance from its excesses.*

> *O'er which the smoke of unremitting fires*
> *Hangs permanent, and plentiful as wreathes*
> *Of vapour glittering in the morning sun.*[8]

This passage captures the sense of awe which these unfamiliar places still evoked – not yet totally sullied, they had a fantastical quality if viewed from sufficient distance. The same, almost magical air is conveyed by James Bourne's watercolour *Manchester from Kersal Moor* (1806), in which the few smoking chimneys are objects of attraction, matching in prominence the towers of churches (Fig. 13.2). In the foreground is a bucolic scene high above the great curve of the Irwell, and the view is framed by woods and fields. In 1852 William Wyld painted (under commission from Queen Victoria who had visited Manchester the previous year) a panorama from almost the same viewpoint (Fig. 13.3). The contrast is startling, for in the later view can be seen not only many more churches and monumental buildings, but also over 150 chimneys. Their smoke rises vertically and then is smudged by a light easterly wind into a dark, hazy pall lying over a city bathed in a strange yellow light as the sunshine

Fig. 13.4 A View of the Town of Warrington from a House near Atherton's Quay, *by D Donbavand (painted c. 1772): a meticulously-detailed depiction of one of Lancashire's earliest industrial centres, which is an invaluable historical record and also reminds us of the rural or country town setting of the first phase of the Industrial Revolution.*

Fig. 13.5 Lowerhouse printworks, Burnley *(unknown artist, c. 1830): a superb portrayal of the romantic view of great industrial buildings, seen from the countryside and looking across a faintly hazy urban area to the hills beyond. Views such as this can be contrasted with 'warts and all' images such as that of St Helens (Fig. 8.9).*

filters through a smoky veil. The landscape is transformed, but there is no doubt that the dramatic quality of the smoke, light and buildings, and the sense of the interplay of man and nature, meant that this was perceived as an attractive view in which even the gross pollution had high aesthetic qualities. It is not harshly realistic, but romantically optimistic. The queen would not have wanted anything else.

Other artists found that industrial elements were an asset to a scene rather than a detraction. Donbavand's colourful and informative view of Warrington from the south (1762), a sort of Canaletto of the Mersey, gives as much prominence to the riverside warehouses and the cones of the glassworks as to Bank Hall, the grand house of the Patten family who owned these industries (Fig. 13.4). For some artists the visual drama of industrial buildings made them a worthy object in their own right – subjects as varied as lime kilns and aqueducts appear in paintings. The engravings in *Lancashire Illustrated* (1831) predictably include town halls and country houses, but also cotton mills in Union Street, Manchester, and the steam-engine manufactory and ironworks of Messrs. Rothwell, Hicks & Co. at Bolton.[9] The Lowerhouse printworks at Burnley was portrayed in about 1830, with two immensely tall chimneys providing the visual focus of the scene (Fig. 13.5). From one emerges a wisp of smoke, but the hills and moors beyond are clear, as in an 18th-century French landscape painting. If the building were a cathedral or a castle this would be a romantic view of the most conventional sort – yet factories were deemed equally appropriate for the artist's brush (Fig. 13.6). Liverpool was a favourite subject for artists and engravers, the many pictures of vessels on the Mersey revealing plenty of full sail and white-capped waves but also recording much detail of townscapes, including the long line of waterfront with Edge Hill and Toxteth Park behind. The city's splendid public buildings and docks were frequently portrayed, perhaps most memorably in Ackerman's highly imaginative aerial view of the mid-1840s, designed to emphasise the sprawl of the built-up area and the forests not of chimneys but of masts. In the 1850s and 1860s many Liverpool street scenes were painted by W G Herdman, whose subjects frequently included ordinary people in everyday settings such as the *Gill Street Pig Market* (1867).[10]

Writers, too, sought to portray industrial sites in positive and sometimes hyperbolic terms, particularly in the first half of the 19th century when the dreadfulness of urban squalor was less apparent – or at least not publicised – and could be ignored. Paeans of praise to industrial might and the owners of industry were numerous, while gentle euphemism could conceal stark realities. An 1889 description of Wigan enumerated 11 mining disasters in 15 years, in which 525 men and boys died, and commented, with some understatement, that the list 'will show that the life of a Wigan miner is, taking all things into consideration, by no means one to be envied'. It then took an artistic view of the Kirkless Iron Company at Ince, a vast industrial site which was notoriously dirty and surrounded by man-made mountains of slag: 'Immense furnaces are blazing here from morning until night, and their glare and smoke can be seen for many miles round, lighting up the murky landscape after dark, and imparting a Rembrandt-like hue'.[11]

Local writers, steeped in pride in their own town, were often enthusiasts for industrial progress. They also tended to sycophantic flattery and eternal optimism about the benefits that industry would bestow. A typical example is Peter Whittle's *History of Preston* (1821), where the account of the new gasworks (the first in any provincial town) is longer than the descriptions of churches. At Canal Street mills, he tells us, 'a fine steam-engine house presents itself ... This erection forms a majestic appearance. The mechanism of the powerful steam-engine is said to surpass any in the kingdom, for beauty and cleanliness', while the great mill at Frenchwood, close to the house of its owner, Samuel Horrocks MP, was 'of brick, ornamented with a pediment and cupola, mounted by a gilt vane; and possesses seventeen windows in length, by five stories high, with a spiral stair-case, large engine-houses, and other out-offices, highly necessary and useful'.[12]

The early railways likewise inspired lyrical prose, as observers became almost intoxicated with the excitement of steam and heavy engineering. When he describes the Olive Mount Cutting at Wavertree in tones of wonder, Henry Booth uses the particularly significant term 'picturesque'. As we have seen, the search for this attribute had led many travellers to the Lake District in the previous half century, but here that desirable quality could be found in a no less remarkable man-made world:

> the traveller passes through a deep and narrow ravine [and] the prospect is bounded by the perpendicular rock on either side with the blue vault above ... the sides of the rock exhibit already the green surface of vegetation, and present altogether far more of the picturesque in their appearance than might be expected from so recent an excavation.[13]

***Fig. 13.6* Oldham from Glodwick Fields,** *by J H Carse (painted 1831): Carse, who died in 1872, was an Oldham artist who painted local scenes in an appealingly naïve style. The maidens in the fields provide the obligatory human touch, but the real subject is the industrial town, with the splendidly rebuilt parish church of St Mary, finished only the previous year (so still gleamingly-bright) already eclipsed by tall chimneys.*

THE NEGATIVE VIEW

Disenchantment followed, and by the 1840s serious doubts about the character and consequences of industrial progress were being raised by more sensitive and socially-aware commentators. Even Henry Booth, describing Barton-on-Irwell, had mused upon the negative implications of

> a great cotton factory [which] rears its tall sides, with its hundred windows, and the fly-wheel of its steam engine pursuing its continuous revolutions, as if symbolical of that eternal round of labour and care, of abundant toil and scanty remuneration, of strained exertion and

insufficient repose, which ... have been the condition and tenure on which the existence of so large a portion of mankind has depended.[14]

There was growing recognition that the new landscapes of the Industrial Revolution were an integral part of the same phenomenon that produced filth and pollution, child labour and shocking infant mortality. There followed a wealth of description from writers with political and social messages to expound. From their pens comes some of the angriest writing of the 19th century. In the 1880s, for example, the journalist Robert Blatchford railed in the Manchester press against the cruel contrast between the wealthy merchant princes of the city and those unfortunates who lived but metres from the business area:

How shall I attempt to paint the shame of modern Athens – the dwellings of her people? The miles of narrow, murky streets, the involuted labyrinths of courts and passages and covered ways, where a devilish ingenuity seems to have striven with triumphant success to shut out light and air ... the ash-pits filled to overflowing, and shedding their foul contents upon the sloppy walks, close to the cottage doors; the dark, narrow, dilapidated built-in hovels; the rotten bricks, the ruptured cave-spouts, the sinking roofs, the stone floors laid upon sodden earth; the perished woodwork, the damp and blackened walls, the filthy ceilings.[15]

Blatchford's passionate prose echoes, perhaps consciously, the words of Friedrich Engels 40 years earlier. Engels' observation of the human misery of Manchester provided ammunition for an evolving political philosophy, codified with Karl Marx in the improbable setting of Chetham's Library. His famous description of Little Ireland, on the banks of the grossly polluted Medlock, bears repetition not only for its political significance, but also for its evocation of the urban slum in the days before byelaws, building controls and state intervention. On the brink of the noxious flow stood

In a rather deep hole ... and surrounded on all four sides by tall factories and embankments covered with buildings ... two groups of about two hundred cottages ... in which live about four thousand human beings ... masses of refuse, offal and sickening filth lie among the standing pools in all directions, the atmosphere is poisoned by the effluvia from these and laden and darkened by the smoke of a dozen tall factory chimneys. A horde of ragged women and children swarm about here, as filthy as the swine that thrive upon the garbage heaps and in the puddles ... The race that lives in those ruinous cottages ... must really have reached the lowest stage of humanity.[16]

A decade later, Elizabeth Gaskell published *North and South*, in which the stark reality of 'Milton' is described: 'Near to the town, the air had a faint taste and smell of smoke ... Here and there a great oblong many-windowed factory stood up, like a hen among her chickens, puffing out black unparliamentary smoke'.[17] In *Hard Times* (1854), Charles Dickens painted a lurid portrait of the landscape of Coketown, for which Preston was the inspiration:

It was a town ... of brick that would have been red if the smoke and ashes had allowed it; but as matters stood it was a town of unnatural red and black like the painted face of a savage. It was a town of machinery and tall chimneys, out of which interminable serpents of smoke trailed themselves for ever and ever, and never got uncoiled. It had a black canal in it, and a river that ran purple with ill-smelling dye, and vast piles of building full of windows where there was a rattling and a trembling all day long, and where the piston of the steam-engine worked monotonously all day long, like the head of an elephant in a state of melancholy madness.[18]

Other observers could not conceal the distaste they felt for Lancashire and its people. A guidebook published in 1842 noted the coaly filthiness of Wigan, where the pavements were 'covered thickly with dark dust which the feet of the crowd of passengers kept continually in motion', and found Bolton tolerable only at night when the scene was illuminated by 'thousands of lights proceeding from the windows of the factories, which opened out before us in the shape of a crescent'. The harshest condemnation, though, was reserved for Burnley, 'most unpicturesque of towns, with a hard, cold appearance; tall chimneys smoke, and a population looking as little pleasing as their place of residence'.[19]

Such comments were echoed after the First World War, when the industrial areas were plunged into economic crisis and the reputation of Lancashire was as dark as its soot-stained buildings. In 1927 the writer H V Morton, who usually travelled in picture postcard counties, was prepared to be revolted by 'Black England', the land between the Mersey and the Ribble. He anticipated 'an England of crowded towns, of tall chimneys, of great mill walls, of canals of slow, black water … of grey, hard-looking little houses in interminable rows', and expected Wigan to be a place of 'dreary streets and stagnant canals and white-faced Wigonians dragging their weary steps along dull streets haunted by the horror of the place in which they are condemned to live'. He was touched nonetheless by the drama of the industrial scene, standing 'impressed and thrilled by the grim power of these ugly chimneys rising in groups, by the black huddle of factories, and the still, silent wheels at pit-mouth and the drifting haze of smoke'.[20] Other writers were more appalled, particularly if they spent longer absorbing the landscape, its fearsome qualities and its impact upon the denizens of this hellish world. The most celebrated temporary resident was George Orwell, whose *The Road to Wigan Pier* contains powerful descriptions of the landscape as a backcloth against which injustice took place – it was not so much the aesthetics that mattered, as the daily impact of such an environment on the lives of 50,000 people:

> the monstrous scenery of slag-heaps, chimneys, piled scrap-iron, foul canals, paths of cindery mud criss-crossed by the prints of clogs … row after row of little grey slum houses running at right angles to the embankment [for] in the industrial areas one always feels that the smoke and filth must go on for ever and that no part of earth's surface can escape them … frightful landscapes where your horizon is ringed completely by jagged grey mountains, and underfoot is mud and ashes and overhead the steel cables where tubs of dirt travel slowly across miles of country. Often the slag-heaps are on fire, and at night you can see the red rivulets … winding this way and that, and also the slow-moving blue flames of sulphur, which always seem on the point of expiring and always spring out again.[21]

Only occasionally is there is a break in the unremitting gloom and overwhelming bleakness. Morton was astonished by the survival of so much countryside, noting that 'London is much more distant from a real wood than Warrington', while in *Shabby Tiger* the usually gloomy Manchester novelist Howard Spring reminds us that south-east Lancashire had a grand physical setting, before revisiting the theme of despoliation:

> under the sky, an immensity of blue … there seemed no limit to the vast perspectives that opened out before their vision. Hill upon hill the country stretched away, and on every hill there was a crenellation of smoking chimneys – chimneys that had been smoking for generations, and for generations depositing their grime upon the seeming fair face of Heaton Park.[22]

Between the wars artists turned again to industrial landscapes. The paintings of L S Lowry (Fig. 13.7) captured the image of teeming masses of little people, going

about their mundane business beneath sunless skies, in the shadow of monolithic buildings. The sense of individuals being insignificant dots in a vast townscape is forcefully conveyed, and others experienced the same oppressive feeling. Priestley wrote of Manchester in the early 1930s that 'the city always looks as if it had been built to withstand foul weather. There is a suggestion of the fortress about it. You always seem to be moving, a not too happy dwarf, between rows of huge square black warehouses'.[23] Artists observed the forlorn character of industrial decline and physical decay. Even in the 1920s the romantically desolate quality of industrial landscapes was re-emerging (Fig. 13.8) as a poignant sense of loss was conveyed, and by the 1950s this haunted, bittersweet feeling was strong. Mid-Victorian paintings emphasised the dynamism of industrial landscapes, but those a hundred years later, such as Kenneth Gribble's *Park Parade, Ashton* (1958), reveal a static melancholy (Figs 13.9, 13.10). The Cumberland poet Norman Nicholson wrote movingly of the collapse of industry and its visual aftermath. In *Cleator Moor* (1944), he contrasted the vast profits made in the heyday of the area, and the frantic activity of the 1940s' war effort, with the desperate poverty and dereliction of the 1930s when

> The pylons rusted on the fells,
> The gutters leaked beside the walls,
> And women searched the ebb-tide tracks
> For knobs of coal or broken sticks.[24]

ABOVE: *Fig. 13.7* **A Street Scene: St Simon's Church, 1928,** *by L S Lowry. The church was built in 1847 and, like almost any public building in almost any south Lancashire town, it swiftly became blackened by smoke. Lowry's unmistakeable style and no less distinctive subject matter have, in the past 40 years, become synonymous with Salford and its townscape, though most people outside the city only became aware of this image after the disappearance of the areas and lifestyles depicted.*

Fig. 13.8 **Near Greenwood's Mill [Blackburn]**, *by Charles Holmes (1868-1936): painted in 1928, at the time when economic decline was afflicting Lancashire, this image of melancholy beauty, with its literally rose-tinted sense of a tranquil idyll, reflects changing perceptions of the industrial landscape and heritage.*

*Fig. 13.9 **Millbottom I,** by James Purdy (1899–1972). Painted in 1935, in the sunset years of the Lancashire cotton industry, this painting of a characteristic textile town scene at the end of the day is both visually arresting and also, in retrospect, highly charged with symbolism. The portrayal of the dramatic impact of the 'red brick giants', the great and brilliantly illuminated mills, is outstanding.*

*Fig. 13.10 **View of Preston in 1952,** by Charles Cundall RA, RWS (1890–1971): an unusual image of the industrial town, commissioned for the 1952 Preston Guild. Cundall chose to paint a positive view, drawing attention to the railway as a symbol of activity, and to the great public buildings; but almost all the smoke comes from locomotives, not belching chimneys, a subtle hint that all was not well with the town's cotton trade?*

In *Weeds*, he evokes the derelict landscapes of west Cumberland and Furness, reminding us that we have not in reality vanquished nature and that she will reclaim her own:

> *And they have their uses, weeds.*
> *Think of the old, worked-out mines –*
> *Quarries and tunnels, earth scorched and scruffy,*
> *torn up railways, splintered sleepers,*
> *And a whole Sahara of grit and smother and cinders.*
>
> *But go in summer and where is all the clutter?*
> *For a new town has risen of a thousand towers,*
> *Sparkling like granite, swaying like larches,*
> *And every spiky belfry humming with a peal of bees.*
> *Rosebay willow herb:*
> *Only a weed!*[25]

THE BIRTH OF 'HERITAGE'

Given the evidence for the character of industrial landscapes, the 20th-century desire to sweep away the legacy of the past is not hard to understand. The environment *was* degraded, the housing *was* poor, the derelict industrial sites *were* unappealing to the eye. The past was seen as a heavy burden, which dragged down those individuals and communities aspiring to a better future. The answer seemed clear: the burden had to be shed, by making a clean break with what had gone before and getting rid of that unwelcome legacy. Communities could be physically reinvented by cleansing them of physical and social grime and providing a bright and wholesome environment, a process that would generate social and economic rebirth. Across the region, industrial landscapes and townscapes were swept away. Towering mills fell to the demolition squads and whole districts of terraced housing were razed, but in the process the ways of life and the sense of belonging also vanished. Cultural and social patterns that went back five generations dissolved and disintegrated. Change was deeply disruptive and unsettling.

Nostalgia for an idealised past emerged as the physical evidence disappeared, while to later generations the old landscapes, just like the old lifestyles, were a matter of history, not of experience. From this combination of an emotional attachment to the times that were receding, and historical curiosity about something never personally encountered, stems much of the present fascination with 'heritage'. When there were 350 mills in Oldham alone, nobody worried about saving even a few for posterity, but when only a few were left each of the survivors became a much treasured piece of history, labelled as an architectural gem. They always *were* architectural masterpieces, but until the late 20th century they had no scarcity value to make them special.

Concern for heritage emerged in the 1950s when, for example, the term 'industrial archaeology' was first coined and volunteer groups began to take action to preserve evidence of industrial and transport history. During the early 1970s, with widespread popular rejection of the excesses of 1960s housing and urban renewal strategies, the notion that wider policies of conservation and rehabilitation were feasible and desirable took hold. Soon, heritage became a business – it could attract resources, visitors, spending power, profit. Thereafter it was ubiquitous, appearing in places where even 20 years before the very thought would have been laughable. History and archaeology became leisure interests, the subject of popular books and television programmes, and history actively engaged a much larger percentage of the population than ever before. The growth in family history research and local history contributed to the 'grassroots' appeal of industrial heritage, because the past was no longer peopled only by the influential elite. The history and experience of 'ordinary people' was of equal interest and value, and the places with which they were associated – mills and mines, cottages and courts – held in correspondingly higher regard.

Railways and canals were among the earliest targets for preservation. The narrow-gauge Ravenglass and Eskdale Railway, originally built for iron ore traffic, was already attracting visitors in the 1880s under the implausible slogan 'the route to the Alps'.[26] During the First World War it was converted to a miniature railway for tourists, in which unexpected shape it has operated ever since. From 1958, when the line was threatened with closure, it has been run by a private company that grew from the preservation society that fought for its survival. In 1973 enthusiasts reopened the Lakeside and Haverthwaite branch, built by the Furness Railway to connect with Windermere steamers and closed in 1965. These projects could draw upon the tourist potential of the Lake District, but more adventurous was the East Lancashire Railway, which reopened the line from Bury to Rawtenstall in 1987 with extensive assistance from local authorities (Fig. 13.11). Their involvement stemmed from a perception that, in an area which had lost much of its traditional industry in the previous 40 years, investment in tourism would be rewarded by new employment opportunities. By 2002 the line was carrying 120,000 passengers a year and a 19km (12-mile) extension to Heywood was completed, making this Britain's longest preserved railway.

The canals extending south from Manchester into Cheshire and the Peak District pass through attractive landscapes, and in the late 1960s the Peak Forest and Macclesfield Canals enjoyed a renaissance as pleasure waterways. This new role soon extended to the Bridgewater, Leeds and Liverpool, and Lancaster Canals, and led directly to the extremely costly projects for the restoration of the Rochdale and Huddersfield Canals, the most spectacular in England, which were reopened in 2000–1.[27] That these waterways, once ink-black and thronged with industrial traffic, should now be popular for leisure boating reflects the curious turn of fate which industrial Lancashire has experienced, a reincarnation exemplified by the restoration of the Manchester, Bolton and Bury Canal which is now under way. Of the landscape through which it once passed, J B Priestley said in 1934 that 'the ugliness was so complete that it is almost exhilarating. It challenges you to live there'.[28] Today industry has largely disappeared from the Irwell valley and hill slopes once stripped bare by fumes from collieries and chemical works are clothed in naturally regenerated woodland. The rationale for the restoration of the canal from the Irwell at Salford to the southern edge of Bury exhibits hard-nosed pragmatism, as well as sentiment. British Waterways claims that it will 'act as a focus for urban and rural regeneration in the area, attracting investment and creating jobs as well as increased opportunities for local companies' and has the potential to 'link and form a spine to a large number of recreation, countryside, heritage and tourism initiatives'.[29]

The preservation of textile mills, waterwheels and steam engines forms another important dimension to the interpretation of the region's past. Given its central importance for a century and half, as well as the intrinsic splendour of some surviving engines, it was to be expected that the rapid disappearance of steam power in the 1960s would stimulate preservation projects. However, some industrial sites had other assets, including an attractive natural setting and well preserved older buildings, which encouraged their rebirth as historic attractions. Tellingly, the preservation of the giant, red-brick mills has not found favour – they are too large and their locations are often unappealing – but at Helmshore and Styal, the two most important examples of mill preservation in the region, these reservations certainly do not apply. The historical importance of the whole community at Styal, with its charming planned village constructed by the Greg family, one of the most enlightened and philanthropic of all textile employers, gave preservation a special impetus, while acquisition by the National Trust in 1939 (as its earliest significant industrial property) guaranteed its respectability (Fig. 13.12). At Helmshore, and Queen Street Mill at Harle Syke in Burnley, both run by Lancashire County Museums, mills are preserved intact. The former includes a very complete water-powered site, while the latter is a fine example of a medium-sized steam-powered mill – and one of the few places where the deafening din of a vast roomful of working looms can now be experienced.

Fig. 13.11 Steam train crossing Summerseat viaduct, East Lancashire Railway: *Britain's longest preserved railway runs from Rawtenstall to Heywood via Bury, and is widely regarded as an important element in the economic and social regeneration of an area that has experienced severe industrial contraction since the 1920s.*

Fig. 13.12 Oak Cottages, Quarry Bank Mill, Styal: *though certainly not representative of the cotton industry as a whole, the mill at Styal and its associated model village is of outstanding interest historically, socially and architecturally. Its present ownership by the National Trust has ensured that it is particularly well-preserved. These cottages were built by the Greg family in 1819–22.*

BELOW: *Fig. 13.13 Wigan Pier and Trencherfield Mill*: *the greatest of all Lancashire's industrial cliches has had an unexpected, and highly successful, reincarnation as a major tourist attraction. The very notion that Wigan might attract visitors (other than, perhaps, Old Etonian campaigners for social justice such as himself) would have astonished George Orwell.*

Visitor centres and museums seek to interpret and recreate lives and landscapes, rather than simply presenting a surviving building and its fittings. The best-known is Wigan Pier, with its 1986 museum entitled 'The Way We Were' housed in a group of canalside buildings around Trencherfield Mill (Fig. 13.13). It is an area rich in industrial history, but the museum – as befits a place redolent of myth and inter-war popular culture – is 'heritage with a difference, a historical exhibition enlivened by actors, trained to record authentically the sight, sense, smell and feel of the past. Part theatre, part museum, each visit is a unique experience … all part of the entertainment and education that make up … *The Way We Were*'.[30] In contrast, the Greater Manchester Museum of Science and Industry at Castlefield emphasises the instructive role of its work, rather than the theatrical dimension. It sprawls across a vast site, exploiting the potential, both architectural and historical, of a variety of buildings including the world's oldest surviving railway station, long ranges of warehouses and great, glass-roofed market halls. Wigan Pier and Castlefield take different approaches and probably serve different markets, generating increasingly divergent images of the reality of the industrial past.

The industrial past can now be the subject of pride, not shame, because it is gone for good: people need no longer fear the realities, but can be comfortable with the real or imagined memory. Local and community initiatives have helped to protect surviving monuments, threatened with demolition or in urgent need of restoration, and in the more rounded and truthful instances have tried to avoid sentimentalising the past. For example, an important group of museums and heritage centres in west Cumberland seeks not only to celebrate the economic and social history of the area, but also to demonstrate something of the hardships faced by those who worked in mining and heavy industry (Fig. 13.14). The Beacon, Whitehaven's new museum, sits dramatically on the harbour wall, using its physical setting to highlight themes of both 'looking out' on the area's maritime history (including its links with America and the Atlantic trade) and 'looking in' at the social history of the town, its development and people, through to recent times. Above the town is the Haig Pit Museum. The colliery, the largest in Whitehaven, opened in 1918 and closed in 1986. Some of the pithead buildings, including the headgear and winding engine house, are now a Scheduled Ancient Monument. They have been restored as a visitor centre that tells the story of mining in the west Cumberland coalfield and draws special attention to the exceptional harshness of the work. A major theme is the terrible safety record of the mines in the area, some of the most dangerous in Europe.

The idea of 'heritage' has also been important in a wider sense, helping to shape schemes for the restoration of derelict land and abandoned sites. While the examples cited above are essentially visitor attractions, the reuse of buildings and the redevelopment of former industrial land is now a key theme in planning policies. Albert Dock in Liverpool (*see* p.224) acted as an inspiration for other places, though the results elsewhere have been mixed because few had the ready-made advantage of such magnificent architecture. At Lancaster, the restoration of St George's Quay was based around an excellent range of 18th- and 19th-century buildings, but at Salford Quays virtually all existing structures were demolished and redevelopment has focused on the docks as a setting for some masterpieces of modern architecture, including The Lowry and the Imperial War Museum North (Fig.13.15). Yet so powerful is the lure of the past as a selling

Fig. 13.14 Florence Mine, Egremont: although still a working iron mine, the last in the region, the Florence Mine is also increasingly seen as a heritage site in which, unusually, a comparatively accurate 'real life' experience of industry can be obtained by visitors.

Fig. 13.15 Salford Quays: The Lowry (1997–2000), centrepiece of the ambitious and costly scheme to regenerate the docklands on both banks of the Ship Canal. Its shining, reflective surfaces, and the no less dramatic qualities of the Imperial War Museum North on the opposite bank, provide the maximum contrast with the image of Salford immortalised by the artist after whom the arts centre is named.

RE-USING THE ARCHITECTURAL HERITAGE

The successful conversion of redundant buildings depends partly on location. Demand for city-centre residential properties has prompted schemes in central Manchester that are highly successful commercially and sensitive to the existing townscape, whereas re-use of similar buildings

in less favoured towns, such as those of north-east Lancashire, is frequently unviable. Here are four examples of conversions that exploit 'heritage' architecture and the availability of large redundant structures. The photo (above) shows the most famous, and still perhaps the most successful, the pioneering conversion of Liverpool's Albert Dock warehouses. Rescued from an ignominious fate in the late 1960s, when it was proposed that the buildings should be bulldozed into the dock basins and car parking laid out on the site, the country's largest group of Grade I listed buildings is now an internationally important tourist destination and forms an outstanding piece of late 20th-century townscape within an equally impressive mid-19th-century skin.[32] Albert Dock's success as a tourist attraction and cultural icon had a powerful psychological impact upon Liverpool; it is often seen as a key element in the revival of the city's self-esteem.

In Manchester, rationalisation in the financial sector made the spectacular headquarters of the Refuge Assurance Company (built in three stages in 1891–5, 1910–12 and 1932) redundant in the late 1980s. Its central location and lavish opulence made it an obvious candidate for conversion, and in 1996 it was reborn as the prestigious Palace Hotel (left), retaining the sumptuous internal fittings of stained glass, faience, marble and bronze.[33]

In the second half of the 20th century, numerous churches and chapels were declared surplus to ecclesiastical requirements. Demolition was the inevitable fate of many, particularly the 'off the peg' products of mid-Victorian fervour, but in the 1990s conversion and re-use of churches was increasingly favoured, especially if listed status brought pressure for retention. St Mark's church, Preston (right), solidly built in sandstone and with a tall square 'landmark' tower, was constructed in 1868 and closed in 1981. It then stood derelict (though Grade II* listed) for over 10 years while a variety of possible uses – as well as schemes for demolition of all but the tower – were considered. Eventually, changing fashions produced an answer and in the mid-1990s it was converted into 25 'luxury' flats.

The Canal Mill at Botany Bay, just outside Chorley, was built in 1856. Cotton manufacturing there ended in early 1960s, and the mill was then used for keeping chickens, storing vehicle parts and as a repair workshop. In 1994, empty and threatened with demolition, it was bought by a local businessman who already ran a successful antiques salesroom at nearby Eccleston. Botany Bay (below) is now a 'unique retail and heritage experience', with five floors of antiques and other sales outlets, 'Dickensian-style shops' and a Victorian market place. Visitors can 'step back in time' to a Victorian penny arcade and enjoy the memorabilia and collectibles on view – including aircraft, tanks and tractors. The mill, adorned with distinctively incongruous red and green corner turrets, is conveniently alongside the M61, a useful form of free advertising.[34]

point that at Buckshaw Village, the new community developed on the site of the Royal Ordnance factory at Euxton near Chorley, there is a 'faux heritage' scheme – a block of apartments designed from scratch as a replica cotton mill converted into flats.

When we consider awareness of the industrial past and its present legacy, it is clear that for the great majority of people 'the past is a foreign country. They do things differently there'.[31] We do not have to work in appalling conditions in mines or mills, and the ways of life revealed in heritage centres and museums, no matter how vividly portrayed and shockingly revealed, are part of history. Unavoidably, the past is presented in such a way that we can observe and learn about it, but we cannot experience its reality, no matter how often the tourist literature claims that we can and do. The industrial buildings and landscapes we visit are clean and safe. Since the Clean Air Acts of the 1950s and 1960s the atmosphere is clear, no longer opaque with clouds of smoke, and following the concerted effort to clean the rivers their water is no longer a treacly flow of dyes, grease, toxic chemicals, waste acid and stinking refuse. If these were still the realities, industrial heritage as we now understand the term would never have emerged.

We are in a position akin to that of observers two centuries ago, during the first phase of the Industrial Revolution. We can appreciate buildings, machinery and industrial landscapes without having to experience the filth, the human tragedies of child mortality and endemic disease, the unbreathable air and undrinkable water. Two centuries ago industry could be appreciated for its aesthetic and architectural qualities, and for the joyous spectacle of watching machinery working in a way that seemed almost magical. Now we can adopt the same perspectives, reinforced with our powerful new sense of history. Defying the injunction of *Lancashire Illustrated* of 1843, we now have plenty of 'time to bestow inquiry or reflection on the past'.

NOTES

1   Anon. 1843, 4
2   Priestley 1934, 274
3   Wordsworth 1904, 5
4   For background, see Klingender 1968
5   Booth 1830, 52
6   Cooke Taylor 1842, 21–2
7   Priestley 1934, 278
8   Wordsworth 1904, 876
9   Austin *et al.* 1831, 69–70 & 86
10 For the artistic and literary context of urban landscapes, see Nenadic in Waller 2000
11 Anon. 1890, unpag.
12 Whittle 1821, 100–10
13 Booth 1830, 51
14 Booth 1830, 57
15 Blatchford 1889, 2
16 Engels 1969, 93
17 Gaskell 1855, ch.7 ('unparliamentary': recent legislation had sought to reduce smoke emissions)
18 Dickens 1854, ch.5
19 Redding & Taylor 1842, 151, 160, 190
20 Morton 1927, 186–7
21 Orwell 1937, ch.1; ch.7
22 Spring 1934, ch. 8 pt.2
23 Priestley 1934, 255
24 Nicholson 1994, 16
25 Ibid, 340–1
26 Joy 1990, 220
27 For an account of canal restoration see Gibson 2002
28 Priestley 1934, 262
29 www.britishwaterways.co.uk/site/ManchesterBoltonBuryCanal
30 Wigan Metropolitan Borough Council publicity leaflet, 1989
31 Hartley 1953
32 Hughes 1999, 56–7; Jarvis & Smith 1999
33 Hartwell 2001, 180–1
34 www.lancshistory.co.uk/chorley/botanybay

14

'A Sort of National Property'?

*… persons of pure taste … by their visits (often repeated) to the Lakes … testify
that they deem the district a sort of national property, in which every man
has a right and interest who has an eye to perceive and a heart to enjoy.*[1]

The poet William Wordsworth's often-quoted phrase articulated for the first time
the idea that the nation as a whole might claim an interest in local landscapes.

He was writing to urge conservation (specifically, to restrain the activities of
new villa-building landowners), but the conception that land may be viewed as 'a
sort of national property' lies behind other important processes of landscape
change, particularly in the 20th century. Wordsworth used the phrase in relation
to the Lake District, but the intention in this chapter is wider – to examine the
impact of external perceptions of the North West, not only in terms of
conservation, but also through national planning for land use, communications,
defence and security. In exploring the meaning of landscape, this final chapter
focuses on the landscape as it is perceived and controlled by distant authorities,
where statutory powers reflect national perceptions of what is meet and proper
for the landscape as a whole.

STATE PLANNING FOR ECONOMIC GROWTH

Until the 1850s central government played no direct part in landscape change,
but by the 20th century it had emerged as an active participant, shaping and
dictating the form of development. As a result, landscape change has increasingly
taken place within the framework of theoretical or abstract policies, translated
into practical effect by decisions at local level. The first local planning controls
were introduced from 1909, and after 1947, when the Town and Country
Planning Act greatly strengthened and extended the scope of the planning
system, they became the context within which all decisions about landscape were
made. It is easy to forget the radical and unprecedented nature of this change,
but for over half a century a huge variety of decisions affecting landscape, from
grand strategies concerning green belts, housing, new towns and National Parks
to the minutiae of development control, have stemmed from the planning role of
central government and its implementation locally.[2]

Shaping the modern industrial landscape

Industrial north-west England, 'the workshop of the world', was compelled to
reinvent itself in the 1920s and 1930s; half a century later it underwent a second and
no less difficult rebirth. The years from 1920 to 1975 showed that central
government intervention, reinforced by vigorous campaigning from local authorities,
was a vital factor in encouraging new industries and determining their location. A
wide variety of financial inducements, including regional development aid and

Fig. 14.1 Lillyhall, near Workington:
a recent industrial estate occupies land which
was formerly damaged by colliery workings.
Beyond the industrial units the rough ground
and very large flat fields extending into the
middle distance are land restored after the
closure of Wythemoor Head opencast mine,
which covered more than 3sq km.

provision of sites and infrastructure, distorted the patterns which would have emerged under an overtly laissez-faire system. In 1934, when unemployment in Maryport, at 57.5 per cent, was higher than in Jarrow, west Cumberland was one of four districts in Britain designated as Special Areas, eligible for direct government assistance (Fig. 14.1). Between 1945 and 1948 this principle was extended under the Development Area scheme to Wigan, St Helens, Merseyside and north-east Lancashire. However, a persistent problem faced by those seeking to remodel the regional economic structure was that the locations perceived to be most in need of help (west Cumberland and east Lancashire) were also those least attractive to new investment. Private capital tended to gravitate to the north–south axis through Lancashire, which was given definition in the 1950s and 1960s by the construction of the M6.[3]

In one important respect the North West, despite its reputation as a stronghold of traditional industries, was an innovator. The world's first industrial estate, laid out between 1897 and 1920 at Trafford Park, next to the newly opened Manchester Ship Canal, served as an inspiration for others in the 1920s and 1930s.[4] On Merseyside, for example, new trading estates were developed in the 1930s at Kirkby, Aintree and Speke, their success reinforcing the message that infrastructure improvements and, if possible, financial incentives were essential to attract new industry. The motor industry, perceived as a source of long-term economic security, encouraged governments after 1945 to focus on vehicle production as the basis of the economic revival of Merseyside. Leyland's inter-war transformation from small cotton-manufacturing town to centre of vehicle production served as an inspiration for drawing more car plants to the region.[5] International car firms were paid massive subsidies and received other incentives to locate on Merseyside, the outcome being the Vauxhall plant at Ellesmere Port and the huge Ford factory at Halewood (which by 1975 employed over 14,000 people).

Government strategic planning and financial encouragement, using Development Area assistance, also further boosted the established petrochemical industry along the lower Mersey after 1945. By the 1970s a chain of chemical plants, refineries and storage depots extended from Widnes and Runcorn to the edge of Birkenhead, and a new industrial zone grew on both banks of the Ship Canal below Trafford Park, where the Irlam steelworks had been among the first new industries to locate beside the canal. In the 1940s and 1950s chemical refineries, petrochemical plants and a huge gas complex at Partington transformed the landscape of the south bank, which is now dominated by tall metal chimneys, tangled webs of electricity power lines, storage tanks and pipelines (Fig. 14.2). But on the north bank the site of the huge steelworks which for 70 years towered above Irlam is now an industrial estate, for what was brand-new in the early 20th century had become an undesirable dinosaur at its end.

Reordering the transport network

Among the most influential aspects of landscape change in the 20th century has been the reshaping of the transport infrastructure, a dimension of public policy for almost a century since the state accepted the principle of paying for roads. The contraction of the industrial base in the 1920s and 1930s and the simultaneous growth of motor transport resulted in large reductions in the railway network. Rural branches and lines serving industrial areas were equally vulnerable to piecemeal closure: the intricate network of lines serving the iron and coal centres of west Cumberland had already gone by the end of the 1930s, its raison d'être having evaporated. After 1950, however, the nationalised system instigated a long-term programme of closures, of which the notorious Beeching cuts were only one phase. By 1975, for example, only the coastal line survived in west Cumbria, while in south Lancashire the railways withdrew entirely from Rossendale, the Leigh and Atherton area and most smaller cotton towns between Bolton and Ashton under Lyne. Elsewhere, larger stations were closed and their adjacent goods yards, rendered redundant by changing patterns of freight handling, were eyed eagerly by property developers. Butler Street goods yard in central Preston became the car park for a 1980s shopping centre, while the station at Blackpool Central and its impressive sprawl of sidings and excursion platforms became the region's largest car park, served by a new road built along the former railway line.[6]

The post-war expansion of commercial air traffic also had major consequences for the landscape. Manchester Corporation opened a municipal airfield at Barton in 1930, the year that Liverpool began work on that at Speke, while Blackpool Council opened an airfield at Stanley Park (now the site of the zoo) in 1927, moving to the present location at Squires Gate in 1932. From the early 1950s Manchester airport mushroomed, swallowing almost the entire parish of Ringway and parts of several others. Its multi-storey car parks, flyovers and access roads, terminal buildings, service depots and ground-level car parks

Fig. 14.2 Chemical works at Weston Point, Runcorn, a dramatic example of the visual impact of 20th-century industrialisation. Overlooking the broad middle reach of the Mersey estuary, the works is one of the most prominent elements in the almost continuous belt of refineries, chemical and petrochemical plants, power stations and storage facilities which extends down the river from Irlam to Tranmere.

Fig. 14.3 Manchester International Airport from the east: *the airport's voracious appetite for land, not only for runways and aprons but also for sprawling car parks, road networks and service facilities, is immediately apparent – and the second runway (foreground) extends twice as far again into the Cheshire countryside, off the picture to the left.*

make it perhaps the largest single feature of the man-made landscape in the entire region (Fig. 14.3).[7]

Perhaps the most significant change was the creation of the modern road network. The last private turnpike trusts were dissolved only two decades before the advent of the motor age which would have transformed their fortunes, so modern road building was entirely paid for by the public purse. Lancashire County Council was early in the field, constructing bypasses at places such as Garstang and Poulton-le-Fylde in the decade from 1922 and widening and straightening inter-urban roads. The Preston to Blackpool road via Kirkham is a classic example of late 1920s design, with four lanes (but no central reservation), sharp curves and numerous junctions. Some towns, including Bolton, Blackburn and Rochdale, built sections of ring road to take through traffic away from congested central streets. In 1923 the county and a consortium of major boroughs agreed to build the East Lancashire Road, in order to link Liverpool and Manchester via St Helens. Completed in 1934, it was among the first British arterial roads of the modern age. Its landscape impact was dramatic: designed for speed, its very direct alignment (almost all entirely new) ruthlessly ignored the existing grain of the countryside. Wide enough for dual carriageways and with deep cuttings, it foreshadowed the impact of the post-war motorways.[8]

Its success encouraged the county council in the late 1930s to plan a much more ambitious network of new roads, and it was from these designs, via the seminal 1949 report *A Road Plan for Lancashire*,[9] that the post-war highway strategy emerged under government auspices. Britain's first stretch of motorway, the M6 Preston bypass, was opened in December 1958 and for the next 40 years the regional network grew steadily, based on the north–south axis of the M6 from Warrington to Carlisle and the east–west route, the M62 from Liverpool to Hull (Fig. 14.4). Two important motorway schemes were partly intended to revive the depressed areas of east Lancashire: the M66 into Rossendale (which had the unanticipated consequence of making this a commuter area for Manchester, its semi-derelict stone farmhouses and barns converted into highly desirable country homes); and the M65 from Preston to Colne, linking a string of mill towns and – contrary to intentions – reinforcing Preston's role as the economic focus of Lancashire. Unlike any earlier transport network, the motorway system was built under a rational strategy and pre-determined plan.

Motorways have transformed the landscapes through which they run. With their exceptional width, ruling gradient of no more than 1 in 25 and curves of large radius, they do not fit readily into existing landscapes and require monumentally large earthworks. This is most dramatically illustrated by the Lune gorge at Tebay, where, in contrast to the main railway line (1846), the M6, though terraced on two levels to reduce the excavation of the hillside, is visually inescapable. At Windy Hill, the summit of the M62 above Rochdale, the motorway runs in a massive cutting over 35m (100 feet) deep, a great slot carved through the crest of the Pennines. Nowhere is a motorway reticent or self-effacing. Where they cross the lowlands, as in the stretch of the M6 from Penrith to Carlisle or at the foot of Farleton Fell near Burton in Kendal, the great roads disrupt the structure of landscape, dividing farms and fields, diverting byroads, culverting watercourses and creating massive physical barriers. Motorway interchanges also consume many acres. Croft interchange on the M6 and M62 near Warrington is over a kilometre across, while the Worsley interchange at the junction of the M60, M61 and A580 is the largest in Britain, covering over 500ha (2 sq. miles) and with 15 separate sets of slip roads (Fig. 14.5).[10]

Motorway architecture in the region includes some impressive bridges and viaducts, from the graceful, slanting overbridge spanning the M6 cutting at Scorton village, and the soaring footbridge that carries the Pennine Way over the summit cutting of the M62, to the great viaducts, such as Thelwall and Gathurst on the M6 (1963), Barton Bridge (1960) and Rakewood on the M62, near Rochdale (1971). The irony is that the aesthetic quality of the structures was often at its best in the most attractive landscapes, which nonetheless suffered serious damage from motorway building.

Motorways intrude on the landscape as ribbons of pollution from noise and light. It is possible to stand on the remotest summits of the lonely Bowland fells and, if the wind is from the west, to hear the distant hum and rumble of traffic on the M6 10km (6 miles) away. At night, across the region, the skeins of bright lights, the interwoven loops of orange dots, the floodlights of service stations and

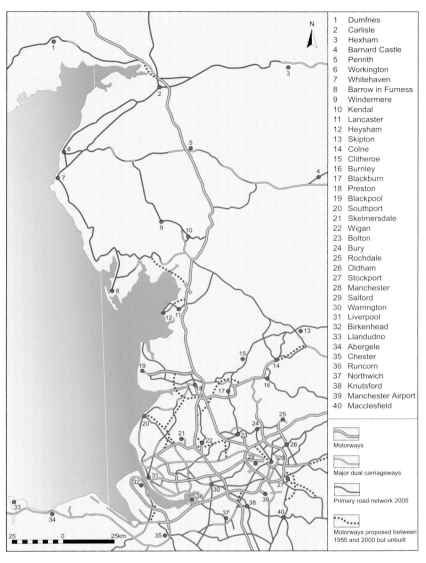

1	Dumfries
2	Carlisle
3	Hexham
4	Barnard Castle
5	Penrith
6	Workington
7	Whitehaven
8	Barrow in Furness
9	Windermere
10	Kendal
11	Lancaster
12	Heysham
13	Skipton
14	Colne
15	Clitheroe
16	Burnley
17	Blackburn
18	Preston
19	Blackpool
20	Southport
21	Skelmersdale
22	Wigan
23	Bolton
24	Bury
25	Rochdale
26	Oldham
27	Stockport
28	Manchester
29	Salford
30	Warrington
31	Liverpool
32	Birkenhead
33	Llandudno
34	Abergele
35	Chester
36	Runcorn
37	Northwich
38	Knutsford
39	Manchester Airport
40	Macclesfield

Motorways

Major dual carriageways

Primary road network 2005

Motorways proposed between 1955 and 2000 but unbuilt

Fig. 14.4 The motorway and main road network: the post-1945 infrastructure of major highways is the latest in a succession of transport networks, each overlaying its predecessors, and has been a powerful determinant of new geographies of economic activity and demographic change, as well as a highly visible feature of the region's landscape.

the beams of thousands of headlights proclaim the presence of these roads from afar.

The landscape impact of the motorway and trunk road network extends well beyond the roads themselves, particularly in the southern half of the region. Motorways increased the accessibility of nodal points, which already acted as magnets for development, reinforcing the commercial vigour and physical growth of towns such as Warrington and Bury. Land adjacent to motorway interchanges now carries retail parks and superstores, office developments, warehousing and distribution centres (as at Bamber Bridge and Walton Summit near Preston, Fig.14.6) or large new industrial estates (as at Heywood and Bury, and at Slattocks near Middleton). Motorways and associated new roads isolate portions of farmland, rendering them redundant for serious agriculture and ripe for commercial development. The built-up area is thus extended and 'rounded off', inexorably generating further pressure to release even more land for growth. The synergy between the two key aspects of central government planning – improving the infrastructure and channelling the location of industry – has thus been a powerful force in shaping landscape change across the region in the past hundred years, particularly in industrial Lancashire.[11]

THE UPLANDS AS A NATIONAL RESOURCE

National planning has also had a major impact on upland environments. Apparently empty and of little economic value, the northern uplands have been viewed as suitable locations for activities needed to contribute to the nation's good. Major changes in upland land use have resulted, as the political imperatives of succeeding generations have been deemed to outweigh purely local concerns. The urgent need for fresh drinking water for towns and cities led to the construction of reservoirs in upland valleys; government policy to increase domestic timber production in order to reduce reliance on imports resulted in the afforestation of mountain and moorland with coniferous plantations; while, most recently, the drive to increase the amount of electricity generated from renewable resources has spawned the wind farms that form the latest striking addition to the landscape of the North West.

Water supply

Proximity to the industrial towns of south and east Lancashire ensured that the Pennine hills were identified early as potential sources of water to serve the needs of the growing urban populations. The first large-scale water supply scheme was that in the Longdendale valley, east of Stalybridge, where Manchester Corporation constructed a flight of five reservoirs between 1848 and 1884. In this era of sanitary reform, water supply schemes for other towns quickly followed, resulting in a rash of reservoir construction on gathering grounds in the Pennines. Liverpool constructed a series of reservoirs at Rivington, gathering water from the western edges of the Rossendale moors from 1849; Lancaster drew water from the Wyresdale fells from the early 1850s; Bolton Corporation acquired extensive catchments to the north of the town in 1865. As urban populations, and thus demand for water, increased across the later 19th and 20th centuries, the number of reservoirs and the hectareage assigned to water catchment grew. These were not solely to provide drinking water: the textile mills were thirsty consumers and over half the water supply in many areas went to industrial and trade concerns in the 1880s. While the municipal authorities of the textile towns could look to the moors behind them (Fig. 14.7), other towns had to look further afield. The coastal resorts of the Fylde turned to the Bowland fells, where Stocks Reservoir was constructed between 1923 and 1937. Everywhere, the deliberate depopulation of water catchments accelerated the retreat of settlement from marginal hill farming land on the moors.[12]

OPPOSITE PAGE:

TOP: *Fig. 14.5 Worsley interchange is the largest motorway junction in Britain. The M60 Manchester Outer Ring Road (top to bottom), the M61 to Preston (top left) and the A580 East Lancs Road (foreground left to right) meet in a skein of roads. The huge land-take is apparent, as is the unexpected role of the motorway in creating new wildlife habitats by isolating substantial areas of open ground. On the right is the medieval and 16th century Wardley Hall, on the left one of the numerous golf courses of the conurbation fringe.*

BOTTOM: *Fig. 14.6 Walton Summit interchange near Preston: the triangle of the M6, M65 (bottom left to top right) and M61 (middle distance left to right) holds one of the largest industrial estates in the north of England, a perfect example of the magnetic commercial attraction of motorway interchanges.*

BELOW: *Fig. 14.7 Greenbooth and Naden Reservoirs, near Rochdale. The Norden Brook valley has supplied water to Heywood since the 19th century. The three smaller reservoirs upstream were created by Heywood Waterworks Company in 1846–8 and in 1863; Greenbooth reservoir, in the foreground, was completed in 1962.*

Fig. 14.8 Thirlmere in 1879, before flooding.

Fig. 14.9 Thirlmere from Bull Crag.
This modern view from almost the same position as Fig. 14.8 captures the dramatic landscape change resulting from the conversion of the valley into a reservoir.

The Pennines could not satisfy the thirst of Manchester, so the city council turned to the Lake District, where very high rainfall and deep, narrow valleys provided ideal conditions for water catchment. From the start, Manchester's plans encountered opposition from those wishing to preserve the Lakeland landscape. The battles over Thirlmere and Haweswater are well known. Manchester Corporation had acquired Thirlmere and its fellside catchments in 1877 and, under the terms of the Manchester Corporation Waterworks Act of 1879, obtained power to abstract over 228 million litres (50 million gallons) of water from the lake daily, taking it the 170km (106 miles) to Manchester down a gravity-fed aqueduct. The proposals immediately galvanised the opposition, which was channelled through the Thirlmere Defence Association, the earliest conservation body in the Lake District. Parliament deemed that Manchester's need for water was paramount and construction began. The dam closing the narrow gap at the outflow of the lower of the two natural lakes, opened in 1894, raised the water level by 17.5m (50 feet), creating a single reservoir. Farms at Armboth were destroyed and the valley sides planted with woodland, converting a landscape of pastoral farming into an almost uninhabited water gathering ground (Figs 14.8 and 14.9). As demand for water continued to increase, Manchester Corporation obtained power to purchase the Haweswater, Swindale and Wet Sleddale valleys in 1919, thus acquiring a further catchment of 9,720ha (24,000 acres). A massive dam, on which construction started in 1934, raised the

level of Haweswater by 27.5m (90 feet), flooding the village of Mardale.[13] In 1919 Manchester's predatory approach to Lakeland water provoked a telling comment from Lancashire County Council, concerned about the water needs of its own towns: the upland catchments should, it suggested, be 'treated in the character of a national trust'.[14]

Not all water supply schemes involved wholesale landscape change. Water has been taken from very many of the lakes and tarns in the Lake District (Fig. 14.10), often with little noticeable impact upon the landscape, as in the example of Crummock Water, which has supplied industrial Workington and the market town of Cockermouth since the 1890s (Fig. 14.11). Since the balance of opinion has shifted towards conservation from the 1940s, water abstraction has not been allowed to create further large-scale landscape transformations. Manchester Corporation's final Lakeland reservoir, constructed between 1962 and 1967 in the remote and little-visited valley of Wet Sleddale, was much more modest in scale and impact on the landscape.[15]

The impact of reservoir construction and water abstraction from the uplands is not restricted to dams, pumping houses and pipelines. The hydrological consequences have been considerable. On many rivers the flow is now artificially controlled, managed to ensure that heavy demand on a reservoir does not result in a damaging reduction in flow downstream. More subtle, perhaps, have been the consequences for the regional hydrological system: drawing water from the Lake District and Pennines for the conurbations of south Lancashire has resulted in a diversion of water from these uplands to the Mersey river system via the sewers of Greater Manchester and Merseyside.[16] Yet in the popular imagination it is the flooding of farms, cottages, graveyards and fields in the valleys that epitomises the landscape cost of water supply. Communities lost beneath the waters evoke a strong response (Fig. 14.12).

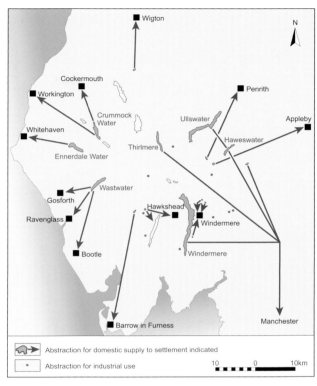

Fig. 14.10 Lake District lakes and tarns modified or created for water supply.

Fig. 14.11 Crummock Water. The lake level was raised by around 1m by the construction of a small dam and a retaining wall along the low-lying shore at the northern end of the lake, to provide water supply for Workington Corporation. Other landscape features resulting from the scheme include the pump house seen here, the canalisation of Park Beck, and some waterlogging of farmland behind the retaining wall.

235

Fig. 14.12 Watergrove Reservoir wall, *showing datestones preserved from houses flooded when the reservoir was constructed in the 1930s.*

Afforestation

To both 19th-century advocates of 'improvement' and 20th-century national planners, afforestation seemed an attractive means of obtaining economic benefit from the fells and moors. Coniferous plantations, mostly of larch, appeared on several Lake District estates in the 19th century, notably near Keswick (the Hospital and Comb plantations at Thornthwaite and Dodd plantation near Mirehouse) and at Grizedale in Furness fells, where Montague Ainslie planted 485ha (1,200 acres) of fell land with larch. Further large-scale planting was undertaken by Manchester Corporation in 1908, when 810ha (2,000 acres) of conifers were planted to protect the water catchments around Thirlmere.[17]

The foundation of the Forestry Commission in 1919, charged with increasing substantially the supply of home-grown timber and given powers of compulsory purchase, resulted in a significant increase in the extent of coniferous plantations in the Lake District. The first state forest there was Thornthwaite Forest, which grew from the core of the Hospital Plantation, acquired in 1919. Most of the land acquired there and elsewhere in the Lake District was former common land enclosed by Parliamentary act and award in the 19th century. The ruler-straight edges to many commercial plantations are more a product of enclosure commissioners in the 19th century than of a love of rectilinearity among foresters of the 20th (Fig. 14.13).

The purchase of all of upper Ennerdale in 1925–6 enabled the creation of a second large forest on rectangular fellside allotments, but further land acquisition in upper Eskdale in 1934 triggered vociferous protests. From the earliest days

Fig. 14.13 Forestry plantations, Whinlatter: *the ruler-straight edges of the plantations are dictated by the boundaries laid across the fells by Parliamentary enclosure.*

forestry plantations had encountered opposition from those who wished to preserve the open, treelesss fells from 'alien' conifers: Wordsworth bemoaned the planting of larch ('this spiky tree' growing into 'nothing but deformity'), anticipating by more than a century the noisy campaign of H H Symonds in the 1930s against the extension of Forestry Commission conifer plantations in the Lake District. Under pressure from the Council for the Preservation of Rural England and the newly formed Friends of the Lake District, the Commission agreed in 1936 not to acquire land for planting in the central 300 square miles of the Lakeland fells. Opposition also eventually thwarted the Commission's plan to create a 'Hardknott Forest Park' in the upper reaches of Eskdale and Dunnerdale. As a result of the pressure to preserve the central fells from afforestation, the more recent expansion of Forestry Commission plantations was restricted to the outer edges of the Lake District, such as Grizedale Forest in the low fells of Furness, and the plantations in the remote valleys of Blengdale and Miterdale in the western fells.[18]

Wind power

Changing government policy is directly related to one of the most recent manifestations of landscape change in the North West. The region's exposure to winds blowing in from the sea attracted the attention of companies seeking to establish wind farms in response to the drive towards increasing electricity generation from renewable resources in the 1990s. Existing planning controls in the National Parks and Areas of Outstanding Natural Beauty deflected the siting of wind farms away from much of the uplands, with the result that clusters of wind turbines are located in two distinct environments – on moorland outside the protected zones of upland landscape and on former industrial 'brown belt' land on the coast. Moorland wind farms, for example, include those on Kirkby Moor, just outside the Lake District National Park boundary north of Ulverston, and Lambrigg Fell, east of Kendal, in the wedge of unprotected hill land between the Lake District and Yorkshire Dales National Parks. 'Brown belt' sites include the string of wind farms along the Cumbrian coast from Siddick, near Workington, in the north to Askam in Furness in the south. As with the other changes in the rural landscape, these restless sentinels on the coasts and hills provoked debate and opposition from those who feared that the rush for renewable energy would result in a proliferation of wind farms on every available hillside and stretch of coast.

MARGINALITY AND NATIONAL SECURITY

The impact on the 20th-century English landscape of two World Wars and the protracted Cold War was considerable. Thousands of hectares of land were requisitioned for military purposes, some temporarily during wartime, others permanently, for use as camps, airfields, training grounds, ammunition factories and stores and, in the arms race of the Cold War, as nuclear installations. No English region escaped the legacy of concrete and wire. In the North West, the perceived remoteness of much of the region, especially Cumbria, attracted national military planners and led to its choice as the site of potentially dangerous activities. Moreover, the region's western location made it comparatively secure from attack from continental Europe.

The first military use where remoteness from centres of population played a part was in the location of ammunition factories and stores. The earliest structure – and one of the most extensive – was the Gretna cordite factory, constructed as a result of the shell shortage during the First World War. The Ministry of Munitions took charge of production in 1915, acquiring by compulsory purchase a 14km (9-mile) swathe of land around Gretna, straddling the Scottish

Fig. 14.14 Broughton Moor
ammunition dump. Storage bunkers and
access roads are spread out across the site but
have not completely obscured the field
boundaries of the earlier agricultural landscape.

border between Longtown and Dornock. The vast factory complex was completed in the following year. Proximity of rail links, where the lines converged to cross the Esk and Eden rivers, was a major attraction when choosing the site, but the low population levels around the Solway mosses were another important consideration. The factory's legacy survives in the new townships of Gretna and Eastriggs, built to house munitions workers, and in the continued military use of an extensive tract of land near Longtown.[19]

During the Second World War a series of munitions works was established in west Cumberland, where remoteness and high levels of unemployment went hand-in-hand. The Admiralty constructed a major naval armaments depot at Broughton Moor (Fig. 14.14) and also stored munitions in a neighbouring mine at Camerton. Further down the coast a TNT factory was established at Sellafield and another ordnance factory at Drigg. In industrial Lancashire, by contrast, armaments factories were sited close to centres of population, as at Risley Moss outside Warrington and the vast Royal Ordnance factory at Euxton, between Leyland and Chorley.

The wartime acquisition of land by the state for military purposes was to be of major significance in determining the location of Cold War nuclear establishments. Plutonium production was planned by a team of chemists based at the armaments factory at Risley, and other existing military sites in the North West played a crucial role in the heady race to create the British atomic bomb in the late 1940s. A disused poison gas factory at Springfields, in the Fylde near Preston, was converted to become the nation's first uranium plant in 1946. The experimental and potentially dangerous nature of the nuclear technology, combined with a desire for maximum secrecy, dictated that the site chosen for the first nuclear reactor should be remote from major concentrations of population. A site in the Scottish Highlands was considered, but ultimately rejected on the grounds that a greenfield site with poor communications and an insufficiently large local labour force was impractical. In 1947 it was decided to construct the reactor on the former TNT factory at Sellafield, which was renamed Windscale. The chimney of the air-cooled reactor pile quarantined since the fire of 1957 still stands.[20]

When the British government decided to invest in nuclear energy in 1955, the first nuclear power station (also supplying plutonium for the weapons programme) was built adjacent to the Windscale reactor at Calder Hall. The complex that grew on and around the site of the former wartime factory at Sellafield is the major nuclear landscape in Britain, its cooling towers and sheer extent dominating the south-west Cumbrian coastal strip (Fig. 14.15).[21] Geographical inertia, bolstered by local support for a contentious technology in an area with few other employment opportunities, has seen the transition from TNT production to plutonium production power generation and finally to nuclear reprocessing in one notorious location.

Fig. 14.15 Sellafield: successive generations of nuclear technology have created a vast industrial complex in the west Cumbrian countryside.

The landscape impact of military control over large hectarages of land in remote areas is also seen elsewhere. Another product of the Cold War was the Spadeadam rocket testing site, set in coniferous plantations in the empty moorlands of north-east Cumbria. Built in 1957 to test the British Intermediate Range Ballistic Missile, the 3,600ha (9,000-acre) complex has served a series of functions for which a remote location was a paramount consideration, whether this was the roar of engines on the test plinths at Priorlancy or the roar of aircraft flying over the RAF's Electronic Warfare Tactics Range established on the site in 1976.[22]

The North West had relatively few military airfields, because it was distant from mainland Europe and inconvenient for the short-range bombers, while much of the area was too hilly or mountainous. Nevertheless, some extensive tracts of agricultural land were commandeered at, for example, Great Orton and Kirkbride on the Solway plain; Warton and Samlesbury in mid-Lancashire; and (largest of all) Burtonwood between Warrington and Prescot. From 1942 Burtonwood was the main American airforce base in western Europe, and by 1945 had a resident population of 17,000. From 1948 Burtonwood played a central role in the Cold War, as the largest military establishment in the 'Free World' outside America itself. It was the gateway to Europe for many thousands of US conscripts, and a temporary home to tens of thousands more – by 1953 it had become a piece of Middle America transplanted, complete with baseball facilities and hamburger joints. With its associated storage depots and warehousing, the base covered over 1,000ha (2,470 acres), but by 1965, as American attention turned to Vietnam, Burtonwood was run down. The site was considered for a new international airport to replace Manchester and Liverpool, but eventually the M62 was built along the main runway and part of the area has now been used for a major commercial and residential development.[23]

NATURE RESTORED

'Nature is never spent' wrote Gerard Manley Hopkins in the poem quoted at the beginning of this book. Human activity channels, restricts or encourages nature, so that the landscape may be viewed as the product of a creative tension between society and natural processes. Where the intensity of human activity decreases, it is not long before plants and animals re-colonise abandoned land, smothering the works of mankind.

The re-advance of nature is vividly apparent in abandoned slate workings in the Lake District. The slopes of Lingmoor Fell in Great Langdale are pock-marked with the waste from slate quarrying and mining, which reached its peak in the late 19th century. At Banks Quarry (right) older waste heaps already lie under a blanket of bracken; scrubby woodland is advancing and trees have colonised even the most extensive and recent quarry waste.

On the Royal Society for the Protection of Birds' reserve at Leighton Moss, near Silverdale, man and nature have worked together to restore the natural habitats of an area of wetland (below). Leighton Moss, a finger of mossland at the head of Morecambe Bay, had been reclaimed for agriculture in the 19th century but required constant pumping to keep the water table in

check. When pumping stopped after the First World War, wetland habitats returned and by the 1960s there were 70ha (173 acres) of Phragmites reed beds. Since the RSPB established the reserve in 1963 the extent of reed fen has increased to 84ha (207 acres) and further wetland areas are in the process of being restored. The driving force behind the human encouragement of wetland here has been the desire to preserve the last breeding ground of the bittern (Botaurus stellaris) in North West England.

The deliberate restoration of land scarred by industrial waste or dereliction has transformed former coal-mining landscapes in both Lancashire and west Cumbria. Lunar landscapes of colliery waste have vanished, to be replaced by farmland or country parks. The legacy of Garswood Hall colliery, near Ashton in Makerfield, which closed in 1958, included dramatic slag heaps known as the 'Three Sisters' (below). They were levelled and planted with trees in the late 1960s as part of a programme to convert an industrial wasteland into an area with facilities for leisure and recreation. A racing circuit and a lake for angling and sailing were created soon after reclamation, but cuts in public expenditure in the 1980s caused low levels of maintenance. The resulting landscape is a semi-natural mixture of grassland and scrubby woodland, which has become a popular recreation area (bottom).

CONSERVING TREASURED LANDSCAPES

Finally, the concept of land and landscape as 'a sort of national property' can also be explored in the direction intended by Wordsworth when he first used the phrase: the incorporation of aesthetic appreciation of landscape into conservation policies and government thinking. The roots of the conservation movement are to be found in the uplands, where, as we have seen, the major landscape transformations of reservoir building and afforestation collided with the aesthetic and recreational love affair with the fells. By the late 20th century, most landscapes in the uplands of north-west England were protected from further large-scale development through being designated as National Parks or Areas of Outstanding Natural Beauty. The National Parks campaign was a product of the 1920s, when urban expansion, increasing concern for nature conservation and the outdoor movement combined to create a focus on the future of the countryside. One of the first significant actions of the Council for the Preservation of Rural England (CPRE), founded in 1926, was to call for an enquiry into the need for National Parks to preserve nature and scenery and to improve recreational facilities. The Addison Committee, appointed by the Labour government in 1929, recommended the establishment of a series of National Parks, including the Lake District. Although none was established until after the Second World War, considerable momentum built during the 1930s, particularly in the Lake District, where a powerful rambling-based lobby, the Friends of the Lake District (founded in 1934), complemented – and cajoled – the landowner-dominated CPRE. The agreement reached with the Forestry Commission in 1936, discussed above, was a landmark in controlling landscape change in an area which was a candidate for National Park status.[24]

Both CPRE and the Friends of the Lake District were instrumental in establishing in 1936 the Standing Committee on National Parks. The Committee spearheaded the campaign that eventually bore fruit in the National Parks and Access to the Countryside Act of 1949. This paved the way for the designation both of National Parks and of 'conservation areas' (which became known as Areas of Outstanding Natural Beauty or AONBs). Most of them were areas of 'wild country' in the uplands: the Peak District and Lake District parks were designated in 1951 and the Yorkshire Dales in 1954. Four further areas in the North West were designated as AONBs, in which the priority was to control development in order to protect scenic beauty: the Forest of Bowland and Solway Coast AONBs in 1964; Arnside and Silverdale in 1972; and the North Pennines in 1988. The 1949 Act also gave statutory powers to the recently created Nature Conservancy, enabling areas of land to be designated and protected as Nature Reserves.[25]

By the mid-20th century, therefore, the shape of the countryside was increasingly being dictated by national policies, mediated through specialist civil servants and local authority officers. Successive planning acts gave local authorities the power to determine in broad outline future patterns of land use. In practice, planning policies have tended to concentrate development in certain areas, and to limit development in much of the region's countryside. The statutory framework of National Parks and AONBs centres on tight control over even small-scale development, and on striving for a balance between economic, conservation and access policies. Other special places, protected from change, are scattered across both town and countryside: Nature Reserves (including coastal dunes and peat mosses, limestone pavements, and ancient woodland), Sites of Special Scientific Interest; urban conservation areas; scheduled archaeological monuments and listed historic buildings.

The countervailing forces of development and preservation, have thus dominated the late 20th century, resulting in the creation of two trajectories of landscape change. On the one hand are areas (mainly on the urban fringes) in which large-scale, often wholesale, re-writing of the landscape is permitted in response to economic stimuli; on the other are the National Parks, AONBs and other conservation areas, where even modest change is strictly controlled and curtailed. The zone of active landscape change in the early 21st century is hemmed in between an almost fossilised countryside and an increasingly protected townscape.

Recent generations are the first for whom preservation of the 'ordinary' past has become an obsession. Earlier generations had no hesitation about changing the everyday landscape by stripping away the legacy of the past, and even outstanding historic monuments would readily be demolished without compunction in the name of progress. Thus much of the rich legacy of timber-framed architecture in south Lancashire was ruthlessly demolished between 1800 and 1950. As late as 1935 there was a serious proposal to demolish Manchester Cathedral and build a modern re-placement set in a large formal park, as part of a complete reconstruction of the city centre. That such a scheme would surely now be unthinkable is testimony to the late 20th-century revolution in how landscape and conservation issues are perceived.

It could be argued, however, that landscape and conservation policies tend to be driven by a series of implicit and largely unquestioned assumptions about what constitutes 'good' landscape. For example, ecological understanding that the natural climax vegetation was a mixed deciduous woodland has been taken on board to the extent that the assumptions that more woodland is by definition desirable (and that native species are better than introduced ones) are rarely challenged. The Red Rose and Mersey 'community forests' seek to re-create native deciduous woodlands for recreational purposes. Yet, as we have seen, it could be argued that the very openness of much of the landscape of the North West, both in its windswept lowlands and its bleak moors and fells, is a key element in its distinctive character.

There also exists a set of assumptions about the ideal character of the landscape to be conserved. As this book has demonstrated, landscapes are the result of long-term evolution over several millennia, punctuated by short bursts of massive transformation. To state that the aim of conservation policies is to preserve landscapes therefore begs several questions. Is the aim merely to stop landscape change in its tracks or to restore the landscape character of the past? If the latter, at what point in time did the ideal landscape exist? Conservation policies suggest that current perceptions see that ideal as being a 'human-scale' landscape of a golden age before the introduction of modern materials and machinery. It is, in short, the lost landscape of the comparatively very recent past, evoked by Victorian photographs. Yet this landscape, its residual elements protected from change and even mimicked by modern building styles, was merely one incarnation in a sequence of human activity stretching back over six millennia.

NOTES

1 de Selincourt 1906, 92
2 For an overview, see Sheail 2002, 12–45
3 For regional policies see McCord & Thompson 1998, 375–6, 392–400; Phillips & Smith 1994, 315–20; Freeman et al. 1966, chs 8–10
4 Nicholls 1996
5 Hunt 1990, ch.9
6 Holt 1986 (esp. 238–72); Joy 1990
7 Caruana & Simmons 2000
8 Whiteley in Crosby 1998, ch6
9 Drake 1949
10 Yeadon in Crosby 1998, ch.7
11 Crosby 1998, ch.8
12 Walters 1936, 98–102, 107–9; White 1993, 181; Hassan 1985, 542
13 Berry & Beard 1980, 6–12; Marshall & Walton 1981, 207–12
14 Sheail 2002, 73
15 Hoyte 1996
16 Harvey in Johnson 1985, 122–42, 139
17 Berry & Beard 1980, 13–14
18 Ibid, 13–20, plates 21–4; Vaughan 2003, 35–6, 41; Sheail 2002, 94–8
19 Brader 2001
20 Arnold 1992, 8–18; Pocock 1977, 5–19
21 Ibid, 33–48
22 www.raf.mod.uk/spadeadam
23 Crosby 2002, 161–5
24 Sandbach 1978, 498–514
25 Sheail 1998, 21–45; Sheail 2002, 103–45

Bibliography

Adams, J 1988 *Mines of the Lake District Fells*. Clapham: Dalesman Books

Andrews, C B 1936 *The Torrington Diaries, containing the tours through England and Wales of the Hon. John Byng (later fifth Viscount Torrington) between the years 1781 and 1794, Volume III*. London: Eyre & Spottiswoode

Andrews, M 1989 *The Search for the Picturesque: landscape aesthetics and tourism in Britain 1760–1800*. Aldershot: Scolar Press

Anon. 1843 *The Pictorial History of the County of Lancaster*. London: George Routledge

Anon. 1876 *Extracts from a Lancashire Diary 1663–1678*. Manchester: T Sowler

Anon. 1890 *Lancashire – the Premier County of the Kingdom: cities and towns, historical, statistical, biographical*. London: Historical Publishing Company

Anon. 1990 *Haslingden Grane: a valley, its landscape and its people*. Preston: Lancashire County Planning Department

Appleby, A B 1978 *Famine in Tudor and Stuart England*. Liverpool: Liverpool University Press

Armstrong, A M, Mawer, A, Stenton, F M and Dickins, B 1950–2 *The Place-Names of Cumberland* (English Place-Names Society vols 20–22). Cambridge: Cambridge University Press

Arnold, L 1992 *Windscale 1957: anatomy of a nuclear accident*. London: Macmillan

Ashmore, O 1982 *The industrial archaeology of North-West England* (Chetham Society 3rd series 29). Manchester: Chetham Society

Austin, S, Harwood, J, Pyne, G and Pyne, C 1831 *Lancashire Illustrated*. London: H & R Fisher and P Jackson

Bailey, J and Culley, G 1805 *General View of the Agriculture of Northumberland, Cumberland & Westmoreland*, 3rd edn. London: G & W Nicol [reprinted Gateshead: Frank Graham, 1972]

Bailey, R N and Cramp, R J 1988 *Corpus of Anglo-Saxon Stone Sculpture Volume II: Cumberland, Westmorland and Lancashire North of the Sands*. Oxford: Oxford University Press for the British Academy

Baldwin, J R and Whyte, I D (eds) 1985 *The Scandinavians in Cumbria*. Edinburgh: Scottish Society for Northern Studies

Barker, T and Harris, J 1993 *A Merseyside Town in the Industrial Revolution: St Helens 1750–1900*. London: Cass

Barrow, G W S 1975 'The pattern of lordship and feudal settlement in Cumbria', *Journal of Medieval History* **1**, 117–38

Beattie, D 1992 *Blackburn: the development of a Lancashire cotton town*. Halifax: Ryburn Publishing

Beck, H M 1984 *Gaping Gill: 150 years of exploration*. London: Hale

Beck, J 1953 'The church brief for the inundation of the Lancashire coast in 1720', *THSLC* **105**, 91–105

Berry, G and Beard, G 1980 *The Lake District: a century of conservation*. Edinburgh: Bartholomew

Bewley, R H 1992 'Excavations on two crop-marked sites in the Solway Plain, Cumbria: Ewanrigg settlement and Swarthy Hill 1986–1988', *CW2* **92**, 23–47

Bewley, R H 1993 'Survey and excavation at a crop-mark enclosure, Plasketlands, Cumbria', *CW2* **93**, 1–18

Binns, J 1851 *Notes on the Agriculture of Lancashire with suggestions for its improvement*. Preston: Dobson & Son

Blatchford, R 1889 'Modern Athens, A City of Shame', *Sunday Chronicle*, 5 May 1889, 2

Bonsall, C, Sutherland, D, Tipping, R and Cherry, J 1989 'The Eskmeals Project: late Mesolithic settlement and environment in north-west England', in Bonsall, C (ed.) *The Mesolithic in Europe*. Edinburgh: John Donald, 175–205

Booth, H 1830 *An Account of the Liverpool and Manchester Railway*. Liverpool: Wales and Baines

Borsay, P 1989 *The English Urban Renaissance: Culture and Society in the Provincial Town, 1660–1770*. Oxford: Oxford University Press

Bouch, C M L 1948 *Prelates and People of the Lake Counties: a history of the Diocese of Carlisle 1133–1933*. Kendal: Titus Wilson

Bowden, M (ed.) 2000 *Furness Iron: The Physical Remains of the Iron Industry and Related Woodland Industries of Furness and Southern Lakeland*. London: English Heritage

Boyson, R 1970 *The Ashworth Cotton Enterprise: the rise and fall of a family firm*. Oxford: Clarendon Press

Brader, C 2001 'Timbertown Girls: Gretna female munitions workers in World War I', unpublished PhD thesis, University of Warwick

Brown, J 1767 *Description of the Lake at Keswick*. Newcastle: [first published in the *London Chronicle*, April 1766]

Butler, D M 1999 *The Quaker Meeting Houses of Britain*. 2 vols. London: Friends Historical Society

Caffrey, H C 2002 'Almshouses: an enduring concept of care', unpublished MA dissertation, University of Lancaster

Calladine, A and Fricker, J 1993 *East Cheshire Textile Mills*. London: RCHME

Camden, W 1610 *Britain or a chorographicall description of the most flourishing kingdoms ....* London: George Bishop

Caruana, V and Simmons, C 2000 'The promotion and development of Manchester Airport, 1929–1974: the local authority initiative', *The Local Historian* **30 (3)**, 165–177

Chambers, F M (ed.) 1993 *Climate Change and Human Impact on the Landscape*. London: Chapman & Hall

Champness, J 1989 *Lancashire's Architectural Heritage: an anthology of fine buildings*. Preston: Lancashire County Planning Department

Clark, S E 1994 'Perceptions of the Boundaries of the Lake District from the 18th century to the designation of the National Park', unpub. Diploma dissertation, Lancaster University

Clarke, J 1787 *A Survey of the Lakes of Cumberland, Westmorland and Lancashire*. London: the author

Clarke, S 1900 *Clitheroe in its railway days*. Clitheroe: Clitheroe Advertiser

Collier, S 1991 *Whitehaven 1660–1800*. London: HMSO

Colligan, J H 1905 'Penruddock Presbyterian meeting-house', *CW2* **5**, 150–71

Collingwood, W G 1895 *Thorstein of the Mere: saga of the Northmen in Lakeland*. London: Edward Arnold

Coney, A 1992 'Fish, fowl and fen: landscape and economy on seventeenth-century Martin Mere', *Landscape History* **14**, 51–64

Coney, A 1995 'Liverpool dung: the magic wand of agriculture', *Lancashire Local Historian* **10**, 15–26

Cooke Taylor, W 1842 *Notes of a Tour in the Manufacturing Districts of Lancashire*. London: Duncan and Malcolm

Cooper, M P and Stanley, C J 1990 *Minerals of the English Lake District: Caldbeck Fells*. London: Natural History Museum Publications

Cooper, W H 1984 *Mountain Painter: an autobiography*. Kendal: Frank Peters

Cotton, C 1681 *The Wonders of the Peake*. London: Joanna Brome

Cowell, R W and Innes, J B 1994 *The Wetlands of Merseyside* (North West Wetlands Survey 1). Lancaster: Lancaster University Archaeological Unit

Crosby, A G 1988 *Penwortham in the Past*. Preston: Carnegie Press

Crosby, A G (ed.) 1993 *Lancashire Local Studies: essays in honour of Diana Winterbotham*. Preston: Carnegie Press

Crosby, A G 1994 'The towns of medieval Lancashire: an overview', *CNWRS Regional Bulletin: Lancaster University*, new series **8**, 7–18

Crosby, A G (ed.) 1998 *Leading the Way: A history of Lancashire's roads*. Preston: Lancashire County Books

Crosby, A G 2000 *Hutton: a millennium history*. Lancaster: Carnegie Publishing/Hutton Parish Council

Crosby, A G 2002 *A History of Warrington*. Chichester: Phillimore and Warrington Borough Council

Crosby, A G 2003 *Colne (South), 1910: historical essay*. Consett: Alan Godfrey Maps

Crossthwaite, J F 1881 *A Brief Memoir of Major-General Sir John G Woodford*. London: Kent & Co

Cunningham, C 1981 *Victorian and Edwardian Town Halls*. London: Routledge & Kegan Paul

Curwen, J C 1812 'President's report', *Proceedings of Workington Agricultural Society, 1812*, 107

Darley, G 1975 *Villages of Vision*. London: Architectural Press

Davis, E 2002 'Clay drainage tile and pipe manufacture at Johnby Waithes, Greystoke, *c.* 1851–1909', *CW3* **2**, 261–75

de Selincourt, E (ed.) 1906, *Wordsworth's Guide to the Lakes: the fifth edition 1835*. Oxford: Oxford University Press [reprinted 1970]

Deakin, D (ed.) 1989 *Wythenshawe: the Story of a Garden City*. Chichester: Phillimore

Defoe, D 1971 *A Tour through the Whole Island of Great Britain*. Harmondsworth: Penguin [first published 1724–6]

Denton, T 2003 *A Perambulation of Cumberland 1687–8 including descriptions of Westmorland, the Isle of Man and Ireland*, ed. A J L Winchester with M Wane (Surtees Society 207/CWAAS Record Series 16). Woodbridge: Boydell Press

Dickens, C 1854 *Hard Times: for these times*. London: Bradbury & Evans

Dilley, R S 2000 'The enclosure awards of Cumberland: a statistical list', *CW2* **100**, 225–39

Done, A and Muir, R 2001 'The landscape history of grouse shooting in the Yorkshire Dales', *Rural History* **12**, 195–210

Drake, J 1949 *Road Plan for Lancashire: a report on existing and proposed road communications within the administrative county*. Preston: Lancashire County Council

Edwards, B J N 1998 *Vikings in North West England: the artifacts* (CNWRS Occasional Paper 36). Lancaster: CNWRS

Elliott, G 1960 'The enclosure of Aspatria', *CW2* **60**, 97–108

Elliott, G 1973 'Field systems of north-west England', in Baker, A R H and Butlin, R A (eds) *Studies of Field Systems in the British Isles*. Cambridge: Cambridge University Press, 41–92

Engels, F 1969 *The Condition of the Working Class in England*. London: Granada [first published 1844]

Farrall, T 1929 *Betty Wilson's Cummerland Teals*, 7th edn. Carlisle: J C Mason [first published 1876]

Fellows-Jensen, G 1985 *Scandinavian Settlement Names in the North West*. Copenhagen: CA Reitzels Forlag

Ferguson, R 1856 *The Northmen in Cumberland and Westmorland*

Ferguson, R S (ed.) 1877 *Miscellany Accounts of the Diocese of Carlile, with the terriers delivered to me at my primary visitation, by William Nicholson late bishop of Carlile* (CWAAS Extra Series 1)

Freeman, T W, Rodgers, H B and Kinvig, R H 1966 *Lancashire, Cheshire and the Isle of Man* (Regions of the British Isles). London: Nelson

Gardner, W H (ed.) 1982 *Poems and Prose of Gerard Manley Hopkins*. Harmondsworth: Penguin

Garnett, M E 1988 'The great rebuilding and economic change in south Lonsdale 1600–1730', *THSLC* **137**, 55–75

Garnett, W J 1849 'Prize Report: Farming of Lancashire', *Journal of Royal Agricultural Society of England* **10** (1), 1–49

Garside, P and Jackson, B n.d. *Model Guide to Lancashire Mental Hospital Records*. Preston: Lancashire County Council

Gaskell, E 1855 *North and South*. Leipzig: Bernhard Tauchnitz [first serialised in *Household Words*, 1854]

George, S 2000 *Liverpool Park Estates: their legal basis, creation and early management* (Liverpool Historical Studies 16). Liverpool: Liverpool University Press

Gerard, J 1894 *Stonyhurst College*. Belfast: M Ward

Gibson, K 2002 *Pennine Dreams: the story of the Huddersfield Narrow Canal*. Stroud: Tempus

Graham, T H B 1907 'An old map of Hayton', *CW2* **7**, 42–51

Graham, T H B 1913 'The townfields of Cumberland Part II', *CW2* **13**, 1–31

Greenall, R L 2000 *The Making of Victorian Salford*. Lancaster: Carnegie Publishing

Hadfield, C and Biddle, G 1970 *The Canals of North West England*. 2 vols; Newton Abbot: David & Charles

Hale, W G and Coney, A 2005 *Martin Mere: Lancashire's lost lake*. Liverpool: Liverpool University Press

Hall, D, Wells, C E and Huckerby, E 1995 *The Wetlands of Greater Manchester* (North West Wetlands Survey 2). Lancaster: Lancaster University Archaeological Unit

Hall, R 1977 'An early Cockermouth charter', *CW2* **77**, 75–81

Hallam, J S, Edwards, B J N, Barnes, B and Stuart, A J 1973 'The remains of a late-glacial elk associated with barbed points from High Furlong, near Blackpool, Lancashire', *Proceedings of the Prehistoric Society* **39**, 100–28

Hankinson, A 1972 *The First Tigers: the early history of rock climbing in the Lake District*. London: Dent

Hankinson, A 1988 *A Century on the Crags: the story of rock climbing in the Lake District*. London: Dent

Hannavy, J 1990 *Historic Wigan: two thousand years of history*. Preston: Carnegie Press

Harford, I 1994 *Manchester and its Ship Canal Movement: class, work and politics in late Victorian England*. Keele: Ryburn

Harrison, S, Wood, J and Newman, R 1998 *Furness Abbey, Cumbria*. London: English Heritage

Hartley, L P 1953 *The Go-Between*. London: Hamilton

Hartwell, C 2001 *Pevsner Architectural Guides: Manchester*. London: Penguin Books

Hartwell, C, Hyde, M and Pevsner, N 2004 *Lancashire: Manchester and the South-East* (The Buildings of England). New Haven and London: Yale University Press

Hassan, J A 1985 'The growth and impact of the British water industry in the nineteenth century', *Economic History Review*, new ser **38 (4)**, 531–47

Heap, D 1964 *Potholing: beneath the Northern Pennines*. London: Routledge & Kegan Paul

Hewitson, A 1883 *History of Preston*. Preston: Preston Guardian

Higham, M C 1991 'The mottes of north Lancashire, Lonsdale and south Cumbria', *CW2* **91**, 79–90

Higham, N 1986 *The Northern Counties to AD 1000* (Regional History of England). London: Longman

Higham, N J 2004 *A Frontier Landscape; the North West in the Middle Ages*. Macclesfield: Windgather Press

Higham, N J and Jones, G D B 1975 'Frontiers, forts and farmers: Cumbrian aerial survey 1974–5', *Archaeological Journal* **132**, 16–53

Higham, N and Jones, B 1985 *The Carvetii* (Peoples of Roman Britain). Gloucester: Alan Sutton

Hill, D 1984 *In Turner's Footsteps*. London: John Murray

Hill, J 1997 *Nelson: Politics, Economy, Community*. Edinburgh: Keele University Press

Hindle, P 1998 *Roads and Tracks of the Lake District*. Milnthorpe: Cicerone Press

Hindle, P 2001 *Roads and Tracks for Historians*. Chichester: Phillimore

Hobbes, T 1678 *De Mirabilibus Pecci: being the wonders of the Peak in Darby-shire ... in English and Latine*. London

Hobsbawm, E 1969 *Industry and Empire*. Harmondsworth: Penguin

Hodgkinson, D, Huckerby, E, Middleton, R and Wells, C E 2000 *The Lowland Wetlands of Cumbria* (North West Wetlands Survey 6). Lancaster: Lancaster University Archaeology Unit

Holden, R N 1998 *Stott and Sons: architects of the Lancashire Cotton Mill*. Lancaster: Carnegie Publishing

Holland, E G 1986 *Coniston Copper*. Milnthorpe: Cicerone Press

Holt, G O 1986 *A Regional History of the Railways of Great Britain: Volume 10 The North West* (revised by G Biddle). Newton Abbot: David & Charles

Holt, J 1795 *A General View of the Agriculture of the County of Lancaster*. London: G Nicol

Housman, J 1800 *Topographical Description of Cumberland, Westmorland, Lancashire and part of the West Riding of Yorkshire*. Carlisle: F Jollie

Howard-Davis, C 1996 'Seeing the sites: survey and excavation on the Anglezarke uplands, Lancashire', *Proceedings of Prehistoric Society* **62**, 133–66

Hoys, D 1955 *Below Scafell*. London: Oxford University Press

Hoyte, P 1996 'Water from Lakeland: a study of two small reservoirs', unpublished Diploma dissertation, University of Lancaster

Hughes, E 1965 *North Country Life in the Eighteenth Century Volume II: Cumberland and Westmorland* (University of Durham Publications). London: Oxford University Press

Hughes, Q 1999 *Liverpool: city of architecture*. Liverpool: The Bluecoat Press

Hunt, D 1990 *The History of Leyland and district*. Preston: Carnegie Press

Hunt, D 1992 *A History of Preston*. Preston: Carnegie Publishing and Preston Borough Council

Hutton, J 1781 *A Tour to the Caves in the Environs of Ingleborough and Settle in the West Riding of Yorkshire*. London: Richardson & Urquhart

Hutton, R 1997 *The Stations of the Sun: a history of the ritual year in Britain*. Oxford: Oxford University Press

James, F G 1956 *North Country Bishop: a biography of William Nicolson*. New Haven: Yale University Press

Jarvis, A 1991 *Liverpool Central Docks 1799–1905*. Stroud: Alan Sutton and National Museums and Galleries on Merseyside

Jarvis, A and Smith, K (eds) 1999 *Albert Dock: Trade and Technology*. Liverpool: National Museums and Galleries on Merseyside and University of Liverpool

Jennings, N 2003 *Clay Dabbins: vernacular buildings of the Solway Plain* (CWAAS Extra Series 30). Kendal: CWAAS

Johnson, R H (ed.) 1985 *The Geomorphology of North-West England*. Manchester: Manchester University Press

Jones, R M and Rees, D B 1984 *The Liverpool Welsh and their Religion*. Liverpool: Modern Welsh Publications

Joy, D 1990 *A Regional History of the Railways of Great Britain: vol 14 The Lake Counties*. Newton Abbot: David and Charles

Kadish, S 2003 'Manchester synagogues and their architects', *Transactions of the Ancient Monuments Society* **47**, 7–32

Kellett, J R 1979 *Railways and Victorian Cities*. London: Routledge & Kegan Paul

Kendal Civic Society 1997 *Bowling Fell: Kendal's First Public Park – its history and development*. Kendal: Kendal Civic Society

Kenyon, D 1991 *The Origins of Lancashire* (Origins of the Shire). Manchester: Manchester University Press

Kermode, D 2003 'The Shepherd's Voice: song and the upland shepherds of 19th- and early 20th-century Lakeland', unpublished MA dissertation, Lancaster University

Kidd, A J 2002 *Manchester*. Edinburgh: Edinburgh University Press

King, C A M 1976 *Northern England* (The Geomorphology of the British Isles). London: Methuen

Klingender, F D 1968 *Art and the Industrial Revolution* (revised edition edited by Arthur Elton). London: Evelyn, Adams & McKay

Knight, C and Burscough, M 1998 *Historic Fulwood and Cadley*. Lancaster: Carnegie Publishing

Knowles, D and Hadcock, R N 1971 *Medieval Religious Houses: England and Wales*. London: Longman

Langton, J and Morris, R J (eds) 1986 *Atlas of Industrialising Britain 1780–1914*. London: Methuen

Law, B R 1999 *Oldham Brave Oldham: an illustrated history of Oldham*. Oldham: Oldham Council

Lawton, R and Pooley, C G 1992 *Britain 1740–1950: an historical geography*. London: Arnold

Leech, R H 1983 'Settlements and groups of small cairns on Birkby and Birker Fells, Eskdale, Cumbria. Survey undertaken in 1982', *CW2* **83**, 15–23

Lemmey, R 2003 'A study of the structure and chronology of the drystone walls of Troutbeck in Westmorland', unpublished MA dissertation, University of Lancaster

Lewis, J 2000 *The Medieval Earthworks of the Hundred of West Derby* (British Archaeological Reports British Series 310). Oxford: John & Erica Hedges Ltd

Little, A G 1890 'The Black Death in Lancashire', *English Historical Review* **5**, 524–30

Lord, T C 2004 '"One on two and two on one": preliminary results from a survey of dry stone walls on the National Trust estate at Malham', in White, R and Wilson, P (eds), *Archaeology and Historic Landscapes of the Yorkshire Dales*. Leeds: Yorkshire Archaeological Society, 173–86

Machin, R 1977 'The Great Rebuilding: a reassessment', *Past & Present* **77**, 33–56

MacRaild, D M 1998 *Culture, Conflict and Migration: the Irish in Victorian Cumbria*. Liverpool: Liverpool University Press

Marsh, J P 2000 'Landed society in the far North West of England', unpublished PhD thesis, University of Lancaster

Marshall, J D 1958 *Furness and the Industrial Revolution*. Barrow: Barrow in Furness Corporation

Marshall, J D 1971 *Old Lakeland*. Newton Abbot: David and Charles

Marshall, J D and Walton, J K 1981 *The Lake Counties from 1830 to the mid-twentieth century: a study in regional change*. Manchester: Manchester University Press

Martin, J D 1993 'Wasdale Hall', *CW2* **93**, 269–82

McCarthy, M 1993 *Carlisle: history and guide*. Stroud: Alan Sutton

McCord, N and Thompson, R 1998 *The Northern Counties from AD 1000* (Regional History of England). London: Longman

McNamee, C 1997 *The Wars of the Bruces: Scotland, England and Ireland 1306–1328*. East Linton: Tuckwell Press

Middleton, R, Wells, C E and Huckerby, E 1995 *The Wetlands of North Lancashire* (North West Wetlands Survey 3). Lancaster: Lancaster University Archaeological Unit

Mills, A D 1976 *The Place-Names of Lancashire*. London: Batsford

Millward, R 1955 *Lancashire: an illustrated essay on the history of the landscape*. London: Hodder and Stoughton

Moore, J R 2003 'Periclean Preston, public art and the classical tradition in late-nineteenth century Lancashire', *Northern History* **40**, 299–323

Morris, C (ed.) 1982 *The Illustrated Journeys of Celia Fiennes 1685–c.1712*. London: Macdonald

Morris, R 1989 *Churches in the Landscape*. London: Dent

Morton, H V 1927 *In Search of England*. London: Methuen

Murdoch, J 1984 *The Discovery of the Lake District: a northern Arcadia and its uses*. London: Victoria and Albert Museum

Newman, R (ed.) 1996 *The Archaeology of Lancashire: present state and future priorities*. Lancaster: Lancaster University Archaeological Unit

Nicholas, R 1945 *The City of Manchester Plan, 1945*. Manchester: Manchester Corporation

Nicholls, R 1996 *Trafford Park: the first hundred years*. Chichester: Phillimore

Nicholson, N 1994 *Collected Poems* (ed. N Curry). London: Faber & Faber

O'Neill, C 2000 'Visions of Lakeland: tourism, preservation and the development of the Lake District, 1919–1939', unpublished PhD thesis, University of Lancaster

Orwell, G 1937 *The Road to Wigan Pier*. London: Gollancz and Left Book Club

Otley, J 1825 *A Concise Description of the English Lakes and adjacent mountains with general directions to tourists*, 2nd edn [first published 1823]. Keswick: the author

Parker, C 2001 'W. G. Collingwood's Lake District', *Northern History* **38** (**2**), 295–313

Parkinson-Bailey, J 2000 *Manchester: an architectural history*. Manchester: Manchester University Press

Parsons, M 1993 'Pasture farming in Troutbeck, Westmorland, 1550–1750', *CW2* **93**, 115–30

Pearson, S 1985 *Rural Houses of the Lancashire Pennines, 1560–1760* (RCHME Supplementary Series 10). London: HMSO

Pennington, W 1970 'Vegetation history in the north-west of England: a regional synthesis', in Walker, D and West, R G (eds) *Studies in the Vegetational History of the British Isles*. Cambridge: Cambridge University Press, 41–79

Perriam, D R and Robinson, J 1998 *Medieval Fortified Buildings of Cumbria* (CWAAS Extra Series 29). Kendal: CWAAS

Pevsner, N 1967 *Cumberland and Westmorland* (The Buildings of England). Harmondsworth: Penguin

Pevsner, N 1969a *Lancashire 1: the Industrial and Commercial South* (The Buildings of England). Harmondsworth: Penguin

Pevsner, N 1969b *Lancashire 2: the Rural North* (The Buildings of England). Harmondsworth: Penguin

Phillips, C B and Smith, J H 1994 *Lancashire and Cheshire from AD 1540* (Regional History of England). London: Longman

Philpott, R A 1989 *Historic Towns of the Merseyside Area: a survey of urban settlement to c.1800*. Liverpool: National Museums and Galleries on Merseyside

Phythian-Adams, C 1996 *Land of the Cumbrians: a study in British provincial origins AD 400–1120*. Aldershot: Scolar Press

Plumtre, J 1992 *James Plumtre's Britain: the journals of a tourist in the 1790s* (ed. I Ousby). London: Hutchinson

Pocock, R F 1977 *Nuclear Power: its development in the United Kingdom*. Woking: Unwin Brothers for Institution of Nuclear Engineers

Pollard, S 1997 *Marginal Europe*. Oxford: Clarendon Press

Pooley, C and Irish, S 1984 *The Development of Corporation Housing in Liverpool 1869–1945* (CNWRS Resource Paper). Lancaster: CNWRS

Pope, R (ed.) 1989 *Atlas of British Social and Economic History since c.1700*. London: Routledge

Porter, J 1975 'A forest in transition: Bowland, 1500–1650', *THSLC* **125**, 40–60

Porter, J 1978 'Waste land reclamation in the sixteenth and seventeenth centuries: the case of south-eastern Bowland, 1550–1630', *THSLC* **127**, 1–23

Potter, T W and Andrews, R D 1994 'Excavation and survey at St Patrick's chapel and St Peter's church, Heysham, Lancashire 1977–8', *Antiquaries Journal* **74**, 55–134

Priestley, J B 1934 *English Journey*. London: Heinemann

Rawlinson-Ford, J and Fuller-Maitland, J A 1931 *John Lucas's History of Warton Parish, compiled 1710–1740*. Privately published

Rawnsley, H D 1903 *Lake Country Sketches*. Glasgow: James MacLehose

RCHME 1997 *Belle Isle, Windermere* (Historic Building Report)

Rea, A 1886 *The Beckside Boggle and other Lake Country Stories*. London: T Fisher Unwin

Redding, C and Taylor, C W 1842 *An illustrated itinerary of the County of Lancaster*. How & Parsons

Richardson, H (ed.) 2001 *English Hospitals 1660–1948: a survey of their architecture and design*. London: English Heritage

Ritchie-Noakes, N 1984 *Liverpool's Historic Waterfront: the world's first mercantile dock system*. London: RCHME

Roberts, B K 1972 'Village plans in County Durham: a preliminary statement', *Medieval Archaeology* **16**, 33–56

Roberts, D S 1999 'Thomas de Quincey's "Danish origin of the Lake Country Dialect"', *CW2* **99**, 257–65

Roberts, E A M (ed.) 1998 *A History of Linen in the North-West* (CNWRS Occasional Paper 38). Lancaster: CNWRS

Rollinson, W 1963 'Schemes for the reclamation of land from the sea in North Lancashire during the eighteenth and nineteenth centuries', *THSLC* **115**, 133–45

Rollinson, W (ed.) 1989 *The Lake District Landscape Heritage.* Newton Abbot: David and Charles

Rumney, A W 1911 *The Dalesman.* Kendal: Titus Wilson

Ruskin, J 1903–12 *The Works of John Ruskin* (ed. E T Cook and A Wedderburn), 36 vols. London: Allen

Sandbach, F R 1978 'The early campaign for a National Park in the Lake District', *Transactions of the Institute of British Geographers*, new ser **3**, 498–514

Searle, C E 1993 'Customary tenants and the enclosure of the Cumbrian commons', *Northern History* **29**, 126–53

Sharples, J 2004 *Pevsner Architectural Guides: Liverpool.* New Haven and London: Yale University Press

Sheail, J 1998 *Nature Conservation in Britain: the formative years.* London: Stationery Office

Sheail, J 2002 *An Environmental History of Twentieth-century Britain.* Basingstoke: Macmillan

Sheppard, J 1974 'Metrological analysis of regular village in Yorkshire', *Agricultural History Review* **22**, 118–35

Shotter, D 1997 *Romans and Britons in North-west England* (CNWRS Occasional Paper 34), 2 edn. Lancaster: CNWRS

Shotter, D and White, A 1990 *The Roman Fort and Town of Lancaster* (CNWRS Occasional Paper 18). Lancaster: CNWRS

Simon, E D and Inman, J 1935 *The Rebuilding of Manchester.* London: Longmans

Sister Agnes 1949 *The Story of Skelsmergh.* Kendal: Westmorland Gazette

Smith, A H 1967 *The Place-Names of Westmorland* (English Place-Names Society vols 42–3). Cambridge: Cambridge University Press

Smith, E H 1959 'Lancashire long measure', *THSLC* **110**, 1–14

Spring, H 1934 *Shabby Tiger.* London: Collins

Stell, C 1994 *An inventory of Nonconformist Chapels and Meeting Houses in the North of England.* London: HMSO

Stobart, J 2004 *The first industrial region: north-west England c.1700–60.* Manchester: Manchester University Press

Stockdale, J 1872 *Annales Caermoelenses: or Annals of Cartmel.* Ulverston: William Kitchin

Strickland, T 1995 *The Romans at Wilderspool: the story of the first industrial development on the Mersey.* Warrington: Greenalls Group plc

Summerson, H and Harrison, S 2000 *Lanercost Priory, Cumbria: a survey and documentary history* (CWAAS Research Series 10). Kendal: CWAAS

Sunderland, F n.d. *A Brief History of Tottlebank Baptist Church.* Liverpool: Unity Press

Swain, J T 1986 *Industry before the Industrial Revolution: North-East Lancashire c.1500–1640* (Chetham Society 3rd series 32). Manchester: Manchester University Press for Chetham Society

Tallis, J H and McGuire, J 1972 'Central Rossendale: the evolution of an upland vegetation: I. The clearance of woodland', *Journal of Ecology* **60 (3)**, 721–37

Taylor, H. 1997 *A Claim on the Countryside: a history of the British outdoor movement.* Edinburgh: Keele University Press

Taylor, R F 1965 'The excavation of a bloomery furnace at Hackensall', *THSLC* **117**, 83–8

Taylor, R F 1975 'The coastal salt industry of Amounderness', *TLCAS* **78**, 14–21

Taylor, R F 1983 'Vaccary walling', *Antiquity* **57**, 131

Thelwall, R E 1972 *The Andrews and Compstall, their village.* Chester: Cheshire County Libraries

Thornber, T 2002 *Seen on the Packhorse Trails.* Todmorden: South Pennines Packhorse Trails Trust

Timmins, J G 1977 *Handloom Weavers' Cottages in Central Lancashire* (CNWRS Occasional Paper 3). Lancaster: CNWRS

Timmins, J G 1993 *The last shift: the decline of handloom weaving in nineteenth-century Lancashire.* Manchester: Manchester University Press

Timmins, J G 1998 *Four Centuries of Lancashire Cotton.* Preston: Lancashire County Books

Toulmin Smith, L (ed.) 1906–10 *The Itinerary of John Leland in or about the years 1535–43*, 5 vols (reprinted London: Centaur Press, 1964)

Townend, M 2000 'In search of the Lakeland saga: antiquarian fiction and the Norse settlement in Cumbria', unpublished conference paper, Reinventing the Medieval Past conference, University of York, 18 March 2000

Trescatheric, B 1985 *How Barrow was Built.* Barrow-in-Furness: Hougenai Press

Tupling, G H 1927 *The Economic History of Rossendale* (Chetham Society, new ser 86). Manchester: Chetham Society

Tyson, B 1992 'Murton Great Field, near Appleby: a case-study of the piecemeal enclosure of a common-field in the mid-eighteenth century', *CW2* **92**, 161–82

Vaughan, D W 2003 'The impact of the Forestry Commission in the Lake District, 1919–1979', unpublished MA dissertation, University of Lancaster

VCH Lancs. The Victoria History of the County of Lancaster, (ed. W Farrer and J Brownbill) 8 vols. London: Constable, 1906–1914

Virgoe, J 1994 *A History of Parbold.* Preston: Carnegie Publishing

Virgoe, J 2003 'Thomas Fleetwood and the draining of Martin Mere', *THSLC* **152**, 27–47

Wainwright, A 1955 *A Pictorial Guide to the Lakeland Fells: Book One: the Eastern Fells.* Kentmere: Henry Marshall

Wainwright, A 1964 *Book Six: the North-Western Fells.* Kendal: Westmorland Gazette

Wakelin, M F 1977 *English Dialects: an introduction* (revised edition). London: Athlone Press

Walker, D 1966 'The late Quaternary history of the Cumberland lowland', *Philosophical Transactions of the Royal Society B* **251**, 1–210

Waller, P (ed.) 2000 *The English Urban Landscape.* Oxford: Oxford University Press

Walters, E C S 1936 *The Nation's Water Supply.* London: Nicholson & Watson

Walton, J K 1983 *The English Seaside Resort: a Social History 1750–1914.* Leicester: Leicester University Press

Walton, J K 1987 *Lancashire: a social history, 1558–1939.* Manchester: Manchester University Press

Walton, J K 1989 'Proto-industrialisation and the first industrial revolution: the case of Lancashire', in Hudson, P (ed.) *Regions and Industries: a perspective on the industrial revolution in Britain.* Cambridge: Cambridge University Press, 41–68

Walton, J K 1992 *Wonderlands by the Waves: A History of the Seaside Resorts of Lancashire*. Preston: Lancashire County Books

Walton, J K 1998 *Blackpool*. Edinburgh: Edinburgh University Press

Watson, R C and McClintock, M E 1979 *Traditional Houses of the Fylde* (CNWRS Occasional Paper 6). Lancaster: CNWRS

Watts, M 1978 *The Dissenters I: from the Reformation to the French Revolution*. Oxford: Clarendon Press

Waugh, E n.d. *Poems and Songs* (ed. G Milner). Manchester: John Heywood

Wawn, A 2000 *The Vikings and the Victorians: inventing the old North in nineteenth-century Britain*. Cambridge: D S Brewer

Wells, C 2003 'Environmental changes in Roman north-west England: a synoptic overview of events north of the Ribble', *CW3* **3**, 67–84

West, T 1778 *A Guide to the Lakes in Cumberland, Westmorland and Lancashire*. London: Richardson & Urquhart

West, T 1780 *A Guide to the Lakes ...*, 2nd edn, London: Richardson & Urquhart

White, A (ed.) 1993 *A History of Lancaster 1193–1993*. Keele: Ryburn Publishing

White, A 2003 *Lancaster: a history*. Chichester: Phillimore

White, R 2002 *The Yorkshire Dales: a landscape through time*. Ilkley: Great Northern Books

Whittle, P 1821 *The History of the Borough of Preston*. Preston: the author

Whyte, I D 2003 *Transforming Fell and Valley: landscape and Parliamentary enclosure in north-west England* (CNWRS Occasional Paper 49). Lancaster: CNWRS

Williams, B 1976 *The Making of Manchester Jewry 1740–1875*. Manchester: Manchester University Press

Williams, L A 1975 *Road Transport in Cumbria in the Nineteenth Century*. London: George Allan & Unwin

Williams, M and Farnie, D A 1992 *Cotton Mills in Greater Manchester*. London: Greater Manchester Archaeological Unit and RCHME

Wilmott, T 1997 *Birdoswald: excavations of a Roman fort on Hadrian's Wall and its successor settlements, 1987–92* (Archaeological Report 14). London: English Heritage

Wilson, J 1997 'Patronage and piety: the monuments of Lady Anne Clifford', *CW2* **97**, 119–42

Wimble, G, Wells, C E and Hodgkinson, D 2000 'Human impact on mid- and late Holocene vegetation in south Cumbria, UK', *Vegetation History and Archaeobotany* **9**, 17–32

Winchester, A J L 1979 'Deserted farmstead sites at Miterdale Head, Eskdale', *CW2* **79**, 150–5

Winchester, A J L 1984 'Peat storage huts in Eskdale', *CW2* **84**, 103–15

Winchester, A J L 1986 'Response to the 1623 famine in two Lancashire manors', *Local Population Studies* **36**, 47–8

Winchester, A J L 1987 *Landscape & Society in Medieval Cumbria*. Edinburgh: John Donald

Winchester, A J L (ed.) 1994 *The Diary of Isaac Fletcher of Underwood, Cumberland, 1756–1781* (CWAAS Extra Series 27). Kendal: CWAAS

Winchester, A J L 2000a *The Harvest of the Hills: rural life in northern England and the Scottish Borders, 1400–1700*. Edinburgh: Edinburgh University Press

Winchester, A J L 2000b 'Hill farming landscapes of medieval northern England', in Hooke, D (ed.) *Landscape: the richest historical record*. Birmingham: Society for Landscape Studies, 75–84

Winchester, A J L 2000c *Discovering Parish Boundaries*, 2nd edn. Princes Risborough: Shire Publications

Winchester, A J L 2003 'Demesne livestock farming in the Lake District: the vaccary at Gatesgarth, Buttermere, in the later thirteenth century', *CW3* **3**, 109–18

Winchester, A J L 2005 'The moorland forests of medieval England', in Whyte, I D and Winchester, A J L (eds) *Society, Landscape and Environment in Upland Britain*. Society for Landscape Studies, 21–34

Winstanley, M J (ed.) 2000 *Rural industries of the Lune Valley* (CNWRS Occasional Paper 43). Lancaster: CNWRS

Wood, O 1988 *West Cumberland Coal 1600–1982/3* (CWAAS Extra Series 24). Kendal: CWAAS

Wood, P N 1996 'On the little British kingdom of Craven', *Northern History* **32**, 1–20

Wordsworth, W 1904 *The Poetical Works of Wordsworth* (ed. T Hutchinson; revised edn, ed. E de Selincourt). London: Oxford University Press

Yates, M 1923 *A Lancashire Anthology*. London: University Press of Liverpool/Hodder & Stoughton

Youd, G 1961 'The common fields of Lancashire', *THSLC* **113**, 1–41

Index

Entries in *italics* refer to illustrations.

Picture Credits

Aerial survey acknowledgements
New English Heritage aerial photographs were taken by Peter Horne, David Macleod, Jane Stone and Damian Grady. The Aerial Reconnaissance team would like to thank the following people for their help: a special note of thanks must go to the skills and patience of the pilots Jon Forsyth, Mark Julian, Jim Loose, Chris Penistone, Mick Webb, David Williams and Martin Wood; the aircraft owners Anthony Crawshaw and David Sanders; the NMR cataloguing team Rose Ogle, Katy Groves, Catherine Runciman, Cinzia Bacilieri, Philip Daniels, Geoff Hall; Jon Proudman for all the publication scanning; Sarah Prince for laser copying thousands of aerial photographs to send to the authors; Kate Bould for post reconnaissance administrative support in York.